D1266661

Transmission of information

Transmission of information

A statistical theory of communications

Robert M. Fano

Professor of Electrical Communications
Massachusetts Institute of Technology

The M.I.T. Press
Massachusetts Institute of Technology
Cambridge, Massachusetts

Copyright © 1961
by The Massachusetts Institute of Technology

Second Printing, September, 1963
with corrections

TK
5101
F21

Library of Congress Catalog Card Number: 61-8799
Printed in the United States of America

to Jacqueline

PREFACE

This book is the outgrowth of a series of lecture notes prepared for a graduate course offered by the Electrical Engineering Department of the Massachusetts Institute of Technology. The course was offered for the first time, in seminar form, during the Spring Term 1951, and the first complete set of lecture notes was prepared during the Spring Term 1952.

My interest in Information Theory dates back to the Summer of 1947 when, after completion of my doctorate thesis, I began looking for greener research pastures. It was a propitious time indeed. In the Research Laboratory of Electronics a very active group was just gathering around Professor Norbert Wiener to explore the engineering applications of his theoretical work. Leaders of this group were Professor J. B. Wiesner and Professor Y. W. Lee. I am deeply grateful to them as well as to Professor Wiener for introducing me to the statistical theory of communications.

My curiosity was particularly aroused by Professor Wiener's frequent statement that the information associated with a message depended on the ensemble from which it was selected, and that its average value could be identified with the entropy of the ensemble. This notion was so strange to me that I felt the need of some operational justification for it. By March 1948 I had obtained a justification in terms of message encoding, which turned out to be very similar to a theorem already proved by C. E. Shannon, but still unpublished. It was in this connection that I had the pleasure of meeting Dr. Shannon for the first time. I was so impressed by the scope and profoundness of his work that I have followed in his footsteps ever since. This book is primarily an account of his work and of work inspired by him, either directly or indirectly.

The preparation of lecture notes was interrupted, except for a minor, partial revision, by the development of a new undergraduate course on electromagnetic theory which absorbed most of my effort from 1954 to 1959. Important advances were made in this period which rendered obsolete a good part of my lecture notes. Among these advances was the discovery by J. M. Wozencraft of a decoding procedure which opened the door to the engineering exploitation of Shannon's fundamental coding theorem.

In February 1960, exactly one year ago, I began the preparation of a new set of lecture notes, intended to be the first draft of a book. Because of the obvious growth of interest in the field, I soon became convinced that an unpolished book available in a year from then would be more useful than a more polished book years later. However, in order to achieve such an early publication, the preparation of the copy for photo-offset printing had to begin long before the completion of the manuscript. I am very grateful to the M. I. T. Press for undertaking such a risky operation, and for the help and cooperation I received from the staff of the Press. I am also greatly indebted to Miss Dorothea Scanlon, who typed the entire rough draft from recorded dictation while keeping up at the same time with her other secretarial duties. Her accurate and prompt help has been invaluable to me.

The book is specifically directed to graduate students and engineers interested in electrical communications. It emphasizes the points of view and methods of analysis which are likely to prove most useful to them in their future work. Unfortunately, many important and interesting topics could not be included because of space limitations. They are presented in other books and in original papers which the reader should be able to follow without difficulty once familiar with the material covered here. The entire book, with the exception of the last two chapters and the sections marked with an asterisk, can be covered in one 15-week term with graduate students well grounded in probability theory. Chapter 8 presents mathematical techniques which have proved very useful in connection with more advanced work, and which are not discussed in sufficient detail anywhere else. Chapter 9 consists entirely of very recent, unpublished work.

I am grateful to Dr. A. Feinstein and to Dr. B. Mandelbrot for taking the time to read parts of the first draft and for pointing out mistakes and suggesting corrections. I am also indebted to my students for calling my attentions to a great many misprints, and in particular to Mr. L. Gimpelson, who proofread the final copy.

The writing of this book was made possible by the exceptional research environment and support provided by the Research Laboratory of Electronics. I wish to take this opportunity to express once more my deep appreciation to the Directors of the Laboratory, past and present, to my colleagues, and to my students for providing such a stimulating and enjoyable atmosphere. To Professors Elias, Shannon, and Wozencraft, my closest associates whose work and ideas I have attempted to present in this book, goes a very personal and most sincere thank you.

R. M. Fano

Cambridge, Massachusetts
February 1961

CONTENTS

Chapter 1

THE TRANSMISSION OF INFORMATION

The development of communication theory in the last decade has proceeded along two main lines. The first line stems primarily from the work of Norbert Wiener [1, 2] presented in his two famous books, Extrapolation, Interpolation, and Smoothing of Stationary Time Series and Cybernetics. The second line stems primarily from the work of Claude Shannon [3, 4] presented in his two classical papers, "A Mathematical Theory of Communication" and "Communication in the Presence of Noise." These key contributions to communication theory were published within a period of a few months in 1948 and 1949, and originated in part, at least, from wartime research on automatic fire control, in the case of Norbert Wiener, and on secrecy codes, in the case of Claude Shannon.

Both Wiener and Shannon postulated that the signal (or message) as well as the interfering noise could be properly described only in probabilistic terms, as members of suitably defined ensembles. This is indeed the point of view which distinguishes modern communication theory. However, the mathematical models on which they focussed their attention differ in a very significant way. Wiener assumed, in effect, that the signal in question could be processed only after it had been corrupted by noise. Shannon, on the other hand, assumed that the signal could be processed both before and after its transmission through a noisy channel. The ultimate objective in the two models was basically the same, namely, the faithful reproduction of the original signal. Thus, both Wiener and Shannon studied the influence of delay on the faithfulness of reproduction, but Wiener, because of his interest in automatic control, placed a much greater emphasis on prediction; i.e., on the reproduction of signals with a negative delay.

Although these differences of mathematical models and objectives may appear to be of secondary importance, there is very little overlap between Wiener's original work and that of Shannon, except for their common probabilistic approach. Wiener's work and the branch of communication theory stemming from it are particularly pertinent to the problems of filtering and prediction arising in automatic control. That of Shannon and the corresponding branch of communication theory are of major interest in connection with the efficient utilization of communication channels.

This text is devoted to the second branch of communication theory; i.e., to that originating from Shannon's work. This branch is often referred to as "Information Theory" from the name of the communication measure basic to it. The same term, however, is commonly used also to indicate both of the above branches of communication theory, and primarily in England, an even broader field including certain aspects of semantics, linguistics, neurophysiology, and psychology.

1.1 A Model of a Communication System

The first steps in the presentation of any theory about some aspect of the physical world are always troublesome. It would be desirable, of course, to agree from the start on the aspects to which the theory is to be pertinent, so as to avoid later misunderstandings about the generality of the results obtained from it. This, however, is very seldom possible. In the first place, theories are based on mathematical models; whether a particular model is correct and adequate can be decided only by comparing results of the theory with experimental evidence. In the second place, even the model can seldom be described precisely from the outset. Indeed the development of a suitable model is itself a significant part of the theory. This is just the situation that we are facing in beginning the presentation of our theory of communication.

The block diagram of Fig. 1.1 illustrates a model of a communication system. This model is admittedly rather vague. The purpose of this chapter is to bring this model into sharper focus, by discussing the roles played by the individual parts of the block diagram, and by outlining some of the major results of the theory. The box marked

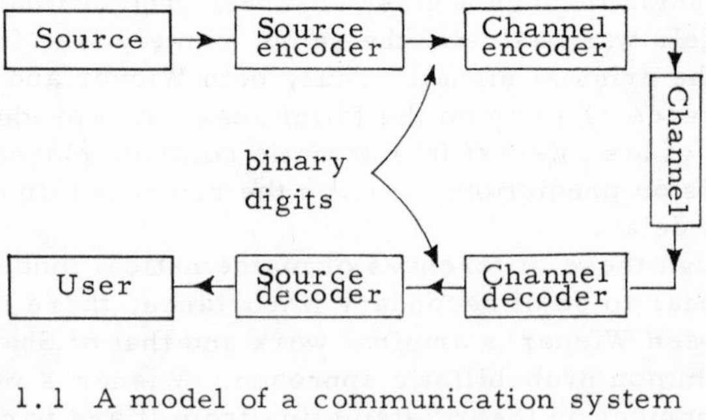

Fig. 1.1 A model of a communication system

"Source" stands for the person or device that generates the information to be transmitted; the box marked "Channel," for the physical means available for transmission; and the box marked "User," for the person or device that receives the information. These three boxes are to be regarded as fixed. The two boxes marked "Source encoder" and "Channel encoder" represent the devices used to transform the output from the source into a signal suitable for transmission through the prescribed channel. The corresponding two boxes marked "Channel decoder" and "Source decoder" represent the devices used to reproduce the desired information from the channel output. These last four boxes are arbitrary, in the sense that they can be made to perform any logically possible operation.

The reason for including two separate encoders and two separate decoders in the block diagram is to make a clear distinction between the encoding and decoding operations that depend on the characteristics of the source-user pair, and those that depend on the characteristics of the channel. The source encoder transforms the source output into a sequence of binary digits, from which the source decoder will in turn generate an acceptable reproduction of the source output. Thus, the input of the channel encoder and the output of the channel decoder consist of binary digits, regardless of the characteristics of the source and of the user. The fact that such an intermediate binary representation of the information to be transmitted can be assumed without any loss of generality is by no means obvious. Indeed, it is one of the major results of the theory, as we shall see later. It implies that the encoding and decoding apparatus pertinent to the channel can be designed and built independently of that pertinent to the source.

The model of a communication process illustrated in Fig. 1.1 is fairly general, and, clearly, can be used to represent a variety of situations of interest. On the other hand, it is too general for certain purposes and too restricted for certain others. For instance, very little can be said about the communication process unless some restriction is placed on the characteristics of the source and of the channel. At the same time, the model is incapable of taking into account the effects of mutual interference (cross talk) between separate communication processes. Therefore, while the model of Fig. 1.1 is very useful for our present purposes, it is but one of the models used in the theory.

1.2. The Object of Communication

The purpose of a communication system such as that illustrated in Fig. 1.1 is to make the source output available to the user; that is, to reproduce the source output at a place convenient to the user. The relative locations of the source and of the user are actually immaterial. The important point is that the prescribed channel must be a link in the transmission chain.

Let us consider critically what we mean by reproducing the output of the source. A little thought indicates that perfect reproduction is never expected. What is expected, instead, is a reproduction satisfactory for certain specific purposes. Indeed, one could claim that the very word reproduction implies the existence of a criterion of acceptability. For instance, we do not expect Western Union to deliver to the addressee a piece of paper looking like the one submitted by the sender. Furthermore, the addressee is inclined to regard a telegraphic message as satisfactory even if some of the letters are incorrect, as long as he can understand its meaning.

The importance of the criterion of acceptability is even more evident in the case of speech communication. The purpose of speech communication is, in some cases, exactly the same as that of telegraphic communication; that is, the reproduction of the speaker's voice is satisfactory so long as the listener is able to write what the speaker is saying. In other cases, the listener is not satisfied unless he can recognize the speaker and appreciate his emotions through the tone and the inflection of his voice. Similiar comments can be made about the transmission of pictures. A picture might be transmitted because of the factual information it contains, as in the case of a map. It may also be transmitted for entertainment or artistic purposes. Clearly the criterion of acceptability depends greatly on the purpose of the transmission.

Similar comments can be made about machine-to-machine communication. For instance, in the transmission of the output of a measuring instrument to, let us say, a computer, both the precision and the accuracy with which the measurements must be received depend on the use the computer will make of them. This is often recognized by quantizing the output of the measuring instrument before transmission to whatever level of precision the computer requires. This quantization is also helpful in preserving the accuracy of the measurement.

The above examples stress the fact that the specification of "the thing" that is transmitted in a communication system must include a fidelity criterion; that is, a criterion of acceptability on the part of the user. Thus "the thing" is not a characteristic of the source alone, but a characteristic of the source-user pair. We shall refer to it as "the information" communicated.

The existence of a criterion of acceptability has a very important consequence. Let us consider some time interval T and list all the possible source outputs during this interval. This listing might not be possible in practice, but it is a well defined conceptual operation. The possible source outputs can then be divided into non-overlapping equivalence classes in such a way that the outputs in each class can be acceptably reproduced as some properly chosen member of the class. In other words, we first select for each class a particular source output to be regarded as representative of the class. Then we assign to each class all source outputs that are equivalent to the representative source output, according to the specified criterion. For instance, if the criterion is a maximum permissible mean-square error, all members of each class must differ from the representative member by less than the stated mean-square error.

The simplest example of division of source outputs into equivalence classes is provided by the process of quantization performed in connection with pulse-code modulation. The source output voltage is first sampled every T seconds (or averaged over each successive time interval T). Each of the resulting voltage samples is then "quantized" by substituting for it the closest voltage value in a discrete set of preselected voltage values. This is equivalent to dividing the possible source outputs over each time interval T into equivalence classes, each consisting of the source outputs whose samples are closest to one of the preselected voltage values. The preselected voltage values are the source outputs representative of the corresponding classes.

If we assume that the possible source outputs over a given time interval have been divided into a discrete set of non-overlapping classes, the process of communication reduces to that of transmitting an indication of the particular class to which the source output belongs in each successive time interval. More precisely, the source encoder identifies the class to which the source output belongs and indicates it to the source decoder, which, in turn, generates the source output representative of the indicated class.

It is often necessary to include a class consisting of all source outputs that are irrelevant to the user, and that, therefore, are equivalent to him. For instance, in the case of speech communication, this class should include all time functions that are not regarded by the user as representing understandable speech sounds. This class makes provisions for the extreme situation in which the user is not at all interested in the source output.

1.3. Source Encoding and Decoding

We saw in the preceding section that the purpose of a communication system is to reproduce the output of the source according to a fidelity criterion specified by the user. The existence of a fidelity criterion suggested visualizing the possible source outputs over any time interval as grouped into non-overlapping classes. Each class would consist of source outputs regarded by the user as equivalent to a preselected output representative of the class. This, in turn, led us to think of the purpose of a communication system as that of indicating to the user the class to which the source output belongs. In other words, we came to the conclusion that the function of the source encoder is to recognize the class to which the source output belongs, and, correspondingly, the function of the source decoder is to generate the representative member of the class. Clearly, the function of the rest of the communication system is to indicate to the source decoder the class to which the source output belongs over the time interval for which the output classes are defined. Of course, this process of indicating the class to which the source output belongs is repeated in each successive interval of time.

The idea of dividing the possible source outputs into a discrete set of classes is of cardinal importance, because it reduces the description of the source output over any prescribed time interval to a simple enumeration of a discrete set of possible events. We shall refer to this set of events, that is, classes, as the set of possible messages over the prescribed time interval.

Let us suppose for the moment that the set of possible messages for a prescribed time interval is finite. If we indicate with M the number of messages in the set, we can assign to each message one of the integers from zero to M-1 . Then we can write the integer corresponding to each particular message as a binary number, thereby associating a sequence of binary digits to each message. For instance, the 27th message in a set of 64 messages would be assigned the binary sequence 011011 . This sequence is obtained by noting that

$$27 = 0 \times 2^5 + 1 \times 2^4 + 1 \times 2^3 + 0 \times 2^2 + 1 \times 2^1 + 1 \times 2^0 \qquad (1.1)$$

Thus, the output from the source can be represented by means of a binary number in each successive time interval, and be transformed thereby into a sequence of binary digits. In this type of encoding, the same number of binary digits must be used to represent each message of a set, regardless of the magnitude of the integer associated with it. Otherwise, it would be impossible to decipher the message numbers once they have been placed in sequence.* The number of binary digits per message is 6 in the above example because the number of messages is

$$M = 2^6 = 64 \qquad (1.2)$$

Clearly 7 digits would be required if M were equal to any integer larger than 64 but smaller than or equal to 128 . In general, the number of digits must be equal to the smallest integer greater than or equal to the logarithm to the base 2 of M .

There is no important conceptual reason for writing the integers associated with the messages as binary numbers. They could be written just as well as ternary numbers, or in any other number system. The important point is that it is possible to transform the source output into a sequence of symbols, that is, digits, selected from a finite alphabet. Then, if these symbols or digits are reproduced correctly at the input of the source decoder, the source decoder will be able to generate an acceptable reproduction of the source output.

The above discussion suggests that the number M of possible messages or, even better, the number of binary digits required to represent each message of the set might provide a useful measure of the amount of information generated by the source relative to the user in the specified time interval. This notion, however, is only partly correct. The number of possible messages does not provide a complete

---

*It is assumed that provisions have been made for identifying the beginning of the first message.

description of the message set. We must, in addition, state the probability with which each particular message is generated by the source. The role played by the message probabilities is best explained in terms of the specific example of a message set illustrated in Fig. 1.2.

Message Number	Binary Number	Message Probability	Binary Code Word	$-\log_2$ of Probability
0	000	1/4	00	2
1	001	1/4	01	2
2	010	1/8	100	3
3	011	1/8	101	3
4	100	1/16	1100	4
5	101	1/16	1101	4
6	110	1/16	1110	4
7	111	1/16	1111	4

Fig. 1.2. Example of fixed-length and of variable-length encoding

The number of possible messages in this example is 8, so that the binary number representing each message contains 3 digits. It is clear, on the other hand, that writing the message number in binary form is just one way of associating a binary code word (i.e., a sequence of binary digits) to each message. The fourth column of Fig. 1.2 shows a different way of associating binary code words to the messages. The number of binary digits in each code word is not the same, but rather it increases as the probability of the corresponding message decreases. More precisely, the number of digits in each code word is equal to the base-2 logarithm of the reciprocal of the message probability. This set of binary code words also has the property that no code word is identical to the beginning of a longer code word. Thus, if these code words are used in a sequence to represent successive messages, it is always possible to recognize where a code word ends in a sequence, and the next one begins.

The average code word length (expected length) for the set of binary code words of Fig. 1.2 is 2.75, which is smaller than the number of digits in the binary numbers shown in the second column. We can conclude, therefore, that the number of binary digits required on the average to represent a message can be reduced by exploiting the fact that the different messages do not occur with the same probability. We shall see in Chapter 3 that the set of code words shown in the fourth column of Fig. 1.2 is optimum in the sense that it yields the smallest possible average number of digits per message. We shall see also that, in an optimum set of code words, the length of each code word is equal to the logarithm to the base 2 of the reciprocal of the message probability (or approximately equal if the logarithm is not an integer).

The example of Fig. 1.2 illustrates that the average number of binary digits that must be transmitted is a function of the message probabilities and, through them, of the number of messages in the set. These probabilities depend, in turn, on the statistical characteristics of the source, and on the manner in which the outputs are grouped into the equivalence classes represented by the messages. On the other hand, for any given fidelity criterion, there are usually many ways in which the source outputs can be grouped into classes. Thus, the average code-word length depends on the manner in which the source outputs are grouped into classes, as well as on the binary representation of the corresponding messages. Furthermore, the resulting average number of binary digits per second generated by the source encoder may depend as well on the time interval used in the grouping of the source outputs into classes. Clearly, the operation of the source encoder can be adjusted, at least in principle, to minimize the average number of output binary digits per second. We are now in a position to state in a preliminary form one of the major results of our theory.

> It is possible, under fairly general conditions, to define a number R for each source-user pair representing the rate at which the source generates information relative to the fidelity criterion specified by the user. This rate is defined as the least average number of binary digits per second that must be transmitted in order to allow the source output to be reproduced according to the specified fidelity criterion.

This concludes our introductory discussion of the characteristics of sources and of the roles played by the source encoder and by the source decoder. We shall now proceed to discuss the characteristics of channels and the roles played by the channel encoder and by the channel decoder. In other words, we shall consider next the problem of transmitting binary digits through the prescribed channel.

1.4. The Means of Communication

The means available for communicating are represented in Fig. 1.1 by the box marked "Channel." A physical channel may be regarded as consisting of a device capable of generating any one of a specified set of physical events and a device capable of observing the event that has been generated. Since energy is absorbed in the observation of any physical event, the existence of a physical channel implies the existence of a medium through which energy can propagate from the device generating the physical event to that observing it.

An obvious example of a communication channel is a pair of wires connected at one end to a voltage source capable of generating a set of distinct time functions, and at the other end to a recording instrument or meter capable of measuring the time variations of the output voltage. Another obvious example can be obtained by substituting for the pair of wires two antennas together with the space between them. A sailor waving two semaphore flags from the deck of a ship and another sailor observing them with a pair of binoculars can be regarded as forming a communication channel. The same can be said about two indians, one moving a blanket over a fire, the other observing the resulting smoke signals. All of these examples involve the propagation of electromagnetic energy, whether in the form of waves guided by a pair of wires, radio waves generated by an antenna, or light waves reflected by the objects in question into the eyes of the observer. Of course, any form of energy propagation can be exploited for communication purposes.

The observation of any physical event is always subject to uncertainties resulting from random disturbances. Even in the absence of man-made disturbances, one has to contend with thermal-agitation noise resulting from the random motion of atoms and molecules in the observing device and in the medium through which the energy propagates. The net result is that the same observation can result from more than one physical event. Thus, an observation can only provide a probabilistic inference about the event that has actually occurred.

Let us consider as a simple example an electrical communication channel involving a voltage source capable of generating pulses of constant amplitude with either positive or negative polarity. Let us assume further that the observation of the pulses is hampered only by the presence of thermal-agitation noise, and that the observation is performed by means of a voltmeter which indicates only whether the output voltage, averaged over a pulse duration, is positive or negative. A mathematical model of this physical channel is illustrated in Fig. 1.3. Because of the presence of thermal-agitation

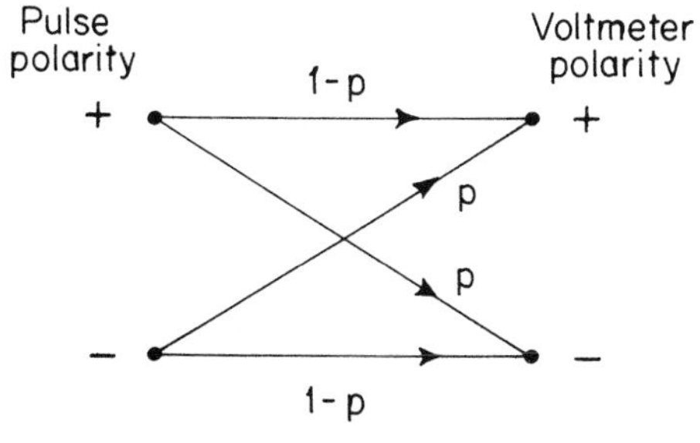

Fig. 1.3. Binary symmetric channel

noise, the indication of the voltmeter will occasionally be negative when the polarity of the transmitted pulse is positive, and will occasionally be positive when the polarity of the pulse is negative. The probability of these two events turns out to be the same, and it can be readily computed from the amplitude of the pulses and that of the noise at the voltmeter terminals. This probability is indicated with p in the diagram of Fig. 1.3. Thus, the probability that the voltmeter's indication will be positive when the pulse is positive and the probability that the voltmeter's indication will be negative when the pulse is negative are each equal to $1 - p$. We shall refer to a channel of this type as a "binary symmetric channel."

Let us suppose next that the output voltmeter indicates not just the polarity of the average output voltage but its actual value. The probability densities of the indication of the voltmeter v when the transmitted pulse is positive and when it is negative are shown in Fig. 1.4.

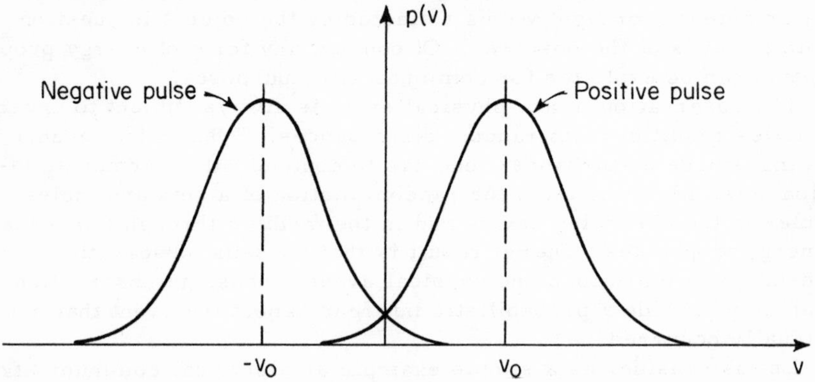

Fig. 1.4. Probability densities for the output voltage in the case of a positive pulse of amplitude v_0, and in that of a negative pulse of amplitude $-v_0$.

Both probability densities are gaussian; their mean values are equal to the signal-pulse amplitudes at the voltmeter's terminals, and their common variance is equal to that of the noise voltage.

A fairly general model of a communication channel is illustrated in Fig. 1.5. The set X represents the set of possible physical

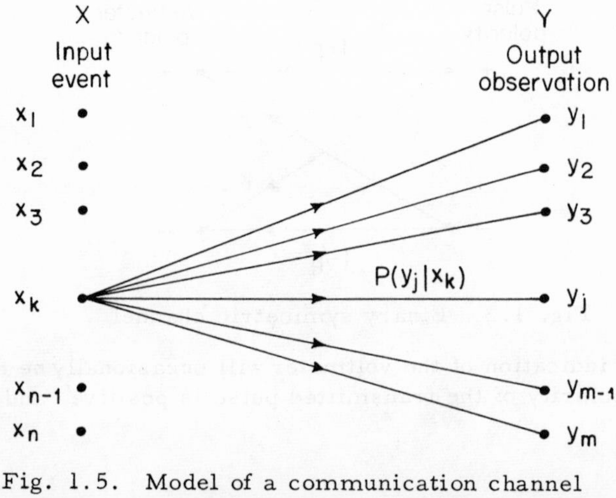

Fig. 1.5. Model of a communication channel

events that can be generated in each successive time interval T. The individual events are represented by x_1, x_2, x_3, . . . , x_k, . . . , x_{n-1}, x_n. The set Y represents the possible results of the observation performed on the input event. The individual results of the observation are represented by y_1, y_2, y_3, . . . , y_j, . . . , y_{m-1}, y_m, where m is in general different from n. The possible observations are related to the possible events by conditional probabilities $P(y|x)$. In particular, the conditional probability $P(y_j|x_k)$ represents the probability that the result of the observation be y_j when the input event is x_k. Clearly, the model of Fig. 1.3 is a special case of the model of Fig. 1.5. In the case of an electrical communication channel, the input events may be pulses with different amplitudes and polarities, they may be sinusoidal signals with the same amplitude but different frequencies, or they may be different but otherwise arbitrary time functions extending over the time interval T. Correspondingly, the set Y represents the possible outputs of a measuring instrument capable of distinguishing the possible input events.

It is assumed, in the model of Fig. 1.5, that the sets X and Y are discrete and finite. Of course, the number of possible output observations need not be the same as the number of possible events. This model can be generalized by allowing the output observations to form a continuum, as in the case of Fig. 1.4. Then, the set of conditional probabilities $P(y_j|x_k)$ must be replaced by the conditional probability density $p(y|x_k)$ for the continuous output variable y, given the input event x_k. The model can be further generalized by allowing the input events to form a continuum represented by the continuous input variable x. In this case, the output variable is related to the input variable by conditional probability densities $p(y|x)$. Such a more general model would be required to represent an electrical communication channel in which the input events are pulses of arbitrary amplitude and polarity and the output observations are the indications of a voltmeter or similar measuring device.

It has been assumed up to now that the conditional probabilities relating the output observations to the input event are the same for successive time intervals. We refer to a channel with this property as a constant channel without memory. A channel with memory would be one in which these conditional probabilities are functions of the preceding input events and/or of the preceding output observations. Channel models including memory of the past are required to represent electrical communication channels involving energy propagation through a dispersive medium. A typical example is provided by high-frequency radio channels exploiting the reflection of electromagnetic waves by the ionosphere in which several propagation paths may be present. As a matter of fact, some dispersion is present in most electrical communication channels. However, a model without memory often provides a satisfactory representation of such physical channels. If the conditional probabilities characterizing the channel are time-dependent, the channel is said to be time-varying.

1.5. Channel Encoding and Decoding

We saw in Sec. 1.3 that, without any loss of generality, the information to be transmitted through a channel can be regarded as consisting of binary digits. Thus the two parameters that characterize the transmission process are:

1. The rate of transmission R measured by the number of binary digits per second input to the channel encoder.
2. The accuracy of reception as indicated by the probability of error per digit $P(e)$; i.e., the probability that any particular binary digit be incorrectly reproduced by the channel decoder.

The theorem that specifies the limitations imposed on these two parameters by the characteristics of the transmission channel was first stated and proved by Shannon in 1948. It has since been extended and refined by Shannon himself and others. This theorem is the most important and most surprising result of our theory. It can be stated approximately as follows:

> For any stationary channel with finite memory, a channel capacity C can be defined having the following significance. For any binary transmission rate R smaller than C , the probability of error per digit can be made arbitrarily small by properly designing the channel encoder and decoder. Conversely, the probability of error cannot be made arbitrarily small when R is greater than C .

This theorem states, in other words, that the presence of random disturbances in a channel does not, by itself, set any limit to the transmission accuracy. Rather, it sets a limit to the binary transmission rate for which arbitrarily high transmission accuracy can be achieved.

Let us examine the encoding and decoding operations that are required to achieve a vanishingly small probability of error for a finite transmission rate. With reference to Fig. 1.6, the input binary digits flow through the encoder in such a way that, at any given time, ν such digits are stored in the encoder. The output from the encoder depends at any given time on the ν binary digits stored in the encoder. Of course, there must be a one-to-one correspondence between the possible outputs from the encoder and the set of events that can be generated in the channel. For instance, if the channel events are sinusoidal pulses of fixed amplitude and adjustable frequency, the output from the encoder must consist of a discrete sequence of values indicating the frequencies of the successive pulses. It is important to note that, if R is the binary transmission rate, each binary digit remains in the encoder for a time $T = \nu/R$ sec . Thus, each binary digit influences the output from the encoder over a time interval T .

The function of the decoder is to determine the binary digits transmitted on the basis of the output from the channel. Since each binary

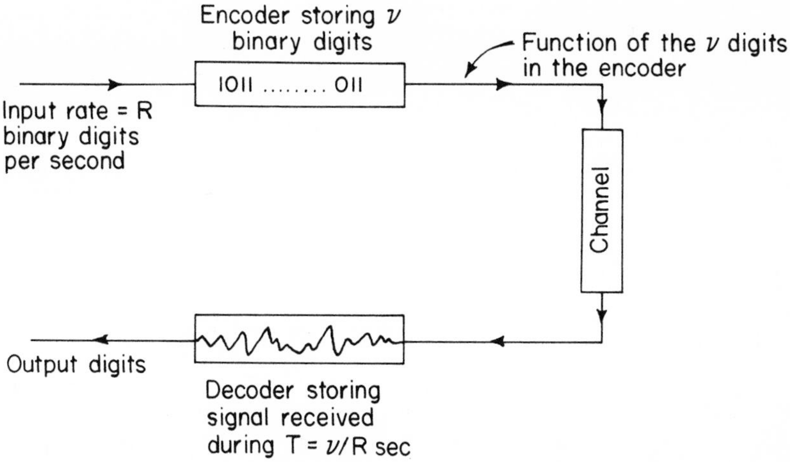

Fig. 1.6. Encoding and decoding of binary digits

digit transmitted influences the input to the channel over a time interval T, the decoder must consider the output from the channel over the corresponding time interval in deciding whether the digit transmitted was a zero or a one. Since the objective is to minimize the probability of error, the decoder generates in each instance the more probable of the two digits. It is easy to see that, disregarding any delay in the channel, T seconds elapse between the time at which a digit is fed to the encoder and the time at which the same digit is reproduced by the decoder. This is the time corresponding to the transmission of ν binary digits.

The probability of error per digit depends strongly on the number ν of binary digits stored in the encoder, as well as on the transmission rate R and on the channel capacity C. We shall see that the expression for this probability of error in the case of a channel with finite memory has this general form:

$$P(e) = K\, 2^{-\nu\alpha/R} \tag{1.3}$$

The factor K is a slowly varying function of ν and R. The exponential coefficient α is independent of ν and is a function of the binary transmission rate R and of the characteristics of the channel. Its dependence on R is of the general form illustrated in Fig. 1.7. The value of α is positive for all values of R smaller than C. It vanishes with a zero derivative for $R = C$. Thus, the probability of error vanishes exponentially with ν for any value of R smaller than C. As a matter of fact, the asymptotic behavior of $P(e)$ is given by

$$\lim_{\nu\to\infty} \frac{\log_2 P(e)}{\nu} = -\alpha/R \tag{1.4}$$

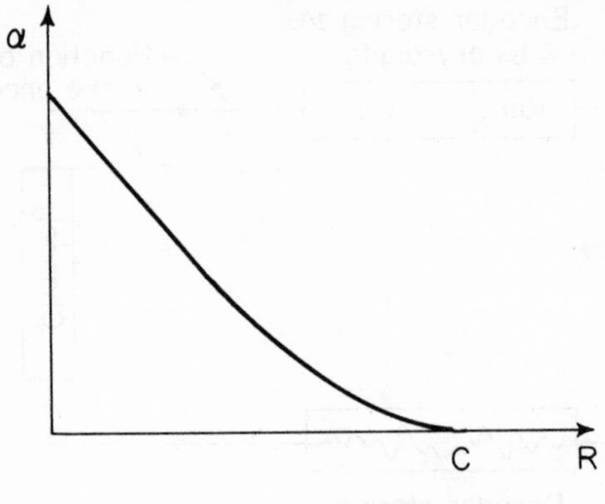

Fig. 1.7. Behavior of the exponential coefficient α as a function of the transmission rate

The origin of the exponential decay of the probability of error with ν cannot be fully discussed at this stage. However, the following argument may be of some help in clarifying the situation. We saw that each digit output from the decoder is decided upon on the basis of the output from the channel over the time interval T corresponding to the transmission of ν binary digits. This implies that the reception of each individual binary digit is hampered by the channel disturbance over the same time interval T.

Let us suppose, for instance, that the channel can be represented by the model of Fig. 1.3. Then, the severity of the disturbance affecting the transmission of each binary digit is measured by the fraction of channel pulses that are received incorrectly over the time interval T associated with the digit. As T is increased, this fraction converges in probability to the conditional probability p indicated in Fig. 1.3, because of the law of large numbers. In other words, the probability that the fraction of pulses received incorrectly during a time interval T will exceed p by any given amount approaches zero as T is increased. Then, if the encoding process makes allowance for an appropriate fraction of the pulses (greater than p) to be received incorrectly, the probability of error will vanish with increasing T. This argument can be generalized to other channels by defining an appropriate measure of the severity of the disturbance.

The central and most difficult question concerns the amount of channel disturbance (fraction of incorrectly received pulses in the above example) that can be tolerated for given values of ν and R. The diagram of Fig. 1.6 indicates that, while each digit influences T seconds of channel signal, the same segment of signal is also influenced by the following $\nu - 1$ digits. It is reasonable to expect the amount of channel disturbance that can be tolerated to decrease with increasing R for a fixed value of $T = \nu/R$. This is indeed the case, and it is responsible for the fact that the exponential factor α decreases with increasing R, as indicated in Fig. 1.7. The surprising result is that the amount of disturbance that can be tolerated is approximately independent of T, and therefore of ν, for any fixed transmission rate R. This is just what makes it possible for the probability of error to vanish with increasing ν for any fixed transmission rate smaller than the channel capacity. Unfortunately, this basic result cannot be further elucidated or made plausible by simple heuristic arguments.

1.6. Transmission Efficiency, Probability of Error, and Equipment Complexity

The form of Eq 1.3 indicates the existence of an exchange relation between ν and α/R, in the sense that the probability of error depends on the product $\nu\alpha/R$, at least for large values of ν. In other words, the probability of error can be reduced by increasing either ν or α/R. We saw that α/R is a function of R for a given channel, and that it increases with decreasing R as indicated in Fig. 1.7. Conversely, the value of α/R increases with increasing channel capacity for a fixed transmission rate R. On the other hand, the complexity of the encoding and decoding devices increases with ν. Thus, the price of decreasing the probability of error for a fixed transmission rate can be paid either in terms of larger channel capacity or in terms of greater equipment complexity and decoding delay. Conversely, a given communication channel can be used more efficiently with the same probability of error at the cost of increasing the complexity of the encoding and decoding equipment and the length of the associated decoding delay. In practice, however, it is usually the equipment complexity, rather than the decoding delay, that limits the value of ν.

The trading of channel capacity for equipment complexity, and vice versa, is very much affected by the manner in which the complexity of the encoding and decoding devices increases with the value of ν. Wozencraft [5] has shown that, in the case of a binary symmetric channel (the channel illustrated in Fig. 1.3), the complexity of a properly designed encoder grows linearly with ν, while the complexity of a properly designed decoder grows in proportion to $\nu \log \nu$. Similar relations between equipment complexity and ν are expected to hold for a large class of channels.

The form of encoding discussed above includes, as special cases, the traditional modulation techniques, namely, pulse-amplitude modulation, pulse-position modulation, and frequency modulation. The main difference between these traditional modulation techniques and the general form of encoding envisioned above lies in the magnitude of the number ν. The value of ν in these traditional forms of modulation is always small, less than 6 or 7. Larger values of ν could in principle be used, except for the fact that the conventional decoding techniques used in connection with these forms of modulation would not be adequate. More precisely, these conventional techniques would lead to inordinately complex decoding equipment. For instance, a frequency-modulation decoder designed for $\nu = 30$ would have to distinguish, in effect, between 2^{30} different frequencies. The only known general procedure for circumventing such an exponential growth of the decoder complexity is that suggested by Wozencraft. It must be stressed, however, that although Wozencraft's procedure leads to a reasonable growth of equipment complexity with ν, the resulting equipment complexity is still rather large for large values of ν. Thus, the practical use of these encoding and decoding techniques hinges on the full exploitation of modern techniques for packaging and mass producing complex data-processing devices.

1.7. Summary and Conclusions

This chapter has been devoted to a preliminary formulation of the communication problem and to a brief survey of the major results of our theory. These results can be summarized as follows: For any given source-user pair and any given channel, two numbers R and C can be defined representing, respectively, the minimum number of binary digits per second required to represent the output from the source, and the maximum number of binary digits per second that can be transmitted through the channel. If the source rate R is smaller than the channel capacity C, it is possible to transmit the source output through the channel according to the fidelity criterion prescribed by the user. Furthermore, the transmission can be achieved by first transforming the source output into a sequence of binary digits, which is later transformed back into a satisfactory reproduction of the source output. These binary digits can, in turn, be transmitted through the channel with a vanishingly small probability of error, provided only that their rate is smaller than the channel capacity. A substantial increase of equipment complexity is the price that must be paid to achieve a vanishingly small probability of error for a transmission rate close to the channel capacity. The minimization of the number of binary digits per second employed to represent the source output requires, similarly, fairly complex data-processing equipment.

In order to appreciate the impact that these results may have on the future of communication engineering, we must discuss briefly the present trends in the demand for communication facilities, and in the technology of data-processing equipment.

The traditional forms of communication are characterized by the fact that the user is a human rather than a machine. They evolved, we might say, as means for extending the range of human senses, as the names telegraph, telephone, and television indicate. For instance, a telephone system serves the function of bridging the space between the speaker and the listener, in an attempt to simulate normal acoustic communication between the two individuals. In other words, the telephone system plays the role of an additional channel connected in cascade to the acoustic channel used in normal conversation. The input and output equipment transforms acoustic energy into electric energy, and vice versa, and shifts the electric signal from the frequency band characteristic of speech to one more appropriate for electromagnetic energy propagation. The important point is that the encoding and decoding operations are performed not within the telephone system but by the speaker and by the listener as in normal conversation. A spoken language may be regarded from this point of view as a form of encoding developed through evolution to meet the needs of human communication. As such, it is capable of overcoming the disturbances normally present in the available acoustic channel, such as the sounds produced by natural phenomena and by other people. The critical part of the decoding operation is performed, of course, by the brain of the listener. Similar comments can be made about telegraph systems. The case of television is somewhat different, but it is still obvious that the brain of the viewer performs a critical decoding function.

The disturbances present in most communication systems are rather similar to the natural disturbances to which human senses are accustomed. This is the reason why traditional communication systems can provide satisfactory operation with a minimum of terminal equipment. It is a common experience that, when confronted by abnormally severe disturbances, we speak more slowly, and use a smaller vocabulary. This is equivalent to reducing the rate of transmission of information. Thus, we adjust automatically the form of encoding to the characteristics of the available channel. Presumably, the nature and the complexity of the decoding operation performed by our brain vary as well with the type and severity of the disturbances. This is evidenced, for instance, by the fact that we find it more tiresome to listen in the presence of severe disturbances.

Machine-to-machine communication is a newcomer among traditional forms of communication. However, some people expect that the volume of communication between digital computers will equal that of speech communication within the next decade. Therefore, in looking at the future, we must pay particular attention to the requirements of this new type of communication.

Machine-to-machine communication does not benefit from the availability of a natural encoding process nor from the availability of a human brain to perform complex decoding operations. Any necessary encoding and decoding operations must be performed within the communication system or within the machines linked by the system. Clearly, the overall transmission accuracy must be comparable to the accuracy of the machines. A high level of accuracy can always be provided with conventional modulation techniques, by repeating each binary digit a sufficiently large number of times. This leads, however, to a grossly inefficient use of communication facilities. On the other hand, the use of complex terminal equipment would permit us to achieve the same accuracy, while utilizing much more efficiently the available communication channel. Clearly, it is a matter of balancing the cost of the communication channel with that of the terminal equipment. Little can be said, at this time, about this balance of costs, because no experimental evidence is available concerning the actual complexity of the necessary terminal equipment. However, as explained below, technological trends seem to indicate a continuous shift of this balance towards the use of more complex terminal equipment.

Digital technology is progressing at a very rapid rate both with respect to the speed and size of components and to mass-production techniques. It is reasonable to assume, therefore, that the size and cost of the terminal equipment that would be required for accurate and efficient communication will steadily decrease for some time in the future. The same cannot be said about the cost of communication channels per unit capacity. Although much progress has been made in developing new communication channels, the installation of the necessary equipment, such as large antennas and underground cables or waveguides, does not lend itself to mass production. Therefore, the cost of channel capacity is not likely to decrease appreciably in the future. This suggests a trend towards a more efficient utilization of channel capacity at the cost of more complex terminal equipment. It is helpful to keep in mind, in this regard, that present-day digital communication systems are usually operated at a rate in the neighborhood of 10 per cent of channel capacity or even less.

There is another important aspect of machine-to-machine communication which is intimately connected with the theoretical results summarized above. Since this new form of communication has requirements considerably different from those of the traditional forms, it becomes more important to dissociate the design of the transmission system from the characteristics of the source and of the user of information. More precisely, the trend seems to be in the direction of general-purpose communication systems, designed to transmit binary digits. It is of cardinal importance in this regard that the requirement that all source outputs be first transformed into binary digits does not by itself place any limit on either the fidelity with which the source output can be reproduced, or on the efficiency of utilization of the communication channel. It does, however, require the development of encoding and decoding techniques that will permit the transmission of speech signals and pictures with as few binary digits as possible.

The problem of representing speech signals and pictures efficiently by means of binary digits has received a great deal of attention, particularly in the last decade. The main difficulty in this problem is the establishing of appropriate fidelity criteria; that is, the determination of which source outputs are to be regarded as equivalent. This problem is extremely interesting, but involves a great many considerations that are outside the scope of this text.

1.8. Selected References

The following list of references includes only key papers mentioned in the text and books believed to be of particular interest to the reader. No attempt is made in this chapter or in the following ones to provide a complete bibliography, because of the availability of the excellent, up-to-date bibliography listed below as Reference 10.

1. N. Wiener, Cybernetics, The Technology Press and John Wiley and Sons, New York, 1948. The introductory chapter presents a very illuminating history of the scientific activities of the 1940's in which the author's work is embedded, and of the origins of the inter-disciplinary research efforts which assumed major proportions in the following decade.

2. N. Wiener, Extrapolation, Interpolation, and Smoothing of Stationary Time Series, The Technology Press and John Wiley and Sons, New York, 1949. This volume is a reprint of a war-time report by the author, and of two related notes by N. Levinson. It presents the theory of statistical filtering and prediction developed by the author in connection with automatic fire control.

3. C. E. Shannon, "A Mathematical Theory of Communication," Bell System Tech. J., 27, 379, 623 (1948). This paper was reprinted in 1949, together with an article by W. Weaver, in a book with the same title published by the University of Illinois Press, Urbana, Ill.

4. C. E. Shannon, "Communication in the Presence of Noise," Proc. I.R.E., 37, 10 (1949). This paper, together with Reference 3 above laid the foundations of the theory presented in this text.

5. J. M. Wozencraft and B. Reiffen, Sequential Decoding, The Technology Press of M.I.T. and John Wiley and Sons, New York, 1961.

6. C. Cherry, On Human Communication, The Technology Press and John Wiley and Sons, New York, 1957. The second chapter presents an historical review of the evolution of the communication sciences.

7. A. Feinstein, Foundations of Information Theory, McGraw-Hill, New York, 1957. A textbook covering the mathematical foundations of Shannon's theory, as extended and refined by the author and other workers.

8. A. I. Khinchin, Mathematical Foundations of Information Theory, Dover, New York, 1957. A translation of two papers, "The Entropy Concept in Probability Theory" (1953) and "On the Fundamental Theorems of Information Theory" (1956), by the famous Russian mathematician presenting the work of Shannon and others in a rigorous mathematical form.

9. L. Brillouin, Science and Information Theory, Academic Press, New York, 1956. Chapters 12 and 13 discuss the relation between information and entropy in physical systems. Chapters 14, 15, and 16 discuss various related questions concerning the measurement of physical quantities.

10. F. L. Stumpers, A Bibliography of Information Theory, I. R. E. Transactions on Information Theory, PGIT-2, Nov., 1953 (original bibliography); IT-1, Sept., 1955 (first supplement); IT-3, June, 1957 (second supplement); IT-6, March, 1960 (third supplement).

Chapter 2

A MEASURE OF INFORMATION

The purpose of the preceding chapter was to provide a general frame of reference for our discussion of communication problems. We saw, in particular, how a typical communication process can be broken into a series of successive operations. We can now proceed to discuss each of these operations in detail, without fear of losing sight of the overall problem. Our first objective will be the definition of a measure of information which has proved to be extremely useful in the study of all of these operations. The rest of this chapter will be devoted to a study of the mathematical properties of this measure, and to interpreting its significance in various communication situations of interest.

2.1. Preliminary Considerations

The operations indicated in the model of a communication system in Fig. 1.1 have an important characteristic in common. The output from each of the boxes is supposed to specify in some sense the input to the same box. This is obviously true, since the input to the user must be a reproduction of the source output within the limits of the fidelity criterion imposed by the user. Let us consider, for instance, the encoding operation illustrated in Fig. 2.1. Let us suppose that message number 3 has been fed to the source encoder, and think of the corresponding binary digits shown in the second column as being generated in succession by the encoder.

Since the code word corresponding to the message number 3 is 011, the first digit generated by the encoder will be 0. Clearly, this digit provides some information about the fact that message 3 is the message that has been fed to the encoder. For instance, the 0 indicates that the input message is one of the four messages 0, 1, 2, 3. The second digit generated by the encoder, 1, restricts further the input message to one of the two messages 2 and 3. Finally, the third digit, 1, uniquely identifies the message.

This process of successively restricting the set of possible messages does not provide a complete description of the manner in which the successive digits specify the input message. Clearly, the message probabilities play some role in the specification of the message, because the situation would be quite different, at least intuitively, if all the messages except 3 had vanishingly small probabilities. How, then, can we state precisely the extent to which each successive digit specifies the input message?

Message Number	Code Word	Message Probabilities Original	After 0	After 1	After 1
0	000	1/4	1/3	0	0
1	001	1/4	1/3	0	0
2	010	1/8	1/6	1/2	0
3	011	1/8	1/6	1/2	1
4	100	1/16	0	0	0
5	101	1/16	0	0	0
6	110	1/16	0	0	0
7	111	1/16	0	0	0

Fig. 2.1. The message probabilities after the generation of each of the digits of the code word corresponding to message 3

From the third column of Fig. 2.1 we see that the probability of message number 3 is 1/8. A simple computation shows that the probability of the same message is 1/6 after the generation of the first digit, 1/2 after the generation of the second digit, and finally 1 after the generation of the third digit, as shown in Fig. 2.1. It is clear from the same figure that the first digit multiplies by 4/3 the probabilities of the messages that are still possible; that is, by the reciprocal of the sum of the original probabilities of the same subset of messages. Similarly, the second digit multiplies by 3 the probabilities of the messages that are still possible after the second digit; that is, by the reciprocal of the sum of the probabilities of the same messages after the first digit. Finally, the third digit multiplies by 2 the probability of message 3; that is, by the reciprocal of its probability after the second digit. Clearly, these successive probability changes provide a complete description of the extent to which each successive digit contributes to the specification of the input message.

Let us consider next the example of Fig. 2.2. Two equiprobable messages are transmitted through the binary symmetric channel of Fig. 1.3 in the form of two sequences of pulses. The sequence corresponding to message 0 consists of three negative pulses, and that corresponding to message 1, of three positive pulses. The polarities of the three successive output pulses are + - +. A simple computation of the message probabilities after the reception of each of the three successive pulses leads to the values given in the last three columns of Fig. 2.2. The symbol p stands for the probability that the polarity of any output pulse be different from that of the corresponding input pulse. Thus, for instance, the probability of the output

Message Numbers	Input Pulse Sequence	Message Probabilities			
		Original	After +	After -	After +
0	- - -	1/2	p	1/2	p
1	+++	1/2	1-p	1/2	1-p

Fig. 2.2. The message probabilities after the reception of each of the pulses of the sequence + - + through the binary symmetric channel of Fig. 1.3

sequence + - + is $p(1 - p)^2$ when the input sequence is + + +, and $p^2 (1 - p)$ when the input sequence is - - - . Then, since the two possible input sequences, + + + and - - -, are a priori equiprobable, the probability of the input sequence + + + after reception of + - + is $[p(1 - p)^2] / [p(1 - p)^2 + p^2 (1 - p)] = 1 - p$.

If the value of p is smaller than 1/2 , the reception of the first pulse increases the probability of message 1 and decreases that of message 0 . The reception of the second pulse, on the other hand, has the opposite effect, and changes the probabilities back to their original values. The reception of the third pulse increases again the probability of message 1 and decreases that of message 0 in the same manner as the reception of the first pulse. Thus, if message 1 is the one actually transmitted, the reception of the first pulse increases its probability, the reception of the second pulse decreases it, and finally the reception of the last pulse increases it again. Again, as in the preceding example, these probability changes represent the extent to which the received pulses specify the input message. Here, however, the probability may decrease as well as increase as a result of the reception of a pulse.

It is desirable, at this point, to disregard temporarily the specific problems in which we are interested, and consider the definition of a measure of information from an abstract point of view. Instead of talking about messages, or symbols, we shall talk about points in some abstract space and about the ensembles of points that result from assigning probability distributions to the corresponding spaces. Thus, we shall remain free later on to give different interpretations to such points and to employ the measure of information defined in terms of them in connection with various aspects of communication problems.

We shall restrict our discussion, for the present, to discrete spaces; that is, to spaces consisting of points which can be arranged into a simple sequence $x_1, x_2, x_3, \ldots$. Continuous spaces will be considered at a later time, so as to prevent the mathematical difficulties inherent in them from obscuring the significance of the new concepts we wish to introduce.

2.2. Review of Basic Definitions

Let us consider two discrete spaces X and Y , and represent by x_k a particular point of the X space and by y_i a particular point of the Y space. The product space XY is defined as a space in which one point, and only one point, corresponds to each pair of points x, y, one in the X space, and the other in the Y space, respectively. This situation is illustrated geometrically in Fig. 2.3, where the product space XY consists of an array of points in the xy plane; each column of points in the array corresponds to a particular point x_k of the X space, and each row of points corresponds to a particular point y_i of the Y space. In other words, the points of the X space and the points of the Y space may be considered as coordinates of the points of the XY space.

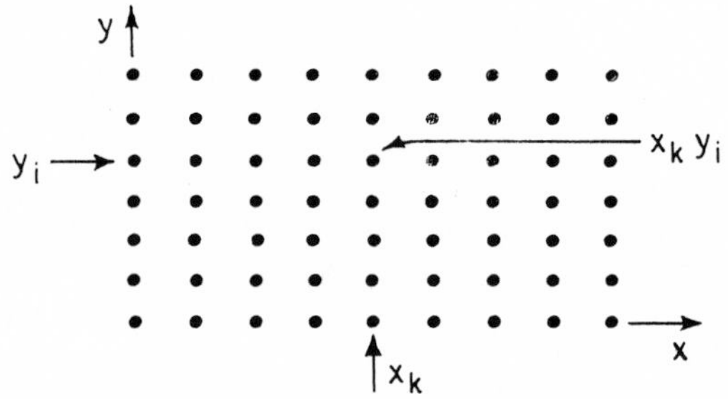

Fig. 2.3. Geometric illustration of the product space XY

The X ensemble is generated by defining a probability distribution P(x) on the X space, which assigns a probability $P(x_k)$ to each particular point x_k of the space.* The Y ensemble or any other ensemble may be generated in a similar manner. In particular, the XY ensemble is generated by assigning a joint probability distribution P(x, y) to the product space XY . The probability distributions P(x) and P(y) are defined in terms of P(x, y) by

$$P(x) \equiv \sum_{Y} P(x, y) \tag{2.1}$$

$$P(y) \equiv \sum_{X} P(x, y) \tag{2.2}$$

---

*The words "set," "space," and "ensemble" are used by most mathematicians as synonyms to indicate the aggregate of all points considered. However, in connection with physics and engineering applications, the word "ensemble" has been frequently used to indicate a space to which a probability distribution is assigned. We shall follow this latter usage.

where the summations are carried out over the Y space or the X space, as indicated. The conditional probability distributions $P(y|x)$ and $P(x|y)$ are defined by

$$P(y|x) \equiv \frac{P(x, y)}{P(x)} \tag{2.3}$$

$$P(x|y) \equiv \frac{P(x, y)}{P(y)} \tag{2.4}$$

It is hardly necessary to add that the sum of the probabilities assigned to all the points of any ensemble must be equal to one; in particular, we have for the product ensemble XY,

$$\sum_{XY} P(x, y) = 1 \tag{2.5}$$

The above relations can be interpreted in terms of Fig. 2.3 as follows. The probability $P(x_k)$ is the sum of the probabilities $P(x_k, y)$ assigned to the points of the column corresponding to x_k. Similarly, the probability $P(y_i)$ is the sum of the probabilities $P(x, y_i)$ assigned to the points of the row corresponding to y_i. For this reason, the probability distributions $P(x)$ and $P(y)$ are often called "marginal." The conditional probability $P(x_k|y_i)$ is equal to the probability $P(x_k, y_i)$ assigned to the point x_k, y_i divided by the sum of the probabilities assigned to the points in the row corresponding to y_i; that is, by $P(y_i)$, provided $P(y_i) \neq 0$. Similarly, the conditional probability $P(y_i|x_k)$ is equal to $P(x_k, y_i)$ divided by the sum of the probabilities assigned to the points of the column corresponding to x_k; that is, by $P(x_k)$, provided $P(x_k) \neq 0$. Thus, in a two-dimensional ensemble, a conditional probability can be thought of as the relative probability of a point with respect to the row or the column to which it belongs.

Higher-order product spaces and the probabilities associated with them can be defined in a similar manner. For instance, let us consider a third discrete space Z of which z_j is a particular point, and the product space XYZ in which each point represents a particular triplet of points $x\ y\ z$. We may think of this product space as a three-dimensional array of points arranged along lines parallel to the x, y and z axes in such a way that the point representing the triplet $x_k\ y_i\ z_j$ is located at the intersection of the three planes $x = x_k$, $y = y_i$, $z = z_j$. Then, if we assign to this triple product space a probability distribution $P(x, y, z)$, we have, by definition,

$$P(x, y) \equiv \sum_{Z} P(x, y, z) \tag{2.6}$$

$$P(y, z) \equiv \sum_{X} P(x, y, z) \tag{2.7}$$

$$P(x, z) \equiv \sum_{Y} P(x, y, z) \tag{2.8}$$

Thus, for instance, $P(x_k, y_i)$ is equal to the sum of the probabilities assigned to the points located on the straight line, parallel to the z axis, formed by the intersection of the plane $x = x_k$ with the plane $y = y_i$. It should be clear by now that

$$P(x) \equiv \sum_{Y} P(x, y) \equiv \sum_{YZ} P(x, y, z) \tag{2.9}$$

so that $P(x_k)$ is the sum of the probabilities assigned to the points of the plane $x = x_k$. Similar expressions can be written for $P(y)$ and $P(z)$.

The conditional probability distribution $P(x|y\ z)$ is defined as the ratio

$$P(x|y\ z) \equiv \frac{P(x, y, z)}{P(y, z)} \tag{2.10}$$

Thus, $P(x_k|y_i\ z_j)$ is equal to the probability assigned to the point $x_k\ y_i\ z_j$ divided by the sum of the probabilities assigned to the points on the straight-line intersection of the planes $y = y_i$ and $z = z_j$. The other conditional probability distributions are defined in a similar manner.

If the conditional probability distribution $P(x|y\ z)$ is independent of the particular pair y, z constituting the condition; that is, if

$$P(x|y\ z) = P(x) \tag{2.11}$$

for all points of the product space XYZ, we say that the X ensemble is statistically independent of the product ensemble YZ, and

$$P(x, y, z) = P(x)\ P(y, z) \tag{2.12}$$

On the other hand, if this is the case,

$$P(y, z|x) \equiv \frac{P(x, y, z)}{P(x)} = \frac{P(x)\ P(y, z)}{P(x)} = P(y, z) \tag{2.13}$$

so that the YZ ensemble is independent of the X ensemble. In other words, the two ensembles are mutually independent. The generalization of this definition of statistical independence to other situations is obvious. It should be noted, however, that the fact that the X ensemble is statistically independent of the Y ensemble and of the Z ensemble, separately, does not necessarily imply that the X ensemble is statistically independent of the product ensemble YZ. In other words, the pair of relations

$$P(x, y) = P(x)\ P(y)\ ; \qquad P(x, z) = P(x)\ P(z) \tag{2.14}$$

does not necessarily imply

$$P(x, y, z) = P(x) P(y, z) \tag{2.15}$$

2.3. A Measure of Information

Let us consider again two discrete spaces, X and Y, and represent by x_k a particular point of X and by y_i a particular point of Y. A probability distribution $P(x, y)$ is given over the product space XY. We wish to define a measure of the information provided by y_i about x_k.

Let us think of x_k as representing the input to one of the boxes of Fig. 1.1 and y_i as the corresponding output. Taking the point of view of an external observer, knowing both input and output, we would like to define a measure of the extent to which y_i specifies x_k; that is, a measure of the amount of information communicated through the box. The two examples of Sec. 2.2 indicate that the information provided by y_i about x_k consists of changing the probability of x_k from the a priori value $P(x_k)$ to the a posteriori value $P(x_k | y_i)$. The measure of this change of probability which turns out to be convenient for our purposes is the logarithm of the ratio of the a posteriori probability and the a priori probability. Thus, we make the following general definition:

> The amount of information provided by the occurrence of the event represented by y_i about the occurrence of the event represented by x_k is defined as

$$I(x_k; y_i) \equiv \log \frac{P(x_k | y_i)}{P(x_k)} \tag{2.16}$$

The base of the logarithm used in this definition fixes the magnitude of the unit of information. The base most commonly used is 2, in which case a unit of information is provided about x_k when its probability is increased by a factor of 2. The natural base e is often used instead of 2, because of its mathematical convenience. The corresponding unit of information is obtained when the probability is increased by a factor equal to e. Clearly, an increase of probability by a factor of 10 yields the unit associated with the use of base 10 logarithms. The names "bit", "nat," and "Hartley" are commonly used to indicate these three units. The name "bit" is a contraction of "binary digit," and the name "nat" is a contraction of "natural unit." The decimal unit has been named in honor of R. V. L. Hartley, because of his pioneering work on communication theory.

The measure just defined has the very important property of being symmetrical with respect to x_k and y_i. This symmetry can be easily demonstrated by multiplying the numerator and the denominator in the ratio of Eq. 2.16 by $P(y_i)$. We obtain

$$I(x_k;y_i) = \log \frac{P(x_k|y_i)\,P(y_i)}{P(x_k)\,P(y_i)} = \log \frac{P(x_k, y_i)}{P(x_k)\,P(y_i)} \qquad (2.17)$$

It follows immediately that

$$I(x_k;y_i) = I(y_i;x_k) \qquad (2.18)$$

In other words, the information provided by y_i about x_k is equal to the information provided by x_k about y_i. For this reason, we shall refer to the measure just defined as the mutual information between x_k and y_i.

The righthand side of Eq. 2.17 suggests interpreting the mutual information just defined as a measure of the statistical constraint between x_k and y_i. In fact, the measure is equal to zero when the two events in question are statistically independent; that is,

$$P(x_k, y_i) = P(x_k)\,P(y_i) \qquad (2.19)$$

The measure is positive when the two events have a larger probability of occurring together than separately. Conversely, the measure is negative when the two events have a smaller probability of occurring together than separately.

Let us consider next the product ensemble XYZ, and represent a particular point of this ensemble by the triplet $x_k y_i z_j$, occurring with probability $P(x_k, y_i, z_j)$.

The mutual information between x_k and y_i for a given z_j is defined, consistently with Eq. 2.16 and Eq. 2.17, by

$$I(x_k;y_i|z_j) \equiv \log \frac{P(x_k|y_i z_j)}{P(x_k|z_j)} = \log \frac{P(x_k, y_i|z_j)}{P(x_k|z_j)P(y_i|z_j)} \qquad (2.20)$$

In other words, the conditional mutual information is defined exactly as in Eq. 2.16, except for the fact that the a priori and the a posteriori probabilities appearing in this equation must be conditioned by the same event z_j. This definition generalizes immediately to the situation in which the mutual information is conditioned by several events.

2.4. Additional Properties of the Measure of Information

Let us consider the product ensemble XYZ of which a typical member is $x_k y_i z_j$, and the mutual information

$$I(x_k;y_i z_j) \equiv \log \frac{P(x_k|y_i z_j)}{P(x_k)} \qquad (2.21)$$

To focus our attention on a particular situation, we may regard x_k as the message input to an encoder, and y_i and z_j as corresponding symbols generated in succession by the encoder. Then, the mutual information of Eq. 2.21 represents the information provided by the output symbols y_i and z_j about the input message x_k. We would like to express this mutual information in terms of the information provided by the first output symbol y_i about the message and the information provided by the second output symbol z_j about the same message.

Multiplying the numerator and denominator of the ratio in Eq. 2.21 by $P(x_k|y_i)$ yields

$$I(x_k;y_iz_j) = \log \frac{P(x_k|y_i)}{P(x_k)} + \log \frac{P(x_k|y_iz_j)}{P(x_k|y_i)}$$

$$= I(x_k;y_i) + I(x_k;z_j|y_i) \tag{2.22}$$

In words, the information provided by the pair y_iz_j about x_k is equal to the sum of the information provided by y_i about x_k and the information provided by z_j about x_k when y_i is known. This result checks perfectly with what our intuition would suggest.

Of course, the order of the two symbols y_i and z_j is immaterial so that

$$I(x_k;y_iz_j) = I(x_k;z_j) + I(x_k;y_i|z_j) \tag{2.23}$$

Then, adding Eqs. 2.22 and 2.23 yields the expression

$$I(x_k;y_iz_j) = \frac{1}{2}\,[\,I(x_k;y_i) + I(x_k;z_j) + I(x_k;y_i|z_j) + I(x_k;z_j|y_i)] \tag{2.24}$$

which is symmetrical in y_i and z_j.

Because of the symmetry of the mutual information, we can regard the mutual information of Eq. 2.21 as representing information provided by x_k about y_i and z_j. Then, interchanging the order of the symbols in each term of Eq. 2.22 yields

$$I(y_iz_j;x_k) = I(y_i;x_k) + I(z_j;x_k|y_i) \tag{2.25}$$

In words, the information provided by x_k about y_i and z_j is equal to the sum of the information provided by x_k about y_i and the information provided by x_k about z_j when y_i is known.

The two expressions given by Eqs. 2.22 and 2.25 permit us to expand in successive steps any mutual information between members of sub-ensembles of an arbitrary product ensemble into a sum of mutual informations between elements of the elementary ensembles constituting the product ensemble. Thus, for instance, we have for the product ensemble XYUV with typical element $x_ky_iu_gv_h$

$$I(x_ku_g;y_iv_h) = I(x_ku_g;y_i) + I(x_ku_g;v_h|y_i)$$

$$= I(x_k;y_i) + I(u_g;y_i|x_k) + I(x_k;v_h|y_i) + I(u_g;v_h|x_ky_i) \tag{2.26}$$

In the special case in which the product ensemble XY is statistically independent of the product ensemble UV, that is,

$$P(x, y, u, v) = P(x, y)\, P(u, v) \tag{2.27}$$

Eq. 2.26 reduces to

$$I(x_k u_g; y_i v_h) = I(x_k; y_i) + I(u_g; v_h) \tag{2.28}$$

In fact, the second and third terms on the righthand side of Eq. 2.26 vanish because of Eq. 2.27, and the conditions in the last term become immaterial also because of Eq. 2.27.

The expression provided by Eq. 2.28 has a very simple interpretation if we regard x and u as independent inputs to two separate channels, and y and v as the corresponding outputs. Then, Eq. 2.28 states that the information provided by the pair of outputs about the pair of inputs is equal to the sum of the informations provided separately by each output about the corresponding input. This result is again just what our intuition would suggest.

Example. The encoding operation described in Fig. 2.1 provides a simple illustration of addition of mutual informations. Let us indicate by u_3 the message fed to the encoder, and by x_0, y_1, z_1 the three successive digits of the corresponding code word. Then, the information provided by the first digit about the message is, from the entries in the third and fourth columns of Fig. 2.1,

$$I(u_3; x_0) = \log \frac{1/6}{1/8} = \log \frac{4}{3} \tag{2.29}$$

The additional information provided by the second digit about the message is, from the entries in the fourth and fifth columns of Fig. 2.1,

$$I(u_3; y_1 \mid x_0) = \log \frac{1/2}{1/6} = \log 3 \tag{2.30}$$

Finally, the additional information provided by the third digit about the message is, from the entries in the fifth and sixth columns of Fig. 2.1,

$$I(u_3; z_1 \mid y_1 x_0) = \log \frac{1}{1/2} = \log 2 \tag{2.31}$$

The total information provided about the message u_3 by the corresponding code word is the sum of the mutual informations given by the Eqs. 2.29, 2.30, and 2.31. Adding these values yields

$$I(u_3; x_0 y_1 z_1) = \log \frac{4}{3} + \log 3 + \log 2 = \log \frac{1}{1/8} = 3 \text{ bits} \tag{2.32}$$

This result indicates that the total information provided about the code word u_3 is equal to the logarithm of the reciprocal of the probability of occurrence of u_3. This follows from the fact that the code word uniquely specifies the message, as discussed in detail in Sec. 2.6.

*2.5 Derivation of the Measure of Information from Postulates

The measure of information defined in Sec. 2.3 can be derived directly from the following four postulates:

Postulate I. Given a product ensemble XY, the measure $I(x_k;y_i)$ of the information provided by y_i about x_k is a once-differentiable function $F(\phi, \theta)$ of the two variables $\phi = P(x_k)$ and $\theta = P(x_k|y_i)$.

Postulate II. Given a product ensemble XYZ, the measure $I(x_k;z_j|y_i)$ of the information about x_k provided by z_j for a given y_i is the same function $F(\phi, \theta)$ in which, however, $\phi = P(x_k|y_i)$ and $\theta = P(x_k|y_iz_j)$.

Postulate III. The measure $I(x_k;y_iz_j)$ of the information provided about x_k by the pair y_iz_j satisfies the relation

$$I(x_k;y_iz_j) = I(x_k;y_i) + I(x_k;z_j|y_i) \tag{2.33}$$

Postulate IV. Given two independent ensembles XY and UV; that is, ensembles for which

$$P(x, y, u, v) = P(x, y)\,P(u, v) \tag{2.34}$$

The measure $I(x_ku_g;y_iv_h)$ of the information about the pair x_ku_g provided by the pair y_iv_h satisfies the relation

$$I(x_ku_g;y_iv_h) = I(x_k;y_i) + I(u_g;v_h) \tag{2.35}$$

These four postulates are suggested by our intuition as conditions that should be satisfied by a useful measure of information. They are sufficient to specify the functional form of the desired measure, apart from a constant multiplier which determines the size of the unit of information. The following derivation** of the functional form of the measure involves two main steps.

The first step consists of showing that the function $F[P(x_k), P(x_k|y_i)]$ originally postulated, must be of the form:

*-Sections marked with an asterisk may be omitted without breaking the continuity of the presentation.

**-This derivation is similar to that presented by P. M. Woodward and I. L. Davies, Proc. I. E. E., 99, Pt. III, 37, 1952.

$$F[P(x_k), P(x_k|y_i)] = G[P(x_k)] - G[P(x_k|y_i)] \tag{2.36}$$

in order to satisfy the requirements set by Postulates II and III. In words, the measure must be the difference between the values assumed by some function $G(\gamma)$ when the a priori probability $P(x_k)$ and the a posteriori probability $P(x_k|y_i)$ are substituted for the variable γ; this result follows, as shown below, from Postulate III (in conjunction with Postulates I and II), which requires the total amount of information provided by y_i and z_j in succession to depend on the a priori probability $P(x_k)$ and on the final a posteriori probability $P(x_k|y_i z_j)$ but not on the intermediate probability $P(x_k|y_i)$.

The second step consists of showing that $G(\gamma)$ must be proportional to $\log \gamma$ in order to meet the requirement set by Postulate IV. Selection of a negative proportionality constant will yield finally

$$I(x_k;y_i) = \log \frac{P(x_k|y_i)}{P(x_k)} \tag{2.37}$$

where the base of the logarithm is arbitrary, as discussed in Sec. 2.3.

A proof of Eq. 2.36 may be obtained as follows. Let, for the sake of brevity,

$$p_0 = P(x_k), \quad p_1 = P(x_k|y_i), \quad p_2 = P(x_k|y_i\ z_j) \tag{2.38}$$

Postulates I, II, and III imply that the function $F(\phi, \theta)$ must satisfy the equation

$$F(p_0, p_2) = F(p_0, p_1) + F(p_1, p_2) \tag{2.39}$$

Differentiation of this equation with respect to p_1 yields

$$\left[\frac{\partial F(\phi,\theta)}{\partial \phi}\right]_{\substack{\phi = p_1 \\ \theta = p_2}} + \left[\frac{\partial F(\phi,\theta)}{\partial \theta}\right]_{\substack{\phi = p_0 \\ \theta = p_1}} = 0 \tag{2.40}$$

Since Eq. 2.40 must be satisfied for all possible values of p_0, p_1, and p_2, the first term must be independent of p_2, and the second one must be independent of p_0. In addition, the two partial derivatives must be equal in magnitude and opposite in sign for $\phi = \theta$. It follows that

$$\frac{\partial F(\phi,\theta)}{\partial \phi} = \left[\frac{dG(\gamma)}{d\gamma}\right]_{\gamma = \phi} \tag{2.41}$$

$$\frac{\partial F(\phi,\theta)}{\partial \theta} = -\left[\frac{dG(\gamma)}{d\gamma}\right]_{\gamma = \theta} \tag{2.42}$$

where $G(\gamma)$ is some once-differentiable function of the single variable γ. Then, integration of these two equations with respect to ϕ and θ yields

$$F(\phi, \theta) = G(\phi) - G(\theta) + K \tag{2.43}$$

where K is an arbitrary constant. Finally, substitution of Eq. 2.43 into Eq. 2.39 shows that $K = 0$, thereby completing the proof of Eq. 2.36.

The second step of the derivation of Eq. 2.37 proceeds as follows. Let again, for the sake of brevity,

$$q_0 = P(u_g), \quad q_1 = P(u_g | v_h) \tag{2.44}$$

Postulate IV, as expressed by Eq. 2.35, requires the function $G(\gamma)$ to satisfy the equation

$$G(p_0 q_0) - G(p_1 q_1) = G(p_0) - G(p_1) + G(q_0) - G(q_1) \tag{2.45}$$

where use is made of the fact that, because of Eq. 2.34,

$$P(x_k, u_g) = P(x_k)P(u_g) = p_0 q_0 \tag{2.46}$$

and

$$P(x_k, u_g | y_i v_h) = P(x_k | y_i)P(u_g | v_h) = p_1 q_1 \tag{2.47}$$

Differentiation of Eq. 2.45 with respect to p_0 yields

$$q_0 \left[\frac{dG(\gamma)}{d\gamma}\right]_{\gamma = p_0 q_0} = \left[\frac{dG(\gamma)}{d\gamma}\right]_{\gamma = p_0} \tag{2.48}$$

Similarly, differentiation with respect to q_0 yields

$$p_0 \left[\frac{dG(\gamma)}{d\gamma}\right]_{\gamma = p_0 q_0} = \left[\frac{dG(\gamma)}{d\gamma}\right]_{\gamma = q_0} \tag{2.49}$$

so that

$$p_0 \left[\frac{dG(\gamma)}{d\gamma}\right]_{\gamma = p_0} = q_0 \left[\frac{dG(\gamma)}{d\gamma}\right]_{\gamma = q_0} \tag{2.50}$$

for all possible non-zero values of p_0 and q_0. It follows that

$$\frac{dG(\gamma)}{d\gamma} = K_1 \frac{1}{\gamma} \tag{2.51}$$

where K_1 is an arbitrary constant, and, by integration,

$$G(\gamma) = K_1 \log \gamma + K_2 \tag{2.52}$$

where K_2 is a second arbitrary constant. Substitution of Eq. 2.52 into Eq. 2.43, with $K = 0$, yields finally

$$F(\phi, \theta) = K_1 \log \frac{\phi}{\theta} \tag{2.53}$$

The value of K_1 may be selected on the basis of convenience alone. Since ϕ represents an a priori probability and θ represents an a posteriori probability, and it would seem appropriate to make the measure of information positive when $\theta > \phi$, we select a negative value for K_1. Furthermore, selecting the magnitude of K_1 is equivalent to selecting the base of the logarithm. Thus

$$F(\phi, \theta) = \log \frac{\theta}{\phi} \tag{2.54}$$

which in turn yields Eq. 2.37.

2.6. The Measure of Self Information

Let us consider again the product ensemble XY, of which the pair $x_k y_i$ is a representative point. Since

$$P(x_k | y_i) \leq 1, \qquad P(y_i | x_k) \leq 1 \tag{2.55}$$

the mutual information between x_k and y_i

$$I(x_k; y_i) = \log \frac{P(x_k | y_i)}{P(x_k)} = \log \frac{P(y_i | x_k)}{P(y_i)} \tag{2.56}$$

satisfies the two inequalities

$$I(x_k; y_i) \begin{cases} \leq \log \dfrac{1}{P(x_k)} \equiv I(x_k) \\ \\ \leq \log \dfrac{1}{P(y_i)} \equiv I(y_i) \end{cases} \tag{2.57}$$

The equal signs hold when, and only when, the corresponding equal signs hold in Eq. 2.55.

The quantity

$$I(x_k) \equiv - \log P(x_k) \tag{2.58}$$

is said to be a measure of the <u>self information</u> of x_k. Similarly, the quantity

$$I(y_i) \equiv - \log P(y_i) \tag{2.59}$$

measures the <u>self information</u> of y_i. In words, the self information of any event is measured by the logarithm of the reciprocal of its probability of occurrence.

The measure of self information can be given two different interpretations, depending on the role played by the event or symbol in question. If x_k represents a message input to an encoder, $I(x_k)$ measures the amount of information that must be provided about x_k in order to specify it uniquely. This follows from the fact that the mutual information between x_k and any other event, such as y_i, becomes equal to the self information of x_k when, and only when, the conditional probability $P(x_k|y_i)$ is equal to 1; that is, when y_i uniquely specifies x_k. In particular, the self information of x_k is the maximum amount of information that can possibly be provided about x_k.

The other interpretation of self information applies, for instance, when we regard y_i as the first symbol of the code word corresponding to the input message x_k. In this particular case, the information provided by y_i about x_k is equal to the self information of the symbol represented by y_i when, and only when, the conditional probability $P(y_i|x_k)$ is equal to 1 , as indicated by Eqs. 2.55 and 2.57. This is the same as saying that the symbol in question represented by y_i is uniquely specified by the message x_k , as expected in a properly designed encoder. In particular, since the information provided by y_i about x_k cannot exceed the self information of y_i, the latter can be interpreted as the maximum amount of information that the symbol y_i is capable of providing.

Example. These two interpretations of the measure of self information can be illustrated with the help of Fig. 2.1. If we indicate with u_3 the third message, and with x_0, y_1, z_1 the three successive digits of the corresponding code word, the amount of information that must be provided about u_3 by the corresponding code word must be equal to the self information of u_3. Thus,

$$I(u_3\,;\,x_0\,y_1 z_1) = I(u_3) = \log \frac{1}{1/8} = 3 \text{ bits} \tag{2.60}$$

in agreement with Eq. 2.32. The self information of the first symbol of the code word, x_0, can be readily evaluated from the message probabilities listed in Fig. 2.1. We obtain

$$I(x_0) = -\log P(x_0) = \log \frac{4}{3} \tag{2.61}$$

This is the same as the value given by Eq. 2.29 for the information provided by x_0 about u_3 , since $P(x_0|u_3) = 1$.

Let us consider next the product ensemble XYZ, of which the triplet $x_k y_i z_j$ is a typical point. The conditional mutual information

$$I(x_k;y_i|z_j) = \log \frac{P(x_k|y_i z_j)}{P(x_k|z_j)} = \log \frac{P(y_i|x_k z_j)}{P(y_i|z_j)} \tag{2.62}$$

satisfies the two inequalities:

$$I(x_k;y_i|z_j) \begin{cases} \leq \log \dfrac{1}{P(x_k|z_j)} \equiv I(x_k|z_j) \\ \\ \leq \log \dfrac{1}{P(y_i|z_j)} \equiv I(y_i|z_j) \end{cases} \quad (2.63)$$

similar to those given in Eq. 2.57. Thus, the conditional self informations

$$I(x_k|z_j) \equiv -\log P(x_k|z_j) \quad (2.64)$$

$$I(y_i|z_j) \equiv -\log P(y_i|z_j) \quad (2.65)$$

can be interpreted in the same manner as the self informations given by Eqs. 2.58 and 2.59. In other words, the conditional self information of an event or symbol can be interpreted either as the amount of information that must be provided about the event in order to specify it uniquely under the stated conditions, or as the maximum amount of information that the event in question is capable of providing under the same stated conditions.

The binary unit of information associated with these two logarithms, namely the bit, can now be interpreted in a more straightforward manner. A bit is the self information of a binary digit when the two possible digits occur with equal probabilities. This interpretation explains why the name of the unit is a contraction of binary digit.

We chose, in our presentation, to define first the measure of mutual information, and then to obtain from it the measure of self information. We could have chosen, just as well, to follow the opposite procedure of defining first the measure of self information, and then obtaining from it the measure of mutual information. In fact, Eq. 2.56 can be rewritten with the help of Eqs. 2.58, 2.59, 2.64, and 2.65, in the form

$$I(x_k;y_i) = I(x_k) - I(x_k|y_i) = I(y_i) - I(y_i|x_k) \quad (2.66)$$

This equation can be interpreted as follows. The information provided by y_i about x_k is equal to the difference between the amounts of information required to specify x_k, before and after y_i becomes known. Similarly, it is equal to the difference between the amounts of information required to specify y_i, before and after x_k becomes known.

The mutual information between x_k and y_i can also be expressed in the following symmetrical form

$$I(x_k;y_i) = I(x_k) + I(y_i) - I(x_k y_i) \quad (2.67)$$

where

$$I(x_k y_i) \equiv -\log P(x_k, y_i) \quad (2.68)$$

is the self information of the point $x_k y_i$ of the product ensemble XY. Conversely,

$$I(x_k y_i) = I(x_k) + I(y_i) - I(x_k ; y_i) \tag{2.69}$$

This last equation states that the self information of the pair $x_k y_i$ is equal to the amount of information required to specify x_k plus the amount of information required to specify y_i, independently of x_k, minus the amount of information about y_i that has already been provided by x_k (or vice versa).

2.7. Information as a Random Variable

The measure of information discussed in the preceding sections can be regarded as random variables*, in the sense that each measure assumes some particular value at each point of the ensemble for which it is defined. In other words, we can look upon a measure of information as a value associated to a random event. The fact that the value itself is a function of the probabilities of the points of the ensemble is immaterial.

We shall have occasion, later on, to deal with various ensemble properties of measures of information. It will be very helpful, therefore, to be able to visualize the probability distributions of the measures, when considered as random variables. As an example, Fig. 2.4 illustrates the probability distribution of the self information of

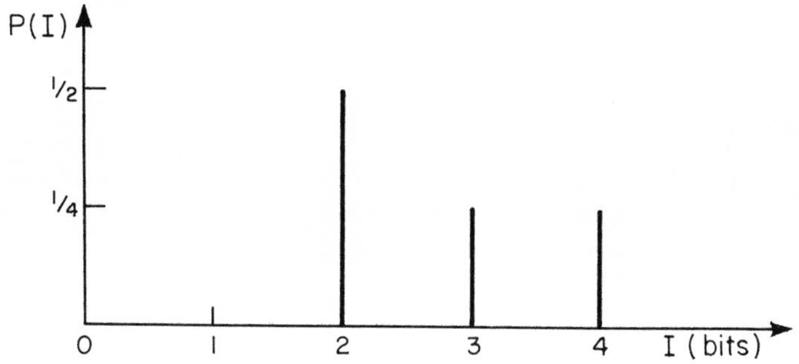

Fig. 2.4. Plot of $P(I) \equiv Pr(I(u) = I)$ for the message ensemble of Fig. 2.1

the messages shown in Fig. 2.1. If we indicate with u any particular message of the ensemble U, the function

$$P(I) \equiv Pr(I(u) = I) \tag{2.70}$$

plotted in Fig. 2.4 is the probability that the message self information $I(u)$ be equal to I. In other words, the function $P(I)$ is the

* Chapters 3 and 4 of Reference 2 (Sec. 2.14) discuss random variables at a level appropriate for the purposes of this section.

probability distribution of the self information of u. Since we are dealing with a discrete ensemble, the self information can assume only a discrete set of values. Thus, the plot of Fig. 2.4 consists of a discrete set of vertical lines whose lengths represent the probabilities that the self information will assume the corresponding values indicated on the I axis. For instance, the vertical line at $I = 3$ has length $1/4$ because the two messages with self information equal to 3 occur each with probability $1/8$, and therefore with a total probability of $1/4$.

The distribution function of the same random variable $I(u)$ is, by definition,

$$F(I) \equiv \Pr[I(u) \leq I] \tag{2.71}$$

the probability that $I(u)$ be smaller than or equal to I. The distribution function for the self information of the messages of Fig. 2.1 is shown in Fig. 2.5. If we regard each vertical line in Fig. 2.4 as

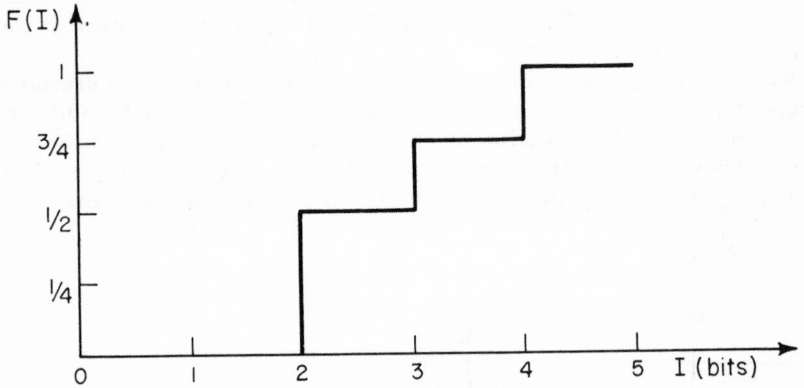

Fig. 2.5. Plot of $F(I) \equiv \Pr[I(u) \leq I]$ for the message ensemble of Fig. 2.1

representing an impulse of weight (that is, area) equal to the height of the line, and remember that an integral of a unit impulse is a unit step, the distribution function can be expressed as the integral

$$F(I) \equiv \int_{-\infty}^{I} p(x)\, dx \tag{2.72}$$

where the probability density $p(x)$ is defined by

$$p(x) \equiv \begin{cases} \infty & \text{for } x = I(u) \\ 0 & \text{otherwise} \end{cases} \tag{2.73}$$

$$\int_{I-\epsilon}^{I+\epsilon} p(x)\, dx \equiv \begin{cases} P(I) & \text{for } I = I(u) \\ 0 & \text{otherwise} \end{cases} \tag{2.74}$$

where ϵ is an arbitrarily small positive number (and smaller than the smallest difference between possible values I).

A frequently used characteristic of the random variable I(u) is its expectation, or average value, defined by

$$E[I(u)] \equiv \int_{-\infty}^{\infty} I\, p(I)\, dI = \sum_{U} P(u)\, I(u) \equiv I(U) \tag{2.75}$$

where the probability density p(I) is defined by Eqs. 2.73 and 2.74, and the summation is evaluated over the points of the ensemble U . We shall use the notation I(U) to indicate the average value of I(u) over the ensemble U . This average value is equal to 2.75 bits for the ensemble of Fig. 2.1.

Another useful characteristic of the random variable I(u) is its variance, defined by

$$\text{Var } I(u) \equiv \int_{-\infty}^{\infty} I^2\, p(I) dI - I^2(U) = \sum_{U} P(u)\, I^2(u) - I^2(U) \tag{2.76}$$

The variance of the self information (in bits) for the ensemble of Fig. 2.1 is equal to 11/16.

Let us consider next the binary symmetric channel illustrated in Fig. 2.6. The probability distribution

$$P(I) \equiv \Pr[I(x;y) = I] \tag{2.77}$$

of the mutual information between input and output symbols is plotted

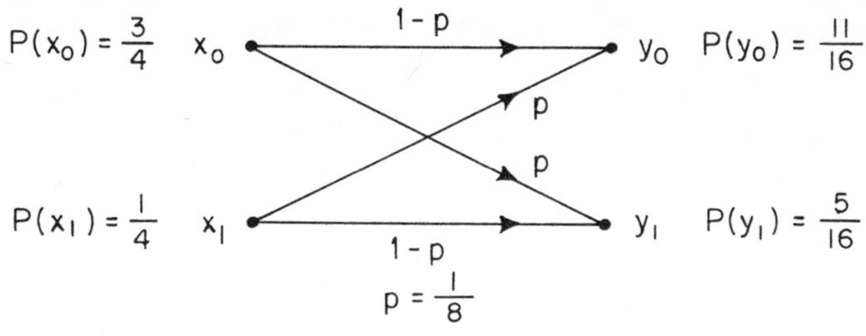

Fig. 2.6. Example of a binary symmetric channel

in Fig. 2.7. Each vertical line corresponds to an xy pair; its height represents the probability of occurrence of the pair, and its position along the I axis represents the corresponding value of the mutual information.

The corresponding distribution function for the mutual information

$$F(I) \equiv \Pr[I(x;y) \leq I] \tag{2.78}$$

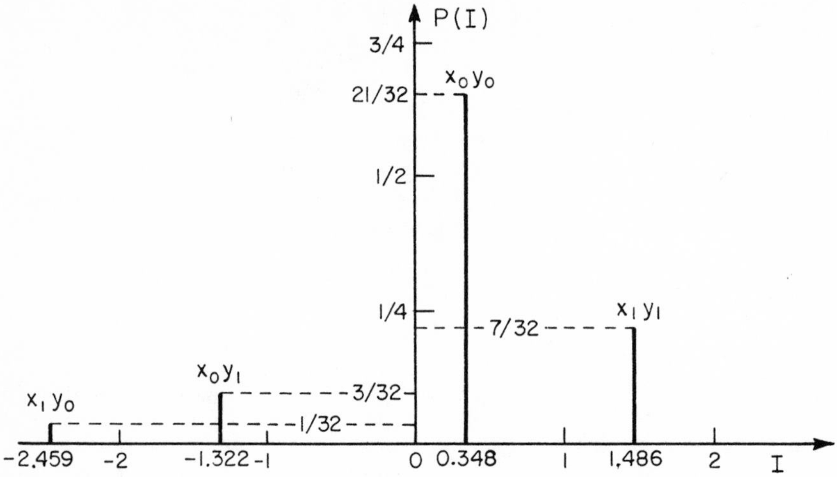

Fig. 2.7. Plot of $P(I) \equiv \Pr[I(x;y) = I]$ for channel of Fig. 2.6

is plotted in Fig. 2.8. Again, we can represent the distribution function in integral form,

$$F(I) \equiv \int_{-\infty}^{I} p(z)\, dz \tag{2.79}$$

where the probability density p(z) is defined by the two equations

$$p(z) \equiv \begin{cases} \infty & \text{for } z = I(x;y) \\ 0 & \text{otherwise} \end{cases} \tag{2.80}$$

$$\int_{I-\epsilon}^{I+\epsilon} p(z)\, dz \equiv \begin{cases} P(I) & \text{for } I = I(x;y) \\ 0 & \text{otherwise} \end{cases} \tag{2.81}$$

where ϵ is an arbitrarily small positive number as in Eq. 2.74.

By analogy to Eq. 2.75, the expectation, or average value, of the mutual information is defined by

$$E[I(x;y)] \equiv \int_{-\infty}^{\infty} I\, p(I)\, dI = \sum_{XY} P(x, y)\, I(x;y) \equiv I(X;Y) \tag{2.82}$$

where the probability density p(I) is defined by Eqs. 2.80 and 2.81, and the summation is evaluated over all points of the product ensemble XY. The notation I(X;Y) is used to indicate the average

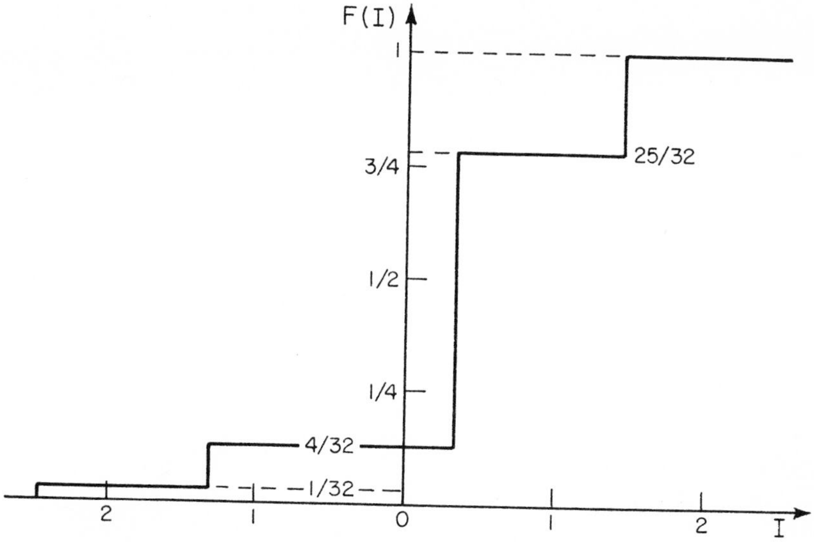

Fig. 2.8. Plot of $F(I) \equiv Pr[I(x;y) \leq I]$ for channel of Fig. 2.6

value of $I(x;y)$ over the product ensemble XY. This average value is equal to 0.353 for the channel of Fig. 2.6.

We shall be interested also in conditional probability distributions, such as

$$P(I|y_i) \equiv Pr[I(x;y_i) = I] \tag{2.83}$$

where y_i is a particular point of the Y ensemble. In the particular case of the channel of Fig. 2.6, the conditional probability distribution for $i = 1$ consists of two vertical lines:

$$P(1.486|y_1) = P(x_1|y_1) = 0.7 \tag{2.84}$$

$$P(-1.322|y_1) = P(x_0|y_1) = 0.3 \tag{2.85}$$

The corresponding conditional expectation is then

$$E[I(x;y_i)] \equiv \sum_X P(x|y_i)\ I(x;y_i) \equiv I(X;y_i) \tag{2.86}$$

which in the particular example considered becomes

$$I(X;y_1) = 0.7 \times 1.486 - 0.3 \times 1.322 = 0.644 \tag{2.87}$$

Clearly, if y_i is a particular symbol received through a channel, $I(X;y_i)$ represents the average amount of information provided by y_i about the transmitted symbol x. We shall see in Sec. 2.9 that this quantity is never negative, in spite of the fact that the mutual information may be negative. It follows that the average value of the mutual information

$$I(X;Y) \equiv \sum_{XY} P(x,y)\ I(x;y) = \sum_{Y} P(y)\ I(X;y) \qquad (2.88)$$

is similarly non-negative.

The following two sections are devoted to a more detailed study of the properties of various average values of measures of information.

2.8. Communication Entropy

We saw in Sec. 2.6 that the self information of a message can be interpreted as the amount of information that must be provided about the message in order to specify it uniquely. Thus, the amount of information that must be provided on the average, in order to specify any particular message of an ensemble X, is the average value of the self information

$$I(X) \equiv - \sum_{X} P(x)\ \log P(x) \equiv H(X) \qquad (2.89)$$

This expression is very basic, so much so that it was used by Shannon as the starting point in his original presentations of the theory. It is identical in form to the expression obtained in statistical mechanics for the thermodynamic quantity known as "entropy" (more precisely, average entropy of a canonical system), if $P(x)$ is taken as the probability of one of the possible states of a system. For this reason, the same name of "entropy" and the corresponding symbol $H(X)$ are used in connection with communication problems to indicate the quantity defined by Eq. 2.89. Thus, $H(X)$ and $I(X)$ stand for the same quantity. As a matter of fact, the connection between average self information and entropy appears to be more profound than a mere mathematical similarity [3]. Although a detailed discussion of such a relationship is beyond the scope of this presentation, it is still worth while mentioning the basic idea involved.

The quantity $H(X)$ may be considered as a measure of the "uncertainty" existing about the message before its reception. On the other hand, thermodynamic entropy is, in a sense, a measure of "disorder;" that is, a measure of how much uncertainty exists about the microscopic state in which a system might be found at a given time. Examples have been presented in which the entropy of a physical system may be decreased by using data available about the microscopic state of the system [3]. It has been verified, however, that the obtainable decrease of entropy cannot be larger, on the average, than the amount of information available (measured in appropriate units) about the state of the system, and that the physical process of obtaining such information results in an increase of entropy equal, at least, to the average amount of information obtained. Thus, as expected, the second law of thermodynamics is not violated by such processes.

The entropy $H(X)$ is non-negative because $I(x)$ is non-negative. Since the product $P(x) \log P(x)$ vanishes only for $P(x) = 0$ and $P(x) = 1$, $H(X)$ is equal to zero when, and only when, $P(x) = 1$ for some point x_k of X. This situation occurs, for instance, when only one message can ever be transmitted, in which case no information can be provided about it as it is completely specified from the start.

The behavior of the entropy $H(X)$ as a function of $P(x)$ is of particular interest when the X space is interpreted as the set of symbols used for encoding purposes. In this case, as discussed in Sec. 2.6, the self information of a particular symbol represents the amount of information that the symbol can provide about the message input to the encoder. Thus, the entropy of an ensemble of symbols represents the amount of information that a symbol can provide, on the average, and, as such, it is a measure of the effectiveness with which the different symbols can be employed. The following property of $H(X)$ is of particular importance in this regard.

Theorem. The entropy $H(X)$ satisfies the inequality

$$H(X) \leq \log M \tag{2.90}$$

where M is the number of points in the X space. The equal sign holds when, and only when, $P(x)$ has the same value $1/M$ for all points of the X space.

Proof. This theorem can be proved with the help of the inequality

$$\ln w \leq w - 1 \tag{2.91}$$

which follows from the fact that the line $u = \ln w$ is tangent to the straight line $u = w - 1$ at the point $w = 1$, while its slope is a monotonically decreasing function of w.

Let us consider the difference

$$H(X) - \log M = \sum_X P(x) \log \frac{1}{P(x)} - \sum_X P(x) \log M$$

$$= \sum_X P(x) \log \frac{1}{M\,P(x)} \tag{2.92}$$

Substitution of the righthand side of Eq. 2.91 in each term of the summation on the righthand side of Eq. 2.92 yields

$$H(X) - \log M \leq \sum_{X} \left[\frac{1}{M} - P(x)\right] \log e = 0 \qquad (2.93)$$

The equal sign holds when, and only when,

$$w = \frac{1}{M\,P(x)} = 1 \qquad (2.94)$$

because this is the value of w for which the equal sign holds in Eq. 2.91.

QED

Example. In the special case of $M = 2$, Eq. 2.89 reduces to

$$H(X) = -[p \log p + (1 - p) \log (1 - p)] \qquad (2.95)$$

where p is the probability of one of the two points of the space. The behavior of $H(X)$ as a function of p is illustrated in Fig. 2.9. The maximum value of $H(X)$, one bit, occurs for $p = 1-p = 0.5$; the curve is symmetrical with respect to this value of p.

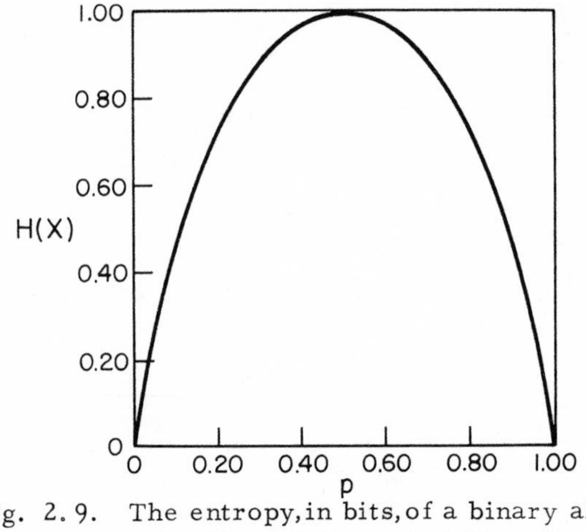

Fig. 2.9. The entropy, in bits, of a binary alphabet as a function of the probability of one of the two symbols

The main significance of the property expressed by Eq. 2.90 may be stated as follows. For any given alphabet of symbols, the amount of information that can be provided, on the average, by one symbol is maximum when all symbols are used with equal probabilities. This maximum amount will be called the "information capacity" or, in short, the "capacity" of the alphabet; it is measured by the logarithm of the number of symbols in the alphabet. Thus, for instance, the capacity of a binary alphabet is equal to one bit.

Let us consider next the product ensemble XY. The average value of the conditional self information is

$$I(Y|X) \equiv -\sum_{XY} P(x, y) \log P(y|x) \equiv H(Y|X) \qquad (2.96)$$

where the summation is extended over all points of the product space XY. We shall refer to this quantity as the conditional entropy of Y for given X, and represent it by the symbol on the righthand side of Eq. 2.96, as well as by that on the lefthand side.

The entropy

$$H(XY) \equiv -\sum_{XY} P(x,y) \log P(x,y) \tag{2.97}$$

of the product ensemble XY is related to $H(X)$ and $H(Y|X)$ by

$$H(XY) = H(X) + H(Y|X) \tag{2.98}$$

This relation can be easily checked by noting that it amounts simply to the average over the XY ensemble of the relation

$$I(xy) = I(x) + I(y|x) \tag{2.99}$$

Theorem. Given a product ensemble XY, the conditional entropy $H(Y|X)$ satisfies the inequality

$$H(Y|X) \leq H(Y) \tag{2.100}$$

in which the equal sign holds when, and only when, y is statistically independent of x; that is, when

$$P(y|x) = P(y) \tag{2.101}$$

Proof. This theorem can be proved by employing again Eq. 2.91. Let us consider the difference

$$H(Y|X) - H(Y) = \sum_{XY} P(x,y) \log \frac{P(y)}{P(y|x)} \tag{2.102}$$

Substitution of the righthand side of Eq. 2.91 for the logarithm in each term of the summation yields

$$H(Y|X) - H(Y) \leq \sum_{XY} P(x,y) \left[\frac{P(y)}{P(y|x)} - 1\right] \log e = 0 \tag{2.103}$$

The equal sign holds when, and only when,

$$w = \frac{P(y)}{P(y|x)} = 1 \tag{2.104}$$

because this is the value of w for which the equal sign holds in Eq. 2.91.

QED

Theorem. Given a product ensemble XYZ, the conditional entropies $H(Z|XY)$ and $H(Z|Y)$ satisfy the inequality

$$H(Z|XY) \leq H(Z|Y) \tag{2.105}$$

in which the equal sign holds when, and only when, z is statistically independent of x for any given y, that is, when

$$P(z \mid yx) = P(z \mid y) \tag{2.106}$$

Proof. The proof of this theorem is almost identical to that of the preceding one; for this reason, the detailed steps are not reproduced here.

These theorems are very important in connection with the encoding of messages. In fact, if we regard x, y, z as successive symbols of a code word, the average amount of information that can be provided by z cannot be increased by making z depend statistically on the identity of preceding symbols; that is, by making the conditional probability $P(z \mid yx)$ differ from $P(z)$. In particular, the information capacity of a given coding alphabet cannot be increased by introducing any interdependence between successive symbols. It follows, as we shall show in detail in Sec. 3.1, that the number of symbols required, on the average, to identify a message of a given ensemble cannot be smaller than the ratio of the entropy of the message ensemble to the capacity of the alphabet employed. In the particular case of binary code words, the entropy of the message ensemble constitutes a lower bound to the average number of binary digits per code word.

It will be shown in the following chapter that this lower bound can be approached as closely as desired by operating on the ensemble formed by sufficiently long sequences of independent messages. This result will provide a precise operational interpretation for the entropy of a message ensemble and, therefore, for the measure of self information defined in Sec. 2.3.

2.9. Average Mutual Information

In addition to the ensemble measures discussed above, the average value of the mutual information between points of different spaces plays an important role in the study of various aspects of communication problems. We wish to investigate its properties and, in particular, its relation to the various entropies that may be defined for the same product ensemble.

Let us consider first the conditional average of the mutual information defined by Eq. 2.86 for the product ensemble XY. We have from this equation

$$I(X;y_i) \equiv \sum_{X} P(x \mid y_i) \log \frac{P(x \mid y_i)}{P(x)} \tag{2.107}$$

Theorem. Given a product ensemble XY, the conditional average $I(X;y_i)$ of the mutual information satisfies the inequality

$$I(X;y_i) \geq 0 \tag{2.108}$$

where the equal sign holds when, and only when,

$$P(x|y_i) = P(x) \tag{2.109}$$

i.e., x is statistically independent of y_i.

Proof. This theorem can be readily proved with the help of Eq. 2.91. We obtain

$$-I(X;y_i) = \sum_X P(x|y_i) \log \frac{P(x)}{P(x|y_i)} \leq \sum_X [P(x) - P(x|y_i)] \log e = 0 \tag{2.110}$$

The equal sign holds when, and only when, the variable w in Eq. 2.91 is equal to 1; that is, when Eq. 2.109 is satisfied.

QED

The property expressed by Eq. 2.108 is particularly significant when y_i represents a symbol received through a noisy channel, and x represents any one of the messages that may have been transmitted. Then, Eq. 2.108 states that the average information provided by the received symbol about the message transmitted is always non-negative. It should be noted, in this regard, that while the information provided by the received symbol about the particular message may be negative, the receiver cannot determine its value because it does not know the identity of the message transmitted. On the other hand, the value of $I(X;y_i)$, which is never negative, can always be determined by the receiver, at least in principle. Thus, we can reconcile our results with the intuitive notion that the information provided by the reception of a symbol should never be negative.

Because of the symmetry property of the mutual information, Eq. 2.108 implies

$$I(x_k;Y) \equiv \sum_Y P(y|x_k) \log \frac{P(y|x_k)}{P(y)} \geq 0 \tag{2.111}$$

This inequality states that if x_k represents the message transmitted through a noisy channel, the average information received through the noisy channel about x_k is non-negative. This checks again with our intuitive notion that the information received cannot be negative when properly evaluated by the transmitter.

Let us consider next the mean value of the mutual information defined by Eq. 2.82,

$$I(X;Y) \equiv \sum_{XY} P(x,y) \log \frac{P(x|y)}{P(x)} = \sum_Y P(y)\, I(X;y) \geq 0 \tag{2.112}$$

The non-negative character of this quantity follows immediately from Eq. 2.111. Its main properties may be readily obtained by averaging Eqs. 2.18, 2.57, 2.108, 2.69, 2.22, and 2.25 over the product ensemble XY. We obtain:

$$I(X;Y) = I(Y;X) \tag{2.113}$$

$$I(X;Y) \leq \begin{cases} H(X) \\ H(Y) \end{cases} \tag{2.114}$$

$$I(X;Y) \geq 0 \tag{2.115}$$

$$H(XY) = H(X) + H(Y) - I(X;Y) \tag{2.116}$$

$$I(X;YZ) = I(X;Y) + I(X;Z|Y) \tag{2.117}$$

$$I(YZ;X) = I(Y;X) + I(Z;X|Y) \tag{2.118}$$

No additional comment is required for all but one of the above equations. Equation 2.116 places in evidence the relation between the average mutual information and the three entropies that pertain to the same product ensemble. We obtain from Eqs. 2.98 and 2.116 the following two alternate expressions for the average mutual information:

$$I(X;Y) = H(X) - H(X|Y) \tag{2.119}$$

$$I(X;Y) = H(Y) - H(Y|X) \tag{2.120}$$

These two expressions are of particular interest when x represents the message transmitted through a noisy communication channel, and y represents the corresponding received signal. In this case Eq. 2.119 states that the average amount of information provided by the received signal about the message is equal to the average amount of information required to specify the message x minus the average amount still required for this purpose after the reception of the signal y. In connection with this interpretation of Eq. 2.119, we refer to the entropy $H(X)$ as the average amount of information transmitted, to $I(X;Y)$ as the average amount received about the transmitted message, and to the conditional entropy $H(X|Y)$ as the average amount lost because of noise, or, in short, as the "equivocation."

Equation 2.120 emphasizes a different way of looking at the average amount of information received; namely, as the difference between the average amount necessary to specify the received signal, and the average amount necessary to specify the same signal when the message transmitted is known. Thus, $H(Y|X)$ is the average amount of information necessary to specify the particular noise disturbance that takes place in the channel so that we may refer to it as the entropy of the channel noise. In other words, $H(Y|X)$ represents the part of the entropy of Y that results from the channel noise.

Returning to Eq. 2.119, one may also say that the difference on the righthand side represents the average change of uncertainty as to which message was transmitted, caused by the reception of y. This interpretation is based on the fact that $H(X|Y)$ may be obtained by averaging over the Y ensemble the entropy (uncertainty) of X conditioned by a particular y_i:

$$H(X|y_i) \equiv - \sum_X P(x|y_i) \log P(x|y_i) \tag{2.121}$$

One should not conclude, however, that the difference $H(X) - H(X|y_i)$ represents the average amount of information provided by the reception of y_i, at least according to the measure of information defined in Sec. 2.3. In fact, we observe, from Eq. 2.107, that

$$I(X;y_i) \neq H(X) - H(X|y_i) \tag{2.122}$$

The difference on the righthand side represents the change of the average amount of information necessary to specify any x, resulting from the imposition of the condition y_i on the X ensemble. On the other hand, $I(X;y_i)$ represents the average change, resulting from the reception of y_i, of the amount of information necessary to specify the particular x that has resulted in the reception of y_i. In other words, $\log P(x)$ is multiplied by $P(x)$ in the summation on the righthand side of Eq. 2.122, and by $P(x|y_i)$ in the summation on the lefthand side.

The basic difference between the two sides of Eq. 2.122 becomes especially evident when y_i specifies a particular x_k; that is, when $P(x_k|y_i) = 1$. We obtain in this case

$$I(X;y_i) = -\log P(x_k) = I(x_k) \tag{2.123}$$

$$H(X) - H(X|y_i) = H(X) \tag{2.124}$$

In words, when y_i uniquely specifies a particular x_k, the average value of the mutual information provided by y_i about the symbols of the X ensemble is equal to the self information of x_k. On the other hand, the reception of y_i changes the entropy of the X ensemble from the value $H(X)$ to zero and, therefore, the difference between a priori and a posteriori entropy is just equal to $H(X)$.

2.10. Extension of the Measure of Mutual Information to Continuous Spaces

Our discussion of measures of information has been limited so far to discrete spaces, for the sake of mathematical simplicity. Many physical channels, however, cannot be adequately represented in terms of discrete spaces. This is the case, for instance, when the input events are pulses of arbitrary amplitude, to which noise pulses are added in the channel. More generally, it is often convenient to represent input events and output observations as time functions over some interval T, which are then described as sums of orthonormal functions of arbitrary amplitudes. In order to study such physical channels, we must therefore extend our measure of mutual information to pairs of points belonging to euclidean spaces of arbitrary dimensionality.

Let us indicate with U a euclidean space of arbitrary dimensionality, and with $\underline{u}$ the vector representing the position of any particular point of U with respect to an arbitrary origin. Since the points of U form a continuum, we cannot assign to each of them a finite probability. However, we can define for such a space a function of the region δU

$$P(\delta U) \equiv Pr(\underline{u} \in \delta U) \tag{2.125}$$

representing the probability that the point $\underline{u}$ belongs to the region δU. This is an additive function of the region δU in the sense that

$$P(\delta U_1 + \delta U_2) = P(\delta U_1) + P(\delta U_2) \tag{2.126}$$

where δU_1 and δU_2 represent two non-overlapping regions of U. Of course,

$$P(U) = 1 \tag{2.127}$$

since $\underline{u}$ belongs, by definition, to the space U.

The significance of the additive function $P(\delta U)$ can be best understood by thinking of the probability as being distributed through the space U, just as if it were some sort of material. More precisely, we could identify, by analogy, the probability in any region δU with the mass of the material in the same region. Of course, the total mass of the material in the space would be equal to 1, just as the total probability. Then, by analogy, the function $P(\delta U)$ would represent the mass of material in the region δU.

The analogy with a space distribution of material of total mass equal to 1 suggests introducing a probability density

$$p(\underline{u}) \equiv \lim_{\delta U \to 0} \frac{P(\delta U)}{\delta U} \tag{2.128}$$

analogous to the mass density, defined in the limit when the volume δU shrinks to zero about the point $\underline{u}$. We shall assume that the limit exists at every point of the space. Points possessing a finite probability of occurrence can be treated in the same manner as point masses; that is, as regions of vanishingly small dimensions containing a finite probability. We shall assume, furthermore, that the probability density $p(\underline{u})$ is piecewise continuous throughout the space U; that is, continuous except over a discrete number of surfaces separating different regions of U. We can then express the probability associated with any particular region δU in terms of the probability density as the integral

$$P(\delta U) = \int_{\delta U} p(\underline{u})\, dU \tag{2.129}$$

where dU is a differential element of volume of U.

Let us consider next a second euclidean space V and indicate with $\underline{v}$ the vector indicating the position of a particular point of the space with respect to an arbitrary origin. A probability density $p(\underline{v})$ can be defined in a similar manner for this space. The probability that $\underline{v}$ belongs to the region δV can then be expressed in the form

$$P(\delta V) \equiv \Pr(\underline{v} \in \delta V) = \int_{\delta V} p(\underline{v})\, dV \tag{2.130}$$

by analogy with Eq. 2.129.

The product space $W \equiv UV$ is a euclidean space of dimensionality equal to the sum of the dimensionalities of U and V. If we regard U and V as subspaces of W with coinciding origins, the vector $\underline{w}$ indicating the position of a particular point of W is the sum of the vectors $\underline{u}$ and $\underline{v}$, indicating the positions of the projections of $\underline{w}$ on the subspaces U and V,

$$\underline{w} = \underline{u} + \underline{v} \tag{2.131}$$

Thus, the single point $\underline{w}$ of the W space represents the pair of points $\underline{u}$ and $\underline{v}$ of the U and V spaces. The distribution of probability over the product space W can be represented in terms of a density $p(\underline{w})$ as discussed above. However, it is more convenient for our purposes to describe the distribution of probability over W as a joint distribution of probability over U and V; that is, in terms of the function

$$P(\delta U, \delta V) \equiv \Pr(\underline{u} \in \delta U, \underline{v} \in \delta V) \tag{2.132}$$

representing the probability that $\underline{u}$ belongs to δU and, simultaneously, $\underline{v}$ belongs to δV. Correspondingly, the probability density over W can be expressed as the joint probability density of $\underline{u}$ and $\underline{v}$ defined by the limit

$$p(\underline{u}, \underline{v}) \equiv \lim_{\substack{\delta U \to 0 \\ \delta V \to 0}} \frac{P(\delta U, \delta V)}{\delta U\, \delta V} \tag{2.133}$$

where the volumes δU and δV shrink simultaneously to the points $\underline{u}$ and $\underline{v}$. We assume again that this limit exists and is piecewise continuous throughout the product space UV. Conversely, the joint probability distribution defined by Eq. 2.132 can be expressed in terms of the joint probability density defined by Eq. 2.133 as the double integral

$$P(\delta U, \delta V) = \int_{\delta U} \int_{\delta V} p(\underline{u}, \underline{v})\, dU dV \tag{2.134}$$

where the two integrals are evaluated over the regions δU and δV.

The probability that $\underline{u}$ belongs to δU can be expressed in terms of the joint probability density defined by Eq. 2.133 as the double integral

$$P(\delta U) = \int_{\delta U} \int_{V} p(\underline{u}, \underline{v})\, dU dV \tag{2.135}$$

from which we obtain, with the help of Eq. 2.128,

$$p(\underline{u}) = \int_{V} p(\underline{u}, \underline{v})\, dV \tag{2.136}$$

where the integral is evaluated over the entire space V. Similarly,

$$p(\underline{v}) = \int_{U} p(\underline{u}, \underline{v})\, dU \tag{2.137}$$

where the integral is evaluated over the entire space U.

The conditional probability that $\underline{u}$ belongs to δU when $\underline{v}$ belongs to δV, is by definition

$$P(\delta U | \delta V) \equiv \frac{P(\delta U, \delta V)}{P(\delta V)} \tag{2.138}$$

The corresponding probability density is defined as the limit

$$p(\underline{u} | \underline{v}) \equiv \lim_{\substack{\delta U \to 0 \\ \delta V \to 0}} \frac{P(\delta U | \delta V)}{\delta U} = \lim_{\substack{\delta U \to 0 \\ \delta V \to 0}} \frac{P(\delta U, \delta V)}{\delta U\ \delta V} \frac{\delta V}{P(\delta V)} = \frac{p(\underline{u}, \underline{v})}{p(\underline{v})} \tag{2.139}$$

where again the volumes δU and δV shrink simultaneously to the points $\underline{u}$ and $\underline{v}$.

We are now in a position to generalize our definition of measure of information. Let us consider the product ensemble UV characterized by the joint probability density $p(\underline{u}, \underline{v})$. The mutual information between any two regions δU and δV of the two spaces U and V is, according to the definition of mutual information given in Sec. 2.3,

$$I(\delta U; \delta V) \equiv \log \frac{P(\delta U, \delta V)}{P(\delta U)\ P(\delta V)} \tag{2.140}$$

This is the amount of information provided by the event "$\underline{v}$ belongs to δV" about the event "$\underline{u}$ belongs to δU," or, conversely, the amount of information provided by the second event about the first one.

> The mutual information between the point $\underline{u}$ and the point $\underline{v}$ is defined as the limit of the mutual information between δU and δV when these two regions shrink simultaneously to the points $\underline{u}$ and $\underline{v}$.

This limit is given by

$$I(\underline{u};\underline{v}) \equiv \lim_{\substack{\delta U \to 0 \\ \delta V \to 0}} I(\delta U;\delta V) \tag{2.141}$$

$$= \lim_{\substack{\delta U \to 0 \\ \delta V \to 0}} \log \frac{P(\delta U, \delta V)\ \delta U\ \delta V}{\delta U\ \delta V\ P(\delta U)\ P(\delta V)} = \log \frac{p(\underline{u}, \underline{v})}{p(\underline{u})\ p(\underline{v})}$$

from which we obtain

$$I(\underline{u};\underline{v}) \equiv \log \frac{p(\underline{u}|\underline{v})}{p(\underline{u})} = \log \frac{p(\underline{v}|\underline{u})}{p(\underline{v})} \tag{2.142}$$

It is important to note that the mutual information between the points $\underline{u}$ and $\underline{v}$ is a function of the probability distribution over the product space UV, but it does not depend in any manner on the positions of the points represented by the vectors $\underline{u}$ and $\underline{v}$. The full significance of this fact will be discussed in the next section.

2.11. Average Mutual Information and Entropy for Continuous Spaces

The conditional expectation of $I(\underline{u};\underline{v})$ for a fixed $\underline{v}$ is, by definition,

$$I(U;\underline{v}) \equiv \int_U p(\underline{u}|\underline{v})\ I(u;v)\ dU \tag{2.143}$$

where the integration is extended over the entire space U, and dU is a differential element of volume of the space.

Theorem. Given a continuous product ensemble UV, the conditional expectation $I(U;\underline{v})$ of the mutual information satisfies the inequality

$$I(U;\underline{v}) \geq 0 \tag{2.144}$$

in which the equal sign holds when, and only when, $p(\underline{u}|\underline{v}) = p(\underline{u})$.

Proof. The proof of this theorem is very similar to the proof of Eq. 2.108, and it is therefore omitted.

The average value of the mutual information over the product ensemble UV is, by definition,

$$I(U;V) \equiv \int_V p(\underline{v})\ I(U;\underline{v})\ dV = \int_V \int_U p(\underline{u},\underline{v})\ I(\underline{u};\underline{v})\ dU\ dV \tag{2.145}$$

It follows from the above theorem that

$$I(U;V) \geq 0 \tag{2.146}$$

where the equal sign holds when, and only when, U and V are statistically independent.

It is instructive to inquire how the average value of the mutual information given by Eq. 2.145 is approached as a limit by the average value of the mutual information between finite regions of the spaces U and V, when the two spaces are successively subdivided into smaller and smaller regions. Let us suppose that the space U is divided into n regions, and the space V is similarly divided into m regions.

Theorem. The average value over the product space of the mutual information between regions δU_k and δV_i,

$$\sum_{i=1}^{m} P(\delta V_i) \sum_{k=1}^{n} P(\delta U_k|\delta V_i) \quad I(\delta U_k;\delta V_i) \tag{2.147}$$

is never decreased by any further subdivision of the regions.

Proof. The statement of the theorem is equivalent to saying that the average value given by Eq. 2.147 is never increased by lumping together any two regions into a single one. In view of the symmetry between the U and V spaces, it is sufficient to show that, for any two regions δU_k and δU_j

$$\begin{aligned} P(\delta U_k|\,\delta V_i)\; I(\delta U_k;\delta V_i) + P(\delta U_j|\,\delta V_i)\; I(\delta U_j;\delta V_i) \\ \geq \; P(\delta U_k + \delta U_j \mid \delta V_i)\; I(\delta U_k + \delta U_j;\delta V_i) \end{aligned} \tag{2.148}$$

which is equivalent to

$$P(\delta U_k|\,\delta V_i) \log \frac{[P(\delta U_k|\,\delta V_i) + P(\delta U_j|\,\delta V_i)]\; P(\delta U_k)}{[P(\delta U_k) + P(\delta U_j)]\; P(\delta U_k|\,\delta V_i)}$$

$$+ P(\delta U_j|\,\delta V_i) \;\log\; \frac{[P(\delta U_k|\,\delta V_i) + P(\delta U_j|\,\delta V_i)]\; P(\delta U_j)}{[P(\delta U_k) + P(\delta U_j)]\; P(\delta U_j|\,\delta V_i)} \leq 0$$

(2.149)

This inequality can be readily proved with the help of Eq. 2.91.

QED

We can conclude that the average value of the mutual information between finite regions given by Eq. 2.147 increases monotonically when the regions are further subdivided and approaches as a limit the average value given by Eq. 2.145. In other words, I(U;V) can be regarded as the maximum average value of the mutual information between regions of the spaces U and V.

Substitution of the expressions given by Eq. 2.142 for $I(\underline{u};\underline{v})$ in Eq. 2.145 yields

$$I(U;V) = H(U) - H(U|\,V) = H(V) - H(V|\,U) \tag{2.150}$$

where

$$H(U) \equiv -\int_U p(\underline{u}) \log p(\underline{u})\, dU \qquad (2.151)$$

$$H(U|V) \equiv -\int_U \int_V p(\underline{u},\underline{v}) \log p(\underline{u}|\underline{v})\, dU\, dV \qquad (2.152)$$

and $H(V)$ and $H(V|U)$ are defined by similar expressions. The expressions for the average value of the mutual information given by Eq. 2.150 are similar in form to those given by Eqs. 2.119 and 2.120 for discrete spaces. However, the entropy and the conditional entropy defined by Eqs. 2.151 and 2.152 cannot be regarded as average values of self informations as in the discrete case. In fact, the self information of the event "$\underline{u}$ belongs to δU" approaches infinity when the region δU shrinks to the point $\underline{u}$. Furthermore, as shown below, while the average mutual information defined by Eq. 2.145 is invariant to any probability-preserving transformation of the spaces U and V, the same is not true for the entropies defined by Eqs. 2.151 and 2.152.

Let us consider a one-to-one transformation of the spaces U and V into the spaces U' and V', and indicate with $\underline{u}'$ and $\underline{v}'$ the points of the U' and V' spaces corresponding to $\underline{u}$ and $\underline{v}$. Let us assume that the transformation leaves invariant the probability of any region of the product space in the sense that

$$P(\delta U', \delta V') = P(\delta U, \delta V) \qquad (2.153)$$

where $\delta U'$ and $\delta V'$ are the regions of U' and V' corresponding to δU and δV. It is clear from Eq. 2.141 that

$$I(\underline{u}';\underline{v}') = I(\underline{u};\underline{v}) \qquad (2.154)$$

because the mutual information depends only on the probabilities associated with the regions, which are, by assumption, invariant to the transformation. On the other hand, the probability densities are not, individually, invariant to the transformation, as evidenced by their very definitions. Thus, $\log p(\underline{u})$ and $\log p(\underline{u}|\underline{v})$ are not invariant to the transformation, and, therefore, the same is true for the entropies defined by Eqs. 2.151 and 2.152.

Let us consider as a simple example a transformation that multiplies by a constant K the volume of every region of U and V,

$$\delta U' = K\, \delta U \qquad \delta V' = K\, \delta V \qquad (2.155)$$

corresponding to a uniform stretching of the two spaces. In this particular case we obtain from Eqs. 2.153 and 2.155 in conjunction with Eqs. 2.128 and 2.139

$$p(\underline{u}') = \frac{1}{K} p(\underline{u}) \quad , \qquad p(\underline{u}'|\underline{v}') = \frac{1}{K} p(\underline{u}|\underline{v}) \qquad (2.156)$$

from which it follows that

$$H(U') = H(U) + \log K \tag{2.157}$$

$$H(U'|V') = H(U|V) + \log K \tag{2.158}$$

Clearly, these entropies transform in such a way that their difference, the average mutual information given by Eq. 2.150, remains invariant as expected.

Example. We shall conclude this discussion of continuous spaces with a simple example. Let U and V be one-dimensional spaces and indicate with x and y the only components of $\underline{u}$ and $\underline{v}$, respectively. The product space UV is then a plane, and x and y can be regarded as cartesian coordinates of the points of this product space. Let us suppose further that x and y - x are gaussianly distributed with mean values equal to zero, and with variances equal to S and N , respectively,

$$p(x) = \frac{1}{\sqrt{2\pi S}} e^{-\frac{x^2}{2S}} \tag{2.159}$$

$$p(y|x) = \frac{1}{\sqrt{2\pi N}} e^{-\frac{(y-x)^2}{2N}} \tag{2.160}$$

It follows that

$$p(x,y) = p(x)\,p(y|x) = \frac{1}{2\pi\sqrt{SN}} e^{-\frac{1}{2N}\left[x^2\left(1+\frac{N}{S}\right)-2xy+y^2\right]} \tag{2.161}$$

$$p(y) = \int_{-\infty}^{\infty} p(x,y)\,dx = \frac{1}{\sqrt{2\pi(S+N)}} e^{-\frac{y^2}{2(S+N)}} \tag{2.162}$$

If we regard x as the amplitude of a pulse input to a channel and y as the amplitude of the corresponding output pulse, y - x is the amplitude of the noise pulse added to the input pulse. The constant S represents the mean-square value of the input-pulse amplitude, and the constant N represents the mean-square value of the noise-pulse amplitude; their sum S + N represents the mean-square value of the output-pulse amplitude.

The average value of the mutual information between x and y is, from Eq. 2.150,

$$I(X;Y) \equiv H(Y) - H(Y|X) \tag{2.163}$$

where

$$H(Y) \equiv - \int_{-\infty}^{\infty} p(y) \log p(y)\, dy \tag{2.164}$$

$$H(Y|X) \equiv - \int_{-\infty}^{\infty} \int_{-\infty}^{\infty} p(x, y) \log p(y|x)\, dx\, dy \tag{2.165}$$

Evaluation of these integrals yields

$$H(Y) = \frac{1}{2} \log \left[2\pi e(S + N)\right] \tag{2.166}$$

$$H(Y|X) = \frac{1}{2} \log (2\pi e N) \tag{2.167}$$

from which we obtain

$$I(X; Y) = \frac{1}{2} \log \left(1 + \frac{S}{N}\right) \tag{2.168}$$

We shall see later on that this is the maximum value that can be assumed by the average mutual information between input and output pulses when the amplitude of the noise pulses is gaussianly distributed with mean-square value equal to N, and the amplitude of the input pulses is required to have a mean-square value equal to S.

* 2.12. Mutual Information Between an Arbitrary Number of Events

We saw in Sec. 2.6, Eq. 2.66 that the mutual information between points of two discrete spaces can be regarded as the difference between the self information of one of the points and the conditional self information of the same point when the other point is given. Indicating with X_1 and X_2 the two spaces, and with x_1 and x_2 the two points in question, we have

$$I(x_1; x_2) = I(x_1) - I(x_1|x_2) = \log \frac{P(x_1, x_2)}{P(x_1)P(x_2)} \tag{2.169}$$

This equation suggests our inquiring about the corresponding difference between mutual informations for a triple product ensemble $X_1\, X_2\, X_3$ consisting of the triplets of points $x_1\, x_2\, x_3$. We have for such a product ensemble

$$I(x_1;x_2) - I(x_1;x_2|x_3) = \log \frac{P(x_1, x_2)}{P(x_1)P(x_2)} - \log \frac{P(x_1, x_2|x_3)}{P(x_1|x_3)P(x_2|x_3)}$$

$$\doteq \log \frac{P(x_1, x_2)\, P(x_1, x_3)\, P(x_2, x_3)}{P(x_1)\, P(x_2)\, P(x_3)\, P(x_1, x_2, x_3)} \tag{2.170}$$

It is very interesting to note that this difference is symmetrical with respect to the three points x_1, x_2, and x_3 just as the difference in Eq. 2.169 is symmetrical with respect to the two points x_1 and x_2. This symmetry suggests that the quantity

$$I(x_1;x_2;x_3) \equiv I(x_1;x_2) - I(x_1;x_2|x_3) = I(x_1;x_3) - I(x_1;x_3|x_2)$$
$$= I(x_2;x_3) - I(x_2;x_3|x_1) \qquad (2.171)$$

can be regarded as a measure of the mutual information between the three points x_1, x_2, and x_3.

Continuing along the same line of thought, we define, for the product ensemble $X_1 \quad X_2 \quad \ldots X_n$, the symmetrical measure

$$I(x_1;x_2;\ldots;x_n) \equiv \log \frac{[\Pi P(x_k, x_i)][\Pi P(x_k, x_i, x_j, x_h] \ldots}{[\Pi P(x_k)][\Pi P(x_k, x_i, x_j)] \ldots} \qquad (2.172)$$

where the products indicated by Π are evaluated over all possible combinations of different subscripts. This measure satisfies the relation

$$I(x_1;x_2;\ldots;x_n) = I(x_1;x_2;\ldots;x_{n-1}) - I(x_1;x_2;\ldots;x_{n-1}|x_n) \qquad (2.173)$$

where x_n can be any one of the points in question. Thus, Eq. 2.172 provides a general definition of the mutual information between an arbitrary number of points.

It can be readily checked from the above definitions that

$$I(x_1x_2 \ldots x_n) = \sum I(x_k) - \sum I(x_k;x_i) + \sum I(x_k;x_i;x_j) + \ldots$$
$$(-1)^{n-1} I(x_1;x_2;\ldots;x_n) \qquad (2.174)$$

where the summations are evaluated over all possible combinations of different subscripts. This equation provides a way of expanding the self information of a point of an arbitrary product ensemble into a sum of mutual informations between points of the individual ensembles.

All the above measures can be averaged over the corresponding ensembles, and corresponding relations can be written between the average measures. Thus, for instance, the average mutual information associated with the product ensemble $X_1 X_2 X_3$ is

$$I(X_1;X_2;X_3) = \sum_{X_1X_2X_3} P(x_1, x_2, x_3) I(x_1;x_2;x_3) = I(X_1;X_2) - I(X_1;X_2|X_3) \qquad (2.175)$$

This average measure of mutual information can be either positive or negative, in contrast with $I(X_1;X_2)$, which is never negative. The same is true for the average value of the mutual information for higher-order product ensembles.

The generalized measure of mutual information discussed in this section was first defined and studied (averaged over the corresponding ensemble) by McGill [4]. He showed that these measures can be used very effectively in analyzing experimental data on the frequencies of occurrence of discrete events, when the traditional techniques of the analysis of variance cannot be employed because no numerical values are associated with the events. More recently, these measures have become of interest in connection with communication channels with multiple inputs and outputs.

2.13. Summary and Conclusions

This chapter has been devoted to the definition of various measures of information and to the study of some of their properties. These measures of information were derived as special cases or generalizations of the fundamental measure of mutual information between two events. This basic measure was originally defined in terms of the change of the probability of one of the events as a result of the observation of the other. More precisely, it was defined as the logarithm of the ratio of the a posteriori probability and the a priori probability of the first event. It was then shown that such a measure is symmetrical in the two events, so that it can be regarded as a measure of the mutual information between the two events.

The self information of an event was then defined as the mutual information between the event in question and the second event, in the special case in which the event in question is uniquely specified by the second event. Thus, the self information of an event could be interpreted as either the amount of information necessary to specify the event uniquely, or as the amount of information that the event can provide about any other event.

The measure of mutual information, originally defined between points of discrete space, was later generalized to continuous spaces by defining the mutual information between two points as the limit of the mutual information between two finite regions when the two regions shrink to the two points in question. On the basis of this definition, the expression for the mutual information between points of continuous spaces turned out to be identical to the corresponding expression for discrete spaces, except for the substitution of probability densities for the corresponding discrete probabilities. On the other hand, performing the same substitution in the expression for the self information of a point belonging to a discrete space did not lead to a meaningful measure of self information. In particular, while it was possible to show that the measure of mutual information between points of continuous spaces is invariant to a one-to-one probability-preserving transformation of the spaces, the same is not true for the measure obtained by substituting the probability density for the corresponding discrete probability in the measure of self information.

Our study of the properties of the average value of the self information led us to the conclusion that the average number of binary digits required to represent the messages of a prescribed ensemble must at least be equal to the average value of the self information of the messages; that is, to the entropy of the ensemble. We shall see in the following chapter that it is always possible to encode the messages in such a way that the average number of binary digits per message will differ from the entropy of the message ensemble by at most one digit. We shall see also that this average number of digits can be made actually equal to the entropy of the message ensemble when the self information of each message is equal to an integral number of bits. In this special case the number of binary digits required to identify any particular message turns out to be equal to the self information of the message.

This important result is a first example of the role played by the measures of information defined above in the study of communication systems. We shall see later that the measure of mutual information will lead to a definition of the capacity of a channel, and that it is possible to transmit through a channel binary digits at any rate smaller than the capacity of the channel with a vanishingly small probability of error. Results of this type provide a precise operational interpretation for the measures of information defined in this chapter. Conversely, these measures, because of their easily understood "physical significance," are very helpful in guiding our thinking through the mathematical derivation of such results.

The material in this chapter can be presented in a more precise and general manner through the use of measure theory [5, 6]. However, the advantages of this approach do not justify, at least for our purposes, the time required to develop the necessary mathematical tools.

The measures of self and mutual information have found useful applications in statistics, as well as in the study of communication systems. These applications are discussed in detail in Reference 6.

2.14. Selected References.

1. W. Feller, An Introduction to Probability Theory and Its Applications, Vol. 1, 2nd edition, John Wiley and Sons, New York, 1957. This is an excellent reference text on the theory of probability for discrete spaces.

2. W. B. Davenport, Jr., and W. L. Root, Random Signals and Noise, McGraw-Hill, New York, 1958. This text, specifically designed for communication engineers, presents the necessary mathematical background at a level appropriate for our discussion.

3. L. Brillouin, Science and Information Theory, Academic Press, New York, 1956. Chapters 12 and 13 discuss the relation between information and entropy in physical systems.

4. W. J. McGill, "Multivariate Information Transmission," Transactions PGIT, 1954 Symposium on Information Theory, PGIT-4, pp. 93-111.

5. H. Cramer, Mathematical Methods of Statistics, Princeton University Press, Princeton, 1951. Chapters 1 through 9 present the aspects of the theory of measure and integration required for a precise discussion of probability in continuous spaces. Chapters 13 and 14 introduce the concept of probability distribution from the measure theory point of view, and Chapter 22 discusses n-dimensional probability distributions.

6. S. Kullback, Information Theory and Statistics, John Wiley and Sons, New York, 1959. The first five chapters of this book discuss the properties of logarithmic measures of information using the tools of measure theory. The rest of the book discusses various applications to statistics.

Chapter 3

SIMPLE MESSAGE ENSEMBLES

The problem of reproducing the output from a given source according to a specified fidelity criterion was formulated in Sec. 1.2 in terms of the concept of equivalence classes. Briefly, the possible source outputs during an appropriate time interval are grouped into classes in such a way that, for each class, a preselected, representative member can be substituted for any other member of the class without violating the fidelity criterion specified by the user. With reference to Fig. 1.1, the source encoder determines the class to which the source output belongs, and transmits a suitable indication of it to the source decoder. The source decoder, in turn, generates the representative member of the class indicated by the source encoder. Repetition of this process in each successive time interval results in the reproduction of the source output according to the specified fidelity criterion.

This formulation has the advantage of separating the problem of transmitting the indication of the class to which the source output belongs from the more complex problem of grouping the possible outputs into equivalence classes. We shall be concerned in this chapter with the more elementary aspects of the transmission problem. More precisely, we shall be concerned with the representation of the messages of a given discrete set by means of sequences of symbols belonging to a prescribed alphabet. Each message may stand for a particular class of source outputs, or it may be directly a source output if the possible source outputs form a discrete set. Our objective will be to construct the sequences of symbols in such a way as to minimize the average number of symbols per message, evaluated over the message ensemble.

We shall assume in this chapter that the transmission probabilities of the messages are known, and that successive messages are statistically independent. Messages and sequences of messages resulting from more complex stochastic processes will be considered in the next chapter.

3.1. Lower Bound on the Average Code-Word Length

Let us consider an ensemble U of M messages, $u_1, u_2, \ldots u_k \ldots u_M$, with corresponding probabilities $P(u_k)$. Each message must be represented by means of a code word consisting of a sequence of symbols belonging to a prescribed alphabet. We shall indicate with D the number of different symbols in the alphabet, and with n_k the number of symbols in the code word corresponding to the message u_k. The average number of symbols per message is, by definition,

$$\bar{n} \equiv \sum_{k=1}^{M} P(u_k)\, n_k \tag{3.1}$$

Our first objective is the determination of a lower bound to $\bar{n}$.

We saw in Sec. 2.8 that the entropy $H(U)$ of the message ensemble represents the average amount of information that must be provided about a message of the ensemble in order to specify it uniquely. We saw, also, in the same section, that the symbols of the prescribed alphabet provide, on the average, a maximum amount of information when they are used with equal probabilities. This maximum value, namely log D, is the capacity of the coding alphabet. Furthermore, Eqs. 2.100 and 2.105 show that statistical dependence of a symbol on the preceding ones cannot increase the average amount of information that the symbol can provide. On the basis of these results we can conclude that

$$\bar{n} \log D \geq H(U) \tag{3.2}$$

from which we obtain

$$\frac{H(U)}{\log D} \leq \bar{n} \tag{3.3}$$

In words, the average number of symbols per message cannot be smaller than the entropy of the message ensemble divided by the capacity of the alphabet. A direct proof of this result is given in Sec. 3.5.

The reasoning involved in obtaining this lower bound suggests general rules for constructing code words with average lengths reasonably close to it. The first rule is that the different symbols of the alphabet must be used with equal probabilities at each position in the code words, so as to maximize the average amount of information provided by them. The second rule is that the probabilities of occurrence of the symbols at each position in the code words should be independent of all preceding symbols. If these rules are exactly followed, the average length of the resulting code words should be equal to the minimum value given by Eq. 3.3. We shall see, however, that only in special cases can the symbol be used with equal probabilities and be made independent of all preceding symbols. These rules for constructing sets of code words are best elucidated in terms of the following specific examples. The encoding procedure employed is similar to that originally suggested by Shannon [1].

3.2. Illustrative Examples

Let us consider the set of eight equiprobable messages shown in Fig. 3.1. The first step in encoding the messages is to divide the set into two equiprobable groups, and to make the first digit a 0

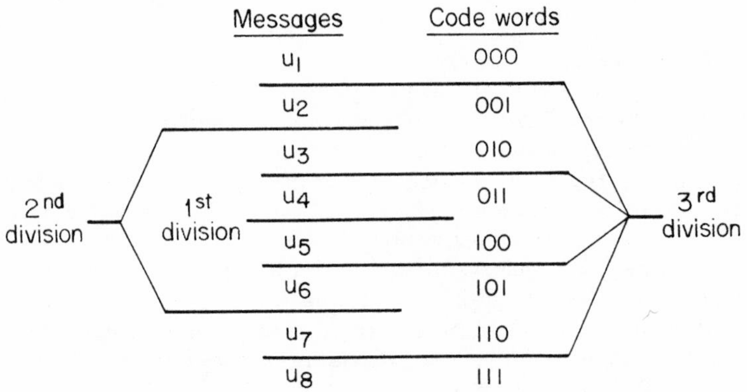

Fig. 3.1. Optimum set of code words for equiprobable messages

for the code words corresponding to the messages of the first group and a 1 for the code words corresponding to the messages of the second group. Thus, the probability that the first digit be a 0 is exactly equal to the probability that the first digit will be a 1.

In deciding upon the second digit we must keep in mind that it must be statistically independent of the first one. This means that the probability of occurrence of a 0 as second digit must be the same whether the first digit is a 0 or a 1; the same must be true for the probability of occurrence of a 1 as second digit. Thus, the second step consists of dividing each of the groups formed in the first step into two equiprobable subgroups as indicated in Fig. 3.1 by the lines marked "2nd division." Then, for each group, a 0 is assigned to the messages of the first subgroup, and a 1 is assigned to the messages of the second subgroup. The four resulting subgroups are, of course, equiprobable.

The third and last step is similar to the second one. Each of the four subgroups shown in Fig. 3.1 is subdivided again into two equiprobable parts, each consisting of a single message, as indicated by the lines marked "3rd division." In each of the subgroups, one of the messages is assigned a 0 as third digit, and the other a 1. Again, this procedure insures that the third digit will be statistically independent of the preceding two, and that 0 and 1 will occur with equal probabilities.

Since the eight messages of Fig. 3.1 are equally probable, the entropy of their ensemble is equal to 3 bits; the capacity of the binary alphabet is equal to 1 bit. Thus, the minimum average number of symbols per message is equal to 3, which is just the number of digits in the code words of Fig. 3.1.

Let us consider next the message ensemble of Fig. 3.2. The message probabilities are no longer equal, but their values are still negative powers of 2. The code words shown in Fig. 3.2 are constructed

Messages	Probabilities	Code Words
u_1	0.25	0 0
u_2	0.25	0 1
u_3	0.125	1 0 0
u_4	0.125	1 0 1
u_5	0.0625	1 1 0 0
u_6	0.0625	1 1 0 1
u_7	0.0625	1 1 1 0
u_8	0.0625	1 1 1 1

Fig. 3.2. Optimum set of code words

again by successively subdividing the message ensemble into equiprobable groups and subgroups. In this case, however, the groups and subgroups do not contain the same number of messages, and the code words do not have the same number of digits. This follows from the fact that a message with probability 1/4 is singled out by two successive divisions of the message ensemble into equiprobable groups, while a message with probability 1/16 is singled out only after four successive divisions into equiprobable groups. The groups and subgroups formed by the successive divisions are clearly indicated by the digits of the code words. Since the message probabilities are negative powers of 2, it is possible to make all groups and subgroups equally probable, and to make each digit statistically independent of the preceding ones. It can be readily checked by inspection that this is true.

Since each digit, whether a 0 or a 1, occurs with probability 1/2, it is capable of providing 1 bit of information about the corresponding message. This amount of information is actually provided because the digit in question is uniquely specified by the corresponding message, as discussed in Sec. 2.6. It follows that the number n_k of digits in each code word must be equal to the self information of the corresponding message. It can be readily checked that this is true for all the code words of Fig. 3.2. We can conclude on this basis that the average number of binary digits per message must be equal to the entropy of the message ensemble, that is, equal to the minimum value given by Eq. 3.3. Both the entropy and the average number of digits are equal to 2.75.

This procedure for constructing code words can be readily generalized to the case of an arbitrary alphabet of D symbols, by successively subdividing the message ensemble into D equiprobable groups and subgroups, instead of just 2. It is clear, on the other hand, that this procedure can be successfully followed only when the message probabilities are negative powers of D, regardless of whether D is equal to 2 or to any other integer. If the message probabilities are not negative powers of D, the successive groups and subgroups cannot be exactly equiprobable, but only approximately so, and the average number of symbols per message cannot be made equal to the minimum value given by Eq. 3.3. Furthermore, when equiprobable groups and subgroups cannot be formed, the procedure does not lead necessarily to a set of code words with the smallest possible average length. A systematic procedure for constructing optimum sets of code words will be presented in Sec. 3.6.

3.3. The Tree Associated with a Set of Code Words

A very useful graphical representation of a set of code words can be obtained by establishing a correspondence between the code words, that is, the messages, and the terminal nodes of a tree. The tree corresponding to the set of binary code words of Fig. 3.2 is illustrated in Fig. 3.3. Starting from the root of the tree, the two branches leading to the first-order nodes correspond to the choice between 0

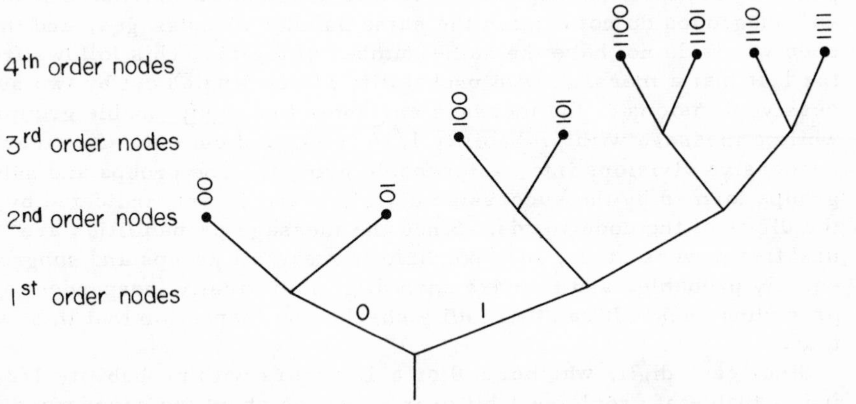

Fig. 3.3. Tree associated with the set of binary code words of Fig. 3.2

and 1 as the first digit of the code words, with the left branch corresponding to 0 and the right branch corresponding to 1. The two branches stemming from each of the first-order nodes correspond to the second digit of the code words, with the left branch indicating again a 0 and the right branch a 1. The same convention applies to the branches between higher-order nodes. Clearly the successive digits of each code word constitute the necessary instructions for climbing from the root of the tree to the terminal node corresponding to the desired message.

Code words can be assigned formally to intermediate nodes as well as to terminal nodes. For instance, the two intermediate nodes of second order in Fig. 3. 3 could be assigned the code words 10 and 11; that is, the first two digits of the code words corresponding to the terminal nodes stemming from them. On the other hand, the code words corresponding to intermediate nodes cannot be used to represent messages; messages can be associated only with terminal nodes. The reason for this is that if we regard a code word as a set of instructions for reaching the node corresponding to a particular message, these instructions would have to include a "stop here" if the node were an intermediate one. Thus, at such an intermediate node three different instructions would be possible; namely, turn left (0), turn right (1), and stop here. In other words, we would have to use at that point a ternary alphabet, contrary to the assumption made.

The requirement that only terminal nodes be assigned to messages is equivalent to the requirement that none of the code words be identical to the first part (prefix) of a longer code word. This condition is automatically met by any set of code words constructed by successive subdivisions of a message ensemble, as in the preceding section. It should be noted also that, if this condition were not met and messages were to be transmitted in succession, it would not be possible, in general, to redivide the resulting sequence of symbols into successive messages in a unique manner.

3.4. The Kraft Inequality [2]

The requirement that messages be represented by terminal nodes of a tree leads to an important theorem on the lengths of the code words assigned to a set of messages. Let D be the number of symbols in the coding alphabet, and $n_1, n_2, \ldots, n_M$ be a prescribed set of M positive integers.

Theorem. The inequality

$$\sum_{k=1}^{M} D^{-n_k} \le 1 \tag{3.4}$$

is a necessary and sufficient condition for the existence of a set of M code words corresponding to terminal nodes of a tree and with lengths equal to the prescribed integers.

Proof. We shall first prove that Eq. 3.4 is a necessary condition. We observe for this purpose that, since the coding alphabet consists of D symbols, there can be up to D branches stemming from each node of the tree. It follows that there can be as many as D^n nodes of order n ; this maximum number is obtained when there are D branches stemming from each node of order smaller than n . On the other hand, the presence of a terminal node of order n_k(smaller than n) eliminates D^{n-n_k} of the possible nodes of order n . We can conclude, therefore, that the prescribed lengths of the code words, that is, the orders of the terminal nodes, must satisfy the inequality

$$\sum_{k=1}^{M} D^{n-n_k} \leq D^n \tag{3.5}$$

for all integers n larger than the largest n_k . Dividing this inequality by D^n yields

$$\sum_{k=1}^{M} D^{-n_k} \leq 1 \tag{3.6}$$

which is the necessary condition stated in the above theorem.

In order to prove that the same condition is sufficient as well as necessary, we must show that a tree with the specified terminal nodes, that is, a set of code words with the specified lengths, can actually be constructed. For this purpose, let us assign the subscripts k in order of increasing code-word lengths so that, for any k ,

$$n_k \leq n_{k+1} \tag{3.7}$$

Let us suppose further that we have succeeded in constructing a tree including all the prescribed terminal nodes of order smaller than m , and that the tree must include w_m terminal nodes of order m . By hypothesis (see Eq. 3.4)

$$\sum_{k=1}^{j} D^{-n_k} + w_m D^{-m} + \sum_{k=j+w_m+1}^{M} D^{-n_k} \leq 1 \tag{3.8}$$

where j is the number of terminal nodes of order smaller than m . Let us multiply this inequality by D^m and transfer the two summations to the righthand side; we obtain

$$w_m \leq D^m - \sum_{k=1}^{j} D^{m-n_k} - \sum_{k=j+w_m+1}^{M} D^{m-n_k} \tag{3.9}$$

On the other hand, the number of available nodes of order m

is D^m minus the number of nodes eliminated by the presence of terminal nodes of lower order; that is,

$$D^m - \sum_{k=1}^{j} D^{m-n_k} \tag{3.10}$$

It follows that the number of available nodes of order m is at least equal to the prescribed number of terminal nodes of the same order, so that all of the latter can be included in the tree. Since this is true for all integers m, we can conclude that a tree with the required terminal nodes can always be constructed step by step, provided only that the orders of the nodes satisfy Eq. 3.4.

QED

The inequality of Eq. 3.4 is a necessary and sufficient condition for the existence of a tree including M terminal nodes of order n_1, n_2, ..., n_M. A tree having these prescribed terminal nodes may or may not have additional terminal nodes. The prescribed set of terminal nodes is said to be complete if there exists a tree having the prescribed terminal nodes and no others; in other words, the prescribed terminal nodes fill the tree completely.

Theorem. The equation

$$\sum_{k=1}^{M} D^{-n_k} = 1 \tag{3.11}$$

is a necessary and sufficient condition for the prescribed set of terminal nodes to be complete.

Proof. That Eq. 3.11 is a necessary condition follows immediately from the reasoning leading to Eq. 3.5. In fact, if the prescribed terminal nodes form a complete set, they must eliminate all nodes of order n, in which case the equal sign holds in Eq. 3.5. Then, dividing this equation by D^n yields Eq. 3.11.

The sufficiency of the condition expressed by Eq. 3.11 can be proved as follows. Since any set of terminal nodes that satisfies Eq. 3.11 also satisfies Eq. 3.4, there exists at least one tree having the prescribed terminal nodes. Let us suppose that this tree has one or more additional terminal nodes besides the prescribed ones. If this were the case, we could insert in the summation on the lefthand side of Eq. 3.11 the terms corresponding to the additional terminal nodes without violating the inequality expressed by Eq. 3.4. This is clearly impossible. It follows that a tree possessing the terminal nodes satisfying Eq. 3.11 cannot possess additional terminal nodes.

QED

Theorem. The equation

$$M = \nu(D-1) + 1 \tag{3.12}$$

where ν is a positive integer, is a necessary and sufficient condition for the existence of a tree with a complete set of M terminal nodes.

Proof. The necessity of Eq. 3.12 can be proved by counting the terminal nodes of a complete tree; that is, a tree in which there are exactly D branches stemming from each intermediate node. Let us think of building the tree in successive steps, and indicate with M_i the number of free nodes present in the tree when the tree is built up to nodes of order i, and with m_i the number of intermediate nodes of order i when the tree is built up to nodes of order higher than i. The number of first-order nodes is

$$M_1 = D = 1 + (D - 1) \tag{3.13}$$

Each of the m_1 intermediate first-order nodes gives rise to D second-order nodes. Thus, the total number of free nodes after building the tree up to second-order nodes is given by

$$M_2 = M_1 + m_1 (D - 1) \tag{3.14}$$

In general,

$$M_{i+1} = M_i + m_i(D - 1) \tag{3.15}$$

from which we obtain, with the help of Eq. 3.13, for the total number of available nodes on the tree,

$$M = 1 + (D - 1) \left[1 + \sum_{i=1}^{n_M - 1} m_i \right] \tag{3.16}$$

where n_M is the order of the highest terminal node of the prescribed set. Since the expression between brackets on the righthand side of Eq. 3.16 is a sum of integers, the number of available terminal nodes must satisfy Eq. 3.12.

In order to prove that Eq. 3.12 is a sufficient as well as necessary condition, we must show that for any number M satisfying Eq. 3.12, there exists a tree with exactly M terminal nodes. This requires, in turn, that there exist an integer n_M and a set of integers m_i $(i < n_M)$ for which the expression between brackets on the righthand side of Eq. 3.16 is equal to the integer ν in Eq. 3.12. The integers m_i are arbitrary except for the limitation

$$0 < m_i \leq D\, m_{i-1} \, ; \quad i < n_M \tag{3.17}$$

Since no restriction is placed on n_M, it is always possible to select the m_i to meet the stated requirement. The integer n_M is just greater than the largest i for which $m_i \neq 0$.

QED

It is important to note that Eq. 3.12 is satisfied by any integer M when D is equal to 2. In other words, complete binary trees can be constructed for any arbitrary number of terminal nodes. This is not true when D is different from 2.

3.5. A Basic Coding Theorem

We shall now proceed to prove the following basic theorem.

> Theorem. Given an ensemble U of M messages with entropy H(U), and an alphabet consisting of D symbols, it is possible to encode the messages of the ensemble by means of sequences of symbols belonging to the prescribed alphabet in such a way that the average number of symbols per message $\overline{n}$ satisfies the inequality
>
> $$\frac{H(U)}{\log D} \leq \overline{n} < \frac{H(U)}{\log D} + 1 \qquad (3.18)$$
>
> The number $\overline{n}$ cannot be made smaller than the lower bound given by Eq. 3.18.

Proof of lower bound. A proof of the lower bound in Eq. 3.18 has already been given in Sec. 3.1. However, because of the importance of this lower bound, it is desirable to give a direct proof of it, without making use of the measures of information defined in Chapter 2. Indicating again with $P(u_k)$ the probability of occurrence of the message u_k, and with n_k the number of symbols in the code word corresponding to the message u_k, we have for the average number of symbols per message

$$\overline{n} = \sum_{k=1}^{M} P(u_k)\, n_k \qquad (3.19)$$

We wish to show that

$$H(U) - \overline{n} \log D \leq 0 \qquad (3.20)$$

when the n_k satisfy Eq. 3.4. Let

$$Q_k = D^{-n_k}, \quad n_k \log D = -\log Q_k \qquad (3.21)$$

We have, then, with the help of Eqs. 2.91 and 3.4,

$$H(U) - \bar{n} \log D = \sum_{k=1}^{M} \left[P(u_k) \log \frac{Q_k}{P(u_k)} \right]$$

$$\leq \sum_{k=1}^{M} P(u_k) \left[\frac{Q_k}{P(u_k)} - 1 \right] \log e = \left[\sum_{k=1}^{M} D^{-n_k} - 1 \right] \log e \tag{3.22}$$

This equation, in conjunction with Eq. 3.4, yields Eq. 3.20.

QED

The proof of the upper bound in Eq. 3.18 is suggested by the following lemma.

Lemma. A necessary and sufficient condition for the existence of a set of code words for which

$$\bar{n} = \frac{H(U)}{\log D} \tag{3.23}$$

is that, for each message u_k,

$$\frac{I(u_k)}{\log D} \equiv \frac{-\log P(u_k)}{\log D} = \text{integer} \tag{3.24}$$

When this condition is satisfied

$$n_k = \frac{I(u_k)}{\log D} \tag{3.25}$$

Proof of Lemma. The equal sign holds in Eq. 3.22 when and only when the equal sign holds in Eq. 2.91. In this special case,

$$Q_k \equiv D^{-n_k} = P(u_k) \tag{3.26}$$

and, therefore,

$$\sum_{k=1}^{M} D^{-n_k} = 1 \tag{3.27}$$

$$n_k = \frac{-\log P(u_k)}{\log D} \tag{3.28}$$

It follows that the equal sign holds in Eq. 3.20 when and only when Eq. 3.28 is satisfied. On the other hand, n_k must be an integer because it represents the number of symbols in the code word associated with u_k. Thus, the condition expressed by Eq. 3.24 is necessary. The same condition is also sufficient because Eq. 3.27 implies Eq. 3.4 which, in turn, is sufficient to insure the existence of code words with the specified lengths. QED

Proof of upper bound. The righthand side of Eq. 3.25 is not, in general, an integer. On the other hand, the above lemma suggests making the number n_k of symbols in the code word corresponding to the message u_k equal to the integer just larger than the righthand side of Eq. 3.25. Let us consider then a set of M integers n_k^* defined by

$$\frac{I(u_k)}{\log D} \leq n_k^* < \frac{I(u_k)}{\log D} + 1 \qquad (3.29)$$

These integers satisfy Eq. 3.4 because Eq. 3.4 is satisfied by the numbers n_k (not necessarily integers) given by Eq. 3.25. Thus, we are assured that a set of code words corresponding to the set of integers n_k^* can actually be constructed. The average number of symbols for such a set of code words must then satisfy the inequality obtained by averaging Eq. 3.29 over the message ensemble, which is just that given by Eq. 3.18. QED

The theorem stated at the beginning of this section provides a direct, operational interpretation for the entropy of a message ensemble. It states, in the case of a binary alphabet, that the average number of binary digits required to represent the messages of a given ensemble U is at least equal to the entropy H(U) of the ensemble, and may exceed it by at most one digit. Thus, if $H(U) \gg 1$, H(U) is a percentagewise accurate estimate of $\overline{n}$, the average number of binary digits required to encode the messages of the ensemble U. Furthermore, we know from Eq. 3.29 that, when the minimization of $\overline{n}$ is our objective, the self information $I(u_k)$ of the message u_k is an accurate estimate (in the same percentagewise sense) of the number of digits in the binary code word representing u_k. These results confirm the appropriateness of our definition of self information.

3.6. Sources of Statistically Independent Messages

We have discussed up to now the encoding of individual messages without reference to the fact that the source output usually consists of a sequence of messages. We have assumed, in effect, that successive messages are encoded separately on the basis of the ensemble formed at that time by the possible output messages. This is perfectly legitimate. However, it may be possible to reduce the average number of symbols per message by taking advantage of the fact that the messages occur in a sequence.

The encoding of sequences of messages is the subject of the next chapter. However, it is desirable to discuss at this point the simple case of sequences of statistically independent messages occurring with fixed probabilities.

Let us segment the message sequence generated by the source into successive sequences of ν messages. If we indicate with M the number of different messages and with U their ensemble, each sequence of ν messages generated by the source is a member of the product ensemble U^ν formed by the M^ν possible sequences of ν messages. Since each message is, by assumption, statistically independent of all preceding messages, the entropy of the product ensemble U^ν is related to the entropy of the ensemble U by

$$H(U^\nu) = \nu H(U) \tag{3.30}$$

Now, let us construct code words of lengths satisfying Eq. 3.4 for the M^ν members of the product ensemble U^ν. If we indicate with $\bar{n}_\nu$ the average number of symbols per code word, the average number of symbols per message is given by

$$\bar{n} = \frac{\bar{n}_\nu}{\nu} \tag{3.31}$$

in view of the fact that each code word represents a sequence of messages. We shall now prove the following theorem.

> Theorem. Given a positive number ϵ, as small as desired, it is possible to find an integer ν and a corresponding set of M^ν code words for which $\bar{n}$, the average number of symbols per message, satisfies the inequality
>
> $$\bar{n} \leq \frac{H(U)}{\log D} + \epsilon \tag{3.32}$$
>
> Conversely, it is impossible to find an integer ν and a corresponding set of code words for which
>
> $$\bar{n} < \frac{H(U)}{\log D} \tag{3.33}$$

Proof. This theorem follows immediately from the fundamental theorem of Sec. 3.5. Substituting $\bar{n}_\nu$ for $\bar{n}$ and $H(U^\nu)$ for H(U) in Eq. 3.18 yields, with the help of Eq. 3.30,

$$\frac{\nu H(U)}{\log D} \leq \bar{n}_\nu < \frac{\nu H(U)}{\log D} + 1 \tag{3.34}$$

and, after division by ν,

$$\frac{H(U)}{\log D} \leq \bar{n} < \frac{H(U)}{\log D} + \frac{1}{\nu} \qquad (3.35)$$

It follows from this equation that Eq. 3.32 can be satisfied by making

$$\nu \geq \frac{1}{\epsilon} \qquad (3.36)$$

Conversely, Eq. 3.33 is inconsistent with Eq. 3.35. QED

The conclusion that we can draw from this theorem is that, when each message is statistically independent of all the preceding ones, encoding sequences of messages rather than individual messages can reduce the average number of symbols per message by at most one symbol.

*3.7. An Optimum Encoding Procedure

The encoding procedure discussed in Sec. 3.2 yields, usually, a fairly satisfactory set of code words, but not necessarily an optimum set. We shall present in this section a systematic encoding procedure discovered by D. A. Huffman [3]. This procedure always yields an optimum set of code words, in the sense that no other set has a smaller average number of symbols per message. We shall first describe the procedure, and then prove that the resulting set of code words is optimum.

Let us consider an ensemble of M messages $u_1, u_2, \ldots, u_M$ occurring with probabilities $P(u_1)$, $P(u_2)$, ..., $P(u_M)$, and an alphabet consisting of D symbols. The following procedure leads to an optimum set of code words.

Step 1. The M messages are arranged in order of decreasing probability as shown in Figs. 3.4 and 3.5.

Step 2. Let m_0 be the integer satisfying the two requirements

$$2 \leq m_0 \leq D \qquad (3.37)$$

$$\frac{M - m_0}{D - 1} = \text{positive integer} \qquad (3.38)$$

Note that $m_0 = 2$ whenever $D = 2$. Group together the m_0 least probable messages and compute the total probability of such a message subset.

Step 3. Construct an auxiliary ensemble of messages from the original ensemble by regarding the subset of m_0 messages formed in Step 2 as a single message with probability equal to the probability of the whole subset. Rearrange the messages of this auxiliary ensemble in order of decreasing probability, as shown in Figs. 3.4 and 3.5.

Step 4. Form a subset of the D least probable messages of the auxiliary ensemble, and compute its total probability.

Code words	Messages	$P(u_k)$
10	u_1	0.25
01	u_2	0.25
00	u_3	0.20
111	u_4	0.15
1101	u_5	0.10
1100	u_6	0.05

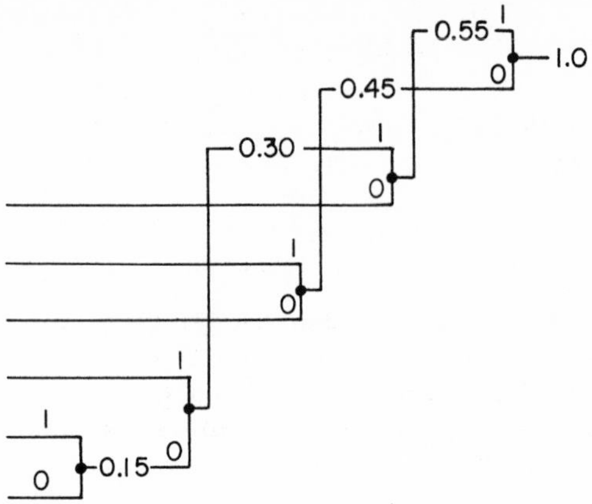

Fig. 3.4. Optimum set of binary code words

Code words	Messages	$P(u_k)$
1	u_1	0.25
0	u_2	0.25
22	u_3	0.20
21	u_4	0.15
201	u_5	0.10
200	u_6	0.05

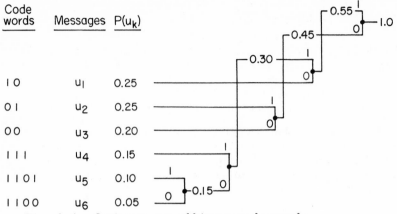

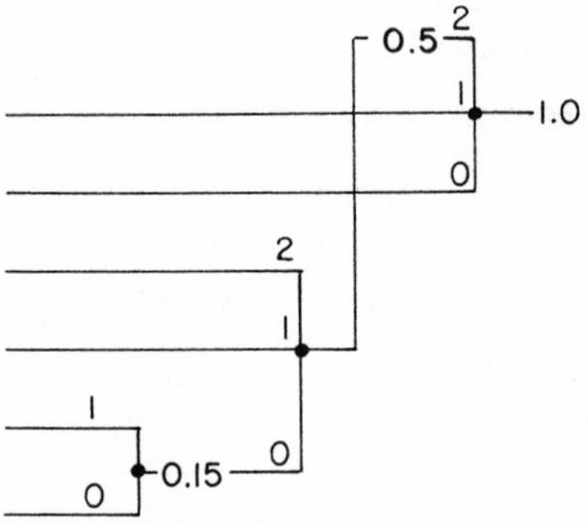

Fig. 3.5. Optimum set of ternary code words

Step 5. Construct a second auxiliary ensemble from the first auxiliary ensemble by regarding the subset of the D messages formed in Step 4 as a single message with probability equal to the total probability of the whole subset. Rearrange the messages of this second auxiliary ensemble in order of decreasing probability.

Step 6. Form successive auxiliary ensembles by repeating Step 4 and Step 5 until a single message of unit probability is left in the ensemble, as illustrated schematically in Figs. 3.4 and 3.5.

Step 7. The preceding steps, when formally carried out by drawing lines joining the messages of successive subsets, yield a tree of which the specified messages are terminal nodes. Code words can then be constructed by assigning different symbols from the prescribed alphabet to the branches stemming from each intermediate node, as shown in Figs. 3.4 and 3.5. Only one of the intermediate nodes may have less than D branches, namely, the one resulting from Step 2.

The set of code words resulting from the above procedure meets the requirement that no word be identical to the prefix of a longer word, since messages are assigned only to terminal nodes of the tree. We shall now prove that the set so obtained is optimum in the sense that no set of code words exists with a smaller average number of symbols per message.

Let n_k represent the number of symbols in the code word corresponding to message u_k. The average number of symbols per message is, by definition,

$$\overline{n} \equiv \sum_{k=1}^{M} P(u_k) n_k \qquad (3.39)$$

We shall first derive various necessary conditions that must be satisfied by the set of code words with the smallest possible value of $\overline{n}$. Next we shall show that these conditions are also sufficient in the sense that all sets of code words that satisfy such necessary conditions are obtainable by means of the above procedure and yield the same value of $\overline{n}$. We shall be able to conclude, then, that no set of code words yields a smaller value of $\overline{n}$, thereby completing the desired proof.

It is convenient, in discussing the details of the proof, to assign the numbers 1 to M to the messages in order of decreasing probability, so that, for instance, u_1 is the most probable message and u_M is the least probable message. In addition, we shall refer to the sequence formed by the first r symbols of a word as the "r^{th} prefix" of the word.

Condition 1. The words, in order of increasing length, must correspond to the messages in order of decreasing probability; that is, for all indices k and j, if

$$P(u_j) \geq P(u_k) \qquad (3.40)$$

it must be

$$n_j \leq n_k \qquad (3.41)$$

This condition is necessary because, if Eq. 3.40 were not satisfied, we could reduce the value of $\overline{n}$ by interchanging the code words corresponding to messages u_k and u_j.

Condition 2. The two least probable messages must correspond to code words of the same length n_M (the maximum length); that is, to nodes of the same order.

This condition is necessary because if only the least probable message corresponded to a terminal node of order n_M, there would be an intermediate node of lower order with a single branch stemming from it; namely, the branch leading to the only node of order n_M. Then, this intermediate node could be changed into a terminal node and the least probable message could be assigned to it, thereby reducing the length of the corresponding code words. In other words, if there were a single code word of length n_M, the last symbol of such a code word would serve no useful purpose and could be eliminated.

> Condition 3. The number $w_t(n_M)$ of terminal nodes of order n_M assigned to messages and the number $w_i(n_M-1)$ of intermediate nodes of order n_M-1 must satisfy the inequality

$$D\, w_i(n_M - 1) - w_t(n_M) < D-1 \tag{3.42}$$

This condition must be satisfied because otherwise at least one of the intermediate nodes of order n_M-1 could be changed into a terminal node, and we could assign to it one of the messages previously assigned to a node of order n_M, thereby reducing the length of the corresponding code word. In other words, since each intermediate node of order n_M-1 can give rise to D nodes of order n_M, the number of available nodes of order n_M must not exceed by more than D-2 the number of messages to be assigned to them. It should be noted, in this connection, that if $w_t(n_M)$ is not a multiple of D, there are many ways in which the messages can be assigned to the available nodes. All such assignments are equivalent in the sense that they yield the same value of $\overline{n}$, the average number of symbols per message. Thus there exists in all cases an optimum set of code words in which D terminal nodes of order n_M stem from each of $w_i(n_M-1) - 1$ intermediate nodes of order n_M-1, and

$$m_0 = w_t(n_M) - D\,[w_i(n_M-1) - 1] > 1 \tag{3.43}$$

terminal nodes of order n_M stem from the remaining intermediate node of order n_M-1.

> Condition 4. There must be D branches stemming from each intermediate node of order smaller than n_M-1.

This condition must be satisfied because otherwise we could construct additional terminal nodes of order smaller than n_M and assign to them messages previously assigned to nodes of order n_M, thereby reducing the lengths of the corresponding code words.

> Condition 5. Suppose we change an intermediate node into a terminal node by eliminating all the branches and nodes stemming from it, and we assign to this node a composite message having a probability equal to the sum of the probabilities of the

messages assigned to the terminal nodes that have been eliminated. Then, if the original tree was optimum for the original ensemble of messages, the new tree must be optimum for the new ensemble of messages.

This condition must be satisfied because otherwise we could decrease the average number of symbols per message for the original ensemble by optimizing the tree for the new ensemble, and then reconnecting to the terminal node corresponding to the composite message the part of the tree that had been eliminated.

We shall now show that for any given message ensemble, all sets of code words that satisfy the above conditions yield the same average number of symbols per message, and that at least one of such sets is obtainable by means of the coding procedure outlined above. We observe, first of all, that Conditions 3 and 4 can be replaced, for our purposes, by the following more stringent condition.

Auxiliary Condition 6. There must be D branches stemming from each intermediate node of order smaller than n_M, except for one node of order n_M-1, for which the number m_0 of branches is given by Eqs. 3.37 and 3.38.

This condition clearly includes Conditions 3 and 4 above, but it is more stringent than Condition 3. On the other hand, the sets of code words that do not satisfy this more stringent condition but satisfy Conditions 3 and 4 yield, for a given message ensemble, the same average number of symbols per message as the sets that satisfy the more stringent condition. In fact, these sets differ only in the assignment of messages to the available nodes of order n_M, as discussed above in connection with Condition 3. In other words, although this more stringent condition is not necessary, we are sure that it is satisfied by at least one optimum set of code words.

Let us proceed by considering first the case of D = 2. In this case Conditions 1 and 2, together with Auxiliary Condition 6, require that the two least probable messages, that is, u_M and u_{M-1}, be assigned to terminal nodes of the same order n_M, and stemming from the same intermediate node of order n_M-1. This is the same as saying that the corresponding code words must have the same length and must be identical but for the last digit. The common prefix of length n_M-1 of these two code words and the corresponding intermediate node of order n_M-1 may be considered as associated to a "combination message" of probability equal to $P(u_M) + P(u_{M-1})$. Then, if we form an auxiliary ensemble by substituting this combination message for u_M and u_{M-1}, we know from Condition 5 that the tree, or set of code words, corresponding to this new ensemble must be optimum in order for the complete tree to be optimum. It follows that the two least probable messages of this auxiliary ensemble must be assigned again to terminal nodes of the same order stemming from the same intermediate node of next lower order. Next, this second pair of messages is again lumped together into a second combination message to form a second auxiliary ensemble consisting of M-2 messages.

It should be clear by now that Conditions 1, 2, and 5, together with Auxiliary Condition 6, require the above procedure to be iterated until the last auxiliary message ensemble consists of a single message, and that this iterative procedure is identical, for D = 2, to that outlined at the beginning of this section. This procedure is uniquely determined by the stated conditions, except when equiprobable messages are present in the original ensemble or in any one of the auxiliary ensembles. In any such case, there can be more than two messages that may be considered as least probable. On the other hand, using different pairs of such messages as least probable is equivalent to interchanging the code words corresponding to equiprobable messages or the prefixes of groups of code words having the same total probability; such interchanges clearly do not change the average number of symbols per message. Thus, for any given ensemble of messages, all trees or sets of code words that satisfy the above necessary conditions have the same average number of symbols per message as the sets resulting from the procedure outlined above. We may conclude, therefore, that, for D = 2, the procedure yields an optimum set of code words.

In the case of $D \neq 2$, Conditions 1 and 2, together with Auxiliary Condition 6, require that m_0 least probable messages be assigned to terminal nodes of order n_M stemming from the same intermediate node of order $n_M - 1$ and that m_0 satisfy Eqs. 3.37 and 3.38. Thus the corresponding m_0 code words must be identical but for the last symbol. Next, Condition 5 requires that the first auxiliary ensemble (formed by lumping together the above m_0 messages into a single combination message having the same total probability) be coded in an optimum manner. On the other hand, Auxiliary Condition 6 requires that the D least probable messages of this auxiliary ensemble be assigned to nodes stemming from the same intermediate node of next lower order; this follows from the fact that, in the final tree, only one intermediate node is permitted to have less than D branches. The same requirement is imposed on all successive auxiliary ensembles. Then, since the number of messages must decrease by D-1 each time a new auxiliary ensemble is formed, and since the last auxiliary ensemble must contain a single combination message, the number m_0 must satisfy the equation

$$1 + \nu(D-1) + (m_0 - 1) = M \tag{3.44}$$

where ν is a non-negative integer. Solving for m_0 yields

$$m_0 = M - \nu(D-1) \tag{3.45}$$

which is equivalent to Eq. 3.38. When the integer m_0 is equal to D, the resulting set of terminal nodes is complete, as discussed in Sec. 3.4.

We can conclude, again, that the conditions stated above uniquely specify an iterative coding procedure, except for possible interchanges of code words between equiprobable messages, and interchanges of prefixes between equiprobable groups of messages. Such interchanges have no effect on the average number of symbols per message. Thus for any ensemble of messages and any alphabet, all the sets of code words that satisfy Conditions 1, 2, 3, 4, and 5 have the same average number of symbols per message. At least one of such sets can be obtained by following the procedure outlined above. We can conclude, therefore, that the coding procedure is optimum for all message ensembles and for all alphabets.

3.8. Summary and Conclusions

We have discussed in this chapter how the messages of a specified ensemble can be represented by sequences of symbols selected from a prescribed alphabet. We saw in particular that the entropy of the message ensemble is a lower bound to the average (over the message ensemble) number of binary digits sufficient to represent the messages of the ensemble. This lower bound can actually be achieved in certain special cases; namely, when the self information of each message (expressed in bits) is an integer. When this is not the case, it is still possible to make the number of binary digits in each code word equal to the integer just larger than the self information of the corresponding message, in which case the average number of binary digits per message will exceed the entropy of the message ensemble by less than one binary digit. Thus, the self information of a message can be regarded as representing the number of binary digits required to identify a message, whenever we wish to minimize the expected (average) value of the number of binary digits. This result provides a most important operational significance for the measure of self information defined in the preceding chapter.

We confined our discussion for the most part to the encoding of discrete message ensembles, without concerning ourselves with the statistical characteristics of the source generating the messages. The matter of the statistical relation between successive messages was touched upon only in Sec. 3.6. We assumed there the simplest type of statistical relation between successive messages, namely, statistical independence. We were able to prove in this simple case that the average number of binary digits per message can be made to approach as closely as desired the entropy of the message ensemble (measured in bits) by encoding sufficiently long sequences of messages. This last result, however, has only limited practical significance, not only because of the assumption that successive messages are statistically independent, but also because no consideration has yet been given to constraints on the rate at which the binary digits generated by the encoder can be transmitted, in relation to the rate at which the messages are generated by the source. The limitations on encoding imposed by the message-generation rate and by the digit-transmission rate will be discussed in the next chapter in connection with our study of stochastic information sources.

3.9. Selected References

1. C. E. Shannon, "A Mathematical Theory of Communication," Bell System Tech. J., 27, 379 (July, 1948). The original encoding procedure developed by Shannon, similar to the one presented in Sec. 3.2, is described in Sec. 9. The same section includes the original proof of the coding theorem discussed in Sec. 3.5.

2. L. G. Kraft, "A Device for Quantizing, Grouping, and Coding Amplitude Modulated Pulses," M.S. Thesis, Electrical Engineering Department, M.I.T. March, 1949.

3. D. A. Huffman, "A Method for the Construction of Minimum Redundancy Codes," Proc. I.R.E., 40, 1098,(Sept., 1952).

Chapter 4

DISCRETE STOCHASTIC SOURCES

We shall discuss in this chapter the problem of encoding the output from a source, when the output consists of a sequence of discrete events. Discrete sources are often encountered in practice, for instance, in connection with telegraphy. Furthermore, continuous sources can be reduced to discrete form by grouping the possible outputs over successive time intervals into equivalence classes, according to the fidelity criterion specified by the user. Such a quantization process is characteristic of the transmission methods known as pulse-code modulation and pulse-position modulation. Thus, the assumption that the source output consists of a sequence of discrete events does not seriously limit the generality of our study.

We saw in Chapter 1 that the channel through which the output from the source must be transmitted places a limitation on the rate of transmission measured in binary digits per second. Thus, it is reasonable to require the source encoder to generate digits, binary or otherwise, at a fixed rate. This requirement, in turn, may place a stringent limitation on the encoding process, depending on the rate at which events are generated by the source. For this reason, we shall distinguish between two main types of sources, controllable-rate sources and fixed-rate sources. A controllable-rate source is one that generates an event when so instructed by the source encoder. The printed text in a telegraph system may be regarded as a controllable-rate source, because no constraint is placed on the time at which each successive letter is transmitted. Conversely, a fixed-rate source is a source that generates events at a fixed, uncontrollable time rate.

A discrete information source can be regarded for our purposes as consisting of a set of rules that, together with the results of successive chance experiments (selections made according to specified probabilities), determine the particular successive events generated by the source. We shall refer to sources of this type as "stochastic."

The first topic in our discussion will be the statistical description of the ensemble of sequences generated by stochastic sources. We shall then focus our attention on the particular class of stochastic sources known as stationary; that is, sources whose statistical description is independent of time. It will be possible, for these sources, to define an entropy per event, representing the average amount of information required to specify each output event. We shall show, in the case of controllable-rate sources, that the entropy so defined is a lower bound to the average number of binary digits per output event by means of which the source output can be uniquely specified, and that this lower bound can be approached as closely as desired by properly designing the encoding process.

Next, we shall turn our attention to the encoding of stationary, fixed-rate sources. We shall show that the source output can again be encoded with a number of binary digits per event as closely as desired to the source entropy, provided we are willing to tolerate a vanishingly small but finite probability of ambiguous encoding.

Finally, we shall discuss in some detail the special case of Markov sources, a class of stochastic sources that provide adequate mathematical models for a variety of physical sources.

4.1. Discrete Stochastic Sources

Let us indicate with $\alpha_1, \alpha_2, \ldots, \alpha_i, \ldots$ the sequence of events generated by the source. Each particular event α_i can be any one of the L letters $a_1, a_2, \ldots, a_k, \ldots, a_L$ of a set A. Although the set of possible letters is the same for all successive events, it will be often convenient to distinguish between the sets of letters corresponding to different events. Thus, we shall indicate with A_i the set of letters corresponding to the ith event α_i, although the members of the set A_i are the same for all integers $i > 0$.

The ensemble of sequences generated by the source is described by the following series of probability distributions:

The probability distribution $P(\alpha_1)$ of the first event, consisting of the probabilities $Pr(\alpha_1 = a_k)$.

The conditional probability distribution $P(\alpha_2 | \alpha_1)$ of the second event, given the first one, consisting of the probabilities $Pr(\alpha_2 = a_j | \alpha_1 = a$

The conditional probability distribution $P(\alpha_i | \alpha_{i-1}, \alpha_{i-2}, \ldots, \alpha_1)$ for the ith event, given the preceding $i-1$ events.

All other probability distributions may be expressed in terms of these. For instance, the joint probability distribution for the first ν events is, by definition,

$$P(\alpha_1, \alpha_2, \ldots, \alpha_\nu) \equiv P(\alpha_1) P(\alpha_2 | \alpha_1) \ldots P(\alpha_\nu | \alpha_{\nu-1}, \ldots, \alpha_1) \tag{4.1}$$

The joint probability distribution for the νth event and the one immediately preceding is then given by

$$P(\alpha_\nu, \alpha_{\nu-1}) = \sum_{A_1 A_2 \ldots A_{\nu-2}} P(\alpha_1, \alpha_2, \ldots, \alpha_\nu) \tag{4.2}$$

where the summation is evaluated over the product ensemble formed by the first $\nu-2$ events. The conditional probability distribution for the νth event, given the event immediately preceding it, is, by definition:

$$P(a_\nu | a_{\nu-1}) \equiv \frac{P(a_\nu, a_{\nu-1})}{P(a_{\nu-1})} \tag{4.3}$$

This description of the ensemble of sequences leads naturally to inquiring about the average amount of information required to specify the successive events of the sequence. The average amount required to specify the first event is given by the entropy

$$H(A_1) \equiv -\sum_{A_1} P(a_1)\log P(a_1) \tag{4.4}$$

The average amount required to specify the second event, after the first one has been specified, is given by the conditional entropy

$$H(A_2 | A_1) \equiv -\sum_{A_1 A_2} P(a_1, a_2)\log P(a_2 | a_1) \tag{4.5}$$

In general, the average amount of information required to specify the ith event, after all preceding events have been specified, is given by

$$H(A_i | A_{i-1} \dots A_1) \equiv -\sum_{A_1 A_2 \dots A_i} P(a_1, a_2, \dots, a_i)\log P(a_i | a_{i-1}, \dots, a_1) \tag{4.6}$$

For the sake of simplicity we shall indicate with

$$H(A_i | A^\nu) \equiv H(A_i | A_{i-1}\ A_{i-2} \dots A_{i-\nu}), \quad i > \nu \geq 0 \tag{4.7}$$

the conditional entropy of the ith event, given the preceding ν events, where the symbol A^ν stands for the product ensemble formed by the preceding ν events.

In view of Eqs. 2.90, 2.100, and 2.105, the above entropies satisfy the inequalities

$$H(A_i | A^\nu) \leq H(A_i | A^{\nu-1}) \leq H(A_i | A^{\nu-2}) \leq \dots \leq H(A_i | A_{i-1}) \leq H(A_i) \tag{4.8}$$

for all integers i and ν, $i > \nu \geq 0$.

4.2. Entropy of a Stationary Source

A source is said to be stationary when the conditional probability distribution of the event a_i, given the ν events preceding it, is independent of i for all integers $\nu < i$; that is,

$$P(a_i | a_{i-1}, a_{i-2}, \dots, a_{i-\nu}) = P(a_j | a_{j-1}, a_{j-2}, \dots, a_{j-\nu}) \tag{4.9}$$

for all integers i and j greater than ν. It follows that, for a stationary source, all probability distributions are invariant to any translation along the sequence that corresponds to increasing or decreasing all the subscripts of the α's by the same integer. In other words, the statistical characteristics of the output from a stationary source are independent of the time origin selected.

Because of Eq. 4.9, the entropies pertaining to the events generated by a stationary source depend only on the relative positions of the events involved in the output sequence of events. For instance,

$$H(A_i | A^\nu) = H(A_j | A^\nu) \tag{4.10}$$

for all integers i and j greater than ν.

Let us consider now the conditional entropies of the successive events generated by the source, when all the preceding events are given, that is, the sequence formed by $H(A_\nu | A^{\nu-1})$ for increasing values of the positive integer ν.

Theorem. For a stationary source, the conditional entropies of successive events, when all the preceding events are given, form a monotonic, non-increasing sequence; that is,

$$H(A_{\nu+1} | A^\nu) \leq H(A_\nu | A^{\nu-1}) \leq H(A_{\nu-1} | A^{\nu-2}) \leq \ldots \leq H(A_2 | A_1) \leq H(A_1) \tag{4.11}$$

Proof. Because of Eq. 4.10, arbitrary, different integers (greater than the number of preceding events that are given) can be substituted for i in each of the entropies in Eq. 4.8. In particular, $\nu+1$ can be substituted for i in the first entropy, ν in the second entropy, $\nu-1$ in the third entropy, and so forth. These substitutions yield Eq. 4.11.
QED

Theorem. The limit

$$\lim_{\nu \to \infty} H(A_\nu | A^{\nu-1}) = H(A | A^\infty) \tag{4.12}$$

exists for every stationary source, where $H(A | A^\infty)$ is a number characterizing the source, which satisfies the inequality

$$0 \leq H(A | A^\infty) \leq \log L \tag{4.13}$$

Proof. The entropy of any discrete ensemble, whether conditional or not, is non-negative and, because of Eqs. 2.90, 2.100, and 2.105, cannot exceed log L, where L is the number of members of the ensemble. On the other hand, because of the theorem expressed by Eq. 4.11, $H(A_\nu | A^{\nu-1})$ is a non-increasing function of the integer ν. It follows that $H(A_\nu | A^{\nu-1})$ must approach, with increasing ν, a limiting value satisfying Eq. 4.13.
QED

The entropy $H(A|A^{\infty})$ is the limiting value of the average amount of information per event required to specify the output of a stationary source. As such, it represents the information rate (per event) of the source. It must be emphasized in this connection that the limit in Eq. 4.12 may not exist if the source is not stationary. In fact, the conditional entropy $H(A_{\nu}|A^{\nu-1})$ of a nonstationary source may oscillate between zero and $\log L$ in an arbitrary manner with increasing ν. It is most important to note that the inequalities in Eq. 4.8 state only that the conditional entropy of the ith event is a non-increasing function of the number of preceding events that are specified; by themselves, they make no statement about the manner in which the conditional entropy of the ith event varies with increasing i.

Let us consider next the entropy of the product ensemble formed by ν successive events. We have from Eq. 2.98

$$H(A^{\nu}) \equiv H(A_1 A_2 \dots A_{\nu}) = H(A_1) + H(A_2|A_1) + H(A_3|A_2 A_1) + \dots + H(A_{\nu-1}|A^{\nu-2}) + H(A_{\nu}|A^{\nu-1}) \tag{4.14}$$

We shall indicate with $H_{\nu}(A)$ the arithmetic mean

$$H_{\nu}(A) \equiv \frac{1}{\nu} H(A^{\nu}) = \frac{1}{\nu} \sum_{j=1}^{\nu} H(A_j|A^{j-1}) \tag{4.15}$$

Theorem. The mean entropy $H_{\nu}(A)$ of a stationary source is a non-increasing function of ν, and

$$\lim_{\nu\to\infty} H_{\nu}(A) = H(A|A^{\infty}) \tag{4.16}$$

Proof. We have from Eqs. 4.11, 4.12, and 4.14

$$H(A^{\nu}) \geq \nu H(A_{\nu}|A^{\nu-1}) \geq \nu H(A_{\nu+1}|A^{\nu}) \tag{4.17}$$

and, therefore,

$$H(A^{\nu+1}) = H(A^{\nu}) + H(A_{\nu+1}|A^{\nu}) \leq \frac{\nu+1}{\nu} H(A^{\nu}) \tag{4.18}$$

from which we obtain, with the help of Eq. 4.15,

$$H_{\nu+1}(A) \leq H_{\nu}(A) \tag{4.19}$$

This equation implies that $H_{\nu}(A)$ is a non-increasing function of ν, and, since it is non-negative, it must approach a limit when ν approaches infinity. The limit in question can be evaluated as follows.

Let ϵ and δ be two positive numbers, as small as desired, and write $H_{\nu}(A)$ in the form

$$H_\nu(A) = \frac{1}{\nu}\left[\sum_{i=1}^{j-1} H(A_i \mid A^{i-1}) + \sum_{i=j}^{\nu} H(A_i \mid A^{i-1})\right] \quad (4.20)$$

We have then, with the help of Eq. 4.11,

$$H_\nu(A) \leq \frac{j-1}{\nu} H(A_1) + \frac{\nu-j+1}{\nu} H(A_j \mid A^{j-1}) \quad (4.21)$$

$$< \frac{j}{\nu} H(A_1) + H(A_j \mid A^{j-1})$$

On the other hand, from Eqs. 4.11 and 4.12, we can always find an integer j for which

$$H(A_j \mid A^{j-1}) < H(A \mid A^\infty) + \epsilon \quad (4.22)$$

Then, for any such integer j, we can find an integer ν for which

$$\frac{j}{\nu} H(A_1) < \delta \quad (4.23)$$

Under these conditions

$$H_\nu(A) < H(A \mid A^\infty) + \epsilon + \delta \quad (4.24)$$

Furthermore, dividing Eq. 4.17 by ν yields, with the help of Eqs. 4.11, 4.12, and 4.15,

$$H_\nu(A) \equiv \frac{1}{\nu} H(A^\nu) \geq H(A_\nu \mid A^{\nu-1}) \geq H(A \mid A^\infty) \quad (4.25)$$

QED

4.3. Encoding of Controllable-Rate, Stationary Sources

We are now in a position to generalize the fundamental theorem presented in Sec. 3.6 to any discrete, stationary source for which the rate at which the output events are generated can be controlled by the source encoder.

Theorem. Given any positive number ϵ, as small as desired, it is possible to encode the sequence of events generated by a discrete, stationary source into a sequence of symbols selected from a prescribed alphabet, in such a way that the ensemble average of the number of symbols per output event satisfies the inequality

$$\bar{n} \leq \frac{H(A \mid A^\infty)}{\log D} + \epsilon \quad (4.26)$$

where $H(A \mid A^\infty)$ is the limiting value of the conditional entropy given by Eq. 4.16 and D is the number of symbols in the encoding alphabet. Conversely, it is impossible to encode the output events in such a way that

$$\bar{n} < \frac{H(A|A^{\infty})}{\log D} \tag{4.27}$$

Proof. Let us segment the output sequence of events into messages, each consisting of ν successive events. Each message is a member of the product ensemble A^{ν} consisting of all possible sequences of ν letters belonging to the set A. The entropy $H(A^{\nu})$ of this ensemble is given by Eq. 4.14. Then, a set of optimum code words can be constructed for the set of possible messages, as discussed in Sec. 3.7. The average number of symbols per message $\bar{n}_{\nu}$ will satisfy the inequality

$$\frac{H(A^{\nu})}{\log D} \leq \bar{n}_{\nu} < \frac{H(A^{\nu})}{\log D} + 1 \tag{4.28}$$

obtained from Eq. 3.18 by identifying the product ensemble A^{ν} with the message ensemble U. Dividing by ν yields, for the average number of symbols per output event, $\bar{n} = \bar{n}_{\nu}/\nu$,

$$\frac{H_{\nu}(A)}{\log D} \leq \bar{n} < \frac{H_{\nu}(A)}{\log D} + \frac{1}{\nu} \tag{4.29}$$

where $H_{\nu}(A)$ is the mean entropy defined by Eq. 4.15. On the other hand, because of Eq. 4.16, it is always possible to find an integer ν such that

$$\frac{H_{\nu}(A)}{\log D} + \frac{1}{\nu} < \frac{H(A|A^{\infty})}{\log D} + \epsilon \tag{4.30}$$

Under these conditions $\bar{n}$ will satisfy Eq. 4.26. Conversely, Eq. 4.27 is inconsistent with Eq. 4.29, because $H_{\nu}(A)$ is never smaller than $H(A|A^{\infty})$, as shown by Eq. 4.25.

QED

Discussion of theorem. This theorem permits us to interpret $H(A|A^{\infty})$, the limiting value of the entropy per event, as the number of binary digits per event required, on the average, to encode the output of a stationary source. Because of its importance, it deserves further, careful discussion.

The theorem is based on two preceding theorems, whose statements are summarized below for the special case of binary encoding.

The first theorem, proved in Sec. 3.5, states that it is always possible to encode a discrete message ensemble by assigning to each message a binary code word of length equal to the integer just larger than, or equal to, the self information of the message expressed in bits. The resulting average (over the message ensemble) code-word length may exceed the entropy of the message ensemble by at most one digit. It follows that, for large values of the entropy, the average code-word length is approximately equal, percentagewise, to the entropy of the message ensemble.

The second theorem, proved in Sec. 4.2, states that, in the case of a discrete, stationary source, the entropy per output event, evaluated over the product ensemble formed by ν successive events, is a non-increasing function of ν, and approaches the value $H(A|A^{\infty})$ when ν approaches infinity. This is equivalent to saying that the entropy of the product ensemble formed by ν successive events is asymptotically equal to $\nu H(A|A^{\infty})$.

The theorem in question was then proved by regarding a sequence of ν successive events as an independent message with a self information

$$I(a_{i+1}\, a_{i+2} \cdots a_{i+\nu}) \equiv - \log P(a_{i+1}, a_{i+2}, \ldots, a_{i+\nu}) \tag{4.31}$$

where a_{i+1} stands for the first event of the sequence. Then, if each of the L^{ν} possible sequences of ν letters is represented by a binary code word of length approximately equal to the self information of the sequence in bits, the number of binary digits employed, on the average, to encode ν output events is approximately equal to the entropy of the ensemble formed by ν successive output events. This entropy is, in turn, asymptotically equal to $\nu H(A|A^{\infty})$, so that the number of binary digits per event, averaged over the ensemble formed by ν successive events, can be made to approach as closely as desired the limiting value $H(A|A^{\infty})$.

It is most important to note that all the averages involved in the theorem are evaluated over the message ensemble (the product ensemble formed by ν successive events). More precisely, each of these averages is the expectation of a random variable, the code-word length, for instance, possessing a well-defined value for each of the messages of the ensemble. Nothing has been said up to now about the mean values of the same random variables over the particular sequence of messages generated by the source. Thus, the theorem makes no statement about the mean length of the successive code words actually generated by the source encoder, but only about the expected length of the code word generated at any particular time, independently of all preceding code words.

In practice, however, we are interested in the mean length of a long sequence of code words, rather than in the expected length of the code word generated at some particular time. The importance of the latter stems from the fact that it coincides with the former in most cases of practical interest. The relation between sequence average and expectation, or ensemble average, is discussed in the next section.

4.4. Ensemble Average and Sequence Average

The following conceptual experiment provides an illuminating interpretation of the concept of expectation, or ensemble average.

Let us imagine that we have available m identical stationary sources; that is, stationary sources described by the same probability distribution. Then let us think of their outputs as segmented synchronously into successive messages, each consisting of a sequence of ν successive events. Let us focus our attention on the particular m messages generated simultaneously by the sources during a particular time interval, and indicate with $I^{(k)}(a^{\nu})$ the self information of the message generated by the kth source; that is, the value given by Eq. 4.31 when $a_{i+1}, a_{i+2}, \ldots, a_{i+\nu}$ are set equal to the particular letters generated by the kth source.

The self information $I^{(k)}(a^{\nu})$ is a random variable defined over the message ensemble; that is, the ensemble formed by the L^{ν} different sequences of ν letters that might be generated by the source. Its expectation, or ensemble average, is, by definition, the entropy $H(A^{\nu})$ of the message ensemble. Since the m sources are, by assumption, identical, the corresponding m random variables have the same probability distribution, and, therefore, the same expectation.

Let

$$J_m \equiv \frac{1}{m} \sum_{k=1}^{m} I^{(k)}(a^{\nu}) \qquad (4.32)$$

be the arithmetic mean of the self informations of the messages simultaneously generated by the m sources. The arithmetic mean J_m is itself a random variable, and its expectation is the same as that of each of the individual self informations, and equal to the entropy $H(A^{\nu})$. Furthermore, if the number of sources is much larger than the number L^{ν} of different messages, we intuitively expect J_m to be approximately equal to $H(A^{\nu})$, for the same reason that we expect the fraction of "heads" to be approximately equal to $\frac{1}{2}$ when we toss a large number of identical, unbiased coins. This intuitive notion is expressed in a precise manner by the two laws of large numbers [1], which are stated below for convenience of reference in terms of the random variables in question.

Weak law of large numbers. For any two positive numbers ϵ and δ there exists an integer μ such that, for $m > \mu$,

$$\Pr(|J_m - H(A^{\nu})| > \epsilon) < \delta \qquad (4.33)$$

In words, the probability that the arithmetic mean J_m will differ from the expectation $H(A^{\nu})$ by more than any finite amount can be made as small as desired by selecting a sufficiently large value of m .

Strong law of large numbers. For any two positive numbers ϵ and δ, there exists an integer μ such that, for any positive integer r, all the r inequalities

$$| J_m - H(A^\nu)| < \epsilon \ ; \ m = \mu + 1, \mu+2, \ldots, \mu + r \qquad (4.34)$$

will be simultaneously satisfied with probability larger than $1 - \delta$.

Roughly speaking, the strong law states that, as the integer m is increased, $| J_m - H(A^\nu)|$ is very likely to become and remain smaller than ϵ, while the weak law states only that the same quantity is very likely to be smaller than ϵ. Both statements, however, permit us to interpret $H(A^\nu)$ as the arithmetic mean of the self informations of the messages simultaneously generated by a large number of sources.

Let us consider next a single, stationary source, and think of its output as being a sequence of messages, each message consisting of ν successive letters. We shall indicate with $I_j(\alpha^\nu)$ the self information of the jth message generated by the source and with

$$J_t \equiv \frac{1}{t} \sum_{j=1}^{t} I_j(\alpha^\nu) \qquad (4.35)$$

the arithmetic mean of the self informations of the first t messages generated by the source.

The value of $I_j(\alpha^\nu)$ depends on the particular sequence of ν letters that constitutes the jth message, and, therefore, $I_j(\alpha^\nu)$ is a random variable defined over the ensemble formed by the L^ν possible messages. The sequence formed by the random variables associated with the successive messages is stationary, because the source is stationary. Thus, the random variables of the sequence have the same probability distribution, although, of course, they may not be statistically independent.

The sequence average of the self information of the successive messages generated by the source is, by definition,

$$< I(\alpha^\nu) > \ \equiv \ \lim_{t \to \infty} J_t = \lim_{t \to \infty} \frac{1}{t} \sum_{j=1}^{t} I_j(\alpha^\nu) \qquad (4.36)$$

if this limit exists. We shall now discuss the significance of this limit and the conditions under which it exists.

Let us consider first a source of statistically independent events. In this case, the random variables $I_j(\alpha^\nu)$ associated with the successive messages are statistically independent, just as if the messages were generated by different sources.

Theorem. The sequence average defined by Eq. 4.36 exists with probability 1 for stationary sources of statistically independent events, and it is equal to the ensemble average $H(A^\nu)$.

Proof. According to the strong law of large numbers, $|J_t - H(A^\nu)|$ remains smaller than any positive number ϵ with probability arbitrarily close to 1 when t approaches infinity. QED

Let us return now to the general case of stationary sources. The generalization of the strong law of large numbers to stationary sequences of non-independent random variables is one of the major results of the ergodic theory [2, 3]. This generalization can be stated for our purposes as follows.

Generalization of the strong law of large numbers. Given any two positive numbers ϵ and δ, there exists an integer μ such that, for any positive integer r and with probability greater than $1 - \delta$, the r inequalities

$$|J_t - \langle I(\alpha^\nu)\rangle| < \epsilon; \quad t = \mu+1, \mu+2, \ldots, \mu+r \tag{4.37}$$

will be satisfied for some number $\langle I(\alpha^\nu)\rangle$. If this number is the same for all source outputs for which the inequalities are satisfied, it coincides with the entropy $H(A^\nu)$, that is, with the common expectation of the random variables $I_j(\alpha^\nu)$.

This generalization of the law of large numbers to stationary sources implies that the sequence average defined by Eq. 4.36 exists with probability 1, that is, for almost all source outputs. If the sequence average is the same for all source outputs for which it exists, it coincides with the ensemble average $H(A^\nu)$. Such an identification of sequence averages with the corresponding ensemble averages is a property of a subclass of stationary sources known as ergodic.

*4.5. Ergodic Sources

A precise statement of the conditions that a source must satisfy in order to be ergodic is beyond the scope of our presentation. However, the following example of a non-ergodic, stationary source will serve to illustrate the basic difference between ergodic and non-ergodic sources.

The source in question is defined as follows. Each event generated by the source may be one of the four letters a_1, a_2, a_3, a_4. The probability distribution $P(\alpha_i)$ is the same for all positive integers i, and it is uniform over the four letters; that is,

$$P(\alpha_i) = \frac{1}{4}; \quad \alpha_i = a_1, a_2, a_3, a_4 \tag{4.38}$$

The conditional probability distribution $P(\alpha_i | \alpha_{i-1})$ is given by

$P(\alpha_i | \alpha_{i-1}) =$ (4.39)

α_{i-1} \ α_i	a_1	a_2	a_3	a_4
a_1	1/2	1/2	0	0
a_2	1/2	1/2	0	0
a_3	0	0	1/4	3/4
a_4	0	0	3/4	1/4

for all positive values of the integer i. The higher-order conditional probability distributions are given by

$$P(a_i | a_{i-1}, a_{i-2}, \ldots, a_{i-j}) = P(a_i | a_{i-1}) \quad \text{for } j > 1 \tag{4.40}$$

In other words, the conditional probability distributions for a_i depend only on the immediately preceding event, if this event is given.

The source is stationary because all probability distributions are independent of i; it can be readily checked that Eq. 4.38 is consistent with Eq. 4.39, in the sense that

$$\sum_{A_{i-1}} P(a_{i-1}) P(a_i | a_{i-1}) = P(a_i) \tag{4.41}$$

Let us suppose that the source output is segmented into successive messages, each consisting of two successive events. The probability distribution for the messages is then given by

$$P(a_{i-1}, a_i) \equiv P(a_{i-1}) P(a_i | a_{i-1}) \tag{4.42}$$

which is, of course, independent of i. Thus, the values of the message probabilities are obtained by multiplying the elements of the matrix in Eq. 4.39 by 1/4. Correspondingly, the message self information has the following three possible values:

$$-\log\frac{1}{8} = 3; \quad -\log\frac{1}{16} = 4; \quad -\log\frac{3}{16} = 2.415 \tag{4.43}$$

which occur with probabilities

$$P(3) = \frac{1}{2}; \quad P(4) = \frac{1}{8}; \quad P(2.415) = \frac{3}{8} \tag{4.44}$$

The entropy of the message ensemble is then

$$H(A_{i-1} A_i) \equiv H(A^2) = \frac{3}{2} + \frac{4}{8} + \frac{3}{8} \times 2.415 = 2.906 \tag{4.45}$$

Let us consider now the sequences that may be generated by the source. It is clear from Eq. 4.39 that there are two types of possible sequences; namely, sequences consisting of the letters a_1 and a_2, and sequences consisting of the letters a_3 and a_4. Since the first event can be any one of the four letters with equal probabilities, the two types of sequences will occur with equal probabilities. We might say that the source consists actually of two different sources having equal probabilities of being turned on.

Let us indicate with S_1 the source that generates the letters a_1 and a_2, and with S_2 the source that generates the letters a_3 and a_4. If the source S_1 is turned on, the message self information $I(a^2)$ can assume only the value 3; that is,

$$\Pr[I(a^2) = 3 | S_1] = 1 \tag{4.46}$$

If source S_2 is turned on, the message self information can assume either one of the two values 4 and 2.415, with probabilities

$$\Pr[I(\alpha^2) = 4 | S_2] = \frac{1}{4}; \quad \Pr[I(\alpha^2) = 2.415 | S_2] = \frac{3}{4} \tag{4.47}$$

Now, as stated in the preceding section, the sequence average defined by Eq. 4.36 exists for almost all the source outputs. However, the value of the sequence average may not be the same for different outputs. In our example, it has one value for the sequences generated by source S_1, and another value for the sequences generated by source S_2. The first value coincides with the conditional expectation of the message self information when source S_1 is turned on; that is,

$$\langle I(a^2) \rangle_1 = 3 \Pr[I(a^2) = 3 | S_1] = 3 \tag{4.48}$$

Correspondingly, the second value coincides with the conditional expectation of the message self information when the source S_2 is turned on; that is,

$$\begin{aligned} \langle I(\alpha^2) \rangle_2 &= 4 \Pr[I(\alpha^2) = 4 | S_2] + 2.415 \Pr[I(\alpha^2) = 2.415 | S_2] \\ &= 2.812 \end{aligned} \tag{4.49}$$

Remembering that these two sources are turned on with equal probabilities, the ensemble average of the sequence averages for the two sources should coincide with the entropy given by Eq. 4.45 and actually does.

The critical characteristic of this stationary source, with respect to the identification of sequence averages with ensemble averages, is that it has two different modes of operation, corresponding to two different stationary sources. This characteristic of the source is immaterial with respect to any ensemble average. In fact, if we regard the ensemble average in question as an arithmetic mean evaluated over the output from a large number of identical sources, approximately half of of the sources would be operating in one mode, and the rest in the other mode. A sequence average, on the contrary, is evaluated over a particular sequence generated by the source, and, therefore, its value depends on the particular mode in which the source is operating.

A stationary source possessing more than one mode of operation is said to be reducible or decomposable. The ensemble of sequences that may be generated by such a source includes two or more sub-ensembles of sequences (other than the entire ensemble) which are, by themselves, stationary. In other words, each of these sub-ensembles constitutes by itself a separate, stationary source. A stationary source that is not reducible is said to be ergodic. Conversely, it can be shown that any stationary source can be regarded as a combination of mutually exclusive ergodic sources, each constituting a different mode of operation of the whole source.

We saw in the preceding section that in the case of an ergodic source, the sequence average defined by Eq. 4.36 exists with probability 1, and it is equal to the ensemble average, that is, to the entropy $H(A^{\nu})$. Thus, for any ergodic source, $H(A^{\nu})$ can be interpreted as the sequence average of the amount of information required to specify successive messages, each consisting of ν events. Then, it follows from Eqs. 4.15 and 4.16 that $H(A|A^{\infty})$, the limiting value of the conditional entropy per event defined by Eq. 4.12, can be interpreted as the sequence average of the amount of information per event required to specify the source output. Finally, in view of the theorem proved in Sec. 4.3, $H(A|A^{\infty})$ (expressed in bits) can be interpreted as the minimum value of the sequence average of the number of binary digits per event that are sufficient to represent the output of a controllable-rate, ergodic source.

4.6. Encoding of Fixed-Rate Sources of Statistically Independent Events

The encoding procedure discussed in Sec. 4.3 is appropriate for controllable-rate sources, that is, when the time rate at which events are generated by the source can be varied by the source encoder. However, the same procedure cannot be used when both the rate at which events are generated by the source, and the rate at which the symbols generated by the source encoder must be transmitted, are fixed. The difficulty encountered in this latter situation can be explained as follows.

The encoding procedure presented above involves segmenting the source output into successive messages consisting of sequences of events of fixed length. Then the set of possible messages is encoded by assigning to each message a code word of length approximately equal to the self information of the message divided by log D, that is, by the capacity of the encoding alphabet. Under these conditions, each symbol generated by the source encoder provides approximately log D bits of information about the source output. Then, if the symbols generated by the source encoder are transmitted at a constant rate, the time required to transmit any particular message becomes approximately proportional to the self information of the message.

Let us suppose that the source generates events, and therefore messages, at a fixed rate. Since, in general, successive messages do not have the same self information, the rate at which messages are transmitted cannot be made equal at all times to the rate at which messages are fed to the source encoder. We may think, at first, that the difference between the two instantaneous message rates can be absorbed by a suitable storage device, if the average rates are equal. It can be shown, however, that with probability 1 any finite storage device will eventually overflow.

Let us then reformulate the encoding problem in a manner appropriate to fixed-rate sources. We shall assume again that the output of the source is segmented into successive messages, each consisting of a fixed number ν of output events. We wish now to encode the set of possible messages in such a way that all the code words corresponding to the messages have the same length, and, therefore, can be transmitted in the same time interval. If each message consists of ν events, and each event can be any one of L different letters, the number of possible messages is L^ν. Then, if a code word must be provided for each message, the length n_ν of the code words must satisfy the relation

$$D^{n_\nu} \geq L^\nu \tag{4.50}$$

so that

$$n_\nu \geq \nu \frac{\log L}{\log D} \tag{4.51}$$

In words, the number of symbols per message generated by the source encoder cannot be smaller than the number of events per message multiplied by the ratio of the information capacities of the two alphabets. Thus, the source encoder can only translate the source output from one alphabet to another, without performing any further reduction of the number of symbols per message.

Clearly, no efficient form of encoding is possible if code words of fixed length must be provided for all possible messages. However, efficient encoding becomes again possible, if the requirement that different code words of fixed length be provided for all the messages is reduced to the requirement that different code words of fixed length be provided for all messages except for a sub-set of messages with a vanishingly small probability of occurrence.

We shall consider in this section the simple case of statistically independent events. Let H(A) be the entropy of the ensemble of possible letters, that is, the expectation of the self information of each event. The self information of a sequence of ν letters is simply equal, in this case, to the sum of the self informations of the ν letters; that is,

$$I(a^\nu) \equiv I(a_1 a_2 \ldots a_k \ldots a_\nu) = I(a_1) + I(a_2) + \ldots + I(a_k) + \ldots + I(a_\nu) \tag{4.52}$$

where

$$I(a_k) \equiv -\log P(a_k) \tag{4.53}$$

is the self information of the letter constituting the kth event of the sequence. The encoding procedure for fixed-rate, statistically independent events is based on the following theorem.

<u>Theorem</u>. Let ϵ and δ be any two positive numbers, and T be the set of sequences a^ν of ν letters for which

$$I(a^\nu) \leq \nu \; [H(A) + \epsilon] \tag{4.54}$$

and indicate with M the number of sequences in T , and with P(T) the probability of occurrence of a sequence belonging to T . Then, if the events are statistically independent, there exists an integer μ such that, for any $\nu > \mu$,

$$P(T) > 1 - \delta \tag{4.55}$$

$$M < 2^{\nu [H(A) + \epsilon]} \tag{4.56}$$

where H(A) is expressed in bits.

Proof. The random variable $I(a^\nu)$ is the sum of ν equally distributed, statistically independent random variables, with expectation equal to H(A). Then, according to the weak law of large numbers (see Sec. 4.4), there exists an integer μ such that, for any $\nu > \mu$,

$$\Pr \left[\left| \frac{1}{\nu} I(a^\nu) - H(A) \right| > \epsilon \right] < \delta \tag{4.57}$$

and, therefore,

$$P(T) > \Pr \left[\left| \frac{1}{\nu} I(a^\nu) - H(A) \right| \leq \epsilon \right] > 1 - \delta \tag{4.58}$$

The upper bound to the number M of sequences in T, given by Eq. 4.56, follows from the very definition of the set T . We have, from Eq. 4.54 and the definition of self information,

$$I(a^\nu) = -\log P(a^\nu) \leq \nu \; [H(A) + \epsilon] \tag{4.59}$$

for all sequences a^ν belonging to T . Thus, the probability of occurrence of any one of the sequences belonging to T satisfies the inequality

$$P(a^\nu) \geq 2^{-\nu [H(A) + \epsilon]} \tag{4.60}$$

where H(A) is expressed in bits. It follows that

$$M \; 2^{-\nu [H(A) + \epsilon]} \leq \sum_T P(a^\nu) < \sum_{A^\nu} P(a^\nu) = 1 \tag{4.61}$$

where A^ν is the set of all sequences a^ν . The desired upper bound to M follows immediately from Eq. 4.61.

QED

This theorem suggests the following encoding procedure. The M sequences of ν letters that belong to the set T of the theorem are represented by different code words of length n_ν , and all the remaining sequences by one and the same code word. Correspondingly, the source encoder segments the source output into messages consisting of ν consecutive letters, and generates for each successive message the corresponding code word. The resulting probability of ambiguous encoding is equal to the probability of occurrence of a sequence that does not belong to the set T .

Theorem. Let ϵ_0 and δ be any two positive numbers. It is possible to encode the output of a fixed-rate source of statistically independent events of entropy H(A) in such a way that the number n of symbols per event and the probability P_a of ambiguous encoding satisfy the inequalities

$$n < \frac{H(A) + \epsilon_0}{\log D} \tag{4.62}$$

$$P_a < \delta \tag{4.63}$$

where D is the number of symbols in the encoding alphabet.

Proof. Using the above encoding procedure, the code-word length n_ν necessary to provide the M+1 different code words satisfies the inequality

$$n_\nu < \frac{\log M}{\log D} + 1 < \nu \frac{H(A) + \epsilon}{\log D} + 1 \tag{4.64}$$

so that the required number of symbols per output event is bounded by

$$n < \frac{H(A) + \epsilon}{\log D} + \frac{1}{\nu} \tag{4.65}$$

On the other hand, according to the preceding theorem, the probability of ambiguous encoding can be made to satisfy the inequality

$$P_a \equiv 1 - P(T) < \delta \tag{4.66}$$

for any positive ϵ by making ν sufficiently large. Then, if ϵ is selected in such a way that

$$\epsilon_0 = \epsilon + \frac{\log D}{\nu} \tag{4.67}$$

Eq. 4.65 reduces to Eq. 4.62.

QED

We can conclude from this theorem that the output of a fixed-rate source of statistically independent events can be encoded with a number of symbols per event as close as desired to, but larger than, the entropy per event divided by the capacity of the encoding alphabet, with a vanishingly small probability of ambiguous encoding. We shall prove next the converse of this result; namely, that the number of symbols per event cannot be made smaller than the entropy per event divided by the alphabet capacity, with a vanishingly small probability of ambiguous encoding.

Theorem. The probability of ambiguous encoding for a fixed-rate source of statistically independent events satisfies the inequality

$$P_a \geq \left[\frac{H(A)}{\log D} - n\right] \frac{\log D}{\log L} \tag{4.68}$$

where H(A) is the entropy per event, n is the number of symbols per event, L is the number of letters in the source alphabet, and D is the number of symbols in the encoding alphabet.

Proof. Let us indicate with W the ensemble of code words, and with A^ν the ensemble of sequences of ν letters represented by the code words. The average amount of information provided by the code words about the sequences can be expressed in the form

$$I(A^\nu;W) = H(A^\nu) - H(A^\nu | W) \tag{4.69}$$

On the other hand, since the events generated by the source are statistically independent,

$$H(A^\nu) = \nu H(A) \tag{4.70}$$

Furthermore,

$$I(A^\nu;W) \leq H(W) \leq n_\nu \log D \tag{4.71}$$

where n_ν is the number of symbols in each code word. It follows that

$$\nu H(A) - H(A^\nu | W) \leq n_\nu \log D \tag{4.72}$$

An upper bound to the conditional entropy $H(A^\nu | W)$ can be readily obtained as follows. Let us indicate with w_0 the code word corresponding to the sequences that do not belong to the set T, and with w_k the code word corresponding to the kth sequence of T. We have, by definition,

$$H(A^\nu | W) = P(w_0)\, H(A^\nu | w_0) + \sum_{k=1}^{M} P(w_k)\, H(A^\nu | w_k) \tag{4.73}$$

The summation on the righthand side is equal to zero, because each of the code words involved uniquely specifies the corresponding sequence. The conditional entropy $H(A^\nu | w_0)$ cannot exceed the logarithm of the number of possible sequences, and $P(w_0)$ is equal to P_a because ambiguous encoding results when, and only when, w_0 occurs. It follows that

$$H(A^\nu | W) = P_a H(A^\nu | w_0) \leq P_a \log L^\nu = \nu P_a \log L \tag{4.74}$$

Finally, substitution of the righthand side of Eq. 4.74 for $H(A^\nu | W)$ in Eq. 4.72 yields

$$\nu H(A) - \nu P_a \log L \leq n_\nu \log D \tag{4.75}$$

from which Eq. 4.68 is readily obtained after replacing n_ν with νn.

QED

*4.7. Encoding of Fixed-Rate, Ergodic Sources

The results of the preceding section can be extended to arbitrary ergodic sources [4, 5] by means of the following process of double segmentation of the source output. The sequence of events generated by the source is first segmented into successive messages, each consisting of ν successive events. Then, the resulting sequence of messages is further segmented into subsequences of t successive messages. The problem to be considered is that of representing the sequences of t messages by means of code words of fixed length. We shall indicate with $H(A^\nu)$ the entropy of the message ensemble, with $I_i(\alpha^\nu)$ the self information of the ith message ($i = 0, 1, \ldots, t-1$) in a sequence of t messages, and with J_t the arithmetic mean of the self informations of the t messages of a sequence; that is,

$$J_t = \frac{1}{t} \sum_{i=0}^{t-1} I_i(\alpha^\nu) \tag{4.76}$$

The generalization to ergodic sources of the encoding procedure discussed in the preceding section is based on the following theorem.

Theorem. Let ϵ and δ be any two positive numbers, and T be the set of sequences of t messages for which

$$J_t \leq H(A^\nu) + \epsilon \tag{4.77}$$

and indicate with M the number of sequences in T, and with P(T) the probability of occurrence of a sequence belonging to T. Then, if the source is ergodic, there exists an integer μ such that, for any $t > \mu$,

$$P(T) > 1 - \delta \tag{4.78}$$

$$M < 2^{t[H(A^\nu) + \epsilon]} \tag{4.79}$$

where $H(A^\nu)$ is expressed in bits.

Proof. The extension of the weak law of large numbers (a special case of the extension of the strong law discussed in Sec. 4.4) to ergodic sources states that† there exists an integer μ such that, for any $t > \mu$,

$$\Pr\left[\,|J_t - H(A^\nu)| > \epsilon\right] < \delta \tag{4.80}$$

It follows that

$$P(T) > \Pr\left[\,|J_t - H(A^\nu)| < \epsilon\right] > 1 - \delta \tag{4.81}$$

† The author is indebted to Dr. A. Feinstein for pointing out that the ergodicity of the ensemble of letter sequences does not necessarily imply that the ensemble of message sequences is ergodic, when each message consists of ν successive letters. It can be shown, however, that, if ν is an integer for which the ensemble of message sequences is not ergodic, the ensemble consists of ν_0 equiprobable, ergodic ensembles, where ν_0 is a divisor of ν. These ergodic ensembles are identical except for a shift in time, corresponding to 1, 2, . . . , ν_0 letters, and therefore their message entropies are equal to $H(A) - \log \nu_0$. It follows that the theorem is still true for the entire ensemble. The author is grateful to Dr. C. E. Shannon for suggesting this result and for his help in proving it. The details of the proof are beyond the scope of this presentation.

The upper bound to the number of sequences in T given by Eq. 4.79 follows from the definition of the set T, and that of the self information $I_i(a^\nu)$. We have from Eq. 4.76

$$- t J_t = - \sum_{i=0}^{t-1} I_i(a^\nu) = \log \prod_{i=0}^{t-1} P(a_{i\nu+1}, a_{i\nu+2}, \ldots, a_{i\nu+\nu}) \tag{4.82}$$

so that, for all message sequences belonging to the set T,

$$\prod_{i=0}^{t-1} P(a_{i\nu+1}, a_{i\nu+2}, \ldots, a_{i\nu+\nu}) \geq 2^{-t[H(A^\nu) + \epsilon]} \tag{4.83}$$

where $H(A^\nu)$ is expressed in bits. It follows that

$$\begin{aligned} M\, 2^{-t\,[H(A^\nu) + \epsilon]} &\leq \sum_{T} \prod_{i=0}^{t-1} P(a_{i\nu+1}, a_{i\nu+2}, \ldots, a_{i\nu+\nu}) \\ &< \sum_{A^{\nu t}} \prod_{i=0}^{t-1} P(a_{i\nu+1}, a_{i\nu+2}, \ldots, a_{i\nu+\nu}) \\ &= \prod_{i=0}^{t-1} \sum_{A^\nu} P(a_{i\nu+1}, a_{i\nu+2}, \ldots, a_{i\nu+\nu}) = 1 \end{aligned} \tag{4.84}$$

where $A^{\nu t}$ is the set of all sequences of t consecutive messages, that is, of all possible sequences of νt letters, and A^ν is the set of all possible sequences of ν letters. The desired upper bound to M follows immediately from Eq. 4.84.

QED

This theorem suggests the following encoding procedure. The M message sequences that belong to the set T of the theorem are represented by different code words of length n_t, and all the remaining sequences by one and the same code word. Correspondingly, the source encoder segments the source output into sequences of t consecutive messages, that is, into sequences of νt consecutive letters, and generates for each successive sequence the corresponding code word. The resulting probability of ambiguous encoding is equal to the probability of occurrence of any one of the message sequences that do not belong to the set T

<u>Theorem.</u> Let ϵ_0 and δ be any two positive numbers. It is possible to encode the output of a fixed-rate, ergodic source with entropy per event $H(A|A^\infty)$ in such a way that the number n of symbols per event and the probability P_a of ambiguous encoding satisfy the inequalities

$$n < \frac{H(A|A^{\infty}) + \epsilon_0}{\log D} \tag{4.85}$$

$$P_a < \delta \tag{4.86}$$

where D is the number of symbols in the encoding alphabet.

Proof. Using the above encoding procedure, the code-word length n_t necessary to provide the M+1 different code words satisfies the inequality

$$n_t < \frac{\log M}{\log D} + 1 < t\,\frac{H(A^{\nu}) + \epsilon}{\log D} + 1 \tag{4.87}$$

so that the required number of symbols per output event is bounded by

$$n < \frac{H(A^{\nu}) + \epsilon}{\nu \log D} + \frac{1}{\nu t} \tag{4.88}$$

On the other hand, according to the preceding theorem, the probability of ambiguous encoding can be made to satisfy the inequality

$$P_a = 1 - P(T) < \delta \tag{4.89}$$

for any positive ϵ by making t sufficiently large.

Next, Eqs. 4.15 and 4.16 state that, for any positive ϵ, $H(A^{\nu})/\nu$ can be made to satisfy the inequality

$$\frac{1}{\nu} H(A^{\nu}) < H(A|A^{\infty}) + \epsilon \tag{4.90}$$

by making ν sufficiently large. Then, substituting the righthand side of Eq. 4.90 for $H(A^{\nu})/\nu$ in Eq. 4.88 yields

$$n < \frac{H(A|A^{\infty}) + \epsilon\,(1 + \frac{1}{\nu})}{\log D} + \frac{1}{\nu t} \tag{4.91}$$

Finally, if ϵ is selected in such a way that

$$\epsilon_0 = \epsilon(1 + \frac{1}{\nu}) + \frac{\log D}{\nu t} \tag{4.92}$$

Eq. 4.91 reduces to Eq. 4.85.

QED

We can conclude from this theorem that the output of a fixed-rate, ergodic source can be encoded with a number of symbols per event as close as desired to, but larger than, the entropy per event of the source, $H(A|A^{\infty})$, divided by the capacity of the encoding alphabet, and that this can be achieved with a vanishingly small probability of ambiguous encoding. The following theorem states the converse of this result; namely, that the number of symbols per event cannot be made smaller than the entropy per event divided by the capacity of the encoding alphabet, and still obtain a vanishingly small probability of ambiguous encoding.

Theorem. The probability of ambiguous encoding for a fixed-rate, ergodic source satisfies the inequality

$$P_a \geq \left[\frac{H(A|A^{\infty})}{\log D} - n\right] \frac{\log D}{\log L} \tag{4.93}$$

where $H(A|A^{\infty})$ is the entropy per event, n is the number of symbols per event, L is the number of letters in the source alphabet, and D is the number of symbols in the encoding alphabet.

Proof. Let us indicate with W the ensemble of code words, and with $A^{\nu t}$ the ensemble of sequences of νt letters represented by the code words. The average amount of information provided by the code words about the sequences can be expressed in the form

$$I(A^{\nu t};W) = H(A^{\nu t}) - H(A^{\nu t}|W) \tag{4.94}$$

On the other hand, since $H(A|A^{\infty})$ is a lower bound to the entropy per event,

$$H(A^{\nu t}) \geq \nu t\, H(A|A^{\infty}) \tag{4.95}$$

so that

$$I(A^{\nu t};W) \geq \nu t\, H(A|A^{\infty}) - H(A^{\nu t}|W) \tag{4.96}$$

Furthermore,

$$I(A^{\nu t};W) \leq H(W) \leq n_t \log D \tag{4.97}$$

where n_t is the number of symbols in each code word. It follows that

$$\nu t\, H(A|A^{\infty}) - H(A^{\nu t}|W) \leq n_t \log D \tag{4.98}$$

The following inequality can be readily obtained by analogy with Eq. 4.74.

$$H(A^{\nu t}|W) \leq \nu t\, P_a \log L \tag{4.99}$$

where P_a is the probability of ambiguous encoding, and L is the number of symbols in the source alphabet. Then, subsitution of the righthand side of Eq. 4.99 for $H(A^{\nu t}|W)$ in Eq. 4.98 yields

$$\nu t\, H(A|A^{\infty}) - \nu t\, P_a \log L \leq n_t \log D \tag{4.100}$$

from which Eq. 4.93 is readily obtained with the help of the identity

$$n_t = \nu t\, n \tag{4.101}$$

QED

*4.8. Markov Sources

A Markov source is characterized by the "states" in which it may find itself, and by the rules governing its transition from any given state to any other state. Letters are generated by the source with probabilities that depend only on the state in which the source happens to be, and the source changes its state, in general, each time a letter is generated. The new state, after the generation of a particular letter, is uniquely specified by the old state and by the particular letter generated, although the letter generated may not be uniquely specified by the two states.

The operation of the source can be illustrated graphically by a diagram such as the one shown in Fig. 4.1. Each node of the diagram represents a state (s_1, s_2, s_3, s_4), and each branch indicates, in

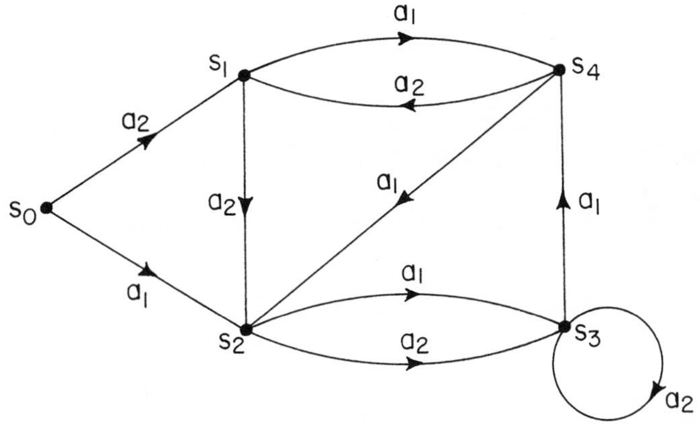

Fig. 4.1. Markov source

the direction of the arrow, the change of state resulting from the generation of a particular letter (a_1, a_2). The state s_0 represents the initial condition of the source when the first letter is generated.

If the letter conditional probabilities $P(a_k | s_j)$ are given for each state of the source, each transition probability $P(s_i | s_j)$ may be computed by adding the probabilities of the letters that result in the transition from state s_j to s_i. For instance, in the case of Fig. 4.1, we have

$$P(s_4 | s_1) = P(a_1 | s_1) \tag{4.102}$$

$$P(s_3 | s_2) = P(a_1 | s_2) + P(a_2 | s_2) = 1 \tag{4.103}$$

The matrix of the conditional probabilities $P(a_k | s_j)$ completely describes the source, and therefore the message ensemble formed by the sequences of letters generated by it.

The sequence of states successively assumed by the source has the important characteristic that each state of the sequence depends only on the identity of the state immediately preceding it. Sequences of this type, known to mathematicians as Markov chains, have been extensively investigated. Some of the properties of Markov chains with a finite number of states are summarized below and in the following two sections, without proof [1].

A state s_i is said to be "persistent" if the probability of an eventual return to s_i is equal to unity; otherwise, the state is said to be "transient." In the case of Fig. 4.1, all states are persistent except for s_0.

A state s_i is said to be "periodic" with period $T > 1$ if a return to s_i is possible only in a number of steps $m = rT$, where r is any positive integer. For instance, all the states in Fig. 4.2 are periodic with period equal to 2. All the states in Fig. 4.1 are aperiodic.

A set of states is said to be "closed" if a one-step transition from any state of the set can lead only to a state of the same set. A chain is said to be "irreducible" if no subset of its states is closed except for the set of all states; otherwise, it is said to be "decomposable."

The chain illustrated in Fig. 4.1 is decomposable because the subset formed by all the states with the exception of s_0 is closed. However, if s_0 were eliminated, the remaining states would form an irreducible chain. In general, if an irreducible subchain is formed by a subset of the states, this subchain may be studied independently of all other states. In fact, once the source has reached one of the

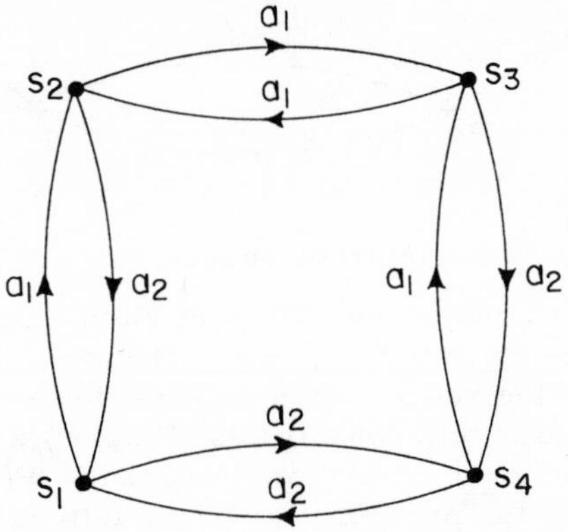

Fig. 4.2. A periodic Markov source

states of the subset, all the states not belonging to it become inaccessible and, therefore, they may be disregarded.

> Theorem. No chain with a finite number of states can consist entirely of transient states; the persistent states contained in the chain can be divided into closed subsets corresponding to irreducible subchains. These closed subsets may be reached from the transient states, but not vice versa, as, for instance, in the case of s_0 in Fig. 4.1.

> Theorem. An irreducible chain (or subchain) with a finite number of states can contain only persistent states. If one of the states is periodic, all the states must be periodic with the same period.

*4.9. Properties of Finite-State, Aperiodic Markov Sources

Let us consider an aperiodic, irreducible Markov source (chain) with a finite number of states, and let $P_m(s_i|s_j)$ be the probability that the source will reach state s_i from state s_j in exactly m steps.

Theorem. For all pairs of states s_i, s_j,

$$\lim_{m \to \infty} P_m(s_i|s_j) = P(s_i) \tag{4.104}$$

The probability distribution $P(s)$ satisfies the set of equations

$$P(s_i) = \sum_S P(s)\, P(s_i|s) \tag{4.105}$$

where the summation extends over all states of the source.

The vanishing of the determinant of the set of linear homogeneous equations given by Eq. 4.105 is insured by the fact that

$$\sum_S P(s|s_j) = 1 \tag{4.106}$$

Thus, the $P(s_i)$ are specified by Eq. 4.105, apart from a constant multiplier, whose value must be such that

$$\sum_S P(s) = 1 \tag{4.107}$$

It can be shown that the values of the $P(s_i)$ so obtained are non-negative in all cases, so that they may be rightfully considered as probabilities.

Two important properties are evidenced by Eq. 4.104. In the first place, the probability of finding the source in any particular state s_i tends to a limit as the number of successive transitions between states increases indefinitely. In the second place, this limit is unique and, in particular, is independent of the state in which the source was initially. These two properties together imply that the sequences of symbols produced by the source tend toward a condition of statistical equilibrium. Furthermore, if the probability of finding the source initially in any particular state s_i is equal to the value of $P(s_i)$ given by Eq. 4.105, this condition of statistical equilibrium exists from the start.

The fact that these properties are distinct, rather than two aspects of the same property, becomes evident when we consider instead a decomposable Markov source, consisting, for instance, of two separate irreducible subchains, C_1 and C_2. Then Eq. 4.104 applies to any two states belonging to the same irreducible chain, but not to states belonging to different chains. Clearly, if s_i belongs to one chain, and s_j belongs to the other chain,

$$P_m(s_i \mid s_j) = 0 \tag{4.108}$$

because the states of one chain cannot be reached from the states of the other chain. Thus, Eq. 4.104 should be rewritten in the form

$$\lim_{m \to \infty} P_m(s_i \mid s_j) = \begin{cases} P(s_i \mid C_1) & \text{if } s_j \text{ belongs to } C_1 \\ \\ P(s_i \mid C_2) & \text{if } s_j \text{ belongs to } C_2 \end{cases} \tag{4.109}$$

where $P(s_i \mid C_1)$ is equal to zero if s_i belongs to C_2, and $P(s_i \mid C_2)$ is equal to zero if s_i belongs to C_1. Correspondingly, the summation in Eq. 4.105 should extend only over the states of the chain to which s_i belongs. Then, if $P(C_1)$ and $P(C_2)$ are the probabilities that the initial state belongs to C_1 and C_2, respectively, the probability of finding the source in state s_i is, in the limit of m approaching infinity,

$$P(s_i) = \begin{cases} P(C_1)\, P(s_i \mid C_1) & \text{if } s_i \text{ belongs to } C_1 \\ \\ P(C_2)\, P(s_i \mid C_2) & \text{if } s_i \text{ belongs to } C_2 \end{cases} \tag{4.110}$$

Furthermore, if the initial state probabilities are equal to the $P(s_i)$ given by Eq. 4.110, the probability of finding the source in any particular state is independent of time. In this case, all statistical characteristics of the ensemble of sequences generated by the source are independent of time, and the source is from the beginning in a stationary condition of operation.

This simple example illustrates how the ensemble of sequences generated by a Markov source may exhibit statistical homogeneity in time, even when the influence of the initial state does not vanish with increasing time. The vanishing of the influence of the initial state, characteristic of irreducible, aperiodic sources with a finite number of states, is responsible for the additional kind of ensemble homogeneity to which we referred in Sec. 4.5 as ergodicity. Thus, ergodicity can be roughly described by saying that almost every sequence generated by the source is "representative" of the entire ensemble of sequences. More precisely, the sequence average of any random variable associated with the state (or with a finite number of successive states) of an ergodic source is equal, with probability 1, to the ensemble average of the same random variable. That is, the sequence of values assumed by such a random variable obeys the strong law of large numbers stated in Sec. 4.4. Clearly this cannot be true for a source consisting of two separate subchains, because only states of one of the subchains can appear in any one particular sequence of states.

Let us consider next decomposable Markov sources possessing transient states as well as several irreducible subchains.

> Theorem. A source which is in a transient state will eventually be, with probability 1, in some persistent state, provided only that the total number of states is finite. If it contains more than one irreducible subchain, the conditional probability $P(C_k | s_j)$ that the source will eventually reach a state belonging to the irreducible chain C_k from a transient state s_j is a solution of the set of equations
>
> $$P(C_k | s_j) - \sum_{S_t} P(s | s_j) \, P(C_k | s) = P_1(C_k | s_j) \qquad (4.111)$$
>
> The summation extends over the subset S_t of all transient states, and $P_1(C_k | s_j)$ is the conditional probability that a state of C_k will be reached from s_j in a one-step transition. Once in a persistent state, the source cannot leave the closed set of persistent states (subchain) to which the first persistent state belongs.

We are now in a position to evaluate the asymptotic behavior of the entropy per letter for an aperiodic Markov source with a finite number of states. We observe, in the first place, that the entropy of the ensemble A of possible letters when the source is in state s_i is, by definition,

$$H(A | s_i) \equiv - \sum_{A} P(a | s_i) \log P(a | s_i) \qquad (4.112)$$

Then, the asymptotic value of the entropy per letter when the length of the sequence of letters approaches infinity is, for an aperiodic, irreducible source,

$$H(A | A^{\infty}) = \sum_{S} P(s) \; H(A | s) \qquad (4.113)$$

where the summation extends over all states of the chain.

The asymptotic behavior of the entropy per letter for a decomposable source may be obtained as the ensemble average of the value given by Eq. 4.113 for its irreducible subchains. The transient states may be disregarded in this averaging process, except for the fact that they control the probability that the source will eventually reach a state of a particular subchain. If the initial state of the source is s_0, the probability $P(C_k | s_0)$ that the source will eventually reach a state of subchain C_k can be computed with the help of Eq. 4.111. Thus, the asymptotic value of the entropy per letter is given by

$$H(A|A^{\infty}) = \sum_{k=1}^{N} P(C_k|s_0) \sum_{S_k} P(s|C_k)\, H(A|s) \qquad (4.114)$$

where S_k is the set of states of the subchain C_k, N is the number of subchains, and $P(s|C_k)$ is the conditional probability of finding the source in state s, on the assumption that a state belonging to the same subchain has been reached.

*4.10. Properties of Finite-State, Periodic Markov Sources

Irreducible periodic sources have a property similar to that expressed by Eq. 4.104.

Theorem. If T is the period of an irreducible, finite-state source, the states can be divided into T subsets, S_0, S_1, ..., S_{T-1}, such that a one-step transition leads from a state of S_k to a state of S_{k+1} (to a state of S_0 if k = T-1). Let r be a positive integer and $P_{rT}(s_i|s_j)$ be the probability that the source will reach state s_i from state s_j in m = rT steps. Then,

$$\lim_{r\to\infty} P_{rT}(s_i|s_j) = P(s_i|S_k) \qquad (4.115)$$

when s_i and s_j belong to the same subset S_k, and

$$\lim_{r\to\infty} P_{rT}(s_i|s_j) = 0 \qquad (4.116)$$

when s_i and s_j belong to different subsets. The $P(s_i|S_k)$ satisfy the set of equations

$$P(s_i|S_k) = \sum_{S_k} P(s|S_k)\, P_T(s_i|s) \qquad (4.117)$$

where the summation extends over all the states of the subset S_k. The existence of suitable solutions for this set of linear homogeneous equations is insured as in the case of Eq. 4.105.

In the periodic case, $P(s_i|S_k)$ represents the asymptotic value of the conditional probability that the source starting from a state of S_k will be found in state s_i, belonging to the same subset, after rT one-step transitions. Then, if $P_0(S_h)$ is the probability that the initial state belongs to S_h, and μ is an integer, $0 \le \mu < T$, the limiting value of the probability of finding the source in state s_i, belonging to S_k, after $m = rT + \mu$ one-step transitions, is given by

$$\lim_{r \to \infty} P_{rT+\mu}(s_i) = P_0(S_h)\ P(s_i | S_k) \tag{4.118}$$

where

$$h = \begin{cases} k - \mu \quad ; & k \geq \mu \\ T + k - \mu\ ; & k < \mu \end{cases} \tag{4.119}$$

Thus, the sequences of the states assumed by a source and those of the symbols generated by it tend to a condition of "periodic" statistical equilibrium. If the initial-state probabilities are proportional to the $P(s_i | S_k)$, the probability $P_m(s_i)$ is, from the start, a periodic function of m.

In the case of finite-state, irreducible periodic chains, the entropy per letter becomes asymptotically a periodic function of the number m of preceding letters generated. We obtain, from Eq. 4.118,

$$\lim_{r \to \infty} H(A_{m+1} | A^m) = \sum_{k=0}^{T-1} P_0(S_h) \sum_{S_k} P(s | S_k)\ H(A | s) \tag{4.120}$$

where h is given by Eq. 4.119, r is an integer, and

$$m = rT + \mu; \qquad 0 \leq \mu < T \tag{4.121}$$

*4.11. Illustrative Example

Let us consider, as an example, the Markov source illustrated in Fig. 4.3. The table on the right side of the figure gives the values of the conditional probabilities $P(a_k | s_j)$, where a_k may be either 0 or 1. The initial state is s_0.

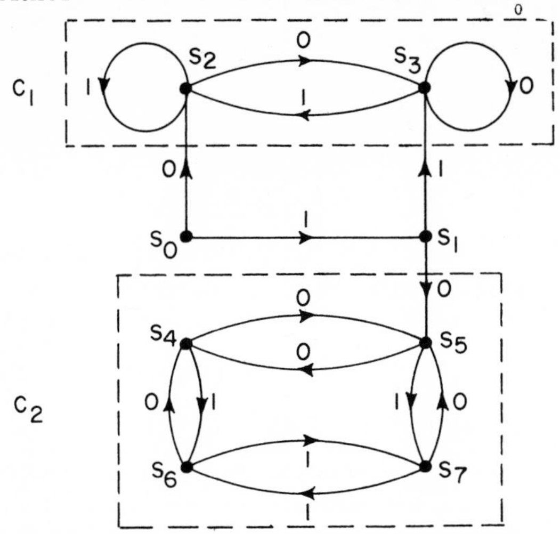

	0	1
s_0	0.2	0.8
s_1	0.5	0.5
s_2	0.7	0.3
s_3	0.6	0.4
s_4	0.3	0.7
s_5	0.6	0.4
s_6	0.9	0.1
s_7	0.2	0.8

Fig. 4.3. An example of Markov source

We observe, in the first place, that states s_0 and s_1 are transient states, because a return to either of them is impossible. The other states form two closed subsets, (s_2, s_3) and (s_4, s_5, s_6, s_7), and, therefore, are persistent states. The subchains C_1 and C_2 corresponding, respectively, to the two closed subsets are irreducible. In addition, s_2 is an aperiodic state, while s_4 is a periodic state, with period $T = 2$. Thus, one of the subchains is aperiodic; the other, periodic.

Considering, first, the aperiodic subchain, we obtain for the asymptotic values of the state probabilities the two equations

$$P(s_2) = 0.3\, P(s_2) + 0.4\, P(s_3) \tag{4.122}$$

$$P(s_3) = 0.7\, P(s_2) + 0.6\, P(s_3) \tag{4.123}$$

which yield, in turn,

$$0.7\, P(s_2) = 0.4\, P(s_3) \tag{4.124}$$

On the other hand,

$$P(s_2) + P(s_3) = 1 \tag{4.125}$$

because the two states form an irreducible aperiodic chain. Thus,

$$P(s_2) = 0.364; \quad P(s_3) = 0.636 \tag{4.126}$$

The states of the periodic subchain may be divided into two subsets $S_0 = (s_4, s_7)$, and $S_1 = (s_5, s_6)$, such that a one-step transition leads from a state of either subset to a state of the other subset. We obtain from the table in Fig. 4. 3

$$\begin{aligned}
P_2(s_4 \mid s_4) &= 0.3 \times 0.6 + 0.7 \times 0.9 = 0.81\\
P_2(s_7 \mid s_4) &= 0.3 \times 0.4 + 0.7 \times 0.1 = 0.19\\
P_2(s_7 \mid s_7) &= 0.2 \times 0.4 + 0.8 \times 0.1 = 0.16\\
P_2(s_4 \mid s_7) &= 0.2 \times 0.6 + 0.8 \times 0.9 = 0.84\\
P_2(s_5 \mid s_5) &= 0.6 \times 0.3 + 0.4 \times 0.2 = 0.26\\
P_2(s_6 \mid s_5) &= 0.6 \times 0.7 + 0.4 \times 0.8 = 0.74\\
P_2(s_6 \mid s_6) &= 0.9 \times 0.7 + 0.1 \times 0.8 = 0.71\\
P_2(s_5 \mid s_6) &= 0.9 \times 0.3 + 0.1 \times 0.2 = 0.29
\end{aligned} \tag{4.127}$$

Substituting these values in Eq. 4.117 yields the two sets of equations

$$\begin{aligned}
P(s_4 \mid S_0) &= 0.81\, P(s_4 \mid S_0) + 0.84\, P(s_7 \mid S_0)\\
P(s_7 \mid S_0) &= 0.19\, P(s_4 \mid S_0) + 0.16\, P(s_7 \mid S_0)
\end{aligned} \tag{4.128}$$

and

$$P(s_5 \mid S_1) = 0.26\, P(s_5 \mid S_1) + 0.29\, P(s_6 \mid S_1)$$

$$P(s_6 \mid S_1) = 0.74\, P(s_5 \mid S_1) + 0.71\, P(s_6 \mid S_1) \qquad (4.129)$$

In addition, it must be

$$P(s_4 \mid S_0) + P(s_7 \mid S_0) = P(s_5 \mid S_1) + P(s_6 \mid S_1) = 1 \qquad (4.130)$$

Thus

$$P(s_4 \mid S_0) = 0.806; \qquad P(s_7 \mid S_0) = 0.184$$

$$P(s_5 \mid S_1) = 0.282; \qquad P(s_6 \mid S_1) = 0.718 \qquad (4.131)$$

It remains to compute the probabilities that the source will eventually reach a state of subchain C_1 or one of subchain C_2. We obtain readily for C_2

$$P(C_2 \mid s_0) = 0.8 \times 0.5 = 0.4 \qquad (4.132)$$

and, therefore, for C_1

$$P(C_1 \mid s_0) = 1 - P(C_2 \mid s_0) = 0.6 \qquad (4.133)$$

We note, in addition, that the initial state of subchain C_2 is necessarily s_5, so that

$$P_0(S_0) = 0\,; \quad P_0(S_1) = 1 \qquad (4.134)$$

We are now in a position to compute the asymptotic value of the entropy per letter for the ensemble of sequences generated by the source. We obtain for the aperiodic subchain C_1

$$H_1(A|A^{\infty}) = -0.364[0.7 \log 0.7 + 0.3 \log 0.3]$$
$$- 0.636[0.6 \log 0.6 + 0.4 \log 0.4] = 0.935 \text{ bit} \qquad (4.135)$$

In the case of the periodic chain C_2, we must first compute the asymptotic values for the two subsets S_0 and S_1. We obtain for S_0 the value

$$-0.806[0.3 \log 0.3 + 0.7 \log 0.7] - 0.184[0.2 \log 0.2 + 0.8 \log 0.8]$$
$$= 0.843 \text{ bit} \qquad (4.136)$$

and for S_1 the value

$$-0.282[0.6 \log 0.6 + 0.4 \log 0.4] - 0.718[0.9 \log 0.9 + 0.1 \log 0.1]$$
$$= 0.611 \text{ bit} \qquad (4.137)$$

Thus, since $P_0(S_0) = 0$ and $P_0(S_1) = 1$, the entropy per letter for the subchain C_2 assumes alternatively the asymptotic values 0.611 and 0.843.

The entropy per letter for the entire chain may be computed by averaging the values determined above for the two subchains. We obtain, with the help of Eqs. 4.132 and 4.133, the two values

$$0.6 \times 0.935 + 0.4 \times 0.843 = 0.898 \quad (4.138)$$

$$0.6 \times 0.935 + 0.4 \times 0.611 = 0.805 \quad (4.139)$$

It may be readily seen by inspection of Fig. 4.3 that the value of 0.898 corresponds to even positions in the sequences of letters generated by the source, while the value 0.805 corresponds to odd positions. We may say, also, that the asymptotic value of the entropy per letter involves two components: an aperiodic component equal to 0.561 and a periodic component alternating between the two values 0.337 and 0.244.

*4.12. The Encoding of Controllable-Rate Markov Sources

Let us turn our attention to the problem of encoding in an efficient manner the sequences of letters generated by controllable-rate Markov sources. We shall restrict our discussion to aperiodic sources, because of their greater practical importance and their simpler asymptotic behavior.

The encoding procedure discussion in Sec. 3.7 may be used in connection with a Markov source, if we identify the alphabet A of letters with the set U of messages. The difference between the present encoding problem and that discussed in Sec. 3.7 is that the letter probabilities $P(a_k|s_i)$ depend on the state of the source, while the message probabilities $P(u_k)$ were assumed to be constant. This requires using a different set of code words for each state of the source. Assuming that the source starts always in the same state, the successive states assumed by the source are uniquely specified by the output letter. Thus, no ambiguity will ever exist as to the set of code words used in any particular instance.

Consider, as an example, the Markov source illustrated in Fig. 4.4, in which s_0 is the initial state. The table on the right side of the figure gives the values of the conditional probability distribution $P(a|s)$.

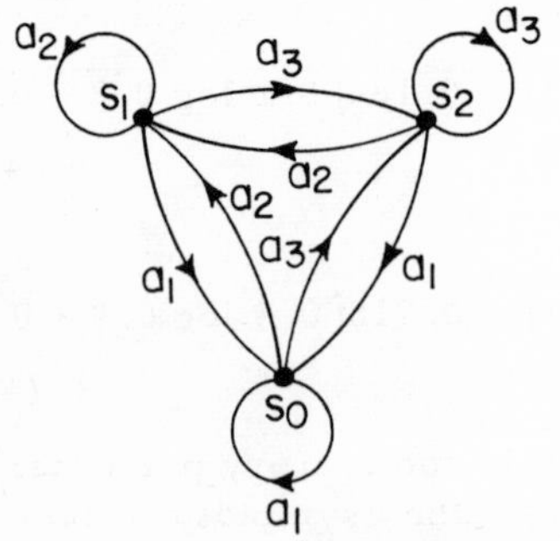

	s_0	s_1	s_2
a_1	0.2	0.3	0.6
a_2	0.4	0.5	0.1
a_3	0.4	0.2	0.3

Fig. 4.4. Markov source

Suppose we wish to represent the output letters by means of binary digits. Following the procedure presented in Sec. 3.7, we obtain for the three different states the three sets of code words shown in Fig. 4.5.

	s_0	s_1	s_2
a_1	10	01	1
a_2	11	1	00
a_3	0	00	01

Fig. 4.5. Binary code words for the states of the source of Fig. 4.4

The state probability distribution P(s) is found to be

$$P(s_0) = 0.355, \quad P(s_1) = 0.344, \quad P(s_2) = 0.301 \qquad (4.140)$$

Using these values, we can compute the over-all average length of the binary code words and the asymptotic value of the entropy per letter. If we define the code efficiency as the ratio of the latter to the former, the efficiency of the above set of code words is equal to 0.978.

General bounds to the average length of the code words may be readily obtained from the results of Sec. 3.5. Let $H(A|s_i)$ be the entropy of the ensemble A when the source is in state s_i, and $\overline{n}(s_i)$ the average number of symbols in the code words for state s_i. We obtain with the help of Eq. 3.18,

$$\frac{H(A|s_i)}{\log D} \leq \overline{n}(s_i) < \frac{H(A|s_i)}{\log D} + 1 \qquad (4.141)$$

Thus, the asymptotic average value of the code length

$$\overline{n} = \sum_S P(s)\, \overline{n}(s_i) \qquad (4.142)$$

satisfies the inequality

$$\frac{H(A|A^\infty)}{\log D} \leq \overline{n} < \frac{H(A|A^\infty)}{\log D} + 1 \qquad (4.143)$$

where $H(A|A^\infty)$ represents as before the asymptotic value of the entropy per letter, given by Eq. 4.113.

The encoding procedure discussed above requires the encoding and decoding devices to store as many sets of code words as there are states of the source. On the other hand, inspection of Fig. 4.5 indicates that in all three sets of code words, two of the words consist of two digits and one of the words consists of a single digit. We know, in addition, that the average code length, while depending on the number of digits in each word, does not depend on the identity of the digits as long as the code words uniquely identify the corresponding letters when the state of the source is known. Thus, the sets of code words shown in Fig. 4.6 are appropriate for our purposes and yield the same average code length as those of Fig. 4.5.

	s_0	s_1	s_2
a_1	10	11	0
a_2	11	0	10
a_3	0	10	11

Fig. 4.6. Alternative sets of code words for the source of Fig. 4.4

These new sets of code words have the important property of being identical except for the correspondence between code words and letters. Comparison with the probability table in Fig. 4.4 shows that the word 0 corresponds in all cases to the letter that has the largest conditional probability when the source is in the state considered. The word 11 corresponds in all cases to the letter that has the next largest conditional probability, and the word 10 corresponds to the letter that has the smallest conditional probability. Thus, if the sets of code words shown in Fig. 4.6 are used, the encoding and decoding devices need to store only one set of code words although they must still store a table indicating, for each state, the correspondence between code words and letters.

The advantages provided by the code words of Fig. 4.6 cannot be obtained in all cases without increasing the average code length because the number of code words having any given length is not the same, in general, for all states, if the sets of code words are optimum. The coding procedure leading to the use of a single set of code words may be described, in general terms, as follows. For each state, let us arrange the letters in order of decreasing probability and indicate with r their rank number ($r = 2$ is the rank of the second most probable letter). Each letter is still represented in general by different code words for different states of the source, but a specific code word is assigned to each rank. Thus, a particular letter a_k is represented in each state by the code word corresponding to the rank r that the letter has for that state. In other words, we encode the ranks of the letters rather than the letters themselves. For instance, in the case of Fig. 4.6, the least probable letter is always represented by the word 10, and the most probable one by the word 0 .

The asymptotic value of the probability $P(r)$ that the source will generate a letter of rank r is given by

$$P(r) = \sum_{S} P(s)\, P(r|s) \qquad (4.144)$$

where $P(r|s)$ is equal to the value of $P(a|s)$ for the letter of rank r in state s, and $P(s)$ is the probability distribution for the states of the source. The average code-word length is given by

$$\bar{n} = \sum_{S} \sum_{r=1}^{L} P(s)\, P(r|s) n_r = \sum_{r=1}^{L} P(r)\, n_r \tag{4.145}$$

where n_r is the number of symbols in the code word assigned to the rank r. Thus, an optimum set of code words may be constructed according to the procedure of Sec. 3.7 by identifying the rank probabilities $P(r)$ with the message probabilities $P(u_k)$.

Bounds for the asymptotic value of $\bar{n}$ may be obtained as follows. Let

$$H(R) \equiv - \sum_{r=1}^{L} P(r) \log P(r) \tag{4.146}$$

be the entropy of the ensemble formed by the different ranks. We have from Eq. 3.18

$$\frac{H(R)}{\log D} \leq \bar{n} < \frac{H(R)}{\log D} + 1 \tag{4.147}$$

where D is the number of letters in the encoding alphabet.

The upper bounds to $\bar{n}$ in Eqs. 4.143 and 4.147 may differ by an appreciable percentage from the corresponding lower bounds, when the entropies $H(A|A^{\infty})$ and $H(R)$ are comparable in magnitude to the capacity $\log D$ of the encoding alphabet. This percent difference, however, can be made as small as desired by encoding messages consisting of ν successive letters, rather than individual letters, as indicated below.

Let us consider the letters generated by a Markov source in pairs rather than one by one. Then a new Markov diagram may be constructed, in which each transition line between states corresponds to the generation of a particular sequence of two letters. For instance, the diagram of Fig. 4.7a would yield that shown in Fig. 4.7b. If L is the number of letters in the source alphabet, the process

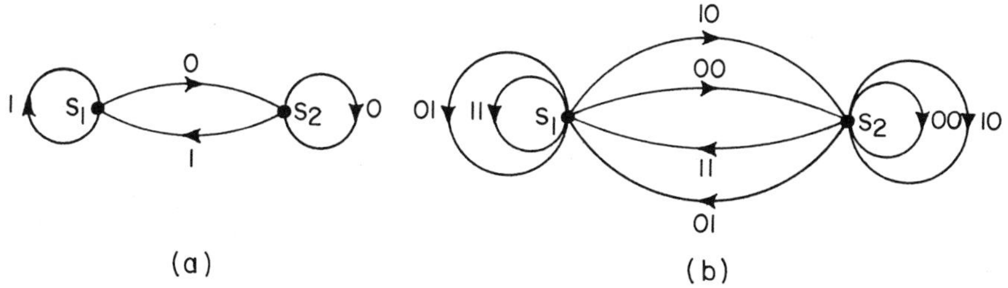

Fig. 4.7. The construction of a diagram for pairs of letters

involved amounts to introducing a new alphabet consisting of L^2 letters, and substituting one of the new letters for each sequence of two original letters. The diagram of Fig. 4.7b represents the Markov source resulting from this substitution.

For each state s we may compute the conditional probabilities $P(\alpha_1, \alpha_2 | s)$, in which α_1 represents the first letter, and α_2 represents the second letter. We can then encode each ordered pair of letters, following either one of the encoding procedures discussed above.

The above process may be readily generalized by considering the output symbols in groups of ν, and constructing a corresponding Markov diagram in which the lines between states represent sequences of ν letters. Optimum code words may then be constructed for these sequences, using the conditional probabilities $P(\alpha_1, \alpha_2, \ldots, \alpha_\nu | s)$.

The asymptotic (stationary), conditional entropy $H(A^\nu | A^\infty)$ of the ensemble of sequences of ν symbols is simply equal to ν times the asymptotic conditional entropy per letter, $H(A | A^\infty)$. This follows from the fact that the letter self informations depend only on the state of the source, and the state probabilities are stationary. Thus, for optimum, state-dependent code words, the average number of symbols per letter will satisfy the inequality

$$\frac{H(A|A^\infty)}{\log D} \leq \bar{n} < \frac{H(A|A^\infty)}{\log D} + \frac{1}{\nu} \tag{4.148}$$

in which the percent difference between the two bounds can be made as small as desired by selecting a sufficiently large value of ν.

It should be mentioned, in closing, that the term "predictive coding" is sometimes used [6] to refer to encoding procedures based on a Markov-source representation of an ensemble of sequences. The reason for such a name is that the first step in the encoding procedure may be considered as a prediction of the next letter, or message, on the basis of the past source output, as represented by the state of the source. Of course, the next letter, or message, cannot be precisely predicted, but only estimated through the specification of a probability distribution, which is then used in constructing an optimum set of code words. The encoder and the decoder perform the same operation of prediction, so that the same set of code words is selected independently by both of them.

4.13. Summary and Conclusions

Four main topics have been covered in this chapter, all pertaining to the encoding of discrete, stochastic sources. We began with a general discussion of the entropy of the successive events generated by a stochastic source. We were able to show, in the important special case of stationary sources, that the entropies of consecutive events, conditioned by all the preceding events, form a monotonic, non-increasing sequence. Because of its monotonic character, the sequence approaches a limit $H(A \mid A^{\infty})$, representing the average amount of information required to specify the next event generated by the source when the infinite past of the source output is known. The main conclusion reached in this chapter is that the number of binary digits per event required to represent the source output is at least equal to $H(A \mid A^{\infty})$, and can be made as close as desired to this value by increasing the length of the sequences of output events for which optimum binary code words are constructed.

In reaching this main conclusion, two different encoding procedures were studied. The first procedure, sometimes referred to as variable-length encoding, consists of segmenting the source output into messages consisting of ν consecutive events, and constructing for each possible message a code word of length proportional to the self information of the message. This form of encoding has the advantage of being always unambiguous. However, since the code-word length varies from message to message, this procedure can be used only when the time rate at which messages are generated by the source can be varied with time to fit the time rate at which the code-word symbols can be transmitted.

The second procedure, sometimes referred to as block encoding, assigns different code words of fixed length to the messages with self information per event not exceeding $H(A \mid A^{\infty}) + \epsilon$, and assigns one and the same code word to the remaining messages. It was shown that, in the case of discrete, ergodic sources, the probability of ambiguous encoding can be made as small as desired for any positive ϵ, by increasing the number of output events in each message. The corresponding number of symbols per output event required to provide the necessary code words is at least equal to $H(A \mid A^{\infty})$, but can be made as close as desired to this value by making ϵ sufficiently small, and the message length sufficiently large. Finally, since a discrete, stationary source that is not ergodic can be regarded as an ensemble of discrete, mutually exclusive, ergodic sources, the same encoding procedure can be readily adapted to non-ergodic, stationary sources.

The fourth and last topic discussed in this chapter was a particularly important class of sources, known as Markov sources. A property of these sources is that the probabilities with which the different letters of the source alphabet may be generated at any given time depend only on the state in which the source is at that time. Because of this property, the asymptotic entropy per event $H(A \mid A^{\infty})$ can be readily computed from the letter probabilities for each state of the source. Furthermore, the source output can be more conveniently encoded by using different sets of code words for different states of the source.

Natural languages, in their written form, are the most familiar examples of discrete, stochastic sources. They have been studied from this point of view by a number of investigators. Particularly pertinent to the subject of this chapter are Shannon's [7] experimental estimation of the entropy of printed English, and Mandelbrot's [8] explanation of experimental results obtained by Zipf on the relative frequencies of occurrence of words. Because of space limitations, this work, as well as the broader areas of speech and picture analysis, cannot be covered in this text. For a critical survey of these areas, see Chap. 1, Ref. 6.

Another important topic omitted from this text is Shannon's work [9] on the encoding of stochastic sources for certain types of fidelity criteria. This work is closely related to the problem of message encoding for transmission through randomly disturbed channel, discussed in the following chapters.

4.14. Selected References

1. W. Feller, An Introduction to Probability Theory and its Applications, 2nd edition, John Wiley & Sons, New York, 1957. The weak and strong laws of large numbers for independent random variables are discussed in Chapter X. Markov chains are discussed in Chapter XV.

2. N. Wiener, Cybernetics, The Technology Press and John Wiley & Sons, New York, 1948. The main results of the ergodic theory are discussed in Chapter II.

3. J. L. Doob, Stochastic Processes, John Wiley & Sons, New York, 1953. The strong law of large numbers for stationary stochastic processes is proved in Chapter X, Section 2. (Familiarity with measure theory is required.)

4. B. McMillan, "The Basic Theorems of Information Theory," Ann. Math. Statistics, 24, 196, 1953.

5. A. I. Khinchin, Mathematical Foundations of Information Theory, translated by R. A. Silverman and M. D. Friedman, Dover, New York, 1957. Chapter II presents a detailed discussion of the encoding of fixed-rate ergodic sources, based on McMillan's [4] original work.

6. P. Elias, "Predictive Coding," Trans. of I.R.E., IT-1, 62, 1955.

7. C. E. Shannon, "Prediction and Entropy of Printed English," Bell System Tech. J., 30, 50, 1951.

8. B. Mandelbrot, "An Informational Theory of the Statistical Structure of Language," in Communication Theory, edited by W. Jackson, Butterworth Scientific Pub., London, and Academic Press, New York, p. 486, 1953.

9. C. E. Shannon, "Coding Theorems for Discrete Source with a Fidelity Criterion," in Information and Decision Processes, edited by R. E. Machol, McGraw-Hill, New York, p. 93, 1960.

Chapter 5

TRANSMISSION CHANNELS

The preceding four chapters have been devoted to a discussion of information sources, and of the encoding of their output into sequences of symbols belonging to a prescribed alphabet. We turn our attention next to the transmission of these symbols through randomly disturbed channels. We shall assume, for the sake of simplicity, that the symbols in question are binary digits. This will not limit in any significant way the generality of our discussion.

We shall study in this chapter various mathematical models of transmission channels. The encoding and decoding of sequences of binary digits for transmission through a prescribed channel will be the main subject of the following chapters.

5.1. Classification of Channels

A transmission channel may be regarded as a transducer which transforms successive input events, each represented by a point x of some space X, into output events, each represented by some point y of some other space Y. The transformation of the point x into the point y is governed by a conditional probability distribution over the Y space for a given point of the X space which describes the random disturbance (noise) present in the channel.

Channels are usually classified according to the characteristics of the input and output spaces, and of the probability distribution governing the transformation from one space to the other. A channel is said to be discrete if the input and output spaces are discrete. It is said to be continuous if the input and output spaces are continuous. If one of the spaces is discrete and the other continuous, the channel is said to be discrete-to-continuous or continuous-to-discrete, as the case may be.

It is clear that in the case of discrete-event spaces, successive events must form a time-discrete sequence. In the case of a continuous space, however, the point representing the current event may be allowed to change only at certain specified times, such as the multiples of a fixed time interval, or it may be free to move continuously with time. A channel with input and output spaces of the latter type is said to be time-continuous. Most physical channels of practical interest are time-continuous. Usually, however, they can be satisfactorily represented by means of time-discrete models.

A channel may possess several input terminals and several output terminals; in this case the spaces X and Y are actually product spaces whose points represent the possible combinations of input events and of output events, respectively. For instance, if the channel possesses two input terminals with corresponding events represented by points of the two spaces X_1 and X_2, the input space X is actually the product space X_1X_2. A channel with a single input terminal and a single output terminal is sometimes called a one-way channel. By contrast, a channel with two input terminals and two output terminals is often referred to as a two-way channel, in view of the fact that it provides means for two-way communication.

A channel in which every input event can be any one of the points of the X space is said to be free from input constraints. Conversely, a channel with input constraints is one in which each input event may be restricted to a subset of the points of the X space depending on the preceding events. For instance, if the events are pulses of arbitrary amplitude, the amplitude of each successive pulse may be constrained by the requirement that the arithmetic mean of the squared magnitude of some specified number of successive pulses be smaller than some given value.

Channels are also classified according to the characteristics of the conditional probability distribution that governs the transformation from the X space to the Y space. A channel in which this conditional probability distribution is the same for all successive input and output events is said to be constant. If, instead, this conditional probability distribution is a function of the preceding events, whether input or output, the channel is said to possess memory. The memory is said to be finite if the dependence extends only to a finite number of preceding events. The conditional probability distribution may also depend on some separate stochastic process. If it does, and if the stochastic process is stationary, the channel is said to be stationary.

Channels can be further subdivided into classes according to special symmetries that may be exhibited by the conditional probability distribution. We shall discuss these symmetries when they become of significance in connection with the evaluation of the information capacity of channels, and in connection with encoding and decoding.

5.2. Discrete, Constant Channels

Of the great variety of possible channels, the most elementary class is clearly that of one-way, discrete, constant channels, that is, of two-terminal channels with discrete input- and output-event spaces related by a fixed conditional probability distribution.

One-way, discrete, constant channels are characterized by the input space X, consisting of L_x points x, the output space Y, consisting of L_y points y, and the conditional probability distribution $P(y|x)$. We shall indicate with ξ_i the ith input event in order of occurrence, and with η_i the corresponding output event. The event

ξ_i may be any one of the points of the X space, that is, of the symbols of the input alphabet. Similarly, η_i may be anyone of the points of the Y space, that is, of the symbols of the output alphabet.

Let us indicate with

$$\xi^n \equiv \xi_1 \xi_2 \ldots \xi_i \ldots \xi_n \tag{5.1}$$

an arbitrary sequence of n input events, and with

$$\eta^n \equiv \eta_1 \eta_2 \ldots \eta_i \ldots \eta_n \tag{5.2}$$

the corresponding sequence of output events. By definition of constant channel, the conditional probability distribution $P(\eta_i | \xi_i)$ is the same for all integers i, independently of all preceding events, and is given by $P(y|x)$ for $\xi_i = x$ and $\eta_i = y$. Thus,

$$P(\eta^n | \xi^n) = \prod_{i=1}^{n} P(\eta_i | \xi_i) \tag{5.3}$$

According to the block diagram of Fig. 1.1, the channel input events are specified by the channel encoder on the basis of the binary digits to be transmitted. For instance, the channel encoder may segment its input into successive messages, each consisting of consecutive binary digits, and assign to each message a particular sequence of n channel events belonging to the input space X. Thus, the statistical characteristics of the sequence of input events depend on the particular transformation of binary digits into channel events performed by the channel encoder. Let $P(\xi^n)$ be the joint probability distribution of n successive input events. The joint probability distribution $P(\eta^n)$ of the corresponding output events can be readily evaluated with the help of Eq. 5.3. We obtain

$$P(\eta^n) = \sum_{X^n} P(\xi^n)\, P(\eta^n | \xi^n) \tag{5.4}$$

where X^n represents the ensemble of input sequences. Indicating with X_i the ensemble of ξ_i, then X^n is the product ensemble $X_1 X_2 \ldots X_i \ldots X_n$ of the n ensembles of the successive input events.

The average value of the mutual information between input and output sequences is given by

$$I(Y^n;X^n) = H(Y^n) - H(Y^n | X^n) \tag{5.5}$$

where Y^n indicates the ensemble of output sequences. Indicating with Y_i the ensemble of η_i, then Y^n is the product ensemble $Y_1 Y_2 \ldots Y_i \ldots Y_n$ of the n ensembles of the successive output events.

The entropy of the ensemble of output sequences may be expressed as the sum of the conditional entropies of the successive events, given the preceding events, as follows:

$$H(Y^n) = H(Y_1) + H(Y_2|Y_1) + H(Y_3|Y_2Y_1) + \ldots + H(Y_n|Y_{n-1} \ldots Y_1) \tag{5.6}$$

where

$$H(Y_i|Y_{i-1} \ldots Y_1) \equiv - \sum_{Y^i} P(\eta^i) \log P(\eta_i|\eta_{i-1} \ldots \eta_1) \tag{5.7}$$

The conditional entropy on the righthand side of Eq. 5.5 may be readily evaluated with the help of Eq. 5.3. We obtain

$$H(Y^n|X^n) = - \sum_{X^nY^n} P(\xi^n, \eta^n) \log P(\eta^n|\xi^n)$$

$$= -\sum_{X_1Y_1} \sum_{X_2Y_2} \cdots \sum_{X_nY_n} P(\xi_1, \eta_1, \xi_2, \eta_2, \ldots \xi_n, \eta_n) \sum_{i=1}^{n} \log P(\eta_i|\xi_i)$$

$$= -\sum_{i=1}^{n} \sum_{X_iY_i} P(\xi_i, \eta_i) \log P(\eta_i|\xi_i) = \sum_{i=1}^{n} H(Y_i|X_i) \tag{5.8}$$

where $H(Y_i|X_i)$, the conditional entropy of the ith output event given the corresponding input event, depends on the probability distribution for the ith input event, and therefore is, in general, different for successive input events.

Substitution of Eqs. 5.7 and 5.8 in Eq. 5.5 yields for the average mutual information between input and output sequences of events

$$I(Y^n;X^n) = \sum_{i=1}^{n} [H(Y_i|Y_{i-1} \ldots Y_1) - H(Y_i|X_i)] \tag{5.9}$$

where $H(Y_i|Y_{i-1} \ldots Y_1)$ reduces to $H(Y_1)$ for $i = 1$. Of course, the value of this average mutual information depends on the probability distribution of the input sequences of events, as well as on the conditional probability distribution $P(y|x)$ characteristic of the channel.

The average mutual information $I(X^n;Y^n)$ measures the amount of information provided, on the average, by the n output events about the corresponding input events. On the other hand, the channel input events are uniquely specified by the binary digits input to the channel encoder. It follows that $I(X^n;Y^n)$ measures as well the amount of information provided, on the average, by the n events output from the channel about the binary digits input to the channel encoder.

We observe next that $I(X^n; Y^n)/n$, the average mutual information per channel event, is a function of n and of the probability distribution $P(\xi^n)$ of the n input events, which can be varied at will through proper choice of the encoding process performed by the channel encoder. Thus, we can define an information transmission capacity for any discrete, constant channel as the maximum value of $I(X^n; Y^n)/n$ evaluated over all possible probability distributions $P(\xi^n)$ and all positive integers n .

$$C \equiv \underset{P(\xi^n),\, n}{\text{Max}} \frac{I(X^n; Y^n)}{n} \tag{5.10}$$

The following two theorems show that this maximum value is obtained, independently of n , when the input events are statistically independent and have the same probability distribution.

Theorem. Let $P(\xi^n)$ be the joint probability distribution of n input events, and $P(\xi_1), P(\xi_2), \ldots, P(\xi_i) \ldots, P(\xi_n)$ be the probability distributions of the individual events. Indicate with $I(X^n; Y^n)$ the average mutual information between the n input events and the corresponding output events, and with $I(X_i; Y_i)$ the average mutual information between the ith input event and the corresponding output event. Then, for any discrete, constant channel,

$$I(X^n; Y^n) \leq \sum_{i=1}^{n} I(X_i; Y_i) \tag{5.11}$$

where the equal sign holds when and only when either the n input events are statistically independent of one another or the output events are statistically independent of the input events (in which case $I(X^n; Y^n) = 0$) .

Proof. We have from Eq. 2.105

$$H(Y_i|Y_{i-1}\, Y_{i-2} \ldots Y_1) \leq H(Y_i) \tag{5.12}$$

where

$$H(Y_i) \equiv - \sum_{Y_i} P(\eta_i) \log P(\eta_i) \tag{5.13}$$

is the entropy of the ith output event. Substitution of Eq. 5.12 in Eq. 5.9 yields Eq. 5.11.

The equal sign holds in Eq. 5.12 and, therefore, in Eq. 5.11 when and only when the output events are statistically independent. In turn, the output events are statistically independent when and only when either the corresponding input events are statistically independent, in which case

$$P(\eta_i | \eta_{i-1} \ldots \eta_1) = \sum_{X_i} P(\xi_i) P(\eta_i | \xi_i) \tag{5.14}$$

or the output events are statistically independent of the input events. QED

Theorem. Let $P(y|x)$ be the conditional probability distribution of a discrete, constant channel, and $P(x)$ be an arbitrary probability distribution over the input space of the channel. The information transmission capacity of the channel is the maximum average value of the mutual information

$$I(X;Y) \equiv \sum_{XY} P(x) P(y|x) \log \frac{P(y|x)}{P(y)} \tag{5.15}$$

evaluated over all possible probability distributions $P(x)$; that is,

$$C = \underset{P(x)}{\text{Max}} \; I(X;Y) \tag{5.16}$$

Proof. It follows from the preceding theorem that the average mutual information $I(X^n;Y^n)$ between n input events and the corresponding output events can be maximized with respect to $P(\xi^n)$ by making the events statistically independent and maximizing independently the mutual information $I(X_i;Y_i)$ for each individual pair of events. On the other hand, $P(\eta_i | \xi_i)$ is equal to $P(y|x)$ for $\xi_i = x$ and $\eta_i = y$, and, therefore, the maximum value of each $I(X_i;Y_i)$ is equal to the righthand side of Eq. 5.16. It follows that the information transmission capacity defined by Eq. 5.10 can be evaluated according to Eq. 5.16. QED

The evaluation of the capacity of a discrete, constant channel according to Eq. 5.16 does not involve any conceptual difficulty, but it may be very laborious. We shall evaluate in the following section the capacities of certain channels for which the maximization procedure is particularly simple. The general maximization procedure will be discussed in Sec. 5.5.

5.3. Uniform, Constant Channels

It is convenient for our purposes to think of the conditional probability distribution $P(y|x)$ characterizing a discrete, constant channel as a matrix

$$\mathscr{P} \equiv \begin{bmatrix} P(y_1|x_1) & P(y_2|x_1) & \ldots & P(y_i|x_1) & \ldots & P(y_{L_y}|x_1) \\ P(y_1|x_2) & P(y_2|x_2) & \ldots & P(y_i|x_2) & \ldots & P(y_{L_y}|x_2) \\ \cdots & \cdots & \cdots & \cdots & \cdots & \cdots \\ P(y_1|x_k) & P(y_2|x_k) & \ldots & P(y_i|x_k) & \ldots & P(y_{L_y}|x_k) \\ \cdots & \cdots & \cdots & \cdots & \cdots & \cdots \\ P(y_1|x_{L_x}) & P(y_2|x_{L_x}) & \ldots & P(y_i|x_{L_x}) & \ldots & P(y_{L_y}|x_{L_x}) \end{bmatrix} \tag{5.17}$$

where L_x and L_y are the numbers of points in the input and output spaces, respectively.

The evaluation of the capacity of a discrete, constant channel becomes particularly simple when the matrix $\mathscr{P}$ of the channel has the following special properties. A channel is said to be uniform from the input when the rows of $\mathscr{P}$ are permutations of the same set of numbers $p_1, p_2, \ldots, p_j, \ldots, p_{L_y}$. The importance of this property stems from the fact that, for any channel possessing it, the conditional entropy

$$H(Y|x_k) = -\sum_{Y} P(y|x_k) \log P(y|x_k) = -\sum_{j=1}^{L_y} p_j \log p_j \tag{5.18}$$

has the same value for all points x_k of X, that is, for all input symbols. This means that when the channel is uniform from the input, the transmission of each of the possible input symbols is disturbed to the same extent by the channel noise.

A channel is said to be uniform from the output when the columns of the matrix $\mathscr{P}$ are permutations of the same set of L_x numbers. The importance of this property for our purposes stems from the fact that, for any channel possessing it, a uniform input probability distribution $P(x) = 1/L_x$ gives rise to a uniform output probability distribution $P(y) = 1/L_y$. This is evident from the relation

$$P(y) = \sum_{X} P(x) \; P(y|x) \tag{5.19}$$

A channel which is uniform from both the input and the output is said to be doubly uniform. The capacity of any such channel can be readily evaluated with the help of the following theorem.

Theorem. The capacity of a discrete, constant channel that is uniform from the input satisfies the inequality

$$C \le \log L_y + \sum_{j=1}^{L_y} p_j \log p_j \tag{5.20}$$

where the numbers p_j are the elements of each of the rows of $\mathscr{P}$. The equal sign holds whenever the channel is uniform from the output as well as from the input, in which case the input and output probability distributions are both uniform.

Proof. Because of Eq. 5.18, the average mutual information between input and output symbols can be written in the form

$$I(X;Y) = H(Y) - H(Y|X) = H(Y) + \sum_{j=1}^{L_y} p_j \log p_j \tag{5.21}$$

On the other hand, we have from Eq. 2.90

$$H(Y) \le \log L_y \tag{5.22}$$

where L_y is the number of points in the output space. Then, in view of Eq. 5.16, substitution of Eq. 5.22 into Eq. 5.21 yields Eq. 5.20.

We know from the theorem embodying Eq. 2.90 that the equal sign holds in Eq. 5.22 when and only when the output probability distribution is uniform, that is, when $P(y) = 1/L_y$ for all output symbols. However, there may or may not exist an input probability distribution $P(x)$ for which $P(y)$ is uniform. If such a probability distribution exists, the equal sign holds in Eq. 5.20.

We saw that if the channel is uniform from the output, a uniform input probability distribution gives rise to a uniform output probability distribution. It follows that, in the case of a doubly uniform channel, the equal sign holds in Eq. 5.20, and the average mutual information is equal to the channel capacity when both input and output probability distributions are uniform. It should be noted that the equal sign may hold in Eq. 5.20 when the channel is not uniform from the output. QED

An example of doubly uniform channel is obtained by setting $L_x = L_y = L$, and

$$P(y_i|x_k) = \begin{cases} 1 - p & ; \quad i = k \\ \dfrac{p}{L-1} & ; \quad i \ne k \end{cases} \tag{5.23}$$

We obtain in this particular case from the above theorem,

$$\begin{aligned} C &= \log L + (1-p) \log (1-p) + p \log \frac{p}{L-1} \\ &= \log L - p \log (L-1) + p \log p + (1-p) \log (1-p) \end{aligned} \tag{5.24}$$

The simplest and best known type of uniform channel is the binary symmetric channel illustrated in Fig. 5.1. Its capacity can be readily obtained from Eq. 5.24 by setting $L = 2$. We have, using base-2 logarithms,

$$C = 1 + p \log p + (1-p) \log (1-p) \text{ bit/event} \tag{5.25}$$

$$\mathscr{P} = \begin{bmatrix} 1-p & p \\ p & 1-p \end{bmatrix}$$

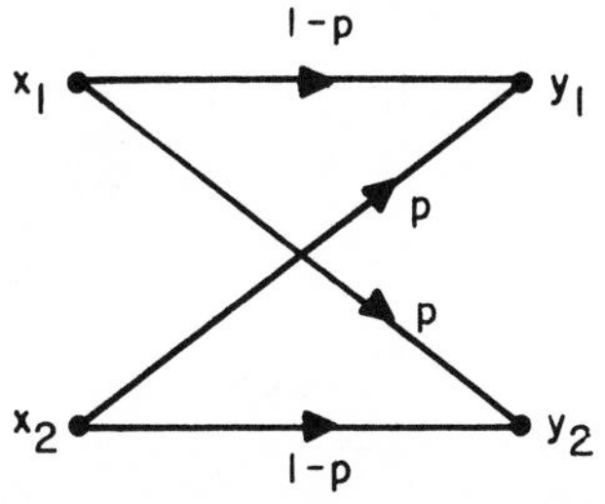

Fig. 5.1. Binary symmetric channel

The behavior of this capacity as a function of p is given by the curve of Fig. 2.9 turned upside down.

A simple channel which is uniform from the input, but not from the output, is illustrated in Fig. 5.2. This channel is identical to the binary symmetric channel illustrated in Fig. 5.1, except for the presence of the output symbol y_3 which may result with

$$\mathscr{P} = \begin{bmatrix} 1-p-q & p & q \\ p & 1-p-q & q \end{bmatrix}$$

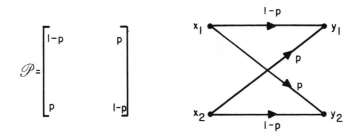

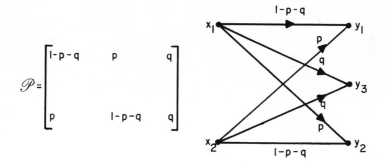

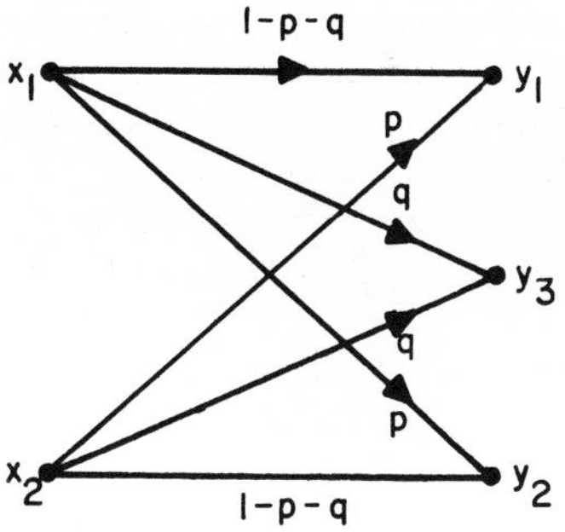

Fig. 5.2. Binary symmetric-erasure channel

probability q from either input symbol. The occurrence of the symbol y_3 in a sequence of output events is equivalent to an event being erased, because the corresponding input event may be x_1 or x_2 with equal probabilities.

The capacity of this special channel can be readily computed because of its special symmetry. Since the channel is uniform from the input, the average mutual information between input and output symbols is given by Eq. 5.21 with $p_1 = 1-p-q$, $p_2 = p$, $p_3 = q$. It follows that the input probability distribution that maximizes $H(Y)$ also maximizes $I(X;Y)$. It can be readily checked that the maximum value of $H(Y)$ occurs when the input symbols are equally probable, in which case

$$P(y_1) = P(y_2) = \tfrac{1}{2}(1-q)\ ; \quad P(y_3) = q \tag{5.26}$$

Thus, the channel capacity is, in bits,

$$C = (1-q)\ [1-\log(1-q)] + (1-p-q)\log(1-p-q) + p\log p \tag{5.27}$$

In the special case of $p = 0$, y_1 can result only from x_1, and y_2 only from x_2, so that the channel is free of disturbances, except for erasures occurring with probability q. The capacity of this erasure channel is, from Eq. 5.27,

$$C = 1 - q \quad \text{bit per event} \tag{5.28}$$

In words, the capacity of a binary erasure channel is equal to the capacity of a noise-free binary channel (one bit) minus the erasure probability q.

*5.4. Convexity of the Average Mutual Information

We shall discuss in this section an important property of the average mutual information between input and output symbols, in preparation for the evaluation, in the following section, of the capacity of an arbitrary discrete, constant channel.

For any given discrete, constant channel, the average mutual information between input and output symbols is a function of the input probability distribution $P(x)$. Let $P_1(x)$, $P_2(x)$, ..., $P_i(x)$, ..., $P_m(x)$ be m different probability distributions, and a_1, a_2, ..., a_i, ..., a_m be a set of m non-negative numbers satisfying

$$\sum_{i=1}^{m} a_i = 1 \tag{5.29}$$

The linear combination

$$P_0(x) \equiv \sum_{i=1}^{m} a_i P_i(x) \tag{5.30}$$

is also a possible probability distribution, because

$$P_0(x_k) = \sum_{i=1}^{m} a_i P_i(x_k) \geq 0 \tag{5.31}$$

and

$$\sum_{k=1}^{L_x} P_0(x_k) = \sum_{i=1}^{m} a_i \sum_{k=1}^{L_x} P_i(x_k) = 1 \tag{5.32}$$

To each probability distribution $P_i(x)$ corresponds a probability distribution over the output space Y given by

$$P_i(y) = \sum_X P_i(x)\, P(y|x) \tag{5.33}$$

We obtain for the probability distribution $P_0(y)$, resulting from the probability distributions defined by Eq. 5.31,

$$P_0(y) = \sum_X \sum_{i=1}^{m} a_i P_i(x) P(y|x) = \sum_{i=1}^{m} a_i\, P_i(y) \tag{5.34}$$

The average mutual information between input and output symbols corresponding to the input probability distribution $P_i(x)$ is given by

$$I_i(X;Y) = H_i(Y) - H_i(Y|X) \tag{5.35}$$

where

$$H_i(Y) \equiv - \sum_Y P_i(y) \log P_i(y) \tag{5.36}$$

$$H_i(Y|X) \equiv - \sum_X P_i(x) \sum_Y P(y|x) \log P(y|x) \tag{5.37}$$

The average mutual information $I_0(X; Y)$ corresponding to $P_0(x)$ is given by similar expressions with the subscript o substituted for the subscript i.

Theorem. For any set of m non-negative numbers a_i satisfying Eq. 5.29,

$$I_0(X; Y) \geq \sum_{i=1}^{m} a_i\, I_i(X; Y) \tag{5.38}$$

Proof. We have from Eq. 5.35

$$\Delta I(X; Y) \equiv \sum_{i=1}^{m} a_i\, I_i(X; Y) - I_0(X; Y)$$

$$= \sum_{i=1}^{m} a_i [H_i(Y) - H_i(Y|X)] - [H_0(Y) - H_0(Y|X)] \tag{5.39}$$

On the other hand, we obtain from Eqs. 5.30 and 5.37

$$H_0(Y|X) \equiv -\sum_X P_0(x) \sum_Y P(y|x) \log P(y|x)$$

$$= -\sum_X \left[\sum_{i=1}^m a_i P_i(x)\right] \sum_Y P(y|x) \log P(y|x)$$

$$= \sum_{i=1}^m a_i H_i(Y|X) \tag{5.40}$$

It follows that

$$\Delta I(X; Y) = \sum_{i=1}^m a_i H_i(Y) - H_0(Y) \equiv \Delta H(Y) \tag{5.41}$$

Next, we expand the righthand side of Eq. 5.41 with the help of Eqs. 5.34 and 5.36:

$$\Delta H(Y) = -\sum_{i=1}^m a_i \sum_Y P_i(y) \log P_i(y) + \sum_Y \left[\sum_{i=1}^m a_i P_i(y)\right] \log P_0(y)$$

$$= \sum_{i=1}^m a_i \sum_Y P_i(y) \log \frac{P_0(y)}{P_i(y)} \tag{5.42}$$

Then, using the inequality (see Eq. 2.91)

$$\ln w \leq w - 1 \tag{5.43}$$

we obtain

$$\Delta H(Y) \leq \sum_{i=1}^m a_i \sum_Y P_i(y) \left[\frac{P_0(y)}{P_i(y)} - 1\right] \log \mathbf{e} = 0 \tag{5.44}$$

and, with the help of Eq. 5.41,

$$\sum_{i=1}^m a_i \; I_i(X; Y) - I_0(X; Y) \leq 0 \tag{5.45}$$

Q. E. D.

Theorem. For any set of m non-negative numbers a_i satisfying Eq. 5.29,

$$I_0(X;Y) \leq H(A) + \sum_{i=1}^{m} a_i I_i(X;Y) \tag{5.46}$$

where

$$H(A) \equiv -\sum_{i=1}^{m} a_i \log a_i \tag{5.47}$$

Proof. Let us expand the logarithm on the righthand side of Eq. 5.42 as follows:

$$\log \frac{P_0(y)}{P_i(y)} = \log \sum_{j=1}^{m} a_j \frac{P_j(y)}{P_i(y)} = \log a_i + \log \sum_{j=1}^{m} \frac{a_j P_j(y)}{a_i P_i(y)} \tag{5.48}$$

The summation on the righthand side of this equation is larger than or equal to 1 because each term is non-negative and the term for $j = i$ is equal to 1. Thus, its logarithm is non-negative and

$$\log \frac{P_0(y)}{P_i(y)} \geq \log a_i \tag{5.49}$$

Then, with the help of this inequality, we obtain from Eqs. 5.41 and 5.42

$$\Delta I(X;Y) = \Delta H(Y) \geq \sum_{i=1}^{m} a_i \sum_{Y} P_i(y) \log a_i = -H(A) \tag{5.50}$$

QED

The first of the above two theorems, namely, that embodying Eq. 5.38, can be given a useful geometric interpretation as follows. Any input probability distribution $P(x)$ can be represented as a point in a Euclidean space by regarding the individual symbol probabilities $P(x_1)$, $P(x_2)$, ..., $P(x_k)$, ..., $P(x_{L_x})$ as the Cartesian coordinates of the point. Since

$$\sum_{k=1}^{L_x} P(x_k) = 1 \tag{5.51}$$

the points representing possible probability distributions must lie on the hyperplane of dimensionality $L_x - 1$ defined by this linear equation. More precisely, since probabilities cannot assume negative values, the locus of such points is the region of the hyperplane bounded by the intersections with the L_x hyperplanes

$$P(x_k) = 0 ; \quad k = 1, 2, \ldots, L_x \tag{5.52}$$

For instance, in the case of a ternary input alphabet, the locus of the points representing possible probability distributions is the equilateral triangle formed by the three straight lines joining the positive unit points on the Cartesian axes.

The value of the average mutual information $I(X; Y)$ can be plotted, for any particular $P(x)$, in the direction normal to the locus of the points representing possible probability distributions, thereby generating a hypersurface of dimensionality $L_x - 1$. Let $P_1(x)$ and $P_2(x)$ be two particular probability distributions. Consider the intersection of the hypersurface with the two-dimensional plane normal to the locus and containing the points representing $P_1(x)$ and $P_2(x)$, as illustrated in Fig. 5.3. Each point of the

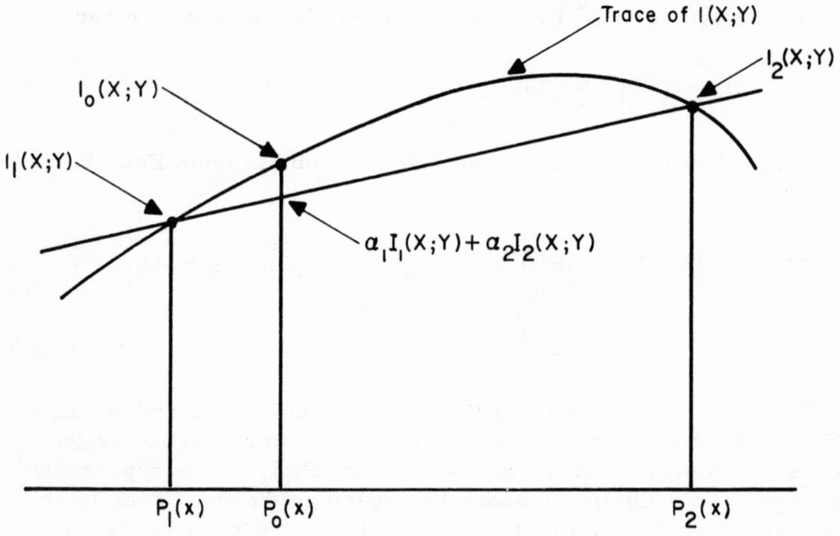

Fig. 5.3. Illustration of the convexity of the average mutual information

segment of straight line between $P_1(x)$ and $P_2(x)$ represents a probability distribution

$$P_0(x) = \alpha_1 P_1(x) + \alpha_2 P_2(x) \tag{5.53}$$

where

$$\alpha_1 + \alpha_2 = 1; \qquad \alpha_1, \alpha_2 \geq 0 \tag{5.54}$$

The trace of the surface $I(X; Y)$ between the points marked $I_1(X; Y)$ and $I_2(X; Y)$ gives the corresponding value of the average mutual information $I_0(X; Y)$, and the segment of straight line between the same two points is a plot of the linear combination $\alpha_1 I_1(X; Y) + \alpha_2 I_2(X; Y)$.

The theorem embodying Eq. 5.38 states that the trace of $I(X; Y)$ between the points marked $I_1(X; Y)$ and $I_2(X; Y)$ in Fig. 5.3 must lie above or on the segment of straight line joining the same two points. Furthermore, since $P_1(x)$ and $P_2(x)$ are arbitrary probability distributions, any segment of the trace of $I(X; Y)$ on a plane normal to the locus of the $P(x)$'s must lie above or on the straight-line segment joining its end points. This implies that the hypersurface $I(X; Y)$ is convex upward. For this reason the average mutual information between input and output symbols is said to be a convex function of the input probability distribution.

> Theorem. The average mutual information $I(X; Y)$ between the input and output symbols of a discrete, constant channel, when regarded as a function of the input symbol probabilities, cannot possess relative minima or saddle points. If it possesses several relative maxima, it must assume the same value at all such maxima and for all linear combinations (with non-negative coefficients satisfying Eq. 5.29) of the corresponding input probability distributions.

Proof. Let us suppose that $I(X; Y)$ has a relative maximum or a relative minimum or a saddle point of value $I_1(X; Y)$ for some input probability distribution $P_1(x)$, and that if $I_1(X; Y)$ is a relative maximum, it is smaller than the largest value of $I(X; Y)$. Then, there must exist a probability distribution $P_2(x)$ for which $I(X; Y)$ assumes a value $I_2(X; Y)$ which is greater than $I_1(X; Y)$. Let $I_0(X; Y)$ be the average mutual information corresponding to the probability distribution $P_0(x)$ defined by Eqs. 5.53 and 5.54. We have

$$\frac{d}{d\alpha_2}\left[\alpha_1 I_1(X; Y) + \alpha_2 I_2(X; Y)\right] = I_2(X; Y) - I_1(X; Y) \geq 0 \tag{5.55}$$

On the other hand, we must also have

$$\frac{d}{d\alpha_2}\left[I_0(X; Y)\right]_{\alpha_2 = 0} = 0 \tag{5.56}$$

because, by assumption, $I(X; Y)$ has a maximum or a minimum or a saddle point at $P_1(x)$. It follows that $I_0(X; Y)$ cannot satisfy

Eq. 5.38 in the immediate vicinity of $P_1(x)$, thereby precluding the existence of relative minima, saddle points, and values of $I(X;Y)$ larger than that of any relative maximum.

The above argument precludes the existence of several relative maxima with different values. If there are m relative maxima with the same value $I_{max}(X;Y)$, corresponding to probability distributions $P_1(x)$, $P_2(x)$, ..., $P_m(x)$, Eq. 5.38, in conjunction with the above argument, requires that the average mutual information $I_0(X;Y)$, corresponding to the family of probability distributions $P_0(x)$ defined by Eqs. 5.29 and 5.30, be equal to $I_{max}(X;Y)$ for all sets of non-negative numbers α_i satisfying Eq. 5.29. QED

*5.5. Capacity Evaluation for Discrete, Constant Channels

We turn now to the evaluation of the capacity of a discrete, constant channel, according to Eq. 5.16. Let us indicate with L_x the number of symbols in the input alphabet X, and with L_y the number of symbols in the output alphabet Y. It is convenient to represent the input probability distribution $P(x)$ as a point in a L_x-dimensional space with Cartesian coordinates $P(x_1)$, $P(x_2)$, ..., $P(x_k)$, ..., $P(x_{L_x})$, as in the preceding section. We stress again that, since these Cartesian coordinates represent probabilities,

$$\sum_{k=1}^{L_x} P(x_k) = 1 \tag{5.57}$$

and

$$P(x_k) \geq 0; \qquad k = 1, 2, \ldots, L_x \tag{5.58}$$

Thus the locus of the points representing probability distributions is the region of the hyperplane defined by Eq. 5.57 bounded by the L_x hyperplanes $P(x_k) = 0$. Our objective is to determine the maximum value assumed by the average mutual information

$$I(X;Y) = H(Y) - H(Y|X) \tag{5.59}$$

within or on the boundaries of the region so defined.

Theorem. For the input probability distribution that maximizes $I(X;Y)$, the conditional average $I(x_k;Y)$ of the mutual information between input and output symbols has the same value for all input symbols x_k for which $P(x_k) \neq 0$, and it is given by

$$I(x_k;Y) = \sum_Y P(y|x_k) \log \frac{P(y|x_k)}{P(y)} = C \tag{5.60}$$

where C is the maximum value of $I(X;Y)$, that is, the channel capacity.

Proof. According to Lagrange's method of indeterminate multipliers [1], the function $I(X;Y)$ of the variables $P(x_1)$, $P(x_2)$, ..., $P(x_{L_x})$ is stationary on the hyperplane defined by Eq. 5.57 when the L_x variables satisfy the set of L_x equations

$$\frac{\partial}{\partial P(x_k)}\left[I(X;Y) + \lambda \sum_{i=1}^{L_x} P(x_i) \right] = 0 \ ; \quad k = 1, 2, \ldots, L_x \tag{5.61}$$

where λ is a constant to be determined with the help of Eq. 5.57. Furthermore, the last theorem of the preceding section states that any such point of stationarity of $I(X;Y)$ within the region defined by Eqs. 5.57 and 5.58 must be a relative maximum of value equal to the largest value of $I(X;Y)$.

Expressing all information measures in natural units and differentiating with respect to $P(x_k)$ yields

$$\frac{\partial H(Y)}{\partial P(x_k)} = \sum_{j=1}^{L_y} \frac{\partial H(Y)}{\partial P(y_j)} \frac{\partial P(y_j)}{\partial P(x_k)} = -\sum_{j=1}^{L_y} [1 + \ln P(y_j)]\, P(y_j|x_k)$$

$$= -\left[1 + \sum_{j=1}^{L_y} P(y_j|x_k) \ln P(y_j) \right] \tag{5.62}$$

$$\frac{\partial H(Y|X)}{\partial P(x_k)} = -\sum_{j=1}^{L_y} P(y_j|x_k) \ln P(y_j|x_k) \tag{5.63}$$

$$\frac{\partial}{\partial P(x_k)} \sum_{i=1}^{L_x} P(x_i) = 1 \tag{5.64}$$

Thus, Eq. 5.61 becomes, with the help of Eq. 5.59,

$$\sum_{j=1}^{L_y} P(y_j|x_k) \ln \frac{P(y_j|x_k)}{P(y_j)} - 1 + \lambda = 0 \tag{5.65}$$

which can also be expressed in the form

$$I(x_k; Y) = C \qquad (5.66)$$

where

$$C \equiv 1 - \lambda \qquad (5.67)$$

is a constant to be determined. Then, multiplying Eq. 5.66 by $P(x_k)$ and adding over k yields, with the help of Eq. 5.57,

$$\sum_{k=1}^{L_x} P(x_k)\, I(x_k; Y) = I(X; Y) = C \qquad (5.68)$$

Since the probabilities $P(x_k)$ satisfy, by assumption, Eq. 5.61, the corresponding value of $I(X; Y)$ is a relative maximum, and, therefore, the constant C is the channel capacity.

QED

The quantity $I(x_k; Y)$ is the conditional expectation (conditional average) of the mutual information between input and output symbols for a particular input symbol x_k. It can be interpreted as the average amount of information received through the channel when the particular symbol x_k is transmitted. This quantity depends on the output probability distribution $P(y)$, which in turn depends on the input probability distribution $P(x)$. Thus, the condition for the existence of a relative maximum of $I(X; Y)$ is that the conditional average of the amount of information received through the channel be the same regardless of the particular symbol input to the channel.

In order to determine [7] a probability distribution $P(x)$ for which $I(X;Y)$ assumes its maximum value C, it is convenient to rewrite Eq. 5.60 in the form

$$\sum_{j=1}^{L_y} P(y_j|x_k)\, [C + \log P(y_j)] = -H(Y|\, x_k); \quad k=1, 2, \ldots, L_x \qquad (5.69)$$

where $P(y_j)$ is given by

$$P(y_j) = \sum_{k=1}^{L_x} P(x_k)\, P(y_j|x_k)\,; \quad j=1, 2, \ldots, L_y \qquad (5.70)$$

Summing this last equation over the output alphabet yields, with the help of Eq. 5.57,

$$\sum_{j=1}^{L_y} P(y_j) = 1 \qquad (5.71)$$

The conditions expressed by Eqs. 5.69, 5.70 and 5.71 form a set of $L_x + L_y + 1$ equations in the same total number of unknowns. (C is one of the unknowns.) Thus, the values of the input probabilities $P(x_1)$, $P(x_2)$, ..., $P(x_{L_x})$ can be evaluated by solving this set of equations, if a solution exists.

If none of the input probabilities so obtained is negative, the corresponding value of I(X; Y) is equal to the channel capacity. If, on the contrary, one of them is negative, the solution is not acceptable because the corresponding point lies outside the region specified by Eq. 5.58. In this case, the largest acceptable value of I(X; Y) occurs on the boundary of such a region that is, on the intersection of the hyperplane defined by Eq. 5.57 with one of the hyperplanes $P(x_k) = 0$. This implies that one of the symbols of the input alphabet must be eliminated by setting its probability equal to zero. There is no simple way of determining which symbol should be eliminated; it is not necessarily the one whose probability turns out to be negative. Thus, we must eliminate one symbol at a time, and evaluate for each of them the maximum value of I(X; Y) according to the above procedure. The largest acceptable value so obtained is the channel capacity. If none of these values is acceptable - that is, if for none of them Eq. 5.58 is satisfied - an additional symbol must be eliminated by setting its probability equal to zero. The maximization procedure is then repeated with each possible pair of symbols eliminated, and the largest acceptable maximum is selected. If no acceptable solution is obtained, additional symbols are eliminated in succession until an acceptable maximum is obtained.

The simultaneous solution of Eqs. 5.69, 5.70 and 5.71 is, in general, very laborious because the set of equations as a whole is transcendental. However, it reduces to the solution of two separate sets of linear equations when the number of input symbols is equal to the number of output symbols, and the determinant $|\mathscr{P}|$ of the channel matrix $\mathscr{P}$ defined by Eq. 5.17 is different from zero.

Let

$$L = L_x = L_y \tag{5.72}$$

be the number of symbols in each of the two alphabets, and $\mathscr{Q}$ be the inverse of $\mathscr{P}$

$$\mathscr{Q} \equiv \mathscr{P}^{-1} \tag{5.73}$$

The elements of $\mathscr{Q}$ are given by

$$q_{jk} \equiv \frac{P_{kj}}{|\mathscr{P}|} \tag{5.74}$$

where P_{kj} is the cofactor of the element $P(y_j|x_k)$ of $\mathscr{P}$. Then, Eq. 5.69 yields

$$C + \log P(y_j) = - \sum_{i=1}^{L} q_{ji} H(Y|x_i) \tag{5.75}$$

from which we obtain, with C and $H(Y|x_i)$ expressed in bits,

$$\sum_{j=1}^{L} P(y_j)\ 2^C = 2^C = \sum_{j=1}^{L} 2^{-\sum_{i=1}^{L} q_{ji} H(Y|x_i)} \tag{5.76}$$

$$C = \log \sum_{j=1}^{L} 2^{-\sum_{i=1}^{L} q_{ji} H(Y|x_i)} \tag{5.77}$$

Then, Eq. 5.70 yields

$$P(x_k) = \sum_{j=1}^{L} q_{kj} P(y_j) = 2^{-C} \sum_{j=1}^{L} q_{kj}\ 2^{-\sum_{i=1}^{L} q_{ji} H(Y|x_i)} \tag{5.78}$$

which is the desired expression for $P(x_k)$ in terms of the elements of the channel matrix .

Theorem. If $L_x > L_y$, the average mutual information $I(X; Y)$ can be made equal to its maximum value C with $L_x - L_y$ of the input-symbol probabilities equal to zero.

Proof. Let us assume that there exists a solution of Eqs. 5.69, 5.70 and 5.71 for which all the $P(x_k)$ are positive. The values of $P(y_j)$ and the value of C that are parts of this solution satisfy Eqs. 5.69 and 5.71. On the other hand, Eq. 5.70 constitutes a set of L_y linear equations in the L_x unknowns $P(x_k)$ when the values of the $P(y_j)$ are specified. Since the number of unknowns is larger than the number of equations, the set of equations has an infinite number of solutions. Then, starting from the assumed solution, we can decrease the value of the probability of any particular symbol x_k until either this probability or the probability of some other symbol x_i becomes equal to zero. This procedure can be repeated in succession, each time holding equal to zero the probabilities that have been previously made to vanish, until $L_x - L_y$ of the input probabilities are equal to zero. At this point the number of $P(x_k)$ that are different from zero is equal to the number of equations, and therefore the solution of the set of equations is unique (unless the rank of the channel matrix $\mathcal{P}$ is smaller than L_y, in which case additional input symbols can be eliminated.) We can conclude, therefore, that there exists a set of L_y input symbols for which the average mutual information can be made equal to the channel capacity when the remaining $L_x - L_y$ input symbols are eliminated by setting their probabilities equal to zero. The particular set of input symbols that can be eliminated must be determined by trying all possible combinations of $L_x - L_y$ symbols and selecting the combination for which the maximum value of $I(X; Y)$ is largest.

QED

5.6. Time-Discrete, Continuous, Constant Channels with Additive Noise

A channel is said to be continuous when the input events and the output events are represented by points of continuous, Euclidean spaces. Since the dimensionality of these spaces is of secondary importance, we shall limit our discussion, for the sake of simplicity, to one-dimensional spaces. Thus, the input space and the output space will be regarded as consisting of the points of two separate straight lines X and Y. We shall label particular points of these two spaces by their algebraic distances x and y from arbitrarily selected origins.

A continuous channel may be either time discrete or time continuous, depending on whether the points representing the input and output events can change their positions only at specified time instants, or are permitted to move continuously with time. Thus, for instance, if the input and output events are rectangular voltage pulses of fixed duration and arbitrary amplitude, the channel is time discrete; the channel would be time continuous if the input and output voltages were permitted to be arbitrary time functions. We shall be concerned in this section with time-discrete channels.

By analogy with discrete channels, a continuous channel with time-discrete events is said to be constant if the conditional probability distribution over the output space for any given point of the input space is the same for all successive pairs of input and output events. We shall assume in what follows that this conditional probability distribution is representable by a density $p(y|x)$.

A continuous channel is said to be disturbed by additive noise if $p(y|x)$ depends on y and x only through their difference; that is, if

$$p(y|x) = q(z) \tag{5.79}$$

where

$$z \equiv y - x \tag{5.80}$$

Noise additivity is a property of continuous channels analogous to the property of uniformity from the input discussed in Sec. 5.3.

In particular, the conditional entropy $H(Y|x)$ of the output space for each point of the input space becomes, for a continuous channel with additive noise,

$$H(Y|x) \equiv -\int_{-\infty}^{\infty} p(y|x) \log p(y|x)\, dy = -\int_{-\infty}^{\infty} q(z) \log q(z)\, dz \tag{5.81}$$

and, therefore, it is independent of x, just as for discrete channels that are uniform from the input. It follows from Eq. 5.81 that the conditional entropy $H(Y|X)$ of a continuous channel with additive noise is independent of the input probability density $p(x)$, and is given by

$$H(Y|X) \equiv \int_{-\infty}^{\infty} H(Y|x)\, p(x)\, dx = -\int_{-\infty}^{\infty} q(z) \log q(z)\, dz \tag{5.82}$$

The definition of the information transmission capacity of a time-discrete, continuous, constant channel is similar to that of a discrete, constant channel. Let $p(\xi^n)$ be the joint probability density of a sequence ξ^n of n input events, and $I(X^n; Y^n)$ be the average mutual information between the sequence of input events and the corresponding sequence of output events. The information transmission capacity per event C is defined as the maximum value of $I(X^n; Y^n)/n$ evaluated over all possible input probability distributions, and all positive integers n,

$$C \equiv \underset{p(\xi^n),\, n}{\mathrm{Max}} \frac{I(X^n; Y^n)}{n} \tag{5.83}$$

The following two theorems, analogous to those stated in Sec. 5.2 for discrete, constant channels, show that this maximum value is obtained, independently of n, when the input events are statistically independent and have the same probability distribution. The proofs of these theorems are omitted because they are very similar to those given in Sec. 5.2.

Theorem. Let $p(\xi^n)$ be the joint probability density of n input events, and $p(\xi_1), p(\xi_2), \ldots, p(\xi_i), \ldots, p(\xi_n)$ be the probability densities of the individual events. Indicate with $I(X^n; Y^n)$ the average mutual information between the n input events and the corresponding output events, and with $I(X_i; Y_i)$ the average mutual information between the ith input event and the corresponding output event. Then, for any time-discrete, continuous, constant channel,

$$I(X^n; Y^n) \leq \sum_{i=1}^{n} I(X_i; Y_i) \tag{5.84}$$

where the equal sign holds when and only when either the input events are statistically independent of one another, or each y_i is statistically independent of the corresponding x_i, in which case $I(\mathbf{X}_i; Y_i) = 0$.

Theorem. Let $p(y|x)$ be the conditional probability density of a time-discrete, continuous, constant channel, and $p(x)$ be an arbitrary probability density over the channel input space. The information transmission capacity of the channel is the maximum average value of the mutual information

$$I(X; Y) \equiv \int_{-\infty}^{\infty} \int_{-\infty}^{\infty} p(x)\, p(y|x) \log \frac{p(y|x)}{p(y)}\, dx\, dy \tag{5.85}$$

evaluated over all possible probability densities $p(x)$; that is,

$$C = \underset{p(x)}{\text{Max}} \quad I(X; Y) \tag{5.86}$$

It is convenient, in evaluating the channel capacity, to express $I(X; Y)$ in the form

$$I(X; Y) \equiv H(Y) - H(Y|X) \tag{5.87}$$

where

$$H(Y) \equiv - \int_{-\infty}^{\infty} p(y) \log p(y)\, dy \tag{5.88}$$

$$H(Y|X) \equiv - \int_{-\infty}^{\infty} \int_{-\infty}^{\infty} p(x)\, p(y|x) \log p(y|x)\, dx\, dy \tag{5.89}$$

For a channel with additive noise, $H(Y|X)$ depends only on $p(y|x)$ and is given by Eq. 5.82. Thus, in this special case, $I(X; Y)$ can be maximized by maximizing $H(Y)$.

It is immediately clear that $H(Y)$ can be made infinitely large unless some constraint is placed on the probability density $p(y)$, either directly or indirectly. Among the many constraints that could be imposed, an upper limit on the mean-square value of x is both mathematically manageable and of great practical significance. In fact, if x represents the amplitude of a voltage pulse, its mean-square value

$$\overline{x^2} \equiv \int_{-\infty}^{\infty} x^2\, p(x)\, dx \tag{5.90}$$

is proportional to the average power associated with the pulse.

Another interesting constraint would be a limitation on the magnitude of x, which would correspond to setting an upper limit to the power of each pulse [2].

We shall assume in what follows, without loss of generality, that the mean value of the additive noise is equal to zero; that is,

$$\bar{z} \equiv \int_{-\infty}^{\infty} z\, q(z)\, dz = 0 \tag{5.91}$$

Then, the mean-square value of y

$$\overline{y^2} \equiv \int_{-\infty}^{\infty} y^2\, p(y)\, dy \tag{5.92}$$

is related to that of x by

$$\overline{y^2} = \int_{-\infty}^{\infty} \int_{-\infty}^{\infty} (x^2 + z^2 + 2xz)\, p(x)\, q(z)\, dx\, dz = \overline{x^2} + N \tag{5.93}$$

where, in view of Eq. 5.91,

$$N \equiv \int_{-\infty}^{\infty} (z - \bar{z})^2\, q(z)\, dz = \int_{-\infty}^{\infty} z^2\, q(z)\, dz \tag{5.94}$$

is the variance of the additive noise. The statistical independence of x and z, required for the validity of Eq. 5.93, follows from the definition of additive noise given by Eqs. 5.79 and 5.80. Thus, setting an upper limit to the mean-square value of x is equivalent to setting an upper limit to the mean-square value of y.

<u>Theorem</u>. Let H(Y) be the entropy of a random variable y with mean-square value $\overline{y^2}$. Then,

$$H(Y) \leq \tfrac{1}{2} \log (2\pi e\, \overline{y^2}) \tag{5.95}$$

where the equal sign holds when and only when p(y) is a gaussian probability density with zero mean and variance equal to $\overline{y^2}$.

<u>Proof.</u> The righthand side of Eq. 5.95 can be evaluated by maximizing H(Y) with respect to the probability density p(y), under the constraint

$$\int_{-\infty}^{\infty} p(y)\, dy = 1 \tag{5.96}$$

and the constraint imposed by Eq. 5.92, according to the calculus of variations [1]. However, a more elegant proof of the theorem can be obtained as follows.

We have for any probability density p(y)

$$\int_{-\infty}^{\infty} p(y) \ln \frac{e^{-y^2/2\overline{y^2}}}{\sqrt{2\pi \overline{y^2}}} dy = -\tfrac{1}{2}\left[1 + \ln (2\pi \overline{y^2})\right] = -\tfrac{1}{2}\ln(2\pi e\, \overline{y^2}) \tag{5.97}$$

Thus,

$$H(Y) - \tfrac{1}{2}\ln(2\pi e\, \overline{y^2}) = \int_{-\infty}^{\infty} p(y) \ln \frac{e^{-y^2/2\overline{y^2}}}{p(y)\sqrt{2\pi \overline{y^2}}} dy \tag{5.98}$$

On the other hand, we have from Eq. 2.91,

$$\ln \frac{e^{-y^2/2\overline{y^2}}}{p(y)\sqrt{2\pi \overline{y^2}}} \le \frac{e^{-y^2/2\overline{y^2}}}{p(y)\sqrt{2\pi \overline{y^2}}} - 1 \tag{5.99}$$

Substitution of this inequality in Eq. 5.98 yields

$$H(Y) - \tfrac{1}{2}\ln(2\pi e\, \overline{y^2}) \le \int_{-\infty}^{\infty} \frac{e^{-y^2/2\overline{y^2}}}{\sqrt{2\pi \overline{y^2}}} dy - \int_{-\infty}^{\infty} p(y)\, dy = 0 \tag{5.100}$$

which proves Eq. 5.95. The equal sign holds in Eq. 5.99 and, therefore, in Eq. 5.100 when and only when the argument of the natural logarithm is equal to 1, that is, when p(y) is a gaussian probability density with zero mean and variance equal to $\overline{y^2}$.

QED

The righthand side of Eq. 5.95 is the maximum value of H(Y) for any specified value of $\overline{y^2}$ when no other restriction is placed on the probability density p(y). However, if y is the output of a channel with a specified noise probability density q(z), there may or may not exist an input probability density p(x) for which

$$p(y) = \int_{-\infty}^{\infty} p(x)\, q(y-x)\, dx\, ; \quad p(x) \ge 0 \tag{5.101}$$

is a gaussian probability density. In the special but very important case in which q(z) is a gaussian probability density, the desired p(x) exists and we have the following theorem.

Theorem. If the additive noise in a time-discrete, continuous, constant channel is gaussianly distributed with zero mean and variance equal to N, and the mean-square value of the input is not allowed to exceed a specified value S, the channel capacity per event is given by

$$C_g = \tfrac{1}{2}\log\left(1 + \frac{S}{N}\right) \tag{5.102}$$

The average mutual information is equal to C_g when and only when the input probability density is gaussian with zero mean and variance equal to S.

Proof. It follows from Eqs. 5.82, 5.87, 5.88, and 5.93 and from the theorem incorporating Eq. 5.95 that the mutual information between input and output events satisfies the inequality

$$I(X;Y) \leq \tfrac{1}{2}\log(2\pi e\,\overline{y^2}) - \tfrac{1}{2}\log(2\pi e\,N) = \tfrac{1}{2}\log\frac{\overline{y^2}}{N}$$

$$\leq \tfrac{1}{2}\log\frac{N+S}{N} \tag{5.103}$$

where the equal sign holds when and only when the output probability density is gaussian with zero mean. On the other hand, y is the sum of two random variables x and z, the latter of which is gaussianly distributed with zero mean. It follows that y is gaussianly distributed with zero mean if and only if x is gaussianly distributed with zero mean.

QED

If the noise is not gaussianly distributed, there does not exist, in general, a probability density p(x) for which p(y) is gaussian, and the evaluation of the maximum value of H(Y) under the constraint imposed by Eq. 5.101 becomes considerably more difficult. However, the maximum value of H(Y) can be bounded as follows. Let, for any one-dimensional ensemble Y,

$$\bar{\sigma}_Y^2 \equiv \frac{1}{2\pi e}\,2^{2H(Y)} \tag{5.104}$$

where H(Y) is expressed in bits, so that

$$H(Y) = \tfrac{1}{2}\log(2\pi e\,\bar{\sigma}_Y^2) \tag{5.105}$$

and define in a similar manner the quantities $\bar{\sigma}_X^2$ and $\bar{\sigma}_Z^2$ in terms of H(X) and H(Z). The quantity $\bar{\sigma}_Y^2$ has been called by Shannon the entropy power of Y because it is equal to the variance of a gaussianly distributed random variable with the same entropy H(Y). It follows from the theorem embodying Eq. 5.95 that the variance σ_Y^2 of y satisfies the inequality

$$\sigma_Y^2 \geq \bar{\sigma}_Y^2 \tag{5.106}$$

Theorem. If y is the sum of two statistically independent random variables x and z with variances σ^2_X and σ^2_Z, and entropy powers $\bar{\sigma}^2_X$ and $\bar{\sigma}^2_Z$, the entropy power $\bar{\sigma}^2_Y$ of y satisfies

$$\bar{\sigma}^2_X + \bar{\sigma}^2_Z \leq \bar{\sigma}^2_Y \leq \sigma^2_X + \sigma^2_Z \tag{5.107}$$

The equal signs hold when and only when x and z are gaussianly distributed.

Proof. The upper bound to $\bar{\sigma}^2_Y$ follows immediately from the theorem embodying Eq. 5.95 in conjunction with Eq. 5.93. The lower bound can be obtained by minimizing H(Y) while holding H(X) and H(Z) fixed. This minimization is rather lengthy, and for this reason it is not reproduced here [2].

Theorem. Consider a time-discrete, continuous, constant channel disturbed by additive noise with zero mean, variance N, and entropy power $\bar{\sigma}^2_N$. If the mean-square value of the input is not allowed to exceed a specified value S, the channel capacity per event C satisfies

$$\tfrac{1}{2}\log\left(1 + \frac{S}{\bar{\sigma}^2_N}\right) \leq C \leq \tfrac{1}{2}\log\frac{N+S}{\bar{\sigma}^2_N} \tag{5.108}$$

where the equal signs hold when and only when the noise is gaussianly distributed, in which case $\bar{\sigma}^2_N = N$.

Proof. The upper bound is obtained by setting H(Y) equal to the righthand side of Eq. 5.95, with $\overline{y^2} = S + N$, which is the maximum value that H(Y) can assume when the constraint imposed by Eq. 5.101 is disregarded. The conditional entropy H(Y|X) is given, in terms of the entropy power of the noise, by

$$H(Y|X) = H(Z) = \tfrac{1}{2}\log(2\pi e\,\bar{\sigma}^2_N) \tag{5.109}$$

The lower bound is obtained by letting p(x) be a gaussian probability density with zero mean and variance equal to S, in which case we have from Eq. 5.107,

$$\bar{\sigma}^2_Y \geq S + \bar{\sigma}^2_N \tag{5.110}$$

Then, with the help of Eq. 5.105, we obtain for the average mutual information

$$I(X;Y) = H(Y) - H(Y|X) \geq \tfrac{1}{2}\log\left(1 + \frac{S}{\bar{\sigma}^2_N}\right) \tag{5.111}$$

QED

The theorem embodying Eq. 5.95 states that the entropy of a random variable with specified mean-square value is largest when the random variable is gaussianly distributed with zero mean. This suggests that the disturbance resulting from an additive noise with zero mean and specified variance should be most severe when the noise is gaussianly distributed. This intuitive notion is stated precisely by the following theorem.

Theorem. Let C be the capacity of a time-discrete, continuous, constant channel disturbed by additive noise with zero mean and variance N, when the mean-square value of the input is not permitted to exceed a specified value S. Let C_g be the capacity of a second channel, identical to the first except for the fact that the noise is gaussianly distributed with zero mean and the same variance N. Then

$$C \geq C_g \tag{5.112}$$

Proof. The capacity of the channel with gaussian noise is given by Eq. 5.102, and the capacity of the channel with arbitrary noise satisfies Eq. 5.108. On the other hand, the entropy power of a random variable cannot exceed the variance of the variable, as stated by Eq. 5.106. It follows that

$$C \geq \frac{1}{2} \log \left(1 + \frac{S}{\overline{\sigma}_N^2}\right) \geq \frac{1}{2} \log \left(1 + \frac{S}{N}\right) = C_g \tag{5.113}$$

QED

5.7. Band-Limited Time Functions

We have discussed up to this point only time-discrete channels, that is, channels in which the input events and the output events occur in discrete time sequences. On the other hand, many channels of practical interest are time continuous in the sense that the point representing the input event and that representing the output event can move continuously with time in their respective spaces. We referred in the preceding section to such channels as time continuous.

While the inputs and outputs of time-continuous channels are continuous (as contrasted with discrete) time functions, they are usually subject to restrictions that make them representable over any finite time interval by a discrete and finite set of variables. For instance, the spectrum of the input voltage of an electrical communication channel is always limited to a finite frequency band, either to avoid interference with other channels, or because the signal energy outside such a band would be greatly attenuated. We shall see below that the family of time functions limited to a frequency band of width W cps, and to a time interval of length T seconds can be represented by $2TW$ independent variables, if such limitations are properly interpreted mathematically. This will reduce the analysis of time-continuous channels to that of time-discrete channels.

Let $u(t)$ be a function of time defined over the time interval $-T/2 < t < T/2$, and $\phi_k(t)$, $k = \ldots, -2, -1, 0, 1, 2, \ldots$, be a complete set of orthonormal functions over the same time interval; that is,

$$\frac{1}{T}\int_{-T/2}^{T/2} \phi_k(t)\ \phi_j(t)\ dt = \begin{cases} 1; & j = k \\ 0; & j \neq k \end{cases} \tag{5.114}$$

Then, under fairly general conditions, we can write, over the interval $-T/2 < t < T/2$,

$$u(t) = \sum_{k=-\infty}^{\infty} x_k\ \phi_k(t) \tag{5.115}$$

where the coefficients x_k are given by

$$x_k = \frac{1}{T}\int_{-T/2}^{T/2} u(t)\ \phi_k(t)\ dt \tag{5.116}$$

The integral

$$S \equiv \frac{1}{T}\int_{-T/2}^{T/2} u^2(t)\ dt = \sum_{k=-\infty}^{\infty} x_k^2 \tag{5.117}$$

is the time average of $u^2(t)$. If $u(t)$ represents a time-varying voltage or current, ST is proportional to the energy that such a voltage or current would dissipate in a resistance during the time interval T. For this reason, we shall refer to S as the average power of $u(t)$.

Let us select as orthonormal functions the sinusoidal functions

$$\phi_k(t) = \cos kqt + \sin kqt \tag{5.118}$$

where k is an integer and

$$q = \frac{2\pi}{T} \tag{5.119}$$

is the angular frequency corresponding to the period T. Then, the righthand side of Eq. 5.115 becomes a Fourier series. (The use of sums of sines and cosines as orthonormal functions, rather than sines and cosines or complex exponentials simplifies notations without introducing complex time functions.) The coefficient x_o represents the average value of u(t),

$$x_o = \frac{1}{T} \int_{-T/2}^{T/2} u(t)\, dt \tag{5.120}$$

and the coefficient x_k is given by

$$x_k = \frac{1}{T} \int_{-T/2}^{T/2} u(t)\,(\cos kqt + \sin kqt)\, dt \tag{5.121}$$

The sum of the two terms corresponding to the same value of $|k|$, namely,

$$x_{|k|}[\cos |k|qt + \sin |k|qt] + x_{-|k|}\,[\cos |k|qt - \sin |k|qt] =$$

$$[x_{|k|} + x_{-|k|}]\cos |k|qt + [x_{|k|} - x_{-|k|}]\sin |k|qt \tag{5.122}$$

is the sinusoidal component of u(t) of frequency $|k|q$. The amplitude of this component is equal to

$$\sqrt{(x_{|k|} + x_{-|k|})^2 + (x_{|k|} - x_{-|k|})^2} = \sqrt{2}\,\sqrt{(x_{|k|}{}^2 + x_{-|k|}{}^2)} \tag{5.123}$$

and its contribution to S, the average power of u(t), is therefore equal to $x_{|k|}{}^2 + x_{-|k|}{}^2$.

Let us turn our attention next to the frequency spectrum of u(t) In order for the frequency spectrum to be specified, u(t) must be defined outside the interval $-T/2 < t < T/2$ as well as inside. It is convenient for our purposes to set u(t) equal to zero outside the interval. Then, a function of time extending over a longer time span can be regarded as the sum of different functions u(t) defined for successive intervals of length T; the same additivity property holds for the Fourier transforms of the same time functions.

The frequency spectrum of u(t) is given by the Fourier transform

$$g(\omega) \equiv \int_{-\infty}^{\infty} u(t)\, e^{-j\omega t}\, dt = \int_{-T/2}^{T/2} u(t)\, e^{-j\omega t}\, dt \tag{5.124}$$

where ω is the angular frequency. Conversely, u(t) is the inverse Fourier transform of $g(\omega)$,

$$u(t) = \frac{1}{2\pi} \int_{-\infty}^{\infty} g(\omega)\, e^{j\omega t}\, d\omega \tag{5.125}$$

Substituting in Eq. 5.124 the Fourier series expression for $u(t)$ yields, after interchanging the operations of summation and integration,

$$g(\omega) = \sum_{k=-\infty}^{\infty} x_k \int_{-T/2}^{T/2} (\cos kq\,t + \sin kq\,t)\, e^{-j\omega t}\, dt \qquad (5.126)$$

and with the help of Eq. 5.122

$$g(\omega) = x_o T \frac{\sin \frac{1}{2}\omega T}{\frac{1}{2}\omega T} + \sum_{|k|=1}^{\infty} \frac{1}{2} T \left\{ [(x_{|k|} + x_{-|k|}) - j(x_{|k|} - x_{-|k|})] \frac{\sin \frac{1}{2}(\omega - |k|q)T}{\frac{1}{2}(\omega - |k|q)T} \right.$$

$$\left. + [(x_{|k|} + x_{-|k|}) + j(x_{|k|} - x_{-|k|})] \frac{\sin \frac{1}{2}(\omega + |k|q)T}{\frac{1}{2}(\omega + |k|q)T} \right\} \qquad (5.127)$$

The first term on the righthand side of Eq. 5.127 is the spectrum of a rectangular pulse of amplitude x_o and width T. Each term in the summation that follows it is the spectrum of a sinusoidal pulse of frequency $|k|q$, with a rectangular envelope of amplitude $\sqrt{2}\,\sqrt{x_{|k|}^2 + x_{-|k|}^2}$ and width T. In other words, the terms of the summation are the spectra of the sinusoidal components of $u(t)$ given by Eq. 5.122, which, of course, vanish outside the interval $-T/2 < t < T/2$. The spectrum of the rectangular pulse of amplitude x_o is centered at $\omega = 0$. The spectrum of each sinusoidal pulse of frequency $|k|q$ consists of two components of similar shape centered at $\omega = |k|q$ and $\omega = -|k|q$, as illustrated in Fig. 5.4. Each of these spectral components is approximately contained within the frequency band of width

$$\Delta\omega \equiv \frac{2\pi}{T} = q \qquad (5.128)$$

between the frequencies at which the spectral magnitude is equal to $2/\pi$ of its peak value. More precisely, 78% of the energy of each component is within such a band.

Let us consider a time function $u(t)$ for which the coefficients x_k differ from zero only for $m_1 \leq |k| < m_2$, where m_1 and m_2 are two non-negative integers. Then the spectrum of $u(t)$ may be regarded as contained within the frequency band $(m_1 - \frac{1}{2})\,q < |\omega| < (m_2 - \frac{1}{2})\,q$, whose width is in cps,

$$W = \begin{cases} (m_2 - m_1)\dfrac{q}{2\pi} = \dfrac{1}{T}(m_2 - m_1)\ ; & m_1 \neq 0 \\[2ex] (m_2 - \frac{1}{2})\dfrac{q}{2\pi} = \dfrac{1}{T}(m_2 - \frac{1}{2})\ ; & m_1 = 0 \end{cases} \qquad (5.129)$$

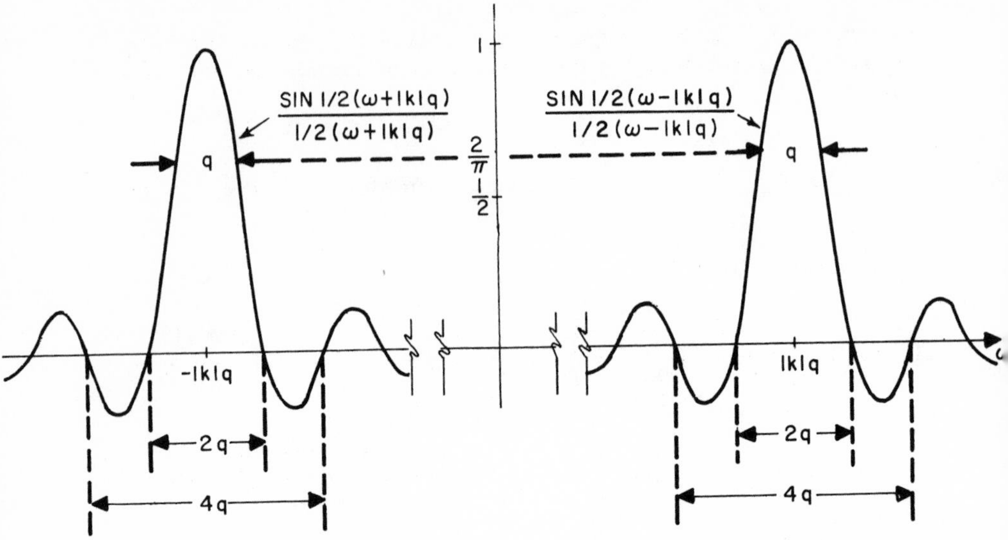

Fig. 5.4. Shape of the spectral components of a sinusoidal pulse of frequency $|k|$ q and width $T = 2\pi/q$

A time function with this property is said to be "band limited," and, by definition, it is completely specified by the

$$2TW = \begin{cases} 2(m_2 - m_1) ; & m_1 \neq 0 \\ 2(m_2 - \frac{1}{2}) ; & m_1 = 0 \end{cases} \tag{5.130}$$

Fourier coefficients x_k with $m_1 \leq |k| < m_2$. In other words, a time function that is band limited in the above sense has two degrees of freedom per unit bandwidth and per unit time.

According to the above definition, the spectrum of a band-limited time function is restricted to a finite frequency band only in an approximate sense. It is well known, in fact, that a time function cannot be strictly limited in time and frequency spectrum simultaneously. On the other hand, it is clear from Eq. 5.128 and Fig. 5.4 that the sharpness of each spectral component, and, therefore, of the band limitation, increases with increasing T . In the limit of T approaching infinity, the spectrum of a band-limited time function completely vanishes outside the frequency band of width W given by Eq. 5.129.

The definition and representation of time-limited and band-limited time functions may be approached also from a different point of view. The spectrum of a function of time $f(t)$ extending in time from $-\infty$ to ∞ may be strictly limited to a finite frequency band. It can be shown, as indicated below, that if the spectrum vanishes outside the band $0 < |\omega| < 2\pi W$, $f(t)$ can be expressed in the form

$$f(t) = \sum_{k=-\infty}^{\infty} f_k \frac{\sin 2\pi W(t - t_k)}{2\pi W(t - t_k)} \tag{5.131}$$

where k is an integer, and

$$t_k = \frac{k}{2W} \tag{5.132}$$

Since

$$\frac{\sin 2\pi W(t_i - t_k)}{2\pi W(t_i - t_k)} = \begin{cases} 1 \ ; & i = k \\ 0 \ ; & i \neq k \end{cases} \tag{5.132}$$

the coefficients f_k are given by

$$f_k = f(t_k) \tag{5.133}$$

that is, they are equal to the values assumed by $f(t)$ at times t_k spaced $1/2W$ seconds apart. Thus, $2W$ uniformly spaced samples per second are sufficient to specify uniquely a time function with a spectrum limited to the band $0 < |\omega| < 2\pi W$. It can be readily checked that the time functions on the righthand side of Eq. 5.131 form an orthonormal set over the infinite time interval, and that their spectra vanish outside the stated frequency band.

The terms of the summation in Eq. 5.131 may be regarded as pulses of identical shape and different amplitudes occurring in succession every $1/2W$ seconds. Each of these pulses extends in time from $-\infty$ to ∞, but is mostly contained within a time interval of width equal to $1/2W$ as shown in Fig. 5.5. More precisely, 78% of the pulse energy is contained in this interval. Thus, if the coefficients f_k differ from zero only for $n_1 \leq |k| < n_2$, where n_1 and n_2 are two positive integers, $f(t)$ is mostly contained within a time interval of length

$$T = (n_2 - n_1) \frac{1}{2W} \tag{5.134}$$

Such a strictly band-limited function is approximately time limited, in the same sense that a strictly time-limited function may be approximately band limited, as discussed above. A comparison of Eqs. 5.127 and 5.131 indicates that the character of the approximation is the same in the two cases.

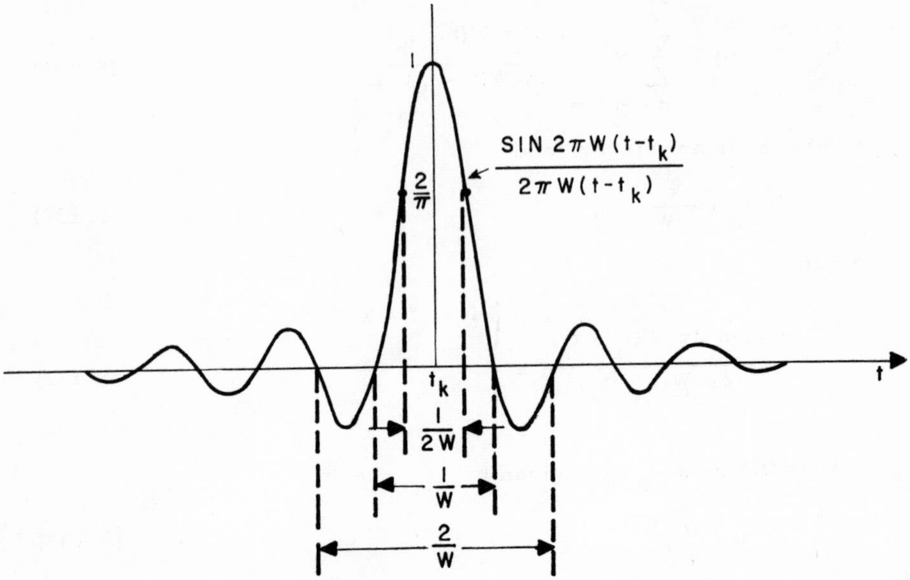

Fig. 5.5. Pulse used in constructing a time function with a spectrum restricted to the band $0 < |\omega| < 2\pi W$

The expansion of a strictly band-limited time function given by Eq. 5.131 can be generalized to the case of an arbitrary frequency band of width W cps, centered at some angular frequency ω_o, that is, to the case of a time function whose spectrum differs from zero only for $\omega_o - \pi W < |\omega| < \omega_o + \pi W$. It can be shown, as indicated below, that under these conditions f(t) can be expressed as

$$f(t) = f_s(t) \sin \omega_o t + f_c(t) \cos \omega_o t \tag{5.135}$$

where $f_s(t)$ and $f_c(t)$ are time functions whose spectra differ from zero only for $|\omega| < \pi W$, and therefore can be expanded, according to Eq. 5.131, into the series

$$f_s(t) = \sum_{k=-\infty}^{\infty} f_{sk} \frac{\sin \pi W (t - t_k)}{\pi W(t - t_k)} \tag{5.136}$$

$$f_c(t) = \sum_{k=-\infty}^{\infty} f_{ck} \frac{\sin \pi W (t - t_k)}{\pi W (t - t_k)} \tag{5.137}$$

The coefficients f_{sk} and f_{ck} are equal to the values assumed respectively by $f_s(t)$ and $f_c(t)$ for $t = k/W$. Thus we have again two coefficients per unit bandwidth (in cps) and per unit time. In communication terminology, the two terms on the righthand side of Eq. 5.135 result from suppressed-carrier modulation of the quadrature carriers $\sin \omega_o t$ and $\cos \omega_o t$ with the modulating signals $f_s(t)$ and $f_c(t)$, respectively. According to a well-known property of Fourier transforms, the spectrum $g(\omega)$ of $f(t)$ is related to the spectra $g_s(\omega)$ and $g_c(\omega)$ of $f_s(t)$ and $f_c(t)$ by

$$g(\omega) = \tfrac{1}{2}[g_c(\omega - \omega_o) + j\, g_s(\omega - \omega_o)] + \tfrac{1}{2}[g_c(\omega + \omega_o) - j\, g_s(\omega + \omega_o)] \qquad (5.138)$$

Thus, if $g_s(\omega)$ and $g_c(\omega)$ differ from zero only for $|\omega| < \pi W$, $g(\omega)$ may differ from zero only for $\omega_o - \pi W < |\omega| < \omega_o + \pi W$.

These results concerning strictly band-limited time functions are known as the sampling theorem. The derivation of Eq. 5.131 is similar to the derivation of Eq. 5.127. Since the spectrum $g(\omega)$ vanishes, by assumption, outside the interval $-2\pi W < \omega < 2\pi W$, it can be expressed as a Fourier series of period $4\pi W$ in the ω-domain (rather than in the time domain). The inverse Fourier transforms of the resulting sinusoidal components of the spectrum (linear combination of $\sin k\omega/2W$ and $\cos k\omega/2W$ for each integer k) are the terms of the summation on the righthand side of Eq. 5.131. The derivation of Eq. 5.135 is identical, except for the fact that two separate Fourier series are required to represent $g(\omega)$.

The main results obtained in this section can be summarized as follows.

> Theorem. A time function that is either strictly time limited and approximately band limited, or strictly band limited and approximately time limited, can be represented in terms of two independent variables per unit time and per unit bandwidth (in cps). The independent variables may be chosen to be, in the first case, the coefficients in the Fourier series representation of the time function, and, in the second case, the values assumed at uniformly spaced time instants by the time function $f(t)$ or by its two quadrature-modulating components $f_s(t)$ and $f_c(t)$.

The two alternate representations of time-limited and band-limited time functions have complementary advantages and disadvantages. The representation based on a strict band limitation has considerable intuitive appeal because it allows us to regard a time function as a discrete sequence of uniformly spaced pulses. On the other hand, the pulses are time limited only in an approximate sense, and, strictly speaking, extend in time from $-\infty$ to ∞.

The representation based on a strict time limitation is more consistent with physical reality because communication signals are often strictly time limited and only approximately band limited. On the other hand, the picture of a time function as a superposition of sinusoidal pulses with rectangular envelopes is not as convenient because the corresponding independent variables, namely, the amplitudes of the sinusoidal pulses, cannot be arranged in a time sequence. We shall see, however, that the latter representation is more generally useful because of its more direct relation to the spectral characteristics of time functions.

Since a time function that is limited, at least approximately, to a time interval T and a bandwidth W can be specified in terms of 2TW independent variables, it can also be represented as a point in a Euclidean space with 2TW dimensions. Let us indicate with u(t) the time function and with $x_1, x_2, \ldots, x_k, \ldots, x_{2TW}$ the independent variables. It is convenient to normalize the variables in such a way that the average power of the time function be expressible in the form

$$S \equiv \frac{1}{T} \int_{-T/2}^{T/2} u^2(t)\, dt = \sum_{k=1}^{2TW} x_k^2 \tag{5.139}$$

In the case of the representation given by Eq. 5.115 the orthonormal functions are normalized in such a way that the coefficients in the expansion already satisfy this requirement. In the case of the representation given by Eq. 5.131, the coefficients f_k must be divided by $\sqrt{2TW}$, because the energy of each term of the summation is equal to $1/2W\ f_k^2$. Similarly, the coefficients f_{sk} and f_{ck} in the expansion given by Eq. 5.135 must be divided by $\sqrt{TW}$ because the individual terms of the two summations have energies equal to $1/W\ f_{sk}^2$ and $1/W\ f_{ck}^2$.

The independent variables $x_1, x_2, \ldots, x_{2TW}$ can be regarded as the Cartesian coordinates of the point representing u(t). Then, if we indicate with $\underline{u}$ the vector distance of the point from the origin, the average power of u(t) is given by

$$S = \sum_{k=1}^{2TW} x_k^2 = \underline{u} \cdot \underline{u} = |\underline{u}|^2 \tag{5.140}$$

In words, the average power of the time function is represented by the square of the distance from the origin of the corresponding point in the 2TW dimensional space. Similarly, the scalar product of two vectors $\underline{u}_1$ and $\underline{u}_2$ representing different time functions $u_1(t)$ and $u_2(t)$,

$$\underline{u}_1 \cdot \underline{u}_2 = \sum_{k=1}^{2TW} x_{1k} \cdot x_{2k} = \frac{1}{T} \int_{-T/2}^{T/2} u_1(t)\, u_2(t)\, dt \tag{5.141}$$

is equal to the cross-correlation coefficient of the two time functions. Vector representations of time functions will be used extensively in the rest of this chapter and in the following chapter.

5.8. Band-Limited Channel with Additive, White, Gaussian Noise

We shall evaluate in this section the capacity of a time-continuous, continuous channel disturbed by additive, white, gaussian noise, under the restriction that the input be a band-limited time function with average power not exceeding some given value S. Many physical channels of practical interest can be adequately represented by such a mathematical model.

An ensemble of time functions is said to be gaussian and stationary if the joint probability density of the values assumed by the time functions at any finite number of time instants is gaussian and independent of the time origin selected. The ensemble is further said to be white if the power density of its spectrum is independent of frequency. The thermal agitation noise present in all physical communication channels can be described mathematically as a gaussian ensemble of time functions, and, in many instances, it can be assumed to be white.

White, gaussian noise has a property of cardinal importance for our purposes. For the sake of emphasis, it is stated below as a theorem. This special property of white noise will be derived in the next section.

> Theorem. Let $n(t)$ be a member of a white, gaussian ensemble, and consider its representation, over the time interval $-T/2 < t < T/2$, by the series of orthonormal functions
>
> $$n(t) = \sum_{k=-\infty}^{\infty} z_k \phi_k(t) \tag{5.142}$$
>
> where the time functions $\phi_k(t)$ satisfy Eq. 5.114. Then, the coefficients z_k are statistically independent, and their individual probability densities are gaussian with zero mean and variance equal to $N_o/2T$, where N_oW is the average power in any frequency band of width W cps.

Let us consider a time-continuous channel for which the input events are described, over any time interval $-T/2 < t < T/2$, by time functions $u(t)$ with spectrum limited to some specified frequency band of width W. The corresponding output events are represented by time functions $v(t)$ related to $u(t)$ by

$$v(t) = u(t) + n(t) \tag{5.143}$$

where $n(t)$ is a member of a white, gaussian ensemble with average power in the specified band equal to $N_o W$. We shall refer to such a channel as a band-limited channel with white, additive, gaussian noise.

The three time functions $u(t)$, $v(t)$, and $n(t)$ can be expressed over the specified time interval as Fourier series. The coefficients x_k in the series for $u(t)$ are given by Eqs. 5.120 and 5.121, and the coefficients y_k and z_k in the series for $v(t)$ and $n(t)$, respectively, by similar expressions. It follows from Eq. 5.143 that these Fourier coefficients are related by

$$y_k = x_k + z_k \tag{5.144}$$

Now, the requirement that the spectrum of $u(t)$ be limited to a frequency band of width W implies, according to the discussion of band-limited time functions in the preceding section, that only $2TW$ of the coefficients x_k can differ from zero, namely, those corresponding to frequencies in the specified band. On the other hand, since the noise $n(t)$ is white as well as gaussian, the coefficients z_k are statistically independent with the result that only the $2TW$ coefficients y_k corresponding to coefficients x_k that can differ from zero provide information about the input time function. In other words, if we indicate with X^{2TW} the product ensemble of the $2TW$ coefficients x_k that can differ from zero, and with Y^{2TW} the product ensemble of the corresponding coefficients y_k, the average amount of information provided by $v(t)$ about $u(t)$ is $I(X^{2TW}; Y^{2TW})$.

Let $\underline{u}$, $\underline{v}$, and $\underline{n}$ be vectors in a $2TW$-dimensional space whose Cartesian components are the $2TW$ Fourier coefficients of $u(t)$, $v(t)$, and $n(t)$ corresponding to frequencies in the specified band. It is convenient in this connection to renumber the components x_k, y_k, and z_k of these three vectors from 1 to $2TW$, by substituting for k an integer i in the range $1 \leq i \leq 2TW$. We have from Eq. 5.144

$$\underline{v} = \underline{u} + \underline{n} \tag{5.145}$$

Then, if we indicate with $p(\underline{u})$ the probability density of $\underline{u}$ and with $q(\underline{n})$ the probability density of $\underline{n}$, we obtain for the conditional probability density $p(\underline{v} \mid \underline{u})$

$$p(\underline{v} \mid \underline{u}) = q(\underline{v} - \underline{u}) = q(\underline{n}) \tag{5.146}$$

and for the probability density of $\underline{v}$

$$p(\underline{v}) = \int_U p(\underline{u})\, q(\underline{v} - \underline{u})\, dU \tag{5.147}$$

where dU is a differential element of volume of the space U of the vector $\underline{u}$. The average mutual information between input and output time functions can now be written in the form

$$I(X^{2TW} ; Y^{2TW}) = I(U ; V) = H(V) - H(V|U) \qquad (5.148)$$

where

$$H(V) = -\int_V p(\underline{v}) \log p(\underline{v})\, dV \qquad (5.149)$$

$$H(V|U) = -\int_N q(\underline{n}) \log q(\underline{n})\, dN \qquad (5.150)$$

and V is the space of the vector $\underline{v}$, N is the space of the vector $\underline{n}$, and dV and dN are the corresponding differential elements of volume.

Theorem. If the input probability distribution is subject to the requirement that the ensemble average of the time average of $u^2(t)$ be at most equal to some value S , that is,

$$\int_U |\underline{u}|^2\, p(\underline{u})\, dU \leq S \qquad (5.151)$$

the capacity of a band-limited channel with additive, white, gaussian noise is

$$C = W \log\left(1 + \frac{S}{N_o W}\right) \text{ information units per second} \qquad (5.152)$$

where W is the width of the specified band in cps, and $N_o W$ is the average noise power in the band.

Proof. The capacity of the channel is defined as

$$C \equiv \max_{T,\ p(\underline{u})} \left[\frac{1}{T} I(U ; V)\right] \qquad (5.153)$$

that is, as the maximum value of the average mutual information per second, evaluated over all values of T , and all probability distributions $p(\underline{u})$ satisfying Eq. 5.151. This maximum value can be determined as follows.

The problem under consideration is very similar to that discussed in Sec. 5.6 in connection with time-discrete, constant channels with additive, gaussian noise. For any value of T , each of the vectors $\underline{u}$, $\underline{v}$, and $\underline{n}$ represents 2TW continuous variables x_i, y_i, and z_i, related by Eq. 5.144 with i substituted for k. The variables z_i are statistically independent and gaussianly distributed with zero mean and variance equal to $N_o/2T$. Thus, we obtain from the theorem incorporating Eq. 5.84.

$$I(U\,;\,V) \le \sum_{i=1}^{2TW} I(X_i\,;\,Y_i) \tag{5.154}$$

where the equal sign holds when and only when the variables x_i are statistically independent. Furthermore, we obtain from Eq. 5.150

$$H(V|U) = 2TW\, H(Z_i) = TW \log\,(2\pi\, e\, N_o/2T) \tag{5.155}$$

where $H(Z_i)$ is the entropy of any one of the variables z_i, and from the theorem incorporating Eq. 5.95

$$H(Y_i) \le \tfrac{1}{2} \log\,(2\pi\, e\, \overline{y_i^2}) \tag{5.156}$$

where $\overline{y_i^2}$ is the mean-square value of y_i. The equal sign holds in Eq. 5.156 when and only when y_i is gaussianly distributed with zero mean and, therefore, with variance equal to $\overline{y_i^2}$. On the other hand, Eqs. 5.154 and 5.155 can be satisfied with the equal sign by selecting $p(\underline{u})$ in such a way that the components x_i of $\underline{u}$ be statistically independent and individually gaussianly distributed with zero mean, in which case the components y_i of $\underline{v}$ are also statistically independent and gaussianly distributed with zero mean. The corresponding average mutual information is then

$$I(U\,;\,V) = \sum_{i=1}^{2TW} H(Y_i) - H(V|U) = \tfrac{1}{2} \log \prod_{i=1}^{2TW} 2\pi\, e\, \overline{y_i^2}$$

$$- TW \log\,(2\pi\, e\, N_o/2T) \tag{5.157}$$

We observe next that the mean-square values of y_i and x_i are related by

$$\overline{y_i^2} = \overline{x_i^2} + N_o/2T \tag{5.158}$$

Furthermore, since the x_i are statistically independent,

$$\int_U |\underline{u}|^2 p(\underline{u})\, dU = \sum_{i=1}^{2TW} \overline{x_i^2} = \sum_{i=1}^{2TW} \overline{y_i^2} - W N_o \tag{5.159}$$

so that we obtain, with the help of Eq. 5. 151,

$$\sum_{i=1}^{2TW} \overline{y_i^2} \leq S + W N_o \tag{5.160}$$

Now, it is well known that under these conditions

$$\prod_{i=1}^{2TW} \cdot \overline{y_i^2} \leq \left[\frac{S + W N_o}{2 T W} \right]^{2TW} \tag{5.161}$$

where the equal sign holds when the $\overline{y_i^2}$ are all equal, and Eq. 5. 160 is satisfied with the equal sign. Finally, substituting the righthand side of Eq. 5. 161 for the product in Eq. 5. 157 yields

$$I(U ; V) = TW \log (1 + \frac{S}{N_o W}) \tag{5.162}$$

which is the maximum value that the average mutual information can assume under the constraint imposed by Eq. 5. 151. Dividing this value by T yields a quantity independent of T, which, therefore, is equal to the channel capacity per second. QED

The expression for the channel capacity in Eq. 5. 152 has become famous among communication engineers since it was first introduced in 1948 independently by N. Wiener and C. Shannon. Because of its conceptual, as well as mathematical simplicity, it has been extensively used and occasionally misused. We must remember that this expression gives the channel capacity only when the noise is gaussianly distributed and white, and the input average power is not permitted to exceed S. Above all, this expression represents the maximum value of the mutual information per second between the input and the output of a channel, and not the information content of a signal, of average power equal to S, mixed with a noise of average power equal to $N_o W$. It turns out [2], however, that if the output of an information source which is gaussianly distributed with average power equal to $S + N_o W$, and whose power spectrum is uniform over a frequency band of width W and vanishes outside such a band, is to be reproduced with a maximum mean-square error equal to $N_o W$, the information rate of the source is given by the righthand side of Eq. 5. 152.

The channel capacity given by Eq. 5. 152 depends on the bandwidth W and on the ratio of S, the allowed average input power, and $N_o W$, the average noise power in the specified frequency band. The behavior of the capacity as a function of W, for fixed S and N_o, is illustrated in Fig. 5. 6. For very small values of W, C increases very fast with W, but it approaches asymptotically a

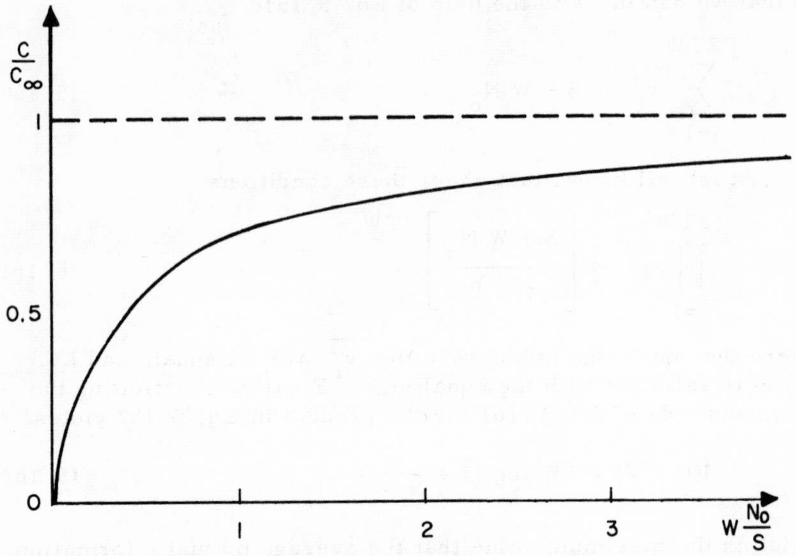

Fig. 5.6. The capacity of a channel with additive, white, gaussian noise as a function of bandwidth

value C_∞ when W approaches infinity. This value can be readily evaluated by noting that

$$\lim_{x\to 0} \frac{1}{x} \ln(1 + x) = 1 \tag{5.163}$$

We obtain

$$C_\infty = \frac{S}{N_o} \log e \tag{5.164}$$

This is the value of the channel capacity when no limitation is placed on the frequency spectrum of the channel input.

The expression in Eq. 5.164 has a very interesting physical interpretation. Our ability to measure any physical quantity is always limited by the presence of thermal-agitation noise. This noise is gaussianly distributed, and its power spectrum has a constant density, at least in the frequency range of interest for communication purposes. The power density N_o is given by

$$N_o = k\, T^o \tag{5.165}$$

where $k = 1.380 \times 10^{-23}$ joule/degree is Boltzmann's constant, and T^o is the absolute temperature of the system in question (a properly defined effective temperature, if the system's temperature is not uniform). Then, it follows from Eq. 5.164 that the signal energy received through a physical communication channel must be at least kT^o joules per nat of information that the signal is capable of providing. In other words, it takes at least kT^o joules of received energy to transmit successfully one nat of information.

The expression given by Eq. 5.152 can also be derived, in the case of input time function with spectrum limited to the band $0 < |\omega| < W$, by expanding such time functions as indicated in Eq. 5.131. It can be shown that, when the input is represented in this manner, the time-continuous channel under consideration reduces to a time-discrete, continuous, constant channel with gaussian additive noise, of the type discussed in Sec. 5.6. The input events of the time-discrete channel are the values assumed by the input time function at successive time instants t_k spaced $1/(2W)$ seconds apart. The corresponding output events are the values assumed at the same time instants by the output time function after having passed through an ideal low-pass filter of bandwidth W. Thus, each output event is the sum of the corresponding input event and the value assumed at the same time instant t_k by the noise after having passed through the same ideal low-pass filter. This value is gaussianly distributed with zero mean and variance $N = N_o W$. The capacity per event of such a time-discrete channel is given by Eq. 5.102, where S is the mean-square value of the input events and N that of the noise. Multiplying this capacity by $2W$, the number of events per second, yields the capacity per second given by Eq. 5.152.

In the case of input time functions with spectra limited to the frequency band $\omega_o - \pi W < |\omega| < \omega_o + \pi W$, the series representation given by Eqs. 5.135, 5.136, and 5.137 reduces the time-continuous channel to two identical, independent, time-discrete channels with input events equal to the values assumed by the two quadrature-modulating time-functions at time instants spaced $1/W$ seconds apart. The capacity per event of each of these channels is still given by Eq. 5.102. Multiplying this value by W, the number of input events per second per channel, gives the capacity per second of each of the two channels, which is one-half of the value given by Eq. 5.152.

This alternate derivation of Eq. 5.152 is somewhat simpler than that based on the Fourier series representation of the time functions involved. The Fourier series formulation, however, is more helpful as an introduction to topics discussed later in this text, and, for this reason, it has been discussed in greater detail.

*5.9. Representation of Stationary, Gaussian Processes

An ensemble of time functions $n(t)$ is said to be a gaussian, random process if the joint probability density of the values assumed by $n(t)$ at any finite number of time instants is a gaussian density function. A gaussian, random process is said to be stationary if these gaussian probability densities are independent of the time origin selected.

The m-dimensional, gaussian probability density of the random variables z_1 , z_2 , . . . , z_k , . . . , z_m is defined by

$$p(z_1, z_2, \ldots z_m) \equiv \frac{e^{-\frac{1}{2|\mathscr{A}|}\sum_{k=1}^{m}\sum_{i=1}^{m} A_{ik} z_k z_i}}{(2\pi)^{m/2}\sqrt{|\mathscr{A}|}} \tag{5.166}$$

where $|\mathscr{A}|$ is the determinant of the correlation coefficients

$$a_{ik} = a_{ki} = \int_{-\infty}^{\infty}\int_{-\infty}^{\infty} z_k z_i \, p(z_k, z_i) \, dz_k \, dz_i \tag{5.167}$$

and $A_{ik} = A_{ki}$ is the cofactor of a_{ik} . We have assumed, without loss of generality, that the mean value of each of the random variables is equal to zero; this can always be obtained by properly selecting the origin with respect to which each random variable is defined.

An important special case of Eq. 5.166 is obtained when all the cross-correlation coefficients vanish, that is, when

$$a_{ik} = \begin{cases} 0 & ; \quad i \neq k \\ \sigma_k^2 & ; \quad i = k \end{cases} \tag{5.168}$$

Then, the determinant of the cross-correlation coefficients is given by

$$|\mathscr{A}| = \prod_{k=1}^{m} \sigma_k^2 \tag{5.169}$$

where σ_k^2 is the variance of z_k , and the cofactor of a_{ik} is given by

$$A_{ik} = \begin{cases} 0 & ; \quad i \neq k \\ \dfrac{|\mathscr{A}|}{\sigma_k^2} & ; \quad i = k \end{cases} \tag{5.170}$$

Under these conditions Eq. 5.166 reduces to

$$p(z_1, z_2, \ldots z_m) = \frac{e^{-\sum_{k=1}^{m} z_k^2/2\sigma_k^2}}{\prod_{k=1}^{m} \sqrt{2\pi}\;\sigma_k} = \prod_{k=1}^{m} \frac{1}{\sqrt{2\pi}\,\sigma_k} e^{-z_k^2/2\sigma_k^2} \tag{5.171}$$

that is, to the product of m one-dimensional, gaussian probability densities. Thus, the vanishing of the cross-correlation coefficient for each pair of distinct random variables implies that the m gaussianly distributed, random variables are statistically independent.

The vanishing of the cross-correlation coefficients can be given a useful geometric interpretation. If we regard the random variables as the Cartesian coordinates of a point in an m-dimensional space, Eq. 5.168 implies that the Cartesian axes coincide with the principal axes of the quadratic hypersurface obtained by equating to a constant the exponent in Eq. 5.166. The coincidence of the two sets of axes may be obtained in all cases (in a number of ways) by an appropriate rotation of the Cartesian axis, that is, by a linear transformation of the variables. We can conclude, therefore, that, for any given m-dimensional, gaussian probability density, there exists a set of m statistically independent linear combinations of the random variables.

Let us consider a stationary, gaussian, random process, and indicate with $n(t)$ a particular time function of the process. Since a gaussian probability density is completely specified by the correlation coefficients defined by Eq. 5.167, a stationary, gaussian process is completely specified by its autocorrelation function

$$R(t - \theta) \equiv \overline{n_t\, n_\theta} = \int_{-\infty}^{\infty} \int_{-\infty}^{\infty} n_t n_\theta\, p(n_t, n_\theta)\, dn_t\, dn_\theta \tag{5.172}$$

where n_t and n_θ are the values assumed by $n(t)$ at any two particular time instants t and θ and $p(n_t, n_\theta)$ is their joint probability density. This auto-correlation function is, of course, the inverse Fourier transform of the power spectrum of the random process.

Let us represent $n(t)$ over the time interval $-T/2 < t < T/2$ as the series of orthonormal functions

$$n(t) = \sum_{k=-\infty}^{\infty} z_k\, \phi_k(t) \;;\quad -\frac{T}{2} < t < \frac{T}{2} \tag{5.173}$$

where the functions $\phi_k(t)$ satisfy Eq. 5.114 and the coefficients z_k are given by

$$z_k = \frac{1}{T} \int_{-T/2}^{T/2} n(t)\, \phi_k(t)\, dt \tag{5.174}$$

Theorem. The joint probability density of the random variables z_k defined by Eq. 5.174 is gaussian.

Proof. It is well known that the joint probability density of independent linear combinations of gaussianly distributed, random variables is gaussian. Then, since the z_k are independent functions of the values assumed by $n(t)$, their joint probability density must be gaussian. For a detailed proof of these statements see Section 8-4 of Reference [3]. QED

Theorem. The random variables z_k defined by Eq. 5.174 are statistically independent if the orthonormal functions $\phi_k(t)$ satisfy the integral equation

$$\int_{-T/2}^{T/2} R(t-\theta)\, \phi_k(\theta)\, d\theta = \lambda_k\, \phi_k(t)\ ; \quad -\frac{T}{2} < t < \frac{T}{2} \tag{5.175}$$

where $R(t-\theta)$ is the autocorrelation function defined by Eq. 5.172 and λ_k is an appropriate constant.

Proof. Since, because of the preceding theorem, the random variables in question are gaussianly distributed, it is sufficient to show that their correlation coefficients vanish when the orthonormal functions satisfy Eq. 5.175. We have for the cross-correlation coefficient a_{ik}, with the help of Eqs. 5.172 and 5.174,

$$\begin{aligned} a_{ik} \equiv \overline{z_i z_k} &= \frac{1}{T^2} \int_{-T/2}^{T/2} \int_{-T/2}^{T/2} \overline{n_t n_\theta}\, \phi_i(t)\, \phi_k(\theta)\, dt\, d\theta \\ &= \frac{1}{T^2} \int_{-T/2}^{T/2} \int_{-T/2}^{T/2} R(t-\theta)\, \phi_i(t)\, \phi_k(\theta)\, dt\, d\theta \end{aligned} \tag{5.176}$$

Then, substituting the righthand side of Eq. 5.175 for the lefthand side yields, with the help of Eq. 5.114,

$$a_{ik} \equiv \overline{z_i z_k} = \frac{1}{T^2} \int_{-T/2}^{T/2} \lambda_k\, \phi_k(t)\, \phi_i(t)\, dt = \begin{cases} 0 & ;\ i \neq k \\ \dfrac{\lambda_k}{T} = \sigma_k^2 ; & i = k \end{cases} \tag{5.177}$$

QED

The following two special cases are of particular importance to us: The power spectrum of the random process is white and T may be finite; T is infinite and the power spectrum of the random process is not necessarily white. The following two theorems pertain, in order, to these two special cases.

Theorem. The random variables z_k given by Eq. 5.174 are statistically independent for any set of orthonormal functions $\phi_k(t)$ when the power spectrum of the random process is white. If the random process has zero mean, each of these random variables has zero mean and variance equal to

$$\sigma_k^2 = \frac{N_o}{2T} \tag{5.178}$$

where N_o is the average power of the random process per unit bandwidth (in cps).

Proof. The autocorrelation function of a random process with a white power spectrum is an impulse function of magnitude equal to the power spectrum density at zero frequency, when this density is regarded as a function of the frequency f (measured in cps), over the doubly infinite interval $-\infty < f < \infty$. It follows that the magnitude of the impulse function is $N_o/2$, and that Eq. 5.175 is satisfied with $\lambda_k = N_o/2$. Finally, since the functions $\phi_k(t)$ form an orthonormal set (they satisfy Eq. 5.114), the correlation coefficient for any pair of random variables z_i and z_k is given by Eq. 5.177.

QED

Theorem. The Fourier coefficients

$$z_k = \frac{1}{T}\int_{-T/2}^{T/2} n(t)\,(\cos kqt + \sin kqt)\,dt \tag{5.179}$$

of a stationary, gaussian process $n(t)$ become statistically independent in the limit of T approaching infinity. If the random process has zero mean, each random variable z_k has zero mean, and its variance σ_k^2 satisfies

$$\lim_{\substack{T\to\infty \\ k\to\infty}} T\sigma_k^2 = N(f) \tag{5.180}$$

where

$$N(f) = \int_{-\infty}^{\infty} R(\tau)\cos 2\pi f\tau \, d\tau \tag{5.181}$$

is the power density spectrum of the random process, and T and k approach infinity in such a way that their ratio, representing the frequency in cps, remains finite, that is,

$$f = \lim_{\substack{T \to \infty \\ k \to \infty}} \frac{k}{T} \tag{5.182}$$

Proof. Since the random variables z_k are gaussianly distributed, it is sufficient to show that the correlation coefficient a_{ik} vanishes for each pair of different $(i \neq k)$ random variables and that the variance of each random variable satisfies Eq. 5.180 when T and k approach infinity in accordance with Eq. 5.182. Under the conditions of the theorem, the lefthand side of Eq. 5.175 becomes

$$\int_{-\infty}^{\infty} R(t-\theta)\,(\cos 2\pi f\theta + \sin 2\pi f\theta)\, d\theta$$

$$= \int_{-\infty}^{\infty} R(\tau)\,[\cos 2\pi f\,(\tau + t) + \sin 2\pi f\,(\tau + t)]\, d\tau$$

$$= \int_{-\infty}^{\infty} R(\tau)\,(\cos 2\pi ft + \sin 2\pi ft)\cos 2\pi f\tau\, d\tau$$

$$= N(f)\,(\cos 2\pi ft + \sin 2\pi ft) \tag{5.183}$$

where $\tau = t - \theta$, and use has been made of Eq. 5.181 and of the fact that the autocorrelation $R(\tau)$ is an even function of τ. On the other hand λ_k, being a function of the integer k, becomes in the limit a function $\lambda(f)$ of the frequency f defined by Eq. 5.182. Thus, Eq. 5.175 can be satisfied by setting

$$\lambda(f) = N(f) \tag{5.184}$$

This implies, in turn, that Eq. 5.177 is satisfied in the limit of T approaching infinity, and that the variance of each random variable satisfies Eq. 5.180 when T and k approach infinity in accordance with Eq. 5.182.

QED

*5.10. Time-Continuous, Gaussian Channels

We shall discuss in this section time-continuous channels disturbed by additive, stationary, gaussian noise with arbitrary power spectrum. In other words, we shall generalize the results obtained in Sec. 5.8 by eliminating the restriction that the power spectrum of the noise be uniform.

Let us represent the gaussian noise $n(t)$ over any particular time interval of length T as in Eq. 5.173, and select as orthonormal functions the solutions of the integral equation given in Eq. 5.175. Then, it follows from the theorem embodying Eq. 5.175 that the coefficients z_k given by Eq. 5.174 are statistically independent as well as gaussianly distributed. The input time function $u(t)$ and the output time function $v(t)$ will be represented in terms of the same set of orthonormal functions.

Let us consider first the special and somewhat artificial case in which only a finite number of the coefficients in the series representation of $u(t)$ are permitted to differ from zero, and furthermore, their mean-square values are specified. It is convenient to relabel these coefficients and the corresponding coefficients in the series for $n(t)$ and $v(t)$ by substituting for k an integer i ranging from 1 to m. Thus, we shall indicate the coefficients in the series for $u(t)$, $v(t)$, and $n(t)$ with x_i, y_i, and z_i, respectively. As in Sec. 5.8, these coefficients may be regarded as the Cartesian components of m-dimensional vectors $\underline{u}$, $\underline{v}$, and $\underline{n}$.

Theorem. If S_i is the prescribed mean square value of x_i, and N_i is the variance of z_i, the maximum value of the average mutual information between $\underline{u}$ and $\underline{v}$ is given by

$$\underset{p(\underline{u})}{\text{Max}}\ I(U\,;\,V) = \sum_{i=1}^{m} \frac{1}{2} \log\left(1 + \frac{S_i}{N_i}\right) \tag{5.185}$$

This value is attained when the components x_i are statistically independent, and are gaussianly distributed with zero mean and variances equal to the prescribed S_i.

Proof. The proof of this theorem is almost identical to that of the first theorem in Sec. 5.8. We know from the theorems embodying Eqs. 5.84 and 5.95 that the average mutual information attains its maximum value when the input x_i are statistically independent and the output y_i are gaussianly distributed with zero mean and variances equal to the prescribed $S_i + N_i$. This maximum value can actually be obtained by assigning to each input coefficient a gaussian probability density with zero mean and variance equal to S_i. Evaluation of the average mutual information for such an input probability distribution yields the righthand side of Eq. 5.185.

QED

The righthand side of Eq. 5.185 depends on the prescribed mean-square values of the x_i, as well as on the variances of the z_i. Let us determine the maximum value that it can attain when neither the number m of components of $\underline{u}$ nor their mean-square value

S_i are specified, but an upper limit is placed on the ensemble average of the time average of $u^2(t)$, that is, on the average input power. Since the righthand side of Eq. 5.185 corresponds to statistically independent x_i, this average power is given by

$$\sum_U |\underline{u}|^2 \; p(\underline{u}) \, dU = \sum_{i=1}^{m} S_i \tag{5.186}$$

Theorem. Let us number the noise components in order of increasing values of their variances, so that

$$N_j \geq N_i \;\; ; \;\; j > i \tag{5.187}$$

and indicate with

$$N(m) \equiv \sum_{i=1}^{m} N_i \tag{5.188}$$

the average noise power associated with the m noise components with the smallest variances. If the average input power is not permitted to exceed some specified value S, the maximum value of the average mutual information between $\underline{u}$ and $\underline{v}$ is given by

$$\operatorname*{Max}_{p(\underline{u})} I(U \,;\, V) = \sum_{i=1}^{m} \frac{1}{2} \log \frac{A}{N_i} \tag{5.189}$$

where

$$A \equiv \frac{S + N(m)}{m} \tag{5.190}$$

and m is the largest integer for which

$$A > N_m \tag{5.191}$$

This maximum value is attained when the input coefficients x_i are statistically independent, and are gaussianly distributed with zero mean and variances given by

$$S_i = \begin{cases} A - N_i & ; \quad i \leq m \\ 0 & ; \quad i > m \end{cases} \tag{5.192}$$

Proof. We know from the preceding theorem that if the mean square values S_i of the input components x_i are specified, the maximum value of the average mutual information is given by the righthand side of Eq. 5.185, where m is the number of input components with mean-square values different from zero. This maximum value is attained when the input components are statistically independent, and are gaussianly distributed with zero mean and variances equal to the prescribed S_i. Thus, we must determine the set of positive numbers S_i that maximizes the righthand side of Eq. 5.185 under the constraint

$$\sum_{i=1}^{m} S_i = S \tag{5.193}$$

Let the subscripts of the noise and input coefficients be assigned in accordance with Eq. 5.187, that is, in order of increasing noise variance. It is clear that if

$$S_j = B > 0 \ ; \ S_i = 0 \ ; \ j > i \tag{5.194}$$

the value of the righthand side of Eq. 5.185 can be increased by interchanging the values of S_j and S_i, that is, by setting

$$S_j = 0 \ ; \ S_i = B > 0 \ ; \ j > i \tag{5.195}$$

It follows that the variances of the input components that maximize the righthand side of Eq. 5.185 satisfy the condition

$$S_i \begin{cases} > 0 \ ; & i \leq m \\ = 0 \ ; & i > m \end{cases} \tag{5.196}$$

In other words, the available average power must be divided among the input components corresponding to the noise components with smallest variances.

Next, we shall show that the value of the righthand side of Eq. 5.185 cannot exceed the value of the righthand side of Eq. 5.189. We have for the difference between these two values, with the help of Eqs. 2.91, 5.188, 5.190, and 5.193,

$$\sum_{i=1}^{m} \frac{1}{2}\left[\log\left(1+\frac{S_i}{N_i}\right) - \log\frac{A}{N_i}\right] = \sum_{i=1}^{m} \frac{1}{2}\log\frac{S_i + N_i}{A}$$

$$\leq \sum_{i=1}^{m} \frac{1}{2}\left[\frac{S_i + N_i}{A} - 1\right]\log e = \frac{1}{2}\left[\frac{S + N(m)}{A} - m\right]\log e = 0 \tag{5.197}$$

The equal sign holds when and only when

$$S_i + N_i = A \;\; ; \;\; S_i > 0 \tag{5.198}$$

for each integer $i \leq m$.

We can conclude that the maximum value of the average mutual information is given by the righthand side of Eq. 5.189 where m is the largest integer for which Eq. 5.191 is satisfied.

QED

The theorem just proved can be interpreted as follows. The variance of each output component y_i is the sum of the variances S_i and N_i of the corresponding input and noise components. On the other hand, since m is the largest integer for which Eq. 5.191 is satisfied, the variances of the output components must be greater than A . It follows that the available average power S is distributed among the input coefficients in such a way as to maximize the smallest among the variances of the output components.

The results obtained so far in this section are valid for any value of the time interval T , provided, of course, the orthonormal functions used in the representation of $n(t)$, $u(t)$, and $v(t)$ satisfy Eq. 5.175 for the particular value of T in question. As discussed in Sec. 5.9, Eq. 5.175 is satisfied by sinusoidal time functions in the limit of T approaching infinity. Thus, in this limit, the components x_i , y_i , z_i of the vectors $\underline{u}$, $\underline{v}$, $\underline{n}$ represent Fourier coefficients, in which case Eqs. 5.185 and 5.189 can be written in terms of the power spectra of $u(t)$ and $n(t)$, as stated in the following theorems.

> Theorem. If $N(f)$ is the power-density spectrum of $n(t)$, and the power-density spectrum $S(f)$ of $u(t)$ is specified, the limit for T approaching infinity of the maximum value of the average mutual information per second between $\underline{u}$ and $\underline{v}$ is
>
> $$\lim_{T\to\infty} \operatorname*{Max}_{p(\underline{u})} \frac{I(U\,;\,V)}{T} = \int_0^{\infty} \log\left(1 + \frac{S(f)}{N(f)}\right) df \tag{5.199}$$
>
> This maximum value is attained when the input $u(t)$ is a stationary, gaussian process with zero mean and power-density spectrum $S(f)$.

Proof. According to the theorem embodying Eq. 5.185, $I(U\,;\,V)$ attains its maximum value for any T when the components x_i of $\underline{u}$ are statistically independent and gaussianly distributed. Thus, $u(t)$ may be regarded as a segment of a stationary, gaussian process over the time interval T . Then, we obtain from the theorem embodying Eq. 5.180

$$\lim_{\substack{T\to\infty \\ i\to\infty}} \log\left(1+\frac{S_i}{N_i}\right) = \log\left(1+\frac{S(f)}{N(f)}\right) \tag{5.200}$$

where T and i approach infinity in such a way that their ratio f, representing the frequency in cps, remains finite as indicated by Eq. 5.182. Correspondingly, $1/T$ represents the increment of frequency between successive terms in the summation in Eq. 5.185, and becomes in the limit the differential df. Thus, we obtain from Eq. 5.182

$$\lim_{\substack{T\to\infty \\ i\to\infty}} \operatorname*{Max}_{p(\underline{u})} \frac{I(U\,;\,V)}{T} = \int_{-\infty}^{\infty} \frac{1}{2}\log\left(1+\frac{S(f)}{N(f)}\right) df \tag{5.201}$$

from which Eq. 5.199 follows immediately in view of the even character of power-density spectra.

QED

<u>Theorem</u>. Let W_B be the region of the frequency spectrum (in general an aggregate of disjoint frequency bands) in which the noise power density is smaller than a specified value B, that is,

$$N(f) \leq B \qquad \text{for} \qquad f \geq 0 \quad \text{in} \quad W_B \tag{5.202}$$

If the average input power is not permitted to exceed some specified value S, the limit for T approaching infinity of the maximum value of the average mutual information per second between u(t) and v(t) is given by

$$\operatorname*{Max}_{S(f)} \int_0^{\infty} \log\left(1+\frac{S(f)}{N(f)}\right) df = \int_{W_B} \log\frac{B}{N(f)}\, df \tag{5.203}$$

where B is a constant satisfying

$$S = 2\int_{W_B} (B - N(f))\, df \tag{5.204}$$

This maximum value is attained when u(t) is a stationary, gaussian process with zero mean and power-density spectrum

$$S(f) = \begin{cases} B - N(f) & ; \quad N(f) < B \\ 0 & ; \quad N(f) \geq B \end{cases} \tag{5.205}$$

Proof. This theorem can be proved by evaluating the maximum value of the righthand side of Eq. 5.199 with respect to the power density S(f) under the constraint

$$\int_{-\infty}^{\infty} S(f)\, df = 2\int_{0}^{\infty} S(f)\, df = S \tag{5.206}$$

It is clear that if the function S(f) that maximizes the righthand side of Eq. 5.199 differs from zero at some frequency at which N(f) is equal to some value B, it must differ from zero over the whole region of the frequency spectrum in which N(f) is smaller than or equal to B. Thus if we indicate with W_B this region of the frequency spectrum,

$$\underset{S(f)}{\text{Max}} \int_{0}^{\infty} \log\left(1 + \frac{S(f)}{N(f)}\right) df = \int_{W_B} \log\left(1 + \frac{S(f)}{N(f)}\right) df \tag{5.207}$$

for some appropriate value of B. On the other hand, we have, following a procedure similar to that used in deriving Eq. 5.197

$$\int_{W_B} \log\left(1 + \frac{S(f)}{N(f)}\right) df - \int_{W_B} \log \frac{B}{N(f)}\, df \le 0 \tag{5.208}$$

where B satisfies Eq. 5.204. The equal sign holds when and only when

$$S(f) + N(f) = B \quad ; \quad S(f) \ge 0 \tag{5.209}$$

It follows that the righthand side of Eq. 5.207 assumes its maximum value when S(f) is given by Eq. 5.205 and B satisfies Eq. 5.204.

QED

The region W_B of the frequency spectrum defined by Eqs. 5.202 and 5.204 may be infinite, as, for instance, when the noise is white. In practice, however, the input power is always specifically restricted to some finite frequency band. This restriction does not invalidate the preceding theorem, except for the fact that the region W_B must be within the specified frequency band. An optimum distribution of input power under these conditions is illustrated in Fig. 5.7, where f_1 and f_2 are the lower and upper limits of the specified frequency band. The solid line in the figure represents the noise-power density, while the input-power density is represented by the difference between the horizontal dashed line and the solid line. The diagram in Fig. 5.7 can be interpreted as follows. Let us regard the signal power as water, and the solid line in the figure as

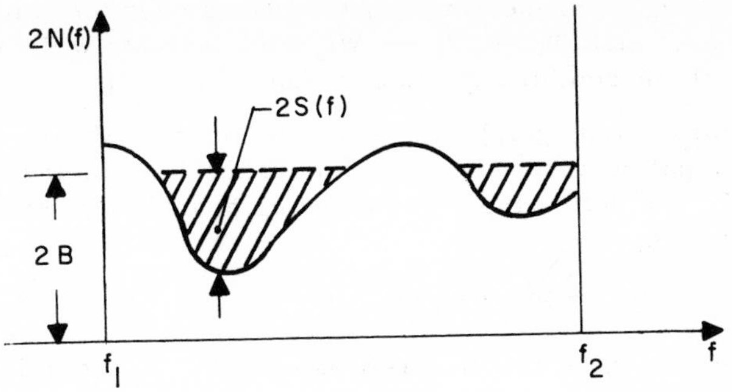

Fig. 5.7. Optimum distribution of input power

the trace of the bottom surface of a container of unit width whose end walls correspond to the frequencies f_1 and f_2. Then, we may think of the water as poured into the container in such a way as to maintain a uniform water level. The final level (measured from the f axis) reached after the total volume S of water has been poured into the container corresponds to the constant 2B.

We are now in a position to determine the capacity of a time-continuous, gaussian channel when the average input power is not permitted to exceed some value S. By definition, the channel capacity is the least upper bound to the average mutual information per second between u(t) and v(t)

$$C \equiv \text{l.u.b.} \frac{I(U;V)}{T} \tag{5.210}$$

This means, by definition of least upper bound, that

$$C \geq \frac{I(U;V)}{T} \tag{5.211}$$

for any T and any input probability distribution for which the average input power does not exceed S and that for any positive ϵ, there exists some time interval T_o and some input probability distribution for which the average mutual information $I_o(U;V)$ satisfies

$$C - \epsilon < \frac{I_o(U;V)}{T_o} \tag{5.212}$$

The channel capacity is defined as the least upper bound to the average mutual information per second rather than as its maximum value, because it turns out that the average mutual information per second has no maxima, but it approaches asymptotically the value given by the righthand side of Eq. 5.207 when T approaches infinity, as shown below.

Let U_1, U_2, and U_o be the ensembles of the vectors $\underline{u}_1$, $\underline{u}_2$, and $\underline{u}_o$ representing time functions over the time intervals T_1, T_2, and $T_1 + T_2$. We shall indicate with V_1, V_2, and V_o the ensembles of the corresponding output vectors.

Lemma. Let $p(\underline{u}_1)$ and $p(\underline{u}_2)$ be the probability densities of the input vectors corresponding to the time intervals T_1 and T_2, and define the corresponding probability density for the vector $\underline{u}_o$ by

$$p(\underline{u}_o) = p(\underline{u}_1)\, p(\underline{u}_2) \qquad (5.213)$$

where the time function represented by $\underline{u}_o$ coincides with the time function represented by $\underline{u}_1$ in the interval T_1 and with that represented by $\underline{u}_2$ in the time interval T_2. Then,

$$I(U_o ; V_o) \geq I(U_1 ; V_1) + I(U_2 ; V_2) \qquad (5.214)$$

Proof. The lefthand side of Eq. 5.214 can be expressed in the form

$$I(U_o ; V_o) = H(U_o) - H(U_o | V_o) \qquad (5.215)$$

On the other hand, it follows from Eq. 5.213 that the entropy of the ensemble U_o is simply the sum of the entropies of the ensembles U_1 and U_2, that is,

$$H(U_o) = H(U_1) + H(U_2) \qquad (5.216)$$

Furthermore, we have, with the help of Eq. 2.105,

$$\begin{aligned} H(U_o | V_o) &= H(U_1 U_2 | V_1 V_2) \\ &= H(U_1 | U_1 V_2) + H(U_2 | V_1 V_2 U_1) \\ &\leq H(U_1 | V_1) + H(U_2 | V_2) \end{aligned} \qquad (5.217)$$

Then, substituting the righthand sides of Eqs. 5.216 and 5.217 for $H(U_o)$ and $H(U_o | V_o)$ in Eq. 5.215 yields

$$\begin{aligned} I(U_o ; V_o) &\geq [H(U_1) - H(U_1 | V_1)] + [H(U_2) - H(U_2 | V_2)] \\ &= I(U_1 ; V_1) + I(U_2 ; V_2) \end{aligned} \qquad (5.218)$$

QED

Theorem. Let $C(T)$ be the value of the average mutual information given by Eq. 5.189 under the conditions stated in the theorem embodying this equation. The capacity per second of a time-continuous, gaussian channel with average input power not exceeding S is given by

$$C = \lim_{T \to \infty} \frac{C(T)}{T} = \int_0^{\infty} \log \left(1 + \frac{S(f)}{N(f)}\right) df \tag{5.219}$$

where $N(f)$ is the power-density spectrum of the gaussian noise, and the power-density spectrum of the input is given by

$$S(f) = \begin{cases} B - N(f) & ; \quad N(f) < B \\ 0 & ; \quad N(f) \geq B \end{cases} \tag{5.220}$$

and the constant B is such that

$$2 \int_0^{\infty} S(f)\, df = S \tag{5.221}$$

This limiting value of the average mutual information per second is obtained when the channel input is a stationary, gaussian process with zero mean and power-density spectrum given by Eq. 5.220.

Proof. We have from the preceding lemma

$$C(T_1 + T_2) \geq C(T_1) + C(T_2) \tag{5.222}$$

from which it follows that, for any positive integer n ,

$$C(nT) \geq n\, C(T) \tag{5.223}$$

This inequality does not necessarily imply that the function $C(T)/T$ increases monotonically with T . However, it implies, as shown below, that the amplitude of the oscillations of this function vanishes when T approaches infinity.

By the very definition of least upper bound, given by Eqs. 5.211 and 5.212, there exist, for any positive ϵ , some value T_o of T for which

$$\frac{C(T_o)}{T_o} > C - \epsilon \tag{5.224}$$

Let us define for any $T > T_o$ an integer n_T such that

$$n_T T_o \leq T < (n_T + 1) T_o \tag{5.225}$$

Then, we obtain from Eqs. 5.222 and 5.223

$$n_T C(T_o) \leq C(n_T T_o) \leq C(T) \tag{5.226}$$

and, with the help of Eq. 5.224,

$$\frac{C(T)}{T} > \frac{C(T)}{(n_T + 1)T_o} \geq \frac{n_T}{n_T + 1} \frac{C(T_o)}{T_o} > \frac{n_T}{n_T + 1} (C - \epsilon) \qquad (5.227)$$

It follows that

$$\lim_{T \to \infty} \frac{C(T)}{T} > C - \epsilon \qquad (5.228)$$

which, together with Eq. 5.211, yields

$$\lim_{T \to \infty} \frac{C(T)}{T} = C \qquad (5.229)$$

This last equation together with the theorem embodying Eq. 5.203 yields the results stated in the theorem.

QED

5.11. Summary and Conclusions

This chapter has been devoted to the study of simple models of communication channels. Sections 5.2 to 5.6 inclusive dealt with time-discrete, constant channels, that is, channels in which input and output events occur in discrete time sequences, and are independently affected by the channel noise. The first major result concerning these channels was that the average mutual information between input and output is maximized by making successive input events statistically independent, in which case the corresponding output events are also statistically independent. This result is very important because it permits the evaluation of the capacity of time-discrete, constant channels by maximizing the average mutual information between each input event and the corresponding output event, independently of all other events.

We focussed our attention first on discrete channels, that is, channels for which the sets of possible input and output events are discrete. We were able, for this class of channels, to develop a procedure for evaluating the channel capacity by maximizing the average mutual information between each input event and the corresponding output event.

We turned our attention next to channels in which the input and output events are represented by continuous variables, and the noise is additive in the sense that the output variable is equal to the input variable plus a random variable representing the noise. The channel capacity was evaluated only in the special case of a gaussianly distributed noise with an upper limit placed on the mean-square value of the input variable. Bounds were obtained for the channel capacity with other types of additive noise and the same limitation on the input variable.

The rest of the chapter was devoted to time-continuous channels disturbed by additive, gaussian noise, when an upper limit is set to the average input power. As the first step in our discussion, we developed means for representing time functions in terms of discrete sets of continuous variables. We were able to show that a time function with spectrum limited to a frequency band of width W can be represented by means of 2W independent variables per second.

The capacity of time-continuous, gaussian channels was evaluated first in the special case of white noise and input spectrum limited to a finite frequency band. In this special case, the channel capacity was found to increase monotonically with the bandwidth and approach asymptotically a value proportional to the ratio of the average signal power and the noise power per cycle of bandwidth. This value is of particular significance because it represents an upper limit to the capacity of a channel in which no disturbance other than thermal agitation noise is present.

The evaluation of the capacity of a time-continuous channel disturbed by additive, gaussian noise with arbitrary power spectrum involved several steps. First, we evaluated the maximum value of the average mutual information between input and output over a finite time interval T . Next, we found the limit of its value divided by T , when T approaches infinity. Finally, we showed that this limiting value is the least upper bound to the average mutual information per second between input and output.

No example of channels with memory has been discussed, because the evaluation of the capacity of such channels is very laborious, when at all possible. If the channel noise depends only on a finite segment of its past input, the channel capacity can be evaluated as the limit of the maximum mutual information per second when the time interval over which it is evaluated approaches infinity [5]. A similar evaluation can be performed if the noise can be represented as a function of the "state" of the channel, the number of such states is finite, and the current state can be determined from the previous state and the last input event [6]. No satisfactory definition of channel capacity has yet been proposed for other channels with memory. The difficulty lies in the fact that unless one of the two conditions mentioned above is met, the channel noise cannot be described without a knowledge of the infinite past history of the channel.

The capacity of a channel, when measured in bits per event or per second, is an upper bound to the number of binary digits per event or per second that can possibly be transmitted through the channel with perfect accuracy. This follows from the fact that the channel capacity is defined as the least upper bound to the average mutual information per event or per second. On the other hand, it is certainly not obvious that a finite number of binary digits per event or per second (smaller than the channel capacity) can in fact be transmitted through the channel with perfect accuracy.

The rest of this volume is devoted to the problem of transmitting binary digits at a finite rate through a specified channel with an arbitrarily small probability of error.

5.12. Selected References

1. I.S. Sokolnikoff and R.M. Redheffer, Mathematics of Physics and Modern Engineering, McGraw-Hill, New York, 1958, Chapter 3, Sections 10 and 15. This reference discusses the maximization of functions of several variables under constraints.

2. C.E. Shannon, "A Mathematical Theory of Communication," Bell System Tech. J., XVII (July and Oct., 1948). The capacity of a time-discrete, gaussian channel with limited peak input power is discussed in Section 25. A proof of Eq. 5.107 is given in Appendix 6.

3. W.B. Davenport, Jr., and W.L. Root, Random Signals and Noise, McGraw-Hill, New York, 1958. The expansion of a general random process in a series of orthonormal functions is discussed in Section 6-4. The aspects of gaussian processes pertinent to this chapter are presented in Sections 8-1 to 8-4.

4. C.E. Shannon, "Communication in the Presence of Noise," Proc. I.R.E., 37, 10 (Jan., 1949). This is the paper in which the results of Section 5.10 were first presented. The rest of the main results of this chapter were first presented in Reference 2 above.

5. A.Feinstein, "On the Coding Theorem and its Converse for Finite-Memory Channels," Information and Control, 2, 25, (April, 1959).

6. C.E. Shannon, "Certain Results in Coding Theory for Noisy Channels," Information and Control, 1, 6 (Sept., 1957).

7. S. Muroga, "On the Capacity of a Discrete Channel. I," Jour. of the Physical Society of Japan, 8, p. 484 (Aug. 1953). This paper discusses in detail the evaluation of the capacity of discrete, constant channels. The material presented in Sec. 5.5 originates from this paper and from Reference 2 above.

Chapter 6

CHANNEL ENCODING AND DECODING

The preceding chapter has been devoted to a discussion of various models of transmission channels and to the evaluation of their information capacity. This capacity was defined as the maximum value of the average mutual information between input and output events that can be obtained by properly selecting the input probability distribution. The capacity expressed in bits sets an upper limit to the number of equiprobable, statistically independent binary digits (per input event or per second as the case may be) that we can hope to transmit through a given channel with perfect accuracy. In fact, the unique identification of such binary digits by the decoder requires that the channel output provide one bit of information about each of them. On the other hand, the fact that the capacity per second of a given channel is greater than the number of binary digits per second that must be transmitted through the channel does not necessarily imply that the digits can be transmitted through the channel with perfect accuracy. That perfect accuracy can be approached as closely as desired for a fairly general class of channels is the major result of the theory presented in this text.

The first theorem asserting the possibility of transmitting messages through randomly disturbed channels with an arbitrarily small probability of error was published by Shannon in 1948. This fundamental theorem has since been refined and extended by Shannon himself and others. A simple example of encoding and decoding capable of insuring an arbitrarily small probability of error is presented in this chapter. Various bounds on the probability of error for discrete, constant channels will be derived in Chapters 7 and 9.

6.1. Block Encoding and Decoding

We shall assume in what follows that the information to be transmitted consists of a sequence of binary digits. With reference to Fig. 1.1, this implies that the source output has already been transformed into a sequence of binary digits from which the source decoder is capable of generating a reproduction of the source output acceptable to the user. Then the function of the channel encoder is to transform the input binary digits into channel input events; the function of the channel decoder, to reproduce the binary digits from the channel output events.

With reference to Fig. 1.6, the channel input is determined at any given time by the binary digits stored in the encoder. The functional dependence of the channel input on such binary digits is to be selected in each case in such a way as to minimize the probability of erroneous decoding of the channel output. The number ν of binary digits on which the channel input depends at any given time is the critical parameter of the encoding process, which, for a given channel and a given transmission rate, controls the minimum probability of error that can be achieved. We shall see for a broad class of channels that the probability of error can be made to vanish exponentially with increasing ν, provided only that the number of binary digits per second to be transmitted is smaller than the channel capacity in bits per second.

A second important parameter of the encoding process is the number of binary digits that enter and leave the encoder simultaneously. At one extreme, the digits may enter and leave the encoder one by one; at the other extreme, ν digits may enter the encoder together at one time, while the ν preceding digits are taken out of it. More precisely, if R is the number of binary digits per second to be transmitted, we may choose to feed the binary digits to the encoder one by one every $1/R$ seconds, or two at a time every $2/R$ seconds, or, in general, μ at a time every μ/R seconds, where $\mu \leq \nu$. Of course, the same number μ of binary digits are taken out of the encoder every μ/R seconds. Clearly, each binary digit remains in the encoder on the average for ν/R seconds, regardless of the value of μ. We refer to the extreme case of $\mu = \nu$, in which all the digits stored in the encoder are changed simultaneously every ν/R seconds, as block encoding. The encoding process is said to be sequential when $\mu < \nu$ because of the sequential character of the dependence of the resulting channel input on its own past. It is clear that if the binary digits enter the encoder μ at a time, each successive block of μ binary digits acts as a single unit in determining the channel input and, therefore, its output. Thus the binary digits must be reconstructed by the decoder in blocks of the same size μ. We shall refer to the corresponding decoding operations as block decoding and sequential decoding, respectively.

Block encoding and decoding has the advantage of making the transmission of each block of ν binary digits independent of that of all preceding and following blocks, at least in the case of constant channels. Because of the resulting analytical simplifications, we shall restrict our discussion to this type of encoding and decoding.

The process of block encoding of binary digits for transmission through a discrete, constant channel with input alphabet X and output alphabet Y can be described as follows. The sequence of binary digits to be transmitted is first segmented into messages consisting of ν successive digits. We shall indicate with m_1, $m_2, \ldots m_i, \ldots m_M$ the points of the resulting message space representing the

$$M \equiv 2^{\nu} \tag{6.1}$$

distinct sequences of ν binary digits. The same symbol M will be used to indicate the message ensemble. The process of encoding consists of assigning to each point of the message space a particular sequence $u = \xi_1 \xi_2 \ldots \xi_n$ of n symbols belonging to the input alphabet X of the channel. Thus a particular assignment of sequences of input symbols to the M possible messages may be regarded as a mapping of the message space M into the product space $U = X^n$ whose points represent the possible sequences of n symbols.

This mapping of the points of the message space into the points of the input-sequence space is indicated schematically on the lefthand side of Fig. 6.1. The output space V on the righthand side of the same figure consists of all the possible sequences $v = \eta_1 \eta_2 \ldots \eta_n$ of n symbols belonging to the output alphabet Y.

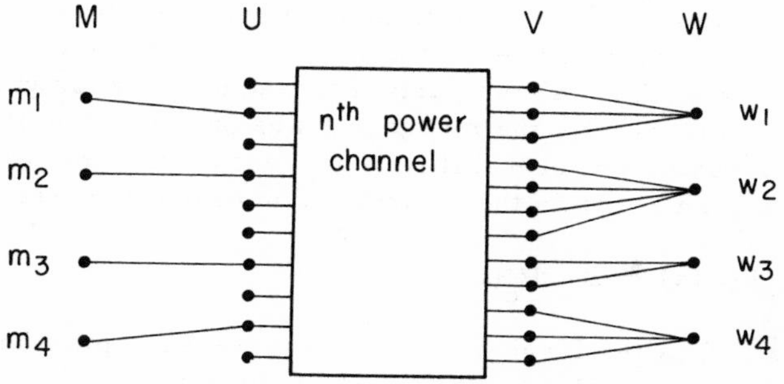

Fig. 6.1. Schematic representation of block encoding and decoding

We shall refer to the resulting channel with input space U and output space V as the nth power of the discrete, constant channel with input alphabet X and output alphabet Y. Since the original channel is constant, the conditional probability distribution defining the nth power channel is, from Eq. 5.3,

$$P(v|u) = \prod_{i=1}^{n} P(\eta_i|\xi_i) \tag{6.2}$$

where ξ_i is some symbol x of the input alphabet X, η_i is some symbol y of the output alphabet Y, and $P(y|x)$ is the conditional probability distribution that defines the channel.

The mapping of the message space M into the input space U defines a conditional probability distribution $P(v \mid m)$ which can be obtained from Eq. 6.2 by identifying each message with the input sequence u corresponding to it. Then if $P(m)$ is the message probability distribution, the probability distribution for the output sequences is given by

$$P(v) = \sum_{k=1}^{M} P(m_k)\, P(v \mid m_k) \tag{6.3}$$

and the conditional probability for the messages given the output sequence v is

$$P(m \mid v) = \frac{P(m)\, P(v \mid m)}{P(v)} \tag{6.4}$$

The objective of the decoding operation is to identify the message transmitted from the evidence provided by the output sequence. Various criteria may be used in this identification process. If the probability distribution of the messages is available to the decoder, the decoder can compute the conditional probability given by Eq. 6.4 for each message m and the particular sequence v output from the channel, and identify the message transmitted as the one for which this a posteriori probability is largest. Then the probability of committing an error in the identification of the message is given by

$$P(e \mid v) \equiv 1 - P_c(m \mid v) \tag{6.5}$$

where $P_c(m \mid v)$ is the largest a posteriori message probability for the particular v received. It is clear from Eq. 6.5 that this decoding procedure minimizes the probability of error.

If, instead, the message probability distribution is not available to the decoder, a reasonable decoding procedure consists of identifying the message transmitted as the one for which the conditional probability $P(v \mid m)$ is largest for the particular v received. This procedure is called maximum likelihood decoding because it selects the message most likely to yield the v actually received. It is important to note that maximum likelihood decoding is equivalent to maximum mutual-information decoding, that is, to selecting the message that maximizes the mutual information

$$I(m; v) \equiv \log \frac{P(v \mid m)}{P(v)} \tag{6.6}$$

for the particular v received. Other decoding criteria may be appropriate when certain errors are in some sense more serious than others.

Any particular decoding procedure may be regarded as a rule for dividing the output space V into M disjoint subsets of points exhausting the entire space, each subset corresponding to a particular message. We shall indicate with w_k the subset of output points corresponding to the message m_k, and with W the discrete space formed by the M subsets. If the output sequence v belongs to the subset w_k, the decoder identifies m_k as the message transmitted. An error is committed whenever the output sequence does not belong to the subset corresponding to the message actually transmitted. This representation of the decoding operation is illustrated schematically on the righthand side of Fig. 6.1. Clearly, the decoding operation may be regarded as a many-to-one mapping of the V space on the W space.

The representation of the encoding and decoding operations shown in Fig. 6.1 suggests regarding the channel together with the encoder and the decoder as forming a new channel with input space M and output space W. Clearly, this channel is constant if the original channel is constant. Its conditional probability distribution

$$P(w \mid m) \equiv \sum_{w} P(v \mid m) \tag{6.7}$$

can be obtained from Eq. 6.2 for any particular encoder and decoder.

<u>Theorem.</u> The average mutual information between M and W cannot exceed the average mutual information between M and V, that is,

$$I(M; W) \equiv H(M) - H(M \mid W) \leq H(M) - H(M \mid V) \equiv I(M; V) \tag{6.8}$$

<u>Proof.</u> Since w is uniquely specified by v,

$$H(M \mid V) = H(M \mid VW) \tag{6.9}$$

On the other hand,

$$H(M \mid VW) \leq H(M \mid W) \tag{6.10}$$

from which we obtain

$$H(M \mid V) \leq H(M \mid W) \tag{6.11}$$

This inequality states that the equivocation of the ensemble M (conditional entropy of M) is greater when W is given than when V is given, as our intuition would suggest in view of the many-to-one mapping of V on W. The desired inequality given in Eq. 6.8 follows immediately from Eq. 6.11.

QED

A discrete model of transmission channel has been used in this preliminary discussion of encoding and decoding to simplify the schematic diagram of Fig. 6.1. The generalization to channels with continuous input and output spaces, either time-discrete or time-continuous, is straightforward. The input and output spaces U and V become continuous spaces, whose points, indicated by vectors $\underline{u}$ and $\underline{v}$, represent the possible input and output time functions over the time interval T devoted to the transmission of each message. Thus the encoding operation may be regarded as a mapping of the M points of the discrete space M into the points of the continuous space U , and the decoding operation as the many-to-one mapping of the points of the continuous space V on the M points of the discrete space W . Clearly, each point w_k of W represents a particular region of the V space, whose points correspond to time functions whose reception is regarded by the decoder as resulting from the transmission of message m_k. The inequality given by Eq. 6.8 is still valid, and the derived channel with input space M and output space W is still discrete. An example of encoding and decoding for transmission through a time-continuous channel is discussed in Secs. 6.3 through 6.6.

6.2. Probability of Error and Equivocation

The probability of error for any particular encoder and decoder is the probability that the output sequence v does not belong to the subset w_k of V corresponding to the transmitted message m_k. Thus it is given by

$$P(e) \equiv \sum_k P(m_k) \sum_{j \neq k} P(w_j | m_k) = \sum_j P(w_j) P(e | w_j) \qquad (6.12)$$

where

$$P(e | w_j) \equiv 1 - P(m_j | w_j) = \sum_{k \neq j} P(m_k | w_j) \qquad (6.13)$$

is the probability of error when the output v belongs to the subset w_j. We wish to relate the probability of error P(e) to the equivocation $H(M|W)$ for the derived channel with input space M and output space W shown in Fig. 6.1.

It is convenient for this purpose to define the entropy

$$H(e) \equiv - P(e) \log P(e) - [1 - P(e)] \log [1 - P(e)] \qquad (6.14)$$

for the binary choice error and no error, and the corresponding condition entropy

$$H(e | W) \equiv - \sum_j P(w_j) \{P(e | w_j) \log P(e | w_j) + [1 - P(e | w_j)] \log [1 - P(e | w_j)]\} \qquad (6.15)$$

when the point of the space W is given.

Theorem. The equivocation $H(M|W)$ satisfies the inequality

$$H(M|W) \le H(e|W) + P(e)\log(M-1) \le H(e) + P(e)\log(M-1) \qquad (6.16)$$

Proof. The equivocation is, by definition,

$$H(M|W) \equiv \sum_j H(M|w_j)\,P(w_j) \qquad (6.17)$$

where

$$H(M|w_j) \equiv -\sum_k P(m_k|w_j)\log P(m_k|w_j) \qquad (6.18)$$

is the equivocation when the output v belongs to the subset w_j. The righthand side of this last equation can be rewritten with the help of Eq. 6.13, in the form

$$H(M|w_j) = -[1 - P(e|w_j)]\log[1 - P(e|w_j)] - P(e|w_j)\log P(e|w_j)$$
$$- P(e|w_j)\sum_{k\neq j}\frac{P(m_k|w_j)}{P(e|w_j)}\log\frac{P(m_k|w_j)}{P(e|w_j)} \qquad (6.19)$$

The summation on the righthand side of Eq. 6.19, (minus sign included), is recognized as the entropy of an ensemble consisting of $M - 1$ points. As such, its value cannot exceed $\log(M-1)$. It follows that

$$H(M|w_j) \le -[1 - P(e|w_j)]\log[1 - P(e|w_j)] - P(e|w_j)\log P(e|w_j)$$
$$+ P(e|w_j)\log(M-1) \qquad (6.20)$$

which when averaged over the ensemble W yields, with the help of Eq. 6.15,

$$H(M|W) \le H(e|W) + P(e)\log(M-1) \qquad (6.21)$$

The desired relation given by Eq. 6.16 follows immediately from Eq. 6.21 in view of the fact that

$$H(e|W) \le H(e) \qquad (6.22)$$

QED

The inequality of Eq. 6.16 can be given the following illuminating interpretation. The equivocation $H(M|W)$ represents the average amount of information required to specify the transmitted message when the subset w to which the output v belongs is known. We may also say that it represents the average amount of information required to correct the errors committed by the decoder, in view of the fact that the decoder generates the message m_k when the output v belongs to w_k. Let us then consider the process of correcting the errors made by the decoder. First of all, we must indicate for each decoded message whether it is correct or incorrect. The average amount of information required for this purpose is measured by the conditional entropy of such a binary choice, given by Eq. 6.15. Whenever the message is incorrect, the correct message must be indicated. Since the number of possible alternatives is $M - 1$, this indication requires at most an amount of information equal to $\log (M-1)$. Furthermore, this indication has to be provided with probability $P(e)$. It follows that the middle part of Eq. 6.16 is an upper bound to the average amount of information that must be provided in order to correct the mistakes made by the decoder, and therefore it is an upper bound to the equivocation.

The relation between equivocation and probability of error given by Eq. 6.16 leads to the following important result concerning the probability of error for transmission rates exceeding channel capacity. This result is known as the converse of the coding theorem.

> Theorem. Let us consider an arbitrary message-decoding procedure for the nth power of a discrete, constant channel, and indicate with W the corresponding partitioning of the output space V into disjoint subsets $w_1, w_2, \ldots, w_M$ associated with the points $m_1, m_2, \ldots, m_M$ of the message space. The probability $P(e)$ that a message be decoded incorrectly has a positive lower bound when the entropy $H(M)$ of the message ensemble exceeds the capacity nC of the nth power channel. More precisely,
>
> $$P(e) \geq P_L > 0 \qquad (6.23)$$
>
> where the lower bound P_L satisfies

$$-P_L \log P_L - (1-P_L) \log (1-P_L) + P_L \log (M-1) = H(M) - nC > 0 \qquad (6.24)$$

Proof. We have from Eq. 6.8 and the definition of channel capacity

$$I(M; W) \equiv H(M) - H(M|W) \leq H(M) - H(M|V) \equiv I(M; V) \leq nC \qquad (6.25)$$

where C is the capacity per event of the given channel. Then it follows from Eq. 6.16 that

$$H(e) + P(e) \log (M-1) \geq H(M) - nC \qquad (6.26)$$

Let

$$F(z) \equiv -z \log z - (1-z) \log (1-z) + z \log (M-1) \qquad (6.27)$$

This function of z coincides with the lefthand side of Eq. 6.26 for $z = P(e)$; it is positive for $z > 0$, and vanishes for $z = 0$. Furthermore,

$$\frac{dF(z)}{dz} = \log \frac{(1-z)(M-1)}{z} > 0 \quad ; \quad 0 \le z < 1 - \frac{1}{M} \qquad (6.28)$$

from which it follows that

$$F(z) < [F(z)]_{z=1-\frac{1}{M}} = \log M \ge H(M) \quad ; \quad 0 \le z < 1 - \frac{1}{M} \qquad (6.29)$$

We can conclude that for any $H(M) - nC > 0$, there exists a positive value P_L of z not exceeding $P(e)$ such that

$$H(e) + P(e) \log (M-1) \ge [F(z)]_{z=P_L} = H(M) - nC \qquad (6.30)$$

QED

This theorem is most readily interpreted when the message ensemble consists of sequences of ν statistically independent, equiprobable binary digits, in which case

$$H(M) = \log M = \nu \text{ bits} \qquad (6.31)$$

Then the theorem states that the probability that a message consisting of ν binary digits be incorrectly decoded cannot be made arbitrarily small for any transmission rate $R = \nu/n$ larger than the channel capacity C. It is known as the converse of the coding theorem for discrete, constant channels, because the latter theorem, which will be proved in Chapter 8, states that the probability of a decoding error can be made arbitrarily small for any transmission rate $R < C$ by increasing n and ν in the same proportions.

A lower bound to $P(e)$ simpler than that provided by Eq. 6.24, but not sufficiently strong to prove the assertion made by the theorem, can be obtained from Eq. 6.26 as follows. Using binary information units, we have, from Eqs. 6.26 and 6.31

$$P(e) \ge \frac{\nu - nC - H(e)}{\log (M-1)} > \frac{\nu - nC - 1}{\nu} = 1 - \frac{C}{R} - \frac{1}{\nu} \qquad (6.32)$$

Thus when ν and n approach infinity while their ratio $R = \nu/n$ remains constant, we obtain

$$\lim_{n \to \infty} P(e) > 1 - \frac{C}{R} \quad ; \quad \text{for } R = \text{constant} \qquad (6.33)$$

The theorems of this section can be readily extended to time-discrete channels with continuous input and output spaces, and to time-continuous channels with additive, stationary noise.

6.3. Decoding of Signals in White Gaussian Noise

We shall consider in this section the encoding and decoding of messages for a time-continuous channel disturbed by additive, stationary, white gaussian noise. This will serve the double purpose of illustrating the processes of block encoding and block decoding outlined in Sec. 6.1, and of providing the background needed in Sec. 6.5 for the evaluation of the probability of error for orthogonal signals.

The diagram in Fig. 6.2 illustrates schematically the process of message transmission by block encoding and decoding in a manner which emphasizes the basic operations that must be performed by the encoder and the decoder. We assume again that the information to be transmitted consists of a sequence of binary digits, and that the sequence is segmented into successive messages, each consisting of ν binary digits. We saw in Sec. 6.1 that the process of encoding involves assigning a distinct sequence of channel input events to each of the $M = 2^\nu$ possible distinct messages. Since we are concerned in this section with a time-continuous channel, we must assign to each of the possible messages a distinct time function (signal) extending over the time interval T corresponding to the transmission of the ν binary digits that constitute the message. Then we can picture the encoder as a selector (switching circuit) that causes the generation of the signal corresponding to the message to be transmitted. We shall indicate with $u_1(t), u_2(t), \ldots, u_M(t)$ the M signals corresponding to the possible sequences of ν binary digits.

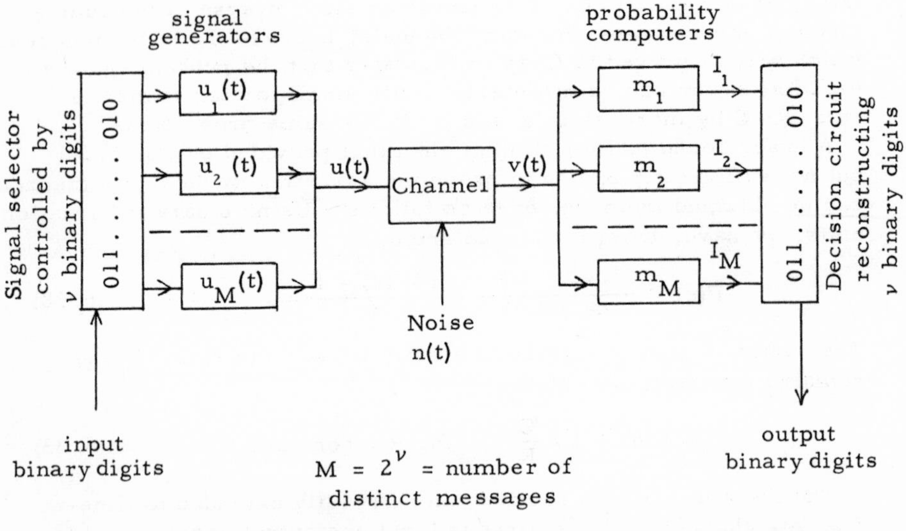

Fig. 6.2. Schematic diagram of message transmission through a time-continuous channel

The discussion of block decoding in Sec. 6.1 was based on the grouping of the possible channel outputs into M subsets, with each subset consisting of the channel outputs that are to be decoded into a particular message according to some specified decoding criterion (maximum a posteriori probability, maximum likelihood, etc.). While such a grouping of the possible channel outputs into subsets provided a convenient representation of the decoding process for the purposes of Sec. 6.1, it did not indicate explicitly the operations to be performed by the decoder.

If v(t) is the channel output resulting from the transmission of a particular message, all the knowledge that v(t) can provide about the message transmitted is contained in the set of M conditional probabilities $P(m_j | v(t))$ $(j = 1, 2, \ldots, M)$, where m_j is the mesage represented by the signal $u_j(t)$. Thus the first operation to be performed by the decoder is the computation of these M conditional probabilities. Actually, it is more convenient to think of the decoder as evaluating the mutual informations (in nats)

$$I_j \equiv I(m_j;v(t)) = \ln \frac{P(m_j | v(t))}{P(m_j)} \quad ; \; j = 1, 2, \ldots, M \qquad (6.34)$$

from which the conditional probabilities can be computed when so desired with the help of the transmission probabilities $P(m_j)$. The evaluation of the I_j is performed by the probability computers on the righthand side of Fig. 6.2.

The function of the decision circuit on the righthand side of Fig. 6.2 is to identify the message transmitted on the basis of the values I_j provided by the probability computers. This identification is made according to whatever decoding criterion has been prescribed. If the criterion is maximum likelihood, that is, maximum mutual information, the decision circuit identifies as message transmitted the one for which the mutual information I_j is largest. If, instead, a maximum a posteriori probability criterion is prescribed, the decision circuit selects the message for which $I_j + \ln P(m_j)$ is largest. Other criteria of practical interest require adding to I_j an appropriate quantity, function of j, and selecting the maximum resulting value.

The schematic diagram in Fig. 6.2 is capable of representing the encoding and decoding operation for a rather large class of channels. We shall discuss below the special case of a time-continuous channel disturbed by additive, white gaussian noise, which is relatively simple from a mathematical standpoint, and at the same time of considerable practical interest. The channel will be assumed to have unity gain. This is equivalent to saying that the input signals and the noise will be referred to the output terminals of the channel; that is, they will be represented as they appear at the output terminals. Such an assumption implies that the channel is not dispersive, and that its gain is either independent of time or is known to the receiver at all times.

Let us represent the signals $u_j(t)$ corresponding to the messages m_j as a series of orthonormal functions over the time interval

$-T/2 < t < T/2$ in which they are defined. We shall assume, further, that only a finite number D of coefficients in such series are permitted to differ from zero, so that the M signals can be represented as vectors $\underline{u}_j$ in a Euclidean space of dimensionality D. Similarly, we shall expand the additive noise $n(t)$ and the channel output $v(t)$ in the same set of orthonormal functions.

It was stated in Sec. 5.8 and proved in Sec. 5.9 that the coefficients in the expansion of $n(t)$ in any series of orthonormal functions over any time interval T become statistically independent when the spectrum of the noise is white. Furthermore, if the noise is stationary and gaussian, and the orthonormal functions are normalized as in Eq. 5.114, each individual coefficient is gaussianly distributed with zero mean and variance

$$\sigma^2 = \frac{N_o}{2T} \tag{6.35}$$

where N_o is the noise power per unit bandwidth (in cps). This suggests, in view of the additivity of the noise, that the mutual information between any message m_i and any particular channel output $v(t)$ should depend only on D of the coefficients in the series expansion of $v(t)$, namely, those corresponding to input signal coefficients that are allowed to differ from zero. In other words, the channel output and the noise, as well as the input signals, can be represented by vectors $\underline{v}$ and $\underline{n}$ in a Euclidean space of dimensionality D.

Theorem. Let $\underline{u}_j$ be a D-dimensional vector whose Cartesian components are the D coefficients in the expansion of $u_j(t)$ in a series of orthonormal functions satisfying Eq. 5.114. Similarly, let $\underline{n}$ and $\underline{v}$ be D-dimensional vectors whose Cartesian components are the corresponding coefficients in the expansions of $n(t)$ and $v(t)$ in the same set of orthonormal functions. If the noise $n(t)$ is additive, stationary, gaussian, and white, the mutual informations defined by Eq. 6.34 are given by

$$I_j = -\frac{T}{N_o} |\underline{v} - \underline{u}_j|^2 - A \tag{6.36}$$

where

$$A \equiv \ln \sum_{k=1}^{M} P(m_k)\, e^{-|\underline{v} - \underline{u}_k|^2 T/N_o} \tag{6.37}$$

and m_j is the message represented by the vector $\underline{u}_j$.

Proof. Let us indicate with x_i, y_i, z_i corresponding coefficients in the expansions of $u(t)$, $v(t)$, and $n(t)$ in series of orthonormal functions, and assign the integers $0 < i \leq D$ to the D coefficients x_i of the signals $u(t)$ that are permitted to differ from zero. Then the noise $n(t)$ can be regarded as the sum of the time function

$$n'(t) \equiv \sum_{i=1}^{D} z_i \phi_i(t) \quad ; \quad -\frac{T}{2} < t < \frac{T}{2} \tag{6.38}$$

represented by the noise vector $\underline{n}$, where $\phi_i(t)$ is the ith function in the orthonormal set, and a second time function

$$n''(t) \equiv n(t) - n'(t) \tag{6.39}$$

Correspondingly, the channel output $v(t)$ resulting from the input signal $u_j(t)$ is the sum of the time function

$$v'(t) \equiv u_j(t) + n'(t) = \sum_{i=1}^{D} y_i \phi_i(t) \tag{6.40}$$

represented by the vector $\underline{v}$, and a second time function

$$v''(t) \equiv v(t) - v'(t) = n''(t) \tag{6.41}$$

Now, since the coefficients z_i are statistically independent, and

$$y_i = z_i \quad ; \quad i \leq 0, \quad i > D \tag{6.42}$$

for the coefficients in the series expansion of $v''(t)$, we have

$$\begin{aligned} P(m_j | v(t)) &= P(m_j | v'(t), v''(t)) \\ &= P(m_j | v'(t)) = P(\underline{u}_j | \underline{v}) \end{aligned} \tag{6.43}$$

In other words, only the coefficients in the series expansion of $v(t)$ that are components of the vector $\underline{v}$ need to be taken into account in evaluating the a posteriori probabilities of the messages.

We have, by definition,

$$P(\underline{u}_j | \underline{v}) \equiv \frac{P(\underline{u}_j)\, p(\underline{v} | \underline{u}_j)}{p(\underline{v})} \tag{6.44}$$

On the other hand, the probability density $q(\underline{n})$ of the noise vector is the product of D gaussian densities each with zero mean and variance σ^2 given by Eq. 6.35, that is,

$$q(\underline{n}) = \prod_{i=1}^{D} \sqrt{\frac{T}{\pi N_o}}\; e^{-z_i^2 T/N_o} \tag{6.45}$$

Since $\underline{n}$ is statistically independent of $\underline{u}$,

$$p(\underline{v} | \underline{u}_j) = q(\underline{v} - \underline{u}_j) = \left(\frac{T}{\pi N_o}\right)^{D/2} e^{-|\underline{v} - \underline{u}_j|^2 T/N_o} \tag{6.46}$$

$$p(\underline{v}) = \sum_{k=1}^{M} P(\underline{u}_k)\, p(\underline{v}\,|\,\underline{u}_k) = \left(\frac{T}{\pi N_o}\right)^{D/2} e^{A} \qquad (6.47)$$

where A is given by Eq. 6.37. Finally, Eq. 6.36 follows immediately from Eqs. 6.34, 6.43, 6.44, 6.46, and 6.47. QED

6.4 Correlation Decoding

The expression for the mutual information I_j given by Eq. 6.36 is useful for certain analytical purposes, but its evaluation cannot be conveniently instrumented, because $T|\underline{v} - \underline{u}_j|^2$ is equal to the mean square difference between v'(t), defined by Eq. 6.40, and $u_j(t)$, rather than to the mean square difference between the entire channel output v(t) and $u_j(t)$. However, an expression whose evaluation can be conveniently instrumented in practice can be readily obtained from Eqs. 6.36 and 6.37 as indicated by the following theorem.

Theorem. Let v(t) be the output of a channel disturbed by additive, white, gaussian noise with power density N_o, and indicate with $u_j(t)$, $-T/2 < t < T/2$, the signal representing the message m_j occurring with probability $P(m_j)$. The mutual information I_j defined by Eq. 6.34 is given by

$$I_j = \frac{2T}{N_o}\left(\rho_j - \tfrac{1}{2} S_{jj}\right) - B \qquad (6.48)$$

where

$$\rho_j \equiv \frac{1}{T}\int_{-T/2}^{T/2} u_j(t)\, v(t)\, dt \qquad (6.49)$$

is the average cross power (cross-correlation coefficient) of the signal $u_j(t)$ and the channel output v(t), and

$$S_{jj} \equiv \frac{1}{T}\int_{-T/2}^{T/2} u_j^2(t)\, dt \qquad (6.50)$$

is the average power of the signal $u_j(t)$. The quantity B, a function of v(t), is given by

$$B \equiv \ln \sum_{k=1}^{M} P(m_k)\, e^{\frac{2T}{N_o}\left(\rho_k - \frac{1}{2} S_{kk}\right)} \qquad (6.51)$$

Proof. The expressions for I_j and A given by Eqs. 6.36 and 6.37 can be rewritten as follows:

$$I_j = -\frac{T}{N_o}\left(|\underline{u}_j|^2 - 2\,\underline{u}_j \cdot \underline{v} + |\underline{v}|^2\right) - A \tag{6.52}$$

$$A = -\frac{T}{N_o}|\underline{v}|^2 + \ln \sum_{k=1}^{M} P(m_k)\, e^{-\frac{T}{N_o}\left(|\underline{u}_k|^2 - 2\underline{u}_k \cdot \underline{v}\right)} \tag{6.53}$$

On the other hand, we have from Eqs. 5.114 and 6.40

$$\underline{u}_j \cdot \underline{v} = \frac{1}{T}\int_{-T/2}^{T/2} u_j(t)\, v'(t)\, dt \tag{6.54}$$

Similarly, we obtain from Eqs. 6.40 and 6.41

$$\frac{1}{T}\int_{-T/2}^{T/2} u_j(t)\, v''(t)\, dt = 0 \tag{6.55}$$

It follows that the scalar product $\underline{u}_j \cdot \underline{v}$ is equal to the average cross power ρ_j defined by Eq. 6.49. Furthermore, substituting $u_j(t)$ for v (t) in Eq. 6.54 yields Eq. 6.50. Finally, we obtain from Eqs. 6.52 and 6.53, with the help of Eqs. 6.49 and 6.50,

$$I_j = \frac{2T}{N_o}\left(\rho_j - \tfrac{1}{2} S_{jj}\right) - \ln \sum_{k=1}^{M} P(m_k)\, e^{\frac{2T}{N_o}\left(\rho_k - \frac{1}{2} S_{kk}\right)} \tag{6.56}$$

which yields Eqs. 6.48 and 6.51. QED

The two most common decoding criteria are maximum likelihood and maximum a posteriori probability, as discussed in Sec. 6.1. The decision operations to be performed by the decoder for these two criteria are specified by the following theorem.

Theorem. For a time-continuous channel disturbed by additive, white, stationary gaussian noise, decoding is accomplished by selecting, among the possible input messages, the message m_k for which

$$\rho_k - K_k > \rho_j - K_j \qquad \text{for all } j \neq k \tag{6.57}$$

where ρ_j is the average cross power defined by Eq. 6.49, and

$$K_j = \tfrac{1}{2} S_{jj} \tag{6.58}$$

when the decoding criterion is maximum likelihood, while

$$K_j = \tfrac{1}{2} S_{jj} - \frac{N_o}{2T} \ln P(m_j) \tag{6.59}$$

when the decoding criterion is maximum a posteriori probability. The average power S_{jj} of the signal representing the message m_j is defined by Eq. 6.50.

Proof. The maximum likelihood criterion requires the decoder to select the message m_j that maximizes the probability density $p(\underline{v} \mid m_j)$, that is, the message most likely to cause the channel output that has actually occurred. On the other hand, we have from Eqs. 6.34, 6.43, and 6.44

$$I_j = \ln \frac{p(\underline{v} \mid m_j)}{p(\underline{v})} \tag{6.60}$$

from which it follows that

$$\begin{aligned} \ln p(\underline{v} \mid m_j) &= I_j + \ln p(\underline{v}) \\ &= \frac{2T}{N_o} (\rho_j - \tfrac{1}{2} S_{jj}) - B + \ln p(\underline{v}) \end{aligned} \tag{6.61}$$

Furthermore, $p(\underline{v})$ and the quantity B given by Eq. 6.51 are independent of j. We can conclude that for any given channel output $\underline{v}$, maximizing $\rho_j - \frac{1}{2} S_{jj}$ is equivalent to maximizing $p(\underline{v} \mid m_j)$.

The criterion of maximum a posteriori probability requires the decoder to select for any particular channel output $v(t)$ the message m_j that maximizes the a posteriori probability $P(m_j \mid v(t))$. On the other hand, we have from Eqs. 6.34, 6.43, and 6.48

$$\begin{aligned} \ln P(m_j \mid v(t)) &= I_j + \ln P(m_j) \\ &= \frac{2T}{N_o} (\rho_j - \tfrac{1}{2} S_{jj}) - B + \ln P(m_j) \end{aligned} \tag{6.62}$$

Again, B is independent of m_j. It follows that B can be disregarded in maximizing the righthand side of Eq. 6.62. QED

It is evident from this theorem that the cross powers ρ_j are the only quantities involved in the decoding operation that depend on the channel output. Thus the probability computers shown in Fig. 6.2 need only evaluate the M numbers ρ_j corresponding to the M possible messages. The M values K_j can be stored in the decision circuit, as biases, for instance.

Since the decoding operation is performed on the cross powers ρ_j, the probability of occurrence of a decoding error depends on their joint probability distribution.

Theorem. Let v(t) be the output of a channel disturbed by additive, white, gaussian noise, and indicate with $u_j(t)$, $-T/2 < t < T/2$, the signal corresponding to the message m_j, and with

$$S_{jk} \equiv \frac{1}{T} \int_{-T/2}^{T/2} u_j(t)\, u_k(t)\, dt \tag{6.63}$$

the average cross power between the signals corresponding to m_j and m_k. The joint conditional probability density $p(\rho_1, \rho_2, \ldots, \rho_M | m_k)$ is gaussian with mean values

$$\overline{\rho}_j = S_{jk} \tag{6.64}$$

and covariances

$$\overline{(\rho_j - \overline{\rho}_j)(\rho_h - \overline{\rho}_h)} = \frac{N_o}{2T} S_{jh} \tag{6.65}$$

Proof. The output vector $\underline{v}$ is related to the input vector $\underline{u}_k$ by

$$\underline{v} = \underline{u}_k + \underline{n} \tag{6.66}$$

and the components z_i of the noise vector $\underline{n}$ are statistically independent and gaussianly distributed with zero mean and variance $N_o/2T$. On the other hand, we have from Eqs. 6.49 and 6.66

$$\rho_j = \underline{u}_j \cdot (\underline{u}_k + \underline{n}) = \underline{u}_j \cdot \underline{u}_k + \underline{u}_j \cdot \underline{n} \tag{6.67}$$

and, with the help of Eq. 5.114,

$$\underline{u}_j \cdot \underline{u}_k = \frac{1}{T} \int_{-T/2}^{T/2} u_j(t)\, u_k(t)\, dt = S_{jk} \tag{6.68}$$

It follows that the random variables ρ_j are linear combinations of the gaussianly distributed random variables z_i and, therefore, are themselves gaussianly distributed.

The mean value of ρ_j is

$$\overline{\rho}_j = S_{jk} + \sum_{i=1}^{D} x_{ji}\, \overline{z}_i = S_{jk} \tag{6.69}$$

where x_{ji} is the ith component of the vector $\underline{u}_j$. The covariance of ρ_j and ρ_h is

$$\overline{(\rho_j - \overline{\rho}_j)(\rho_h - \overline{\rho}_h)} = \overline{(\underline{u}_j \cdot \underline{n})(\underline{u}_h \cdot \underline{n})} = \sum_{i=1}^{D} \sum_{r=1}^{D} x_{ij} x_{rh} \overline{z_i z_r}$$

$$= \sum_{i=1}^{D} x_{ij} x_{ih} \overline{z_i^2} = S_{jh} \frac{N_o}{2T} \qquad (6.70)$$

QED

The encoding and decoding operations discussed above may be conveniently instrumented with pairs of matched filters. Two filters F and F* are said to be matched when the impulse responses h(t) and h*(t) are related by

$$h^*(t) = h(\tau_o - t) \qquad (6.71)$$

where τ_o is an appropriate constant. In other words, the impulse responses of matched filters are obtained from each other by inverting the direction of the time scale and adding an appropriate delay. Since the response of a filter to an impulse occurring at $t = 0$ must vanish for $t < 0$, Eq. 6.71 can be satisfied with a finite τ_o only when h(t) vanishes outside some finite time interval $0 < t < T$, in which case $\tau_o = T$. It is well known that the frequency responses of two filters whose impulse responses satisfy Eq. 6.71 are complex conjugates of each other except for a linear phase shift corresponding to the delay τ_o.

Let us suppose that the signal generators on the lefthand side of Fig. 6.2 are filters F_i with impulse responses equal to the signals $u_j(t)$, and that the signal selector excites with an impulse (an appropriate narrow pulse, in practice) the filter F_k corresponding to the message m_k to be transmitted. Then, if the channel output is fed to a bank of M filters matched to the filters that generate the message signals, the output $f_j(t)$ of the filter F_j^* will be

$$f_j(t) = \int_{-\infty}^{\infty} v(\theta)\, h_j^*(t - \theta)\, d\theta$$

$$= \int_{-\infty}^{\infty} v(\theta)\, h_j(T + \theta - t)\, d\theta \qquad (6.72)$$

It follows that if the exciting impulse occurs at $t = -T/2$ and the impulse response of F_j is

$$h_j(t) = u_j\left(t - \frac{T}{2}\right) \qquad (6.73)$$

the output of the filter F_j^* at $t = T/2$ is

$$f_j\left(\frac{T}{2}\right) = \int_{-T/2}^{T/2} v(\theta)\, u_j(\theta)\, d\theta = \rho_j T \tag{6.74}$$

In other words, the output of F_j^* at $t = T/2$ is equal to the average cross power ρ_j multiplied by T. Thus the probability computers on the righthand side of Fig. 6.2 can be instrumented as filters matched to those employed as signal generators.

The following simple example will illustrate some of the results obtained in this section and in the preceding one. Let us suppose that the D orthonormal functions from which the message signals are constructed are non-overlapping, rectangular pulses of width T/D, that is,

$$\phi_i(t) = \begin{cases} \sqrt{D} & ; \quad t_i - \frac{T}{D} < t \le t_i \, ; \; i = 1, 2, \ldots, D \\ 0 & ; \quad \text{otherwise} \end{cases} \tag{6.75}$$

where

$$t_i = -\frac{T}{2} + i\,\frac{T}{D} \tag{6.76}$$

It can be readily checked that these functions satisfy Eq. 5.114. There are many ways in which the remaining orthonormal functions can be selected so that the same equation is satisfied by the entire set.

With this choice of orthonormal functions, the signals $u_j(t)$ become sequences of pulses of width T/D with arbitrary magnitudes and polarities. The components of the vectors $\underline{u}_j$ are equal to the algebraic amplitudes of the pulses divided by $\sqrt{D}$. The components z_i of the noise vector $\underline{n}$ are given by

$$z_i = \frac{1}{T}\int_{-T/2}^{T/2} n(t)\, \phi_i(t)\, dt = \frac{\sqrt{D}}{T}\int_{t_i - T/D}^{t_i} n(t)\, dt \;;\; i = 1, 2, \ldots, D \tag{6.77}$$

Similarly, the components y_i of the output vector $\underline{v}$ are given by

$$y_i = \frac{\sqrt{D}}{T}\int_{t_i - T/D}^{t_i} v(t)\, dt \tag{6.78}$$

Thus we may regard the channel noise and the channel output as sequences of pulses of width T/D occurring in synchronism with the pulses constituting the input signal. Of course, each output pulse is the sum of the corresponding input pulse and the corresponding noise pulse. Since the components z_i of the noise vector $\underline{n}$ are statistically independent and gaussianly distributed with zero mean and variance given by Eq. 6.35, the amplitudes of the noise pulses are statistically independent and gaussianly distributed with zero mean and variance $N_o D/2T$. It is interesting to note that if we define the effective bandwidth occupied by the pulses as

$$W \equiv \frac{D}{2T} \tag{6.79}$$

the variance of the amplitude of each noise pulse becomes equal to $N_o W$, that is, to the noise power in the bandwidth W. The average cross power ρ_j, defined by Eq. 6.49, is equal to the sum of the products of the amplitudes of the signal pulses and the corresponding amplitudes of the output pulses divided by D.

This pulse model of transmission through a channel disturbed by additive, white, gaussian noise may be very helpful in interpreting the results obtained above, and in reconstructing them from memory. Another advantage of such a model is that pairs of matched filters with impulse responses consisting of successive pulses of constant width can be readily constructed with the help of delay lines with equally spaced taps.

6.5 Orthogonal Signals in White, Gaussian Noise

We shall evaluate in this section the probability of error when the messages are equiprobable and are represented by mutually orthogonal time functions with the same average power S. We shall assume, as in the preceding section, that the channel noise is additive, white, stationary, and gaussianly distributed. Under these conditions we have from Eq. 6.63

$$S_{jk} \equiv \frac{1}{T} \int_{-T/2}^{T/2} u_j(t)\, u_k(t)\, dt = \begin{cases} S \;; & j = k \\ 0 \;; & j \neq k \end{cases} \tag{6.80}$$

It is convenient to select the set of orthonormal functions $\phi_i(t)$ used in the series representation of the noise in such a way that $D = M$ of them are proportional to the M message signals, that is,

$$u_j(t) = \sqrt{S}\; \phi_j(t) \qquad ; \qquad 1 \leq i \leq D = M \tag{6.81}$$

For any such selection of the $\phi_j(t)$, each message vector $\underline{u}_j$ has a single component different from zero, that is,

$$x_{ij} = \begin{cases} \sqrt{S} & ; \quad i = j \\ 0 & ; \quad i \neq j \end{cases} \tag{6.82}$$

where S is the common average power of the signals representing the M messages.

Since the messages are, by assumption, equiprobable, and the corresponding signals have the same average power, it follows from the theorem incorporating Eq. 6.57 that the probability of error is minimized when the channel output is decoded into the message m_j that maximizes the average cross power ρ_j defined by Eq. 6.49. Let m_k be the message actually transmitted. We obtain from Eq. 6.49 with the help of Eqs. 6.80 and 6.81,

$$\rho_j = y_j \sqrt{S} = z_j \sqrt{S} + \begin{cases} S & ; \quad j = k \\ 0 & ; \quad j \neq k \end{cases} \tag{6.83}$$

where y_j is the jth component of the output vector $\underline{v}$, and z_j is the corresponding component of the noise vector $\underline{n}$. Then solving for y_j yields

$$y_j = \frac{\rho_j}{\sqrt{S}} = z_j + \begin{cases} \sqrt{S} & ; \quad j = k \\ 0 & ; \quad j \neq k \end{cases} \tag{6.84}$$

Since the y_j are proportional to the corresponding ρ_j, it follows from the theorem incorporating Eqs. 6.63, 6.64, and 6.65 that for any given transmitted message m_k, the random variables y_j are statistically independent and gaussianly distributed with mean

$$\overline{y_j} = \begin{cases} \sqrt{S} & ; \quad j = k \\ 0 & ; \quad j \neq k \end{cases} \tag{6.85}$$

and variance

$$\sigma^2 = \overline{(y_j - \overline{y}_j)^2} = \frac{N_o}{2T} \tag{6.86}$$

According to our decoding criterion, the decoder must select for any channel output the message that maximizes ρ_j, and therefore

y_j. It follows that if m_k is the message actually transmitted, the channel output will be correctly decoded when the component y_k of the output vector $\underline{v}$ is larger than all the other components y_j of the same vector. Thus the probability of error for any message is

$$P(e) = 1 - \Pr(\text{all } y_j < y_k) \quad ; \quad 1 \leq j \neq k \leq M \tag{6.87}$$

Theorem. Consider an ensemble of M equiprobable messages represented by time functions with the same average power S and mutually orthogonal over a time interval T, and indicate with

$$R \equiv \frac{\log_2 M}{T} \text{ bits/sec} \tag{6.88}$$

the corresponding information rate, that is, the self information per second of the message ensemble. If such messages are transmitted through a time-continuous channel disturbed by additive, white, stationary, gaussian noise with power density N_o having a capacity

$$C = \frac{S}{N_o} \log_2 e \text{ bits/sec} \tag{6.89}$$

the channel output can be decoded with a probability of error

$$P(e) < K\, 2^{-TC\alpha} \tag{6.90}$$

where

$$K \equiv \frac{\sqrt{\log_2 e}}{\sqrt{4\pi CT}} \begin{cases} \left[\dfrac{1}{1 - \sqrt{R/C}} + \dfrac{\sqrt{\log_2 e}}{\sqrt{4\pi RT}\,(2\sqrt{R/C} - 1)}\right]; & \frac{1}{4} < \dfrac{R}{C} < 1 \\[2ex] \left[\dfrac{\sqrt{2}}{\sqrt{1 - 2R/C}} + \dfrac{1}{\sqrt{2} - \sqrt{1 - 2R/C}}\right] \;; & 0 \leq \dfrac{R}{C} \leq \frac{1}{4} \end{cases} \tag{6.91}$$

and

$$\alpha \equiv \begin{cases} \left[1 - \sqrt{\dfrac{R}{C}}\right]^2 \;; & \frac{1}{4} < \dfrac{R}{C} < 1 \\[2ex] \frac{1}{2} - \dfrac{R}{C} \;; & 0 \leq \dfrac{R}{C} \leq \frac{1}{4} \end{cases} \tag{6.92}$$

Proof. The probability that any one component of the output vector $\underline{v}$ be smaller than y_k is given by

$$\Pr(y < y_k) = 1 - \int_{y_k}^{\infty} \frac{1}{\sqrt{2\pi}\,\sigma} e^{-y^2/2\sigma^2}\, dy = 1 - \Pr(y \geq y_k) \tag{6.93}$$

The probability that all the components y_j of $\underline{v}$ with $j \neq k$ be simultaneously smaller than y_k is

$$Q(y_k) \equiv \prod_{\text{all } j \neq k} \Pr(y_j < y_k) = [1 - \Pr(y \geq y_k)]^{M-1} \tag{6.94}$$

in view of the fact that the y_j are statistically independent and equally distributed. It follows that the probability of error can be expressed in the form

$$P(e) = 1 - \int_{-\infty}^{\infty} p(y_k)\, Q(y_k)\, dy_k \tag{6.95}$$

where

$$p(y_k) = \frac{1}{\sqrt{2\pi}\,\sigma} e^{-(y_k - \sqrt{S})^2/2\sigma^2} \tag{6.96}$$

Although the probability of error can be readily evaluated by numerical integration from Eq. 6.95, it is very desirable to estimate its value by means of some readily computable upper bound. It is clear from Eq. 6.94 that the probability $Q(y_k)$ approaches 1 when y_k approaches ∞, and approaches zero when y_k approaches $-\infty$. For values of $Q(y_k)$ close to unity, the following well-known inequality provides a convenient lower-bound approximation

$$Q(y_k) \geq 1 - (M-1)\Pr(y \geq y_k) > 1 - M \Pr(y \geq y_k) \tag{6.97}$$

However, this approximation becomes very poor when $\Pr(y \geq y_k)$ approaches unity. As a matter of fact, the righthand side of Eq. 6.97 becomes negative. A more appropriate lower-bound approximation for such values of $\Pr(y \geq y_k)$ is provided by the trivial inequality

$$Q(y_k) \geq 0 \tag{6.98}$$

Thus we shall approximate $Q(y_k)$ with the function

$$Q_o(y_k) \equiv \begin{cases} 0 & ; \quad y_k \leq a \\ 1 - M \Pr(y \geq y_k) & ; \quad y_k > a \end{cases} \tag{6.99}$$

which is a lower bound to $Q(y_k)$ for all values of y_k. The value of the parameter a will be selected in such a way as to optimize the approximation.

Substituting the lower bound $Q_o(y_k)$ for $Q(y_k)$ in Eq. 6.95 yields

$$P(e) < 1 - \int_a^\infty p(y_k)\,[1 - M \Pr(y \geq y_k)]\, dy_k = P_1 + M P_2 \tag{6.100}$$

where

$$P_1 \equiv \int_{-\infty}^{a} p(y_k)\, dy_k = \int_{-\infty}^{a} \frac{1}{\sqrt{2\pi}\sigma} e^{-(y_k - \sqrt{S})^2/2\sigma^2}\, dy_k \tag{6.101}$$

$$P_2 \equiv \int_a^\infty p(y_k) \Pr(y \geq y_k)\, dy_k \tag{6.102}$$

Let us first evaluate P_1. Making the change of variable

$$t = (y_k - \sqrt{S})/\sigma \tag{6.103}$$

in Eq. 6.101, and using the well-known inequality

$$\int_x^\infty \frac{1}{\sqrt{2\pi}} e^{-t^2/2}\, dt \leq \frac{1}{\sqrt{2\pi}\, x} e^{-x^2/2} \quad ; \quad x > 0 \tag{6.104}$$

we obtain

$$\begin{aligned} P_1 &= \int_{-\infty}^{(a-\sqrt{S})/\sigma} \frac{1}{\sqrt{2\pi}} e^{-t^2/2}\, dt = \int_{(\sqrt{S}-a)/\sigma}^{\infty} \frac{1}{\sqrt{2\pi}} e^{-t^2/2}\, dt \\ &\leq \frac{1}{\sqrt{2\pi}} \frac{\sigma}{\sqrt{S} - a} e^{-(\sqrt{S}-a)^2/2\sigma^2} \quad ; \quad \sqrt{S} - a > 0 \end{aligned} \tag{6.105}$$

The first step in the evaluation of P_2 consists of finding a suitable upper bound to $\Pr(y \geq y_k)$. We obtain from Eq. 6.93, with the help of Eq. 6.104,

$$\Pr(y \geq y_k) = \int_{y_k}^{\infty} \frac{1}{\sqrt{2\pi}\,\sigma} e^{-y^2/2\sigma^2}\, dy \leq \frac{1}{\sqrt{2\pi}} \frac{\sigma}{y_k} e^{-y_k^2/2\sigma^2} \quad ; \; y_k > 0 \tag{6.106}$$

Substitution of this expression in Eq. 6.102 yields, with the help of Eq. 6.96,

$$P_2 \leq \int_a^{\infty} \frac{1}{2\pi y_k} e^{-[(y_k - \sqrt{S})^2 + y_k^2]/2\sigma^2}\, dy_k \quad ; \; a > 0 \tag{6.107}$$

Since the lower limit of integration in this equation is the parameter a, $y_k \geq a$ within the range of integration. It follows that the value of the integral is increased if a is substituted for y_k in the denominator of the integrand. This substitution yields

$$P_2 < \int_a^{\infty} \frac{1}{2\pi a} e^{-[(2y_k - \sqrt{S})^2 + S]/4\sigma^2}\, dy_k$$

$$= \frac{\sigma}{\sqrt{4\pi}\, a} e^{-S/4\sigma^2} \int_{(2a-\sqrt{S})/\sqrt{2}\sigma}^{\infty} \frac{1}{\sqrt{2\pi}} e^{-\theta^2/2}\, d\theta \; ; \quad a > 0 \tag{6.108}$$

where

$$\theta = \frac{2y_k - \sqrt{S}}{\sqrt{2}\,\sigma} \tag{6.109}$$

An upper bound to the integral on the righthand side of Eq. 6.108 can be obtained with the help of Eq. 6.104 when the lower limit of integration is positive. When the lower limit of integration is negative, the entire integral can be set equal to 1, thereby increasing the value of the integral by at most a factor of 2. In conclusion, the probability P_2 can be bounded by

$$P_2 < \begin{cases} \dfrac{\sigma^2}{2\pi a(2a - \sqrt{S})} e^{-[(2a-\sqrt{S})^2 + S]/4\sigma^2} \; ; & \sqrt{S}/2 < a \\[2ex] \dfrac{\sigma}{\sqrt{4\pi}\; a} e^{-S/4\sigma^2} \; ; & 0 < a \leq \sqrt{S}/2 \end{cases} \tag{6.110}$$

The next step is the optimization of the parameter a. For this purpose, let us indicate with β_1 and β_2 the exponents on the righthand sides of Eqs. 6.105 and 6.110, respectively, and with b_1 and b_2 the corresponding factors by which the exponentials are multiplied. Then substituting for P_1 and P_2 in Eq. 6.100 the corresponding upper bounds given by Eqs. 6.105 and 6.110 yields

$$P(e) < b_1 \, e^{\beta_1} + b_2 \, e^{\beta_2 + \ln M} \tag{6.111}$$

The value of the parameter a should be adjusted to minimize the righthand side of this inequality. This, however, leads to a rather involved expression for a. Actually, we are not so much interested in obtaining the smallest possible upper bound as in obtaining a simple bound which is still reasonably good. Thus it would seem reasonable to adjust the value of a in such a way that

$$\beta_1 = \beta_2 + \ln M \tag{6.112}$$

Since the righthand side of Eq. 6.111 is primarily controlled by the two exponentials, equating the two exponents approximately minimizes the whole expression.

Substituting for β_1 and β_2 in Eq. 6.112 the corresponding exponents in Eq. 6.105 and 6.110 yields, with the help of Eq. 6.86,

$$\ln M - [(2a - \sqrt{S})^2 + S] \frac{T}{2N_o} = -(\sqrt{S} - a)^2 \frac{T}{N_o} \quad ; \quad \tfrac{1}{2} < \frac{a}{\sqrt{S}} < 1 \tag{6.113}$$

$$\ln M - S \frac{T}{2N_o} = -(\sqrt{S} - a)^2 \frac{T}{N_o} \quad ; \quad 0 < \frac{a}{\sqrt{S}} \le \tfrac{1}{2} \tag{6.114}$$

from which we obtain

$$a = \begin{cases} \sqrt{S} \sqrt{\dfrac{R}{C}} & ; \quad \tfrac{1}{2} < \sqrt{\dfrac{R}{C}} < 1 \\[2ex] \sqrt{S} \left[1 - \dfrac{1}{\sqrt{2}} \sqrt{1 - 2\dfrac{R}{C}} \right] & ; \quad 0 \le \sqrt{\dfrac{R}{C}} \le \tfrac{1}{2} \end{cases} \tag{6.115}$$

where R and C are the information rate and the channel capacity given by Eqs. 6.88 and 6.89.

Finally, substituting for P_1 and P_2 in Eq. 6.100 the righthand sides of Eqs. 6.105 and 6.110, evaluated for the values of the parameter a given by Eq. 6.115, yields Eq. 6.90. QED

The time functions employed to represent the M possible messages have been assumed to be mutually orthogonal over the time interval T, but are otherwise arbitrary. For instance, each message m_k could be represented by a sinusoidal signal of frequency

$$f_k = \frac{n + k}{T} \quad ; \quad 1 \leq k \leq M \tag{6.116}$$

where k is an integer characterizing the M different frequencies and n is a fixed integer. This particular set of mutually orthogonal signals yields a form of encoding that may be called quantized frequency modulation. It should be noted, however, that the decoding procedure is quite different from that commonly used in frequency-modulation receivers.

Another example of mutually orthogonal signals is provided by quantized pulse-position modulation. In this form of encoding, the M signals are non-overlapping pulses of width T/M. These signals are mutually orthogonal over the time interval T because each of them vanishes when any one of the others differs from zero. Again, the decoding procedure assumed in this section differs from that usually employed in pulse-position-modulation receivers.

It can be readily seen that the bandwidth occupied by the signals in these two types of encoding must increase almost exponentially with T for a fixed transmission rate R. In the frequency-modulation case, the spacing between frequencies corresponding to different messages is inversely proportional to T, as indicated by Eq. 6.116, but the number of messages M must increase exponentially with T. In the pulse-position-modulation case, the width of the pulses is directly proportional to T but inversely proportional to M. Therefore, the bandwidth occupied by the pulses is proportional to M/T.

This almost exponential increase with T of the bandwidth occupied by the signals is a general consequence of their mutual orthogonality. In fact, if the M signals are limited to some bandwidth W in the sense discussed in Sec. 5.7, they can be represented by vectors in a space with 2TW dimensions. Then the maximum number of mutually orthogonal vectors that can exist in such a space is just equal to the dimensionality of the space, so that

$$M \leq 2TW \tag{6.117}$$

It follows that for a fixed transmission rate, the product WT must increase exponentially with T.

The requirement that the time functions representing the messages be mutually orthogonal was imposed only for the sake of simplifying the evaluation of the probability of error. Shannon[1] has obtained a similar upper bound to the probability of error for signals (not necessarily orthogonal) limited to a finite bandwidth W. This bound has the same exponential form as that obtained in this section, and the exponent is similarly proportional to T. Furthermore, if the bandwidth is so large that the signal-to-noise ratio within the prescribed frequency band is

$$\frac{S}{N} = \frac{S}{N_o W} \ll 1 \tag{6.118}$$

the exponential coefficient α obtained by Shannon is identical to that given by Eq. 6.92.

6.6. Discussion of Results

The upper bound to the probability of error given by Eqs. 6.90, 6.91, and 6.92 as a function of the time interval T, the channel capacity C, and the transmission rate R, deserves detailed discussion because it is typical of the bounds to the probability of error that have been obtained for many other channels. Some of these bounds will be derived in the following chapters.

The factor K in Eq. 6.90 decreases slowly with increasing T, and is a function of R and C. The exponent in the same equation is negative for any $R < C$, and its magnitude is proportional to T for fixed values of R and C. It follows that for any fixed $R < C$, the probability of error approaches zero with increasing T slightly faster than exponentially. In other words, there is no theoretical limit to the accuracy of transmission that can be achieved, provided only that the transmission rate R is smaller than the channel capacity C.

The exponential factor α, given by Eq. 6.92, is plotted in Fig. 6.3 as a function of R/C. It can be readily checked that the slope

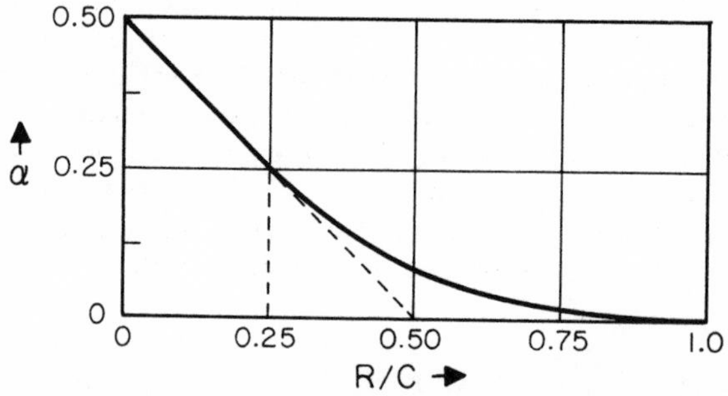

Fig. 6.3. Plot of exponential coefficient α as a function of R/C.

of the curve is continuous at the point $R/C = 1/4$, that is, at the point where the functional dependence of α on R/C changes. For $R/C < 1/4$, α is linearly related to R/C. The continuation of this straight-line part of the plot in Fig. 6.3 intersects the R/C axis at the point 1/2. For $R/C > 1/4$, the value of α continues to decrease with increasing R/C, and vanishes with a zero derivative for $R/C = 1$.

The probability of error is primarily controlled by the magnitude of the exponent αCT. Thus the same probability of error can be obtained either with a relatively large value of α and a relatively small value of CT, or vice versa. It is clear, on the other hand, that a relatively large value of α implies a relatively small value of R/C, that is, a relatively inefficient use of the available channel capacity. Conversely, a relatively large value of CT (the channel capacity per message) implies that the number of messages is relatively large. The relation between the number of messages and the transmission rate is more readily investigated by rewriting Eq. 6.90 in the form

$$P(e) < K2^{-\nu\alpha\frac{C}{R}} \tag{6.119}$$

where ν is the number of binary digits constituting a message, which is related to the number M of distinct messages and to the information transmission rate R by

$$\nu = \log_2 M = RT \tag{6.120}$$

The exponential factor $\alpha C/R$ is plotted in Fig. 6.4 as a function of C/R.

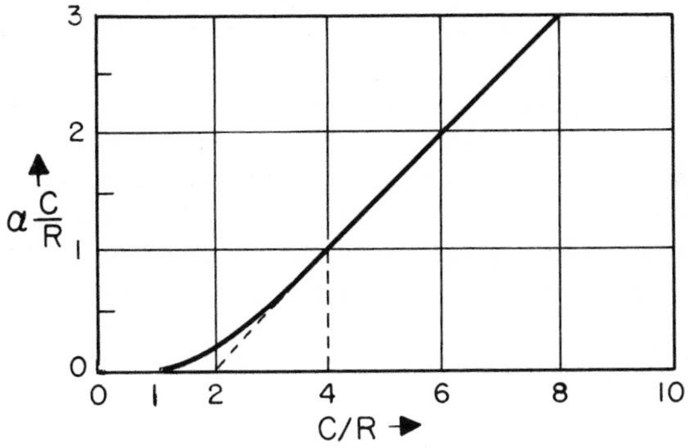

Fig. 6.4. Plot of exponential coefficient $\alpha C/R$ as a function of C/R

Let us suppose that the product $\nu\alpha C/R$ is to be equal to 10. Then for C/R = 4, ν must be equal to 10. This implies that the number of messages must be M = 1024. The corresponding probability of error is approximately 2×10^{-4}. In order to make $\nu = 4$ (corresponding to M = 16), the value of $\alpha C/R$ would have to be increased to 2.5. This value corresponds in Fig. 6.4 to C/R = 7, which implies a rather inefficient use of the channel.

This example indicates that the number of messages M must

be rather large to permit efficient transmission with a reasonably low probability of error. Furthermore, for a fixed channel and a fixed transmission rate, the probability of error decreases roughly exponentially with ν, while the number of messages M increases exponentially with ν, so that M is roughly inversely proportional to the probability of error. Thus efficient transmission with the encoding and decoding procedures discussed in this section requires prohibitively complex terminal equipment. In fact, the encoder must be capable of generating any one of M different time functions, and the decoder must compare the channel output with each of the M possible message signals in order to determine which message is a posteriori most probable.

An approximately linear growth with M of the complexity of the decoding operation can be expected whenever the decoding criterion requires that some function of a message signal and of the channel output, such as the a posteriori probability, be strictly optimized. In order to circumvent such a linear growth with M, strict optimization must be replaced by some approximate, threshold-type optimization.

Aside from the complexity of the decoding operation itself, the fact that both the encoder and the decoder must be capable of generating any one of M different signals (the decoder must be able to compare them with the channel output) presents serious practical difficulties. If the signals are actually stored in some appropriate medium, the capacity of the storage medium must be proportional to the product MT. This practical difficulty can be circumvented by employing message signals that can be generated, when needed, directly from the binary representation of the message to be transmitted. For instance, if the M mutually orthogonal signals $u_k(t)$ of the preceding section are pulses of fixed amplitude and width T/M occurring at M distinct times,

$$t_k \equiv k\frac{T}{M} + \tau \quad ; \quad 1 \leq k \leq M, \ \tau = \text{constant} \tag{6.121}$$

the encoder may consist simply of a pulse generator triggered by a suitable binary counter.

A little thought indicates, however, that in order for any such encoding procedure to be practical, the message signals must be representable as sequences of elementary time functions selected from a finite, and rather small, alphabet. In other words, the time-continuous input space of the channel in question must be first "quantized" into a discrete space consisting of a finite number of distinct time functions extending over some elementary time interval τ_o. Then appropriate message signals can be constructed as sequences of such time functions in successive elementary time intervals of length τ_o. For instance, the elementary time functions may be pulses of fixed shape and different amplitudes.

A similar "quantization" of the channel output space is often required in practice, because the operations to be performed by the decoder are so complex that they are best executed by digital means. For instance, if the input elementary time functions are pulses of different amplitudes, and the channel is of the type assumed in the preceding three sections, the average value of the channel output over each successive elementary time interval may be quantized to a finite number of amplitudes, both positive and negative, not necessarily equal to the number of allowed amplitudes of the input pulses.

For instance, a time-continuous channel disturbed by additive, stationary, white, gaussian noise becomes a binary, symmetric channel when the input pulses differ only in polarity, and only the polarity of the average value of the channel output in each elementary time interval is taken into account by the decoder. If $\sqrt{S}$ is the magnitude of the input pulses and N_o is the power density of the noise, and

$$\frac{2S\tau_o}{N_o} \ll 1 \tag{6.122}$$

the capacity of the binary channel turns out to be

$$C_b = \frac{2}{\pi}\frac{S}{N_o}\log_2 e = \frac{2}{\pi}C \text{ bits/sec} \tag{6.123}$$

where C is the capacity of the time-continuous channel.

The conclusion that we wish to draw from the above arguments is that practical considerations almost always require reducing a time-continuous channel to a discrete channel, as a first step in the design of a suitable encoder and decoder. Various considerations which cannot be discussed at this time are involved in the selection of such a discrete channel. The most important one is, of course, that the capacity of the discrete channel should not be unduly smaller than the capacity of the original channel. We must keep in mind, in this respect, that if the discrete model involves restricting the channel input over any time interval τ_o to L distinct time functions, the capacity per second of the discrete channel is

$$C_d \leq \frac{\log L}{\tau_o} \tag{6.124}$$

6.7. Summary and Conclusions

This chapter has served the purpose of introducing the fundamental concepts of block encoding and block decoding and of illustrating with a simple example the behavior of the probability of error as a function of the information transmission rate and of the number of binary digits that are simultaneously block encoded.

We began our discussion by defining the operation of encoding as a mapping of the M points of the message space into properly selected points of the channel input space, and the operation of decoding as a partition of the channel output space into M subsets. Each of these subsets corresponds to a particular message in the sense that all the channel outputs belonging to it are to be decoded into the corresponding message. It was pointed out in this connection that the probability of occurrence of a decoding error is minimized by including in each subset the channel outputs for which the corresponding message is a posteriori most probable. While such a decoding criterion is the one most commonly employed, the above definition of the decoding operation is not restricted to any particular decoding criterion. For instance, in the case of maximum likelihood decoding, each subset of the output space includes all the channel outputs whose conditional probability, given the corresponding message, is greater than for any other message.

Next, we turned our attention to the relation between the probability of occurrence of a decoding error and the message equivocation, that is, the conditional entropy of the message ensemble given the subset to which the channel output belongs. We first showed that this conditional entropy is at least as great as the conditional entropy of the message ensemble given the channel output itself. Then, we were able to derive an inequality stating that the message equivocation cannot exceed the average amount of information required to correct the errors committed by the decoder. Finally, this inequality was used to show that there exists a finite lower bound to the probability of error when the transmission rate exceeds the channel capacity. This last statement is known as the converse of the coding theorem for randomly disturbed channels.

The remainder of the chapter dealt with the transmission of messages through time-continuous channels disturbed by additive, stationary, white, gaussian noise. We began our discussion of this problem by pointing out that while the representation of the decoding operation in terms of subsets of the channel output space is convenient for analytical purposes, it does not portray the operations that the decoder must perform in practice. Since it is not feasible to store the partitioning of the channel output space, the decoder must compute from the actual channel output the mutual information between the channel output and each of the possible input messages. All the decoding criteria of practical interest can be instrumented by selecting the message that maximizes the sum of the mutual information and an appropriate function of the message. In particular, when the messages are equiprobable, the probability of error is minimized by selecting the message with the largest mutual information.

We showed next that in the particular case of the channel under consideration, the mutual information between the channel output and any one of the possible input messages can be expressed as the sum of the average cross power (cross-correlation coefficient) between the channel output and the signal representing the message, and a quantity independent of the channel output. Thus the decoding operation consists primarily of the evaluation of the average cross powers between the channel output and the possible message signals. In the particular case of equiprobable messages and signals with the same average power, the probability of error is minimized by decoding the channel output into the message with the largest average cross power. We pointed out in this connection that the operations of encoding and decoding can be conveniently instrumented with pairs of matched filters.

Finally, we evaluated an upper bound to the probability of error in the special case of equiprobable, mutually orthogonal signals with the same average power. This upper bound turned out to vanish exponentially with increasing message length for any fixed transmission rate smaller than the channel capacity. We stressed in this connection that such a behavior of the probability of error is typical of that obtained for a large class of randomly disturbed channels. We shall derive in the following chapters similar upper bounds to the probability of error for discrete, constant channels.

For the sake of mathematical simplicity, the discussion in most of this chapter was restricted to time-continuous channels disturbed by additive, stationary, white, gaussian noise. The results obtained can be generalized, with suitable modifications, to the case of non-white noise; some of the results can be generalized to dispersive channels with random impulse responses. Several such topics concerning the decoding of message signals that have been omitted here are discussed in Refs. [2] and [3].

We stressed in the last section that we are often forced in practice to quantize the input and output spaces of time-continuous channels for the sake of simplifying the instrumentation of the channel encoder and of the channel decoder. It is for this reason that discrete channels are of great practical importance in spite of the fact that most physical channels are time continuous. It must be remembered, however, that the capacity of any discrete model of a time-continuous channel will, in general, be smaller than the capacity of the original channel. Thus the construction of a discrete model of a time-continuous channel must be regarded as part of the design of the encoder and of the decoder.

The next three chapters are devoted to the encoding and decoding of messages for transmission through discrete, constant channels. We shall treat first the special case of binary, symmetric channels because of its lesser mathematical complexity. The general case of discrete, constant channels, discussed in Chapter 9, will require special mathematical techniques, which will be presented in Chapter 8.

6.8. Selected References

1. C. E. Shannon, "Probability of Error for Optimal Codes in a Gaussian Channel," Bell System Tech. J., 38, 611, May, 1959.

2. W. B. Davenport, Jr., and W. L. Root, Random Signals and Noise, McGraw-Hill, New York, 1958. Chapter 14 discusses various aspects of the decoding of signals in the presence of additive noise.

3. D. Middleton, Statistical Communication Theory, McGraw-Hill, New York, 1960. Part 4 discusses the same general subject as Ref. 2 above, but in greater detail. Extensive bibliographies are provided at the end of each chapter.

Chapter 7

ENCODING FOR BINARY SYMMETRIC CHANNELS

We shall discuss in this chapter the encoding and decoding of messages for transmission through a binary symmetric channel. The input alphabet of this channel consists of two symbols to which we shall refer as 0 and 1, and its output space consists also of two symbols to which we shall refer similarly as 0 and 1. Either input symbol is transformed by the channel noise into the other symbol with probability p, and remains unchanged with probability $1 - p$, as indicated in Fig. 7.1. We shall refer to p as the "noise probability." The capacity of such a channel in bits per input digit was found in Sec. 5.3 to be

$$C = 1 + p \log_2 p + (1-p) \log_2 (1-p) \tag{7.1}$$

A large part of the literature on encoding and decoding is concerned with the binary symmetric channel because of its great simplicity. Although all the important results obtained about binary symmetric channels have been generalized to broader classes of channels, it is still desirable to focus our attention on this simple channel to prevent extraneous mathematical complications from obscuring the aspects of encoding and decoding in which we are interested. Thus, the relative emphasis given here, as well as elsewhere, to the binary symmetric channel should not be interpreted as an indication that the binary symmetric channel is the channel of greatest practical importance, or even less that the encoding and decoding of messages require, in practice, that a physical channel be reduced to a binary symmetric channel.

Most of the results presented in this chapter were originally obtained by P. Elias [1].

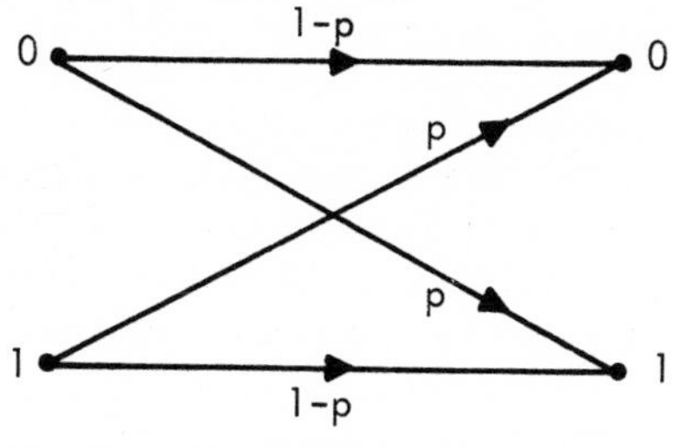

Fig. 7.1. Binary symmetric channel

7.1. The Binomial Distribution

We shall need in our study of binary symmetric channels various bounds on the binomial probability distribution [2]. These bounds are derived in this section, ahead of time, to free our later discussion from as many mathematical details as possible.

Let us consider a sequence of n successive events, each of which may be either an A or a B. In the mathematical literature on the binomial distribution, the events are referred to as trials, and the two possible outcomes of each trial, namely A and B, are referred to as success and failure. The number of different sequences consisting of r events A and of $n - r$ events B is given by the binomial coefficient

$$\binom{n}{r} \equiv \frac{n!}{r!\,(n-r)!} \equiv \binom{n}{n-r} \tag{7.2}$$

We shall find it convenient to express this number in terms of functions that can be more readily evaluated, and with whose behavior we are more familiar. We shall use for this purpose the following theorem.

Theorem. The number $\binom{n}{r}$ of different sequences of r events A and $n - r$ events B satisfies the inequality

$$e^{-\frac{1}{12n\rho(1-\rho)}} < \binom{n}{r} \sqrt{2\pi n\rho(1-\rho)}\; e^{n(\rho\ln\rho + (1-\rho)\ln(1-\rho))} < 1 \tag{7.3}$$

where

$$0 < \rho \equiv \frac{r}{n} < 1 \tag{7.4}$$

Proof. This inequality can be obtained with the help of the Sterling approximation to the factorial expressed [2] by the inequality

$$1 < e^{\frac{1}{12m+1}} < \frac{m!}{\sqrt{2\pi m}\; m^{m}\, e^{-m}} < e^{\frac{1}{12m}} \tag{7.5}$$

where m is any positive integer.

The upper bound in Eq. 7.3 is obtained by substituting for the factorial at the numerator of Eq. 7.2 the upper bound given by Eq. 7.5, and for the factorials at the denominator the corresponding lower bounds given by the same equation. We obtain

$$\binom{n}{r} < \frac{1}{\sqrt{2\pi n\rho(1-\rho)}}\, e^{-n[\rho\ln\rho + (1-\rho)\ln(1-\rho)]}\, e^{\frac{1}{12n} - \frac{1}{12r+1} - \frac{1}{12(n-r)+1}} \tag{7.6}$$

where ρ is defined by Eq. 7.4. The exponent in the last factor on the righthand side of Eq. 7.6 is negative for any positive integer $r < n$,

$$\frac{1}{12n} - \frac{1}{12r+1} - \frac{1}{12(n-r)+1} < \frac{1}{12n} - \frac{1}{12r+1} < 0 \ ; \quad r < n \qquad (7.7)$$

Thus, the last factor on the righthand side of Eq. 7.6 can be set equal to 1, thereby yielding the upper bound in Eq. 7.3.

The lower bound in Eq. 7.3 is obtained, similarly, by substituting for the factorial at the numerator in Eq. 7.2 the smaller of the two lower bounds given by Eq. 7.5, and for the two factorials at the denominator the corresponding upper bounds given by the same equation. These substitutions yield immediately the lower bound in Eq. 7.3.

QED

The number N_k of sequences of n events in which the number of A's is smaller than or equal to some integer k will play an important role in our discussion. Again it is desirable to find for this number upper and lower bounds that can be expressed in terms of more convenient functions. We shall use for this purpose the following theorem.

Theorem. The number N_k of sequences of i events A and $n - i$ events B for which $i \leq k$ satisfies the inequality

$$\binom{n}{k} < N_k \equiv \sum_{i=0}^{k} \binom{n}{i} < \frac{n-k}{n-2k}\binom{n}{k} \ ; \quad k < \frac{n}{2} \qquad (7.8)$$

where k is any positive integer smaller than $n/2$.

Proof. The behavior of the binomial coefficient $\binom{n}{r}$ as a function of k is illustrated in Fig. 7.2 for $n = 20$. This figure suggests that, for $k < n/2$, the upper bound in Eq. 7.8 may be obtained by constructing a geometric progression with $k + 1$ terms in which each term is greater than or equal to the corresponding term of the summation in Eq. 7.8. Let us consider, for this purpose, the ratio of any two successive terms of the summation in Eq. 7.8. We obtain, with the help of Eq. 7.2,

$$\frac{\binom{n}{i-1}}{\binom{n}{i}} = \frac{n!}{(i-1)!(n-i+1)!} \ \frac{i!(n-i)!}{n!} = \frac{i}{n-i+1} < \frac{i}{n-i} < 1 \ ; \ i < \frac{n}{2} \qquad (7.9)$$

Then, letting

$$a \equiv \frac{k}{n-k} \qquad (7.10)$$

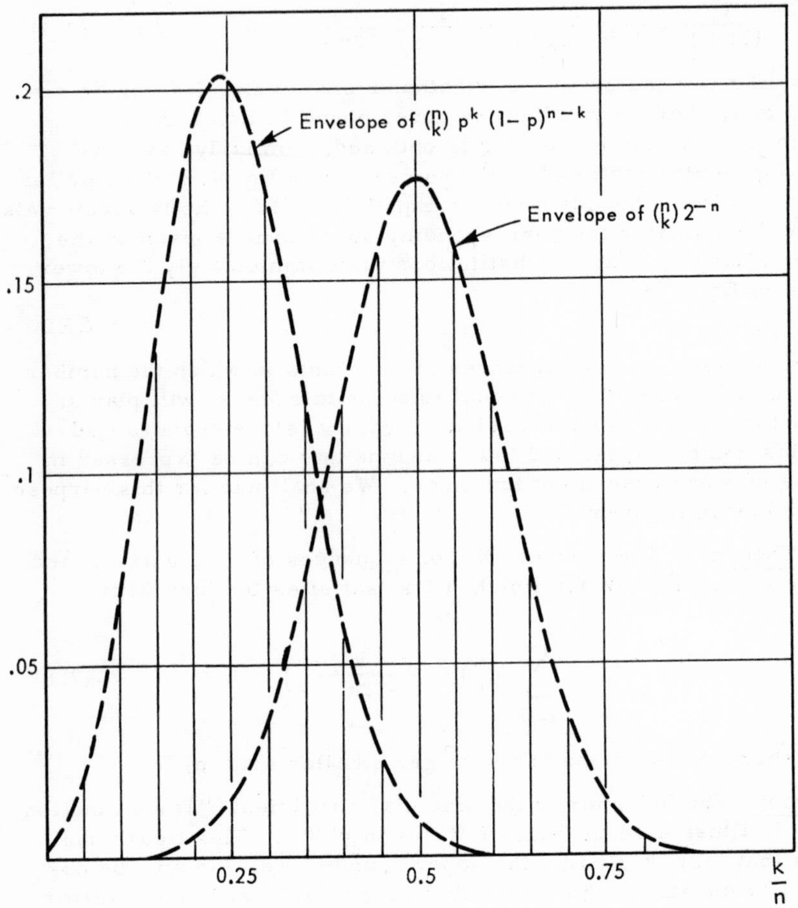

Fig. 7.2. Plots of the normalized binomial coefficient $\binom{n}{k}2^{-n}$, and of the binomial distribution $\binom{n}{k}\, p^{k}(1-p)^{n-k}$, for $n = 20$ and $p = 0.25$

it follows from Eq. 7.9 that

$$\frac{\binom{n}{i-1}}{\binom{n}{i}} < a < 1 \; ; \quad i \leq k < \frac{n}{2} \tag{7.11}$$

and, consequently,

$$\sum_{i=0}^{k} \binom{n}{i} < \binom{n}{k} \left[1 + a + a^2 + \ldots + a^k\right] = \binom{n}{k} \frac{1 - a^{k+1}}{1 - a} \; ; \; k < \frac{n}{2} \tag{7.12}$$

Furthermore,

$$\frac{1 - a^{k+1}}{1 - a} < \frac{1}{1 - a} = \frac{n-k}{n-2k} \tag{7.13}$$

Substitution of the righthand side of this equation in the righthand side of Eq. 7.12 yields the upper bound in Eq. 7.8.

The lower bound in Eq. 7.8 is obtained by noting that all the terms of the summation are positive and that $\binom{n}{k}$ is the largest one, as indicated by Eq. 7.11.

QED

Next, let us suppose that the n events of the sequence are selected independently at random with probabilities

$$P(A) = p < \frac{1}{2} \; ; \quad P(B) = 1 - p \tag{7.14}$$

The probability of occurrence of any particular sequence u consisting of k events A and $n - k$ events B is

$$P(u) = p^k (1 - p)^{n-k} \tag{7.15}$$

Thus the probability that k of the randomly selected events be A's and $n - k$ be B's is .

$$b_k \equiv \binom{n}{k} p^k (1 - p)^{n-k} \tag{7.16}$$

that is, the number of different sequences consisting of exactly k events A and $n - k$ events B, given by Eq. 7.2, multiplied by the probability of occurrence of each of these sequences, given by Eq. 7.15. The probability given by Eq. 7.16 is the kth term of the binomial probability distribution, whose behavior as a function of k is illustrated in Fig. 7.2 for $n = 20$, $p = 1/4$.

We shall be interested in the probability that the number of A's in a sequence of n randomly selected events be greater than some prescribed integer r. This probability is, from Eq. 7.16,

$$\Pr(k > r) = \sum_{k=r+1}^{n} b_k = 1 - \sum_{k=0}^{r} b_k \tag{7.17}$$

Again, we shall find it desirable to bound this probability with more convenient functions of r and p. We shall need for this purpose the following theorem.

Theorem. If the event A occurs with probability p, the probability that the number of A's in a sequence of n statistically independent events will exceed a positive integer $r > np$ satisfies the inequality

$$\frac{p(1-\rho)}{(1-p)\left(\rho+\frac{1}{n}\right)} b_r < \sum_{k=r+1}^{n} b_k < \frac{p(1-\rho)}{\rho - p} b_r \tag{7.18}$$

where

$$p < \rho \equiv \frac{r}{n} \leq 1 \tag{7.19}$$

Proof. The derivation of this inequality is very similar to the derivation of the inequality given by Eq. 7.8. We obtain for the ratio of successive terms of the summation in Eq. 7.18

$$\frac{b_{k+1}}{b_k} = \frac{n!}{(k+1)!\,(n-k-1)!} \frac{k!(n-k)!}{n!} \frac{p^{k+1}(1-p)^{n-k-1}}{p^k(1-p)^{n-k}}$$

$$= \frac{n-k}{k+1} \frac{p}{1-p} < \frac{n-k}{k} \frac{p}{1-p} < 1 \;;\; np < k \leq n \tag{7.20}$$

Then, letting

$$a \equiv \frac{n-r}{r} \frac{p}{1-p} = \frac{p(1-\rho)}{\rho(1-p)} \tag{7.21}$$

it follows from Eq. 7.20 that

$$\frac{b_{k+1}}{b_k} < a < 1 \;;\; p < \rho < \frac{k}{n} \tag{7.22}$$

so that

$$\sum_{k=r+1}^{n} b_k < b_r\, a(1 + a + a^2 + \ldots + a^{n-r-1}) = b_r\, a \frac{1-a^{n-r}}{1-a} \;;\; p < \frac{r}{n} \leq 1 \tag{7.23}$$

Furthermore,

$$a\frac{1-a^{n-r}}{1-a} < \frac{a}{1-a} = \frac{p(1-\rho)}{\rho(1-p)-p(1-\rho)} = \frac{p(1-\rho)}{\rho-p} \quad ; \; p < \rho \leq 1 \qquad (7.24)$$

Substitution of the righthand side of this equation in the righthand side of Eq. 7.23 yields the upper bound in Eq. 7.18. The lower bound in Eq. 7.18 is obtained by noting that all the terms of the summation are positive and that b_{r+1} is the largest one, as indicated by Eq. 7.22.

QED

The last expression for which we shall need upper and lower bounds cannot be given any illuminating interpretation at this time. We shall state and prove the following theorem without any further discussion.

Theorem. Let N_k be the number of different sequences consisting of i events A and $n-i$ events B for which $i \leq k$, and b_k be the binomial term given by Eq. 7.16, and define

$$\rho_c \equiv \frac{\sqrt{p}}{\sqrt{p}+\sqrt{1-p}} \qquad (7.25)$$

Then,

$$b_r N_r < \sum_{k=0}^{r} b_k N_k < \frac{p(1-\rho)^2}{p(1-\rho)^2 - \rho^2(1-p)}\, b_r N_r \; ; \; 0 \leq \frac{r}{n} \equiv \rho < \rho_c \qquad (7.26)$$

$$\sum_{k=0}^{n} b_k N_k < (\sqrt{p} + \sqrt{1-p})^{2n} \qquad (7.27)$$

Proof. The upper bound in Eq. 7.26 can be derived by following the same procedure employed in deriving the upper bounds in Eqs. 7.8 and 7.18. In order to obtain an expression for the ratio of successive terms of the summation in Eq. 7.26, we observe, with the help of Eq. 7.2, that

$$N_k \equiv \sum_{i=0}^{k} \binom{n}{i} > \sum_{i=1}^{k} \binom{n}{i} = \sum_{i=0}^{k-1} \binom{n}{i+1}$$

$$= \sum_{i=0}^{k-1} \binom{n}{i} \frac{n-i}{i+1} > \frac{n-k+1}{k} N_{k-1} > \frac{n-k}{k} N_{k-1} \qquad (7.28)$$

Then, we have for the ratio of successive terms

$$\frac{b_{k-1}N_{k-1}}{b_k N_k} < \frac{b_{k-1}}{b_k}\frac{k}{n-k} = \frac{k}{n-k+1}\frac{1-p}{p}\frac{k}{n-k} < \left(\frac{k}{n-k}\right)^2 \frac{1-p}{p} \tag{7.29}$$

Let

$$a \equiv \left(\frac{r}{n-r}\right)^2 \frac{1-p}{p} = \left(\frac{\rho}{1-\rho}\right)^2 \frac{1-p}{p} \tag{7.30}$$

where

$$\rho \equiv \frac{r}{n} \tag{7.31}$$

It can be readily checked that the parameter a defined by Eq. 7.30 becomes equal to one when ρ is equal to the value ρ_c given by Eq. 7.25. Then, it follows from Eq. 7.29 that

$$\frac{b_{k-1}N_{k-1}}{b_k N_k} < a < 1 \quad ; \quad 0 \leq \rho < \rho_c \tag{7.32}$$

so that

$$\sum_{k=0}^{r} b_k N_k < b_r N_r (1 + a + a^2 + \ldots + a^r) = b_r N_r \frac{1 - a^{r+1}}{1-a} \quad ; \; 0 \leq \rho < \rho_c \tag{7.33}$$

Furthermore,

$$\frac{1-a^{r+1}}{1-a} < \frac{1}{1-a} = \frac{p(1-\rho)^2}{p(1-\rho)^2 - \rho^2(1-p)} \tag{7.34}$$

Substituting the righthand side of this equation in the righthand side of Eq. 7.33 yields the upper bound in Eq. 7.26. The lower bound in the same equation is obtained by noting that all the terms of the summation are positive, and that $b_r N_r$ is the largest one, as indicated by Eq. 7.32.

The derivation of the upper bound given by Eq. 7.27 involves a special technique known as "tilting of probability distributions," which will be discussed in general terms in Sec. 8.2. The upper bound given by Eq. 7.26 is valid only for $r < n\rho_c$ because $b_k N_k$ reaches a maximum value for k slightly larger than $n\rho_c$. It follows that the summation in Eq. 7.26 increases slower than linearly with r, for $r > n\rho_c$.

An upper bound to the lefthand side of Eq. 7.27 could be obtained, in principle, by multiplying the largest term in the summation, or a suitable upper bound to it, by the total number n of terms.

However, no suitable upper bound to the largest term can be readily obtained. The reason for this difficulty is that b_k and N_k vary in opposite directions very fast with k when their product reaches its maximum value, as indicated by the plots of Fig. 7.2. This suggests that we should multiply b_k and divide N_k by an appropriate function $f(k)$, selected in such a way that both $b_k f(k)$ and $N_k/f(k)$ reach their maximum values in the same neighborhood as $b_k N_k$. This is the tilting process referred to above. Since the maximum value of b_k occurs in the vicinity of $k = np$, and we would like $b_k f(k)$ to have a maximum in the vicinity of $k = n\rho_c$, we should select $f(k)$, if possible, so that $b_k f(k)$ have the same functional form as b_k, but with ρ_c substituted for p. This goal can be achieved by selecting

$$f(k) = \left(\frac{1-p}{p}\right)^{k/2} \tag{7.35}$$

In fact,

$$\begin{aligned} b_k f(k) &= \binom{n}{k} p^k (1-p)^{n-k} p^{-k/2} (1-p)^{k/2} \\ &= \binom{n}{k} \rho_c^k (1-\rho_c)^{n-k} (1-p)^{n/2} (\sqrt{p} + \sqrt{1-p})^n \end{aligned} \tag{7.36}$$

We observe, in addition, that

$$f(i) \leq f(k) \quad ; \quad i \leq k \tag{7.37}$$

so that

$$\begin{aligned} \frac{1}{f(k)} N_k &< \sum_{i=0}^{k} \binom{n}{i} p^{i/2} (1-p)^{-i/2} \\ &= \sum_{i=0}^{k} \binom{n}{i} \rho_c^i (1-\rho_c)^{n-i} (1-p)^{-n/2} (\sqrt{p} + \sqrt{1-p})^n \end{aligned} \tag{7.38}$$

It follows that

$$\begin{aligned} \sum_{k=0}^{n} b_k N_k &< (\sqrt{p} + \sqrt{1-p})^{2n} \sum_{k=0}^{n} \binom{n}{k} \rho_c^k (1-\rho_c)^{n-k} \sum_{i=0}^{k} \binom{n}{i} \rho_c^i (1-\rho_c)^{n-i} \\ &< (\sqrt{p} + \sqrt{1-p})^{2n} \left[\sum_{k=0}^{n} \binom{n}{k} \rho_c^k (1-\rho_c)^{n-k} \right]^2 = (\sqrt{p} + \sqrt{1-p})^{2n} \end{aligned} \tag{7.39}$$

which coincides with Eq. 7.27.

The reason why a rough approximation such as extending the upper limit of the summation in Eq. 7.39 from $i = k$ to $i = n$ still yields a reasonably good upper bound, is that the main contributions to both summations come from terms with values of i and k in the vicinity of $n\rho_c$. This is the advantage that results from the tilting of the probability distribution.

QED

7.2. A Lower Bound to the Probability of Error

We shall begin our discussion of binary symmetric channels with the derivation of a lower bound to the probability of error. We shall assume for this purpose that a message set is given consisting of M equiprobable messages $m_1, m_2, \ldots, m_M$. Each of these messages is to be encoded for transmission into a sequence of n binary digits.

We saw in Sec. 6.1 that the operation of encoding may be regarded as a mapping of the message space into the channel input space, consisting, in our case, of the 2^n distinct sequences of n binary digits. We shall indicate with $u_1, u_2, \ldots, u_M$ the M sequences into which the M messages are mapped. In other words, we shall indicate with u_i the sequence of n binary digits input to the channel when the message m_i is transmitted.

The decoding operation may be regarded, as discussed also in Sec. 6.1, as a partitioning of the channel output space into M subsets $w_1, w_2, \ldots, w_M$; in which each subset w_i consists of all the sequences of n binary digits that are to be decoded into the message m_i, corresponding to the input sequence u_i.

Let us indicate with v the channel output sequence. The probability that v will be correctly decoded when the message m_i is transmitted is equal to the conditional probability that v belongs to the subset w_i when the input sequence is u_i. Thus since the messages are equiprobable $(P(m_i) = 1/M)$, the average probability of correct decoding is given by

$$1 - P(e) = \sum_{i=1}^{M} P(m_i) \sum_{w_i} P(v|u_i) = \frac{1}{M} \sum_{i=1}^{M} \sum_{w_i} P(v|u_i) \tag{7.40}$$

where $P(v|u_i)$ is the conditional probability of any particular output sequence v when the input sequence is u_i.

<u>Theorem.</u> The average probability of correct decoding is a maximum for any particular set of input sequences u_1, $u_2, \ldots, u_M$, representing M equiprobable messages, if and only if

$$P(v|u_i) \geq P(v|u_j) \text{ for every } v \text{ in } w_i, \quad 1 \leq j \leq M, \quad 1 \leq i \leq M \tag{7.41}$$

Proof. Let us suppose that Eq. 7.41 is not satisfied for some output sequence v_h belonging to the subset w_i and some input sequence u_j. Then it follows from Eq. 7.40 that the probability of correct decoding can be increased by transferring the output sequence v_h from the subset w_i to the subset w_j. Conversely, transferring any one of the output sequences from one subset to another when condition (7.41) is satisfied cannot increase the average probability of correct decoding. Clearly, Eq. 7.41 is equivalent to the requirement that the subsets w_i be constructed according to the maximum-likelihood criterion; this criterion is equivalent, in our particular case, to the maximum-a posteriori-probability criterion, in view of the fact that the messages are equiprobable.

QED

The following theorem is basic to our evaluation of a lower bound to the probability of error for a binary symmetric channel. We shall indicate with p the probability that either input symbol be transformed by the channel noise into the other output symbol, that is, the noise probability.

Theorem. Let us consider the block encoding of a set of M equiprobable messages into sequences of n binary digits for transmission through a binary symmetric channel, and define

$$N_r \equiv \sum_{k=0}^{r} \binom{n}{k} \tag{7.42}$$

Then, if r is the smallest integer for which

$$\frac{2^n}{M} \leq N_r \tag{7.43}$$

the probability of occurrènce of a decoding error, $P(e)$, satisfies the inequality

$$P(e) \geq \sum_{k=r+1}^{n} \binom{n}{k} p^k (1-p)^{n-k} \tag{7.44}$$

for any assignments of channel input sequences to messages.

Proof. The summation on the righthand side of Eq. 7.40 extends over all output sequences v. Each term of the summation is the conditional probability that a particular sequence v be received when the channel input is the sequence u_i corresponding to the subset w_i to which the sequence v belongs. In the case of a binary symmetric channel this probability is given by

$$P(v|u_i) = p^k (1-p)^{n-k} \tag{7.45}$$

where k is the number of digits in which the sequence v differs from the sequence u_i. In other words, $P(v|u_i)$ is the probability that k particular digits of the sequence u_i be changed by the channel noise.

The righthand side of Eq. 7.45 decreases monotonically with increasing k. On the other hand, there can be at most $\binom{n}{k}$ sequences v that differ from any particular u_i in k digits, and, therefore, at most $M\binom{n}{k}$ terms of the summation on the righthand side of Eq. 7.40 can be equal to the righthand side of Eq. 7.45 for each particular integer k. It follows that the probability of correct decoding cannot exceed the value assumed by the righthand side of Eq. 7.40 when the smallest possible integers k, consistent with the above constraint, are used. Then, if we indicate with r the largest value of k appearing in the summation, we obtain for the probability of correct decoding

$$1 - P(e) \leq \frac{1}{M} \sum_{k=0}^{r} M\binom{n}{k} p^k (1-p)^{n-k} = \Pr(k \leq r) \tag{7.46}$$

The righthand side of this equation is the probability that r or less digits of the input sequence be changed by the channel noise. Thus the probability of error must exceed or be equal to the probability that more than r of the digits of the input sequence be changed by the channel noise, that is,

$$P(e) \geq \Pr(k > r) = \sum_{r+1}^{n} \binom{n}{k} p^k (1-p)^{n-k} \tag{7.47}$$

which coincides with Eq. 7.44.

The number of terms of the summation in Eq. 7.46 must be at least equal to 2^n, that is, to the number of different output sequences of n digits because otherwise there would have to be output sequences v for which $k > r$, in contrast with the above assumption. It follows that

$$2^n \leq \sum_{k=0}^{r} M \binom{n}{k} \tag{7.48}$$

from which Eq. 7.43 follows, with the help of Eq. 7.42.

QED

We envisioned in the above proof a set of M input sequences for which each of the subsets w_i consists of all the output sequences v that differ from the corresponding sequence u_i in r or less digits. Sets of input sequences meeting this requirement exist only for particular values of n and M. For such special sets of input sequences the equal signs hold in Eqs. 7.43 and 7.44. In general, however, the set of input sequences envisioned in the proof does not actually exist, although no realizable set of sequences can yield a probability of error smaller than the righthand side of Eq. 7.44.

The argument used in the above proof is sometimes referred to as "sphere packing." This name results from the following geometric interpretation. Let us consider an n-dimensional space in which the Cartesian coordinates can assume only the two values 1 and 0. It is clear that any sequence of n binary digits can be represented as a point in this space. Furthermore, if k is the number of digits in which two particular sequences differ, the distance between the two corresponding points is equal to $\sqrt{k}$. Then, each of the subsets w_i of output sequences envisioned in the proof of the theorem consists of the set of points within or on a sphere of radius $\sqrt{r}$, centered at the point corresponding to the input sequence u_i. Similarly, all the possible sequences of n binary digits are within or on a sphere of radius $\sqrt{n}$, centered at the origin. We observe, in addition, that the probability that any one sequence be transformed into another sequence by the channel noise, given by Eq. 7.45, decreases monotonically with increasing distance between the points corresponding to the two sequences.

The argument used in proving the theorem corresponds then to fitting M spheres of radius $\sqrt{r}$ into a sphere of radius $\sqrt{n}$ in such a way that all the points corresponding to possible sequences of n digits be within or on one and only one of the M spheres. Each sphere of radius $\sqrt{r}$ includes a number of points N_r, given by Eq. 7.42, and the sphere of radius $\sqrt{n}$ includes 2^n points. It follows that, if M satisfies Eq. 7.43 the probability of error cannot be smaller than the righthand side of Eq. 7.44. Correspondingly, the righthand side of Eq. 7.44 is the probability that any one of the input sequences, represented by the center of one of the spheres, be transformed by the channel noise into an output sequence represented by a point outside the corresponding sphere of radius $\sqrt{r}$.

Such a sphere-packing problem may or may not have a solution, depending on the values of the integers n and M. However, the best possible partition of the 2^n points of a sphere of radius $\sqrt{n}$ into M subsets cannot yield a probability of error smaller than that obtained by assuming that a solution exists for the sphere-packing problem.

Corollary. A sufficient condition for a set of M input sequences to yield the smallest possible probability of error is that it be possible, for some integer r, to partition the space of the output sequences v into subsets w_i in such a way that each w_i contain all the sequences that differ from u_i in less than r digits and no sequence that differs in more than r digits.

Proof. The proof of this corollary is based on the same argument used in proving the preceding theorem. It is clear from Eq. 7.40 that any set of input sequences meeting the condition stated in the corollary yields the same probability of error when the subsets w_i satisfy Eq. 7.45. Conversely, any set of input sequences not meeting the condition of the corollary must yield a larger probability of error because at least one of the terms of the summation in Eq. 7.40 must be equal to the righthand side of Eq. 7.45 for $k > r$ rather than for $k < r$

QED

The rate of information transmission when a set of M equiprobable messages is encoded into n binary digits is, by definition,

$$R \equiv \frac{\log_2 M}{n} \quad \text{bits/channel digit} \tag{7.49}$$

The lower bound to the probability of error given by Eq. 7.44 depends of course on the transmission rate R through the integer r. In order to study further the relation between the lower bound to the probability of error and the lower bound to the transmission rate (implied by Eq. 7.43), it is convenient to obtain new bounds for these quantities expressible in terms of more convenient functions of r and n.

Theorem. Let us consider the block encoding of equiprobable messages for transmission through a binary symmetric channel, and indicate with n the number of digits in the input sequences representing the messages. If the transmission rate R (bits per channel digit) satisfies the inequality

$$R \geq \frac{1}{n}\left[\frac{\log_2 e}{12n\rho(1-\rho)} + \log_2 \sqrt{2\pi n\rho(1-\rho)}\right] + [1 + \rho \log_2 \rho + (1-\rho)\log_2(1-\rho)] \equiv R_L \tag{7.50}$$

for

$$p \leq \rho \equiv \frac{r}{n} \leq \frac{1}{2} \tag{7.51}$$

the probability of error must satisfy the inequality

$$P(e) > \frac{\rho(1-\rho)}{(1-p)(\rho+\frac{1}{n})} \frac{e^{-\frac{1}{12n\rho(1-\rho)}}}{\sqrt{2\pi n\rho(1-\rho)}} 2^{-n\left[\rho\log_2\frac{\rho}{p}+(1-\rho)\log_2\frac{1-\rho}{1-p}\right]} \equiv P_L(e) \tag{7.52}$$

Proof. Substituting the lower bound given by Eq. 7.18, with the help of Eq. 7.16, for the righthand side of Eq. 7.44 yields

$$P(e) > \frac{p(1-\rho)}{(1-p)(\rho+\frac{1}{n})} \binom{n}{r} p^r (1-p)^{n-r} \; ; \; \frac{r}{n} \equiv \rho \geq p \tag{7.53}$$

Then, substituting for $\binom{n}{r}$ in this equation the lower bound given by Eq. 7.3 yields, after some manipulations, the righthand side of Eq. 7.52.

According to the preceding theorem, the value $P_L(e)$ given by Eq. 7.52 is a lower bound to the probability of error when the number M of messages satisfies Eq. 7.43. This inequality can be rewritten, in terms of the transmission rate defined by Eq. 7.49 as follows

$$R \geq \frac{1}{n} \log_2 \frac{2^n}{N_r} = 1 - \frac{1}{n} \log_2 N_r \tag{7.54}$$

On the other hand, substituting for N_r the lower bound given by Eq. 7.8, and for $\binom{n}{r}$ the lower bound given by Eq. 7.3, yields

$$1 - \frac{1}{n}\log_2 N_r < 1 - \frac{1}{n}\log_2 \binom{n}{r} < R_L \; ; \; \rho \leq \frac{1}{2} \tag{7.55}$$

where R_L is the expression on the righthand side of Eq. 7.50. It follows that Eq. 7.54 is satisfied by any transmission rate R larger than or equal to R_L, so that Eq. 7.52 is satisfied whenever the transmission rate satisfies

$$R \geq R_L > 1 - \frac{1}{n}\log_2 N_r \; ; \; \rho \leq \frac{1}{2} \tag{7.56}$$

QED

We are now in a position to discuss the relation between R_L, the lower bound to the transmission rate given by Eq. 7.50, and $P_L(e)$, the lower bound to the probability of error given by Eq. 7.52. Let us indicate with $C(\rho)$ the expression in the second bracket of Eq. 7.50, and with α_L the exponential factor between square brackets in Eq. 7.52. Inspection of Eq. 7.50 indicates that for any reasonably large value of n, R_L is approximately equal to $C(\rho)$. More precisely,

$$\lim_{n\to\infty} R_L = 1 + \rho \log_2 \rho + (1-\rho) \log_2 (1-\rho) \equiv C(\rho) \qquad (7.57)$$

Similarly, inspection of Eq. 7.52 indicates that under the same conditions, $P_L(e)$ is primarily controlled by the product of n and the exponential factor α_L. More precisely,

$$\lim_{n\to\infty} \left[-\frac{1}{n} \log_2 P_L(e) \right] = \rho \log_2 \frac{\rho}{p} + (1-\rho) \log_2 \frac{1-\rho}{1-p} \equiv \alpha_L \qquad (7.58)$$

Thus we can focus our attention on the relation between α_L and C_ρ.

The two quantities $C(\rho)$ and α_L are related to each other through the parameter ρ. The quantity $C(\rho)$ is plotted in Figure 7.3

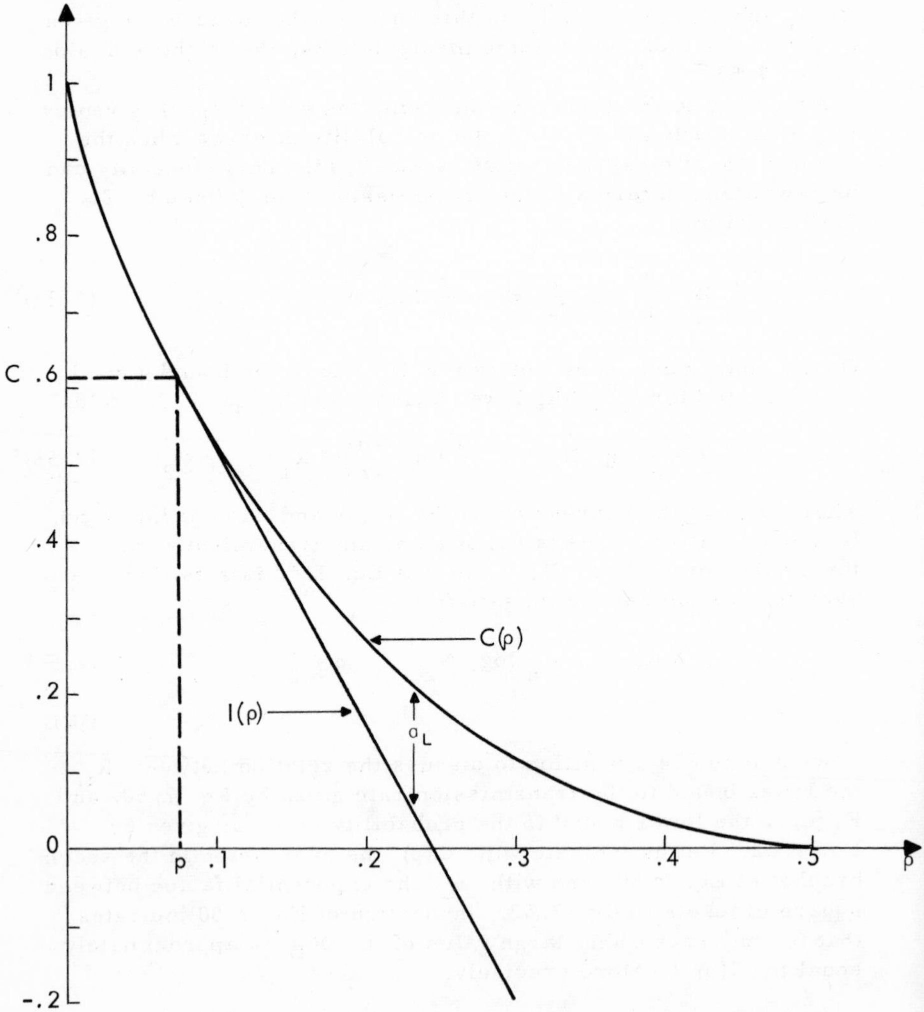

Fig. 7.3. Graphical determination of α_L

as a function of ρ. It is clear that the expression for $C(\rho)$ is identical to the expression for the channel capacity given by Eq. 7.1 with ρ substituted for p. Thus, the channel capacity is represented in Fig. 7.3 by the value assumed by $C(\rho)$ for $\rho = p$.

Next, let us define the quantity

$$I(\rho) \equiv 1 + \rho \log_2 p + (1 - \rho) \log_2 (1 - p) \tag{7.59}$$

This quantity, when plotted as a function of ρ, yields a straight line tangent to the curve $C(\rho)$ at the point $C(\rho) = C$. Then, the exponential factor α_L can be expressed in the form

$$\alpha_L = C(\rho) - I(\rho) \tag{7.60}$$

It follows that α_L is represented in Fig. 7.3 as the difference between the curve $C(\rho)$ and the straight line $I(\rho)$.

It is clear from Fig. 7.3 that the exponential factor α_L is positive for all values of ρ larger than p and vanishes for $\rho = p$; Eq. 7.52 is not valid for $\rho < p$. It follows that $\alpha_L > 0$ for $C(\rho) < C$, so that the lower bound to the probability of error vanishes exponentially with n for any fixed transmission rate $R < C$. Furthermore, it is clear from Fig. 7.3 that the value of α_L increases monotonically from zero with decreasing $C(\rho)$, and therefore with decreasing transmission rate.

It is interesting to note also that the quantity $C(\rho)$ is the average mutual information between input and output digits of a binary symmetric channel, when the input symbols are equally probable and the noise probability is equal to ρ. The quantity $I(\rho)$ can be interpreted in a similar manner. It can readily be checked that $I(\rho)$ is the average mutual information between input and output digits when the mutual informations of the four possible pairs of input and output digits are evaluated with the noise probability equal to p, but they are averaged with respect to a noise probability equal to ρ. Thus the exponential coefficient α_L may be regarded as a measure of the mutual-information tolerance that results from making the transmission rate equal to the capacity that the channel would have if the noise probability were equal to ρ rather than p.

7.3. An Upper Bound to the Probability of Error

Our objective in this section is to derive an upper bound to the probability of occurrence of a decoding error when a set of M messages is encoded into sequences of n binary digits for transmission through a binary symmetric channel. By an upper bound to the probability of error we mean a value $P_U(e)$ depending on the integer n and on the transmission rate

$$R \equiv \frac{\log_2 M}{n} < C \tag{7.61}$$

such that for any n and R there exists a set of M input sequences and a decoding procedure for which the probability of error is smaller than or equal to $P_U(e)$. The following derivation of an upper bound to the probability of error is based on a very interesting technique known as "random coding," which was first used by Shannon in his original proof that the probability of error can be made to vanish for any $R < C$ in the limit of n approaching infinity.

We saw in Sec. 6.1 that block encoding may be regarded as a mapping of the message space into the space U consisting of all possible input sequences of n digits. The mapping, of course, should be selected in such a way as to enable the decoder to recognize the message transmitted with as small a probability of error as possible. Unfortunately, no general procedure has yet been found for constructing an optimum mapping, or even a reasonably good mapping, for arbitrary values of n and $R < C$. However, an upper bound to the probability of error can be obtained by evaluating the average probability of error over the ensemble of mappings generated by a random assignment of input sequences to messages.

The random assignment of input sequences to messages is carried out as follows. For each message m_i an input sequence u_i is constructed by selecting its n digits independently at random with equal probabilities. Thus, the probability that any particular sequence of n digits be assigned to a particular message m_i is equal to 2^{-n} for all sequences and all messages, and the probability that any particular mapping results from such a random procedure is equal to 2^{-nM}

The reason for using this particular random assignment of input sequences to messages is that, in the resulting ensemble of mappings, the n digits input to the channel when any particular message is transmitted are statistically independent and equally probable, irrespectively of the message transmitted. Furthermore, the corresponding n digits output from the channel are similarly statistically independent and equiprobable. It is important to stress that this is true only over the ensemble of mappings defined above, and not for any particular mapping.

This random encoding procedure can be interpreted as follows. A very large number of mappings (ideally infinite) are constructed independently at random according to the above procedure, and copies of such mappings in order of selection are provided to both the encoder and the decoder. It is agreed, then, that the first message will be encoded for transmission according to the first mapping, the second message according to the second mapping, and in general, the νth message according to the νth mapping. Thus although the mappings are constructed at random, the encoder and decoder know the particular mapping to be used in connection with the transmission of each successive message. The frequency with which decoding errors will occur in the transmission of a sequence of messages will converge, because of the law of large numbers, to the average probability of error evaluated over the ensemble of mappings.

We shall assume, in what follows, maximum-likelihood decoding, that is, that any particular output sequence v will be decoded into a message m_i for which

$$P(v|m_i) \geq P(v|m_j) \quad ; \quad 1 \leq j \leq M \tag{7.62}$$

If the M messages are equiprobable, this criterion is equivalent to decoding v into the message that maximizes the a posteriori message probability for the particular v in question.

Theorem. Let $\overline{P}(e)$ be the average probability of error for the ensemble of mappings and the decoding criterion specified above. If the message set consists of M messages, and the corresponding input sequences consist of n digits,

$$\overline{P}(e) \leq \sum_{k=0}^{n} \binom{n}{k} p^k (1-p)^{(n-k)} \left\{ 1 - \left[1 - 2^{-n} \sum_{j=0}^{k} \binom{n}{j} \right]^{M-1} \right\} \tag{7.63}$$

where p is the channel noise probability.

Proof. Let us suppose that a particular sequence u_i representing the message m_i is transmitted, and that a particular sequence v is received which differs from u_i in k digits. Such a sequence v will be correctly decoded into the message m_i if all the input sequences assigned to the other messages by the particular mapping employed differ from v in more than k digits. A decoding error may or may not occur when one or more of the input sequences assigned to other messages differ from v in exactly k digits. We shall make a conservative estimate of the probability of error by assuming that an error will occur whenever such a special situation arises. Since the probability that any particular input sequence is assigned to any particular message m_j by the mapping employed is equal to 2^{-n}, the probability that a sequence that differs from v in more than k digits is assigned to m_j is

$$2^{-n} \sum_{j=k+1}^{n} \binom{n}{j} = 1 - 2^{-n} \sum_{j=0}^{k} \binom{n}{j} \tag{7.64}$$

Furthermore, this probability is independent of the sequences assigned to the other messages. It follows that the probability that all the $M - 1$ sequences assigned by the mapping to other messages differ from v in more than k digits is equal to

$$Q_k \equiv \left[1 - 2^{-n} \sum_{j=0}^{k} \binom{n}{j}\right]^{M-1} \qquad (7.65)$$

On the other hand, the probability that a sequence v be received that differs from the transmitted sequence in k digits is

$$b_k \equiv \binom{n}{k} p^k (1 - p)^{n-k} \qquad (7.66)$$

It follows that the average probability of correct decoding must satisfy the inequality

$$1 - \overline{P}(e) \geq \sum_{k=0}^{n} b_k Q_k \qquad (7.67)$$

Solving this inequality for $\overline{P}(e)$ with the help of Eqs. 7.65 and 7.66, and of the identity

$$\sum_{k=0}^{n} b_k \equiv 1 \qquad (7.68)$$

yields Eq. 7.63.

QED

We shall proceed next to derive an upper bound to the average probability of error that can be more readily interpreted than the righthand side of Eq. 7.63. This upper bound is presented, for the sake of emphasis, as the following theorem.

Theorem. Let M be the number of distinct messages as in the preceding theorem, and

$$R \equiv \frac{\log_2 M}{n} \qquad (7.69)$$

be the corresponding transmission rate in bits per channel digit, and define a parameter ρ related to R by

$$R \equiv \begin{cases} 1 + \rho \log_2 \rho + (1 - \rho) \log_2 (1 - \rho) & ; \quad p \leq \rho < \rho_c \\ 1 + \rho \log_2 \rho_c + (1 - \rho) \log_2 (1 - \rho_c) & ; \quad \rho_c \leq \rho \leq 1/2 \end{cases} \qquad (7.70)$$

where

$$\rho_c \equiv \frac{\sqrt{p}}{\sqrt{p} + \sqrt{1 - p}} \quad ; \quad 1 - \rho_c = \frac{\sqrt{1 - p}}{\sqrt{p} + \sqrt{1 - p}} \qquad (7.71)$$

Then the average probability of error for the ensemble of mappings and the decoding criterion specified above satisfies the inequality

$$\overline{P}(e) < K\, 2^{-n\alpha_U} \tag{7.72}$$

where

$$K \equiv \begin{cases} \dfrac{p}{\sqrt{2\pi n}} \sqrt{\dfrac{1-\rho}{\rho}} \left[\dfrac{1}{\rho - p} + \dfrac{1}{\sqrt{2\pi n}} \sqrt{\dfrac{1-\rho}{\rho}} \dfrac{1-\rho}{(1-2\rho)\left[p(1-\rho)^2 - \rho^2(1-p)\right]} \right] & ;\ p < \rho < \rho_c \\ 1 & ;\ \rho_c \le \rho \end{cases} \tag{7.73}$$

and

$$\alpha_U \equiv \begin{cases} \rho \log_2 \dfrac{\rho}{p} + (1-\rho) \log_2 \dfrac{1-\rho}{1-p} & ;\ p < \rho < \rho_c \\ 1 - 2 \log_2 (\sqrt{p} + \sqrt{1-p}) - R = \rho \log_2 \dfrac{\rho_c}{p} + (1-\rho) \log_2 \dfrac{1-\rho_c}{1-p} & ;\ \rho_c \le \rho \end{cases} \tag{7.74}$$

The exponential factor α_U can also be expressed for $p < \rho \le 1/2$ in the form

$$\alpha_U = R - I(\rho) \tag{7.75}$$

where

$$I(\rho) \equiv 1 + \rho \log_2 p + (1-\rho) \log_2 (1-p) \tag{7.76}$$

Proof. Our objective is to find an upper bound to the righthand side of Eq. 7.63. We observe, for this purpose, that the first two terms of the binomial expansion of the righthand side of Eq. 7.65 constitute a lower bound to Q_k, so that

$$Q_k \ge 1 - (M-1)\, 2^{-n} \sum_{j=0}^{k} \binom{n}{j} > 1 - M 2^{-n} N_k \tag{7.77}$$

where

$$N_k \equiv \sum_{j=0}^{k} \binom{n}{j} \tag{7.78}$$

On the other hand, the righthand side of Eq. 7.77 becomes negative for sufficiently large values of k, while Q_k is never negative because it represents a probability. Thus a more reasonable lower bound for Q_k is given by

$$Q_k \geq Q_k^* \equiv \begin{cases} 1 - M 2^{-n} N_k & ; \quad k \leq r \\ 0 & ; \quad k > r \end{cases} \tag{7.79}$$

where r is an integer to be determined later.

Substituting Q_k^* for Q_k in Eq. 7.63 yields

$$\overline{P}(e) \leq \sum_{k=0}^{n} b_k(1 - Q_k^*) = M 2^{-n} \sum_{k=0}^{r} b_k N_k + \sum_{k=r+1}^{n} b_k \tag{7.80}$$

The last term on the righthand side of Eq. 7.80 is the probability that the number of digits changed by the channel noise, k , be larger than r . The first term on the righthand side of the same equation is M times the joint probability that $k \leq r$ and that a sequence of n digits selected independently at random with equal probabilities will differ from the received sequence in k or less digits.

The next step in our derivation is to substitute for b_k and N_k the upper bounds given by Eqs. 7.3, 7.8, 7.18, and 7.26. We obtain for $p < r/n \equiv \rho < \rho_c$

$$\overline{P}(e) < \left[\frac{1-\rho}{1-2\rho} \frac{p(1-\rho)^2}{p(1-\rho)^2 - \rho^2(1-p)} \frac{1}{\sqrt{2\pi n\rho(1-\rho)}} 2^{-n[1+\rho \log_2 \rho + (1-\rho)\log_2(1-\rho) - R]} \right.$$
$$\left. + \frac{p(1-\rho)}{\rho - p}\right] \frac{1}{\sqrt{2\pi n\rho(1-\rho)}} 2^{-n\left[\rho \log_2 \frac{\rho}{p} + (1-\rho)\log_2 \frac{1-\rho}{1-p}\right]} ; \quad p < \frac{r}{n} \equiv \rho < \rho_c \tag{7.81}$$

The value of the integer r and of the corresponding parameter ρ are, up to this point, unrelated to the transmission rate R . It is clear that if the exponential factor including R in Eq. 7.81 is positive, the first of the two terms between square brackets becomes, for large value of n ., negligibly small compared to the other. Conversely, if the same exponential factor is negative, the second term becomes negligibly small compared to the first one. It is clear that we should make this exponential factor equal to zero by setting

$$R = 1 + \rho \log_2 \rho + (1 - \rho) \log_2(1 - \rho) \equiv C(\rho) \quad ; \quad p < \rho < \rho_c \tag{7.82}$$

This equation establishes a relation between the transmission rate R and the parameter ρ , on which the righthand side of Eq. 7.81 depends. The righthand sides of Eqs. 7.70, 7.72, 7.73, and 7.74 for $p < \rho < \rho_c$ follow immediately from Eqs. 7.81 and 7.82.

The corresponding expressions for $\rho \geq \rho_c$ can be obtained with the help of Eq. 7.27. Setting r = n , and substituting the righthand side of Eq. 7.27 for the remaining summation in Eq. 7.80 yields

$$\overline{P}(e) \leq M\,2^{-n} \sum_{k=0}^{n} b_k N_k < 2^{-n[1-R-2\log_2(\sqrt{p}+\sqrt{1-p})]} \tag{7.83}$$

which agrees with Eqs. 7.72, 7.73, and 7.74 for $\rho_c \leq \rho$.

It is important to note that the exponential factor α_U given by Eq. 7.83 is directly a function of R, rather than being related to it through the parameter ρ. As a matter of fact, the parameter ρ has not been defined for $\rho \geq \rho_c$. It is convenient, on the other hand, to express the relation between α_U and R in terms of the parameter ρ over the entire range $0 \leq R < C$.

We obtain from Eq. 7.71

$$2\log_2(\sqrt{p}+\sqrt{1-p}) = -\log_2 \frac{(1-\rho_c)^2}{1-p} \tag{7.84}$$

Then, substituting for R the expression given by Eq. 7.70 for $\rho \geq \rho_c$ yields

$$\alpha_U = 1 + \log_2 \frac{(1-\rho_c)^2}{1-p} - 1 - \rho\log_2 \rho_c - (1-\rho)\log_2(1-\rho_c)$$

$$= \rho\log_2 \frac{1-\rho_c}{\rho_c} + \log_2 \frac{1-\rho_c}{1-p} = \rho\log_2 \frac{\rho_c(1-p)}{p(1-\rho_c)} + \log_2 \frac{1-\rho_c}{1-p}$$

$$= \rho\log_2 \frac{\rho_c}{p} + (1-\rho)\log_2 \frac{1-\rho_c}{1-p} \tag{7.85}$$

where use has been made of the relation

$$\left(\frac{\rho_c}{1-\rho_c}\right)^2 = \frac{p}{1-p} \tag{7.86}$$

implied by Eq. 7.71.

The expression for α_U given by Eqs. 7.75 and 7.76 follows by inspection from Eqs. 7.70 and 7.74.

QED

The upper bound to the probability of error given by Eq. 7.72 depends primarily on the integer n and on the exponential factor α_U. The factor K given by Eq. 7.73 is of relatively secondary importance; its behavior as a function of ρ is mainly the result of the particular approximations used.

The relation between α_U and R can be interpreted graphically as in the case of α_L in the preceding section. The behavior of R as a function of ρ is illustrated in Fig. 7.4.

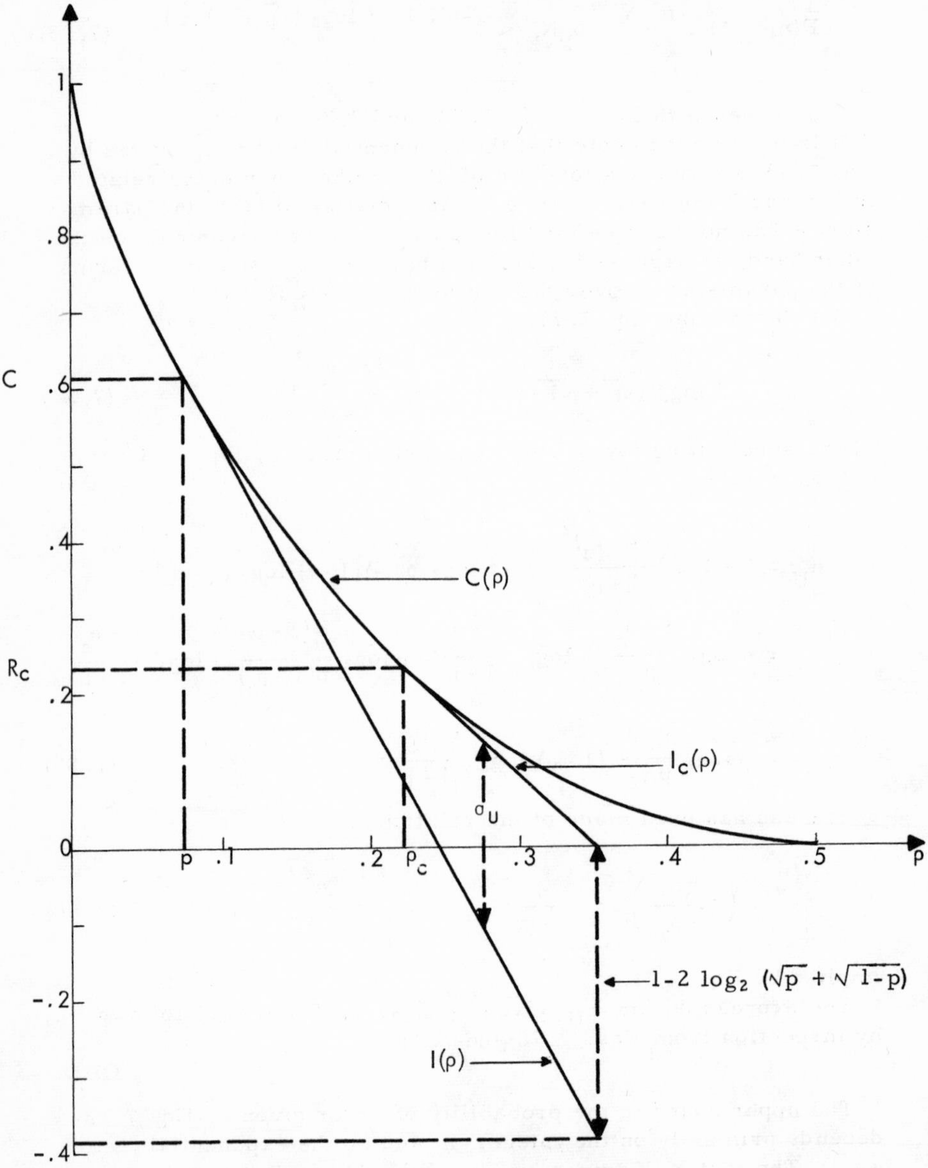

Fig. 7.4. Graphical determination of α_U

For $p < \rho < \rho_c$, R coincides with the curve $C(\rho)$ defined by Eq. 7.82. For $\rho \geq \rho_c$, R coincides with the straight line

$$I_c(\rho) = 1 + \rho \log_2 \rho_c + (1 - \rho) \log_2 (1 - \rho_c) \tag{7.87}$$

This straight line is tangent to the curve $C(\rho)$ at the critical point $\rho = \rho_c$, corresponding to the critical transmission rate

$$R_c = 1 + \rho_c \log_2 \rho_c + (1 - \rho_c) \log_2 (1 - \rho_c) \tag{7.88}$$

According to Eq. 7.77, the exponential coefficient α_U is the difference between the transmission rate R and the linear function $I(\rho)$ given by Eq. 7.76. This function is plotted in Fig. 7.4 as the straight line tangent to the curve $C(\rho)$ at the point $\rho = p$ at which $R = C$. Thus the exponential coefficient α_U is represented in Fig. 7.4 as the distance between the composite curve coinciding with $C(\rho)$ for $\rho < \rho_c$ and with $I_c(\rho)$ for $\rho > \rho_c$, and the straight line $I(\rho)$. It is clear that the exponential coefficient α_U is positive for $0 \leq R < C$ and increases with decreasing R. It follows that the average probability of error can be made as small as desired for any transmission rate $R < C$ by making n sufficiently large.

It is important to note that the relation between α_U and R is identical to the relation between α_L and the limiting value of R_L given by Eq. 7.57 for $p < \rho < \rho_c$. This is evident from Figs. 7.3 and 7.4. Thus for $p < \rho < \rho_c$, the upper bound to the probability of error derived in this section and the lower bound to the probability of error derived in the preceding section have the same exponential behavior with increasing n. However, for $\rho > \rho_c$, $\alpha_U < \alpha_L$. In other words, for any transmission rate $R < R_c$, the upper bound given by Eq. 7.72 diverges exponentially with increasing n from the lower bound given by Eq. 7.52.

It is clear that the upper bound to the average probability of error given by Eq. 7.72 is also an upper bound to the probability of error for some realizable set of M sequences of n digits. In fact, the ensemble of mappings considered in the above theorems must include at least one mapping for which the probability of error is not greater than the average probability of error over the ensemble. An even stronger result is stated by the following theorem.

Theorem. If M messages are encoded into sequences of n digits constructed by selecting the digits independently at random with equal probabilities, the probability that $P(e)$, the resulting probability of error, will be greater than $A\overline{P}(e)$ satisfies the inequality

$$\Pr [P(e) \geq A\overline{P}(e)] \leq \frac{1}{A} \tag{7.89}$$

where A is any constant larger than 1.

Proof. Let g represent any particular mapping and P(g) be the probability distribution for the ensemble of mappings. If $P(e|g)$ is the probability of error for a particular mapping g, the average probability of error over the ensemble of mappings is, by definition,

$$\overline{P}(e) \equiv \sum_{G} P(g)\, P(e|g) \tag{7.90}$$

where G indicates the set of possible mappings. Let G_A be the subset of mappings for which the probability of error satisfies the inequality

$$P(e|g) \geq A\,\overline{P}(e) \quad ; \quad g \text{ in } G_A \tag{7.91}$$

Then, we obtain from Eq. 7.90, with the help of Eq. 7.91,

$$\overline{P}(e) \geq \sum_{G_A} P(g)\, P(e|g) \geq A\,\overline{P}(e) \sum_{G_A} P(g)$$

$$= A\,\overline{P}(e)\, \Pr[P(e) \geq A\,\overline{P}(e)] \tag{7.92}$$

which yields immediately Eq. 7.89.

QED

This theorem implies that the random construction procedure introduced in this section for the purpose of obtaining an upper bound to the probability of error can actually be employed in practice for encoding messages into sequences of binary digits. In fact, such a random encoding procedure will yield, with reasonable probability, a mapping with a probability of error of the same order of magnitude as the average probability of error given by Eq. 7.72.

7.4. Parity-Check Codes

The upper and lower bounds evaluated in the preceding sections provide a reasonably accurate estimate of the probability of error that can be achieved when messages are encoded into sequences of binary digits for transmission through a binary symmetric channel. Furthermore, the theorem embodying Eq. 7.89 permits us to conclude that suitable sequences can be obtained in practice by selecting their digits independently at random.

On the other hand, the use of randomly constructed sequences has the practical disadvantage of requiring the encoder and the decoder to store $n2^{nR}$ binary digits, where n is the length of each sequence and R is the transmission rate in bits per channel digit. Such an exponential growth of the required storage capacity with n is unacceptable in practice. Fortunately, however, it can be easily circumvented through the use of the parity-check codes described below.

Parity-check codes are best defined in terms of modulo-2 sums of binary digits. Let a and b be binary digits. Their modulo-2 sum is, by definition,

$$a \oplus b = \begin{cases} 0 & ; \quad a = b \\ 1 & ; \quad a \neq b \end{cases} \tag{7.93}$$

It can readily be checked that the modulo-2 sum has the associative property

$$a \oplus b \oplus c = (a \oplus b) \oplus c \tag{7.94}$$

and, together with ordinary multiplication, the distributive property

$$(a \oplus b)\, c = a\, c \oplus b\, c \tag{7.95}$$

where c is a third binary digit. Furthermore, it follows from Eq. 7.93 that if

$$a = b \tag{7.96}$$

then

$$a \oplus b = 0 \tag{7.97}$$

In other words, modulo-2 subtraction is identical to modulo-2 addition.

Let $a_1\, a_2\, \ldots\, a_n$ be a sequence of n binary digits. We shall refer to the number of digits in the sequence that are equal to 1 as the weight k of the sequence. It follows from Eq. 7.93 that the modulo-2 sum of the n digits of the sequence is

$$\sum_{i=1}^{n}{}^{\oplus}\, a_i = \begin{cases} 0 & ; \quad k \text{ even} \\ 1 & ; \quad k \text{ odd} \end{cases} \tag{7.98}$$

In other words, the modulo-2 sum of the digits indicates whether the weight of the sequence is even or odd.

It is convenient, in connection with parity-check codes, to regard each message m as a sequence of ν binary digits

$$m \equiv \alpha_1 \alpha_2 \, \ldots \, \alpha_\nu \tag{7.99}$$

so that the number of distinct messages is

$$M = 2^\nu \tag{7.100}$$

An encoding procedure is said to be a parity-check code if it assigns to each message a sequence of binary digits

$$u \equiv \xi_1 \xi_2 \ldots \xi_n \qquad (7.101)$$

constructed as follows. The first ν digits of u are identical to the ν digits constituting the message m , that is,

$$\xi_j = \alpha_j \quad ; \quad 1 \leq j \leq \nu \qquad (7.102)$$

We shall refer to these first ν digits as information digits, in view of the fact that they are identical to the message digits. The remaining $n - \nu$ digits are linear combinations of the same message digits, that is,

$$\xi_{\nu+i} = \sum_{j=1}^{\nu} a_{ij}\alpha_j \quad ; \quad 1 \leq i \leq n - \nu \qquad (7.103)$$

where the coefficients a_{ij} are arbitrary binary digits. We shall refer to these remaining $n - \nu$ digits of u as parity-check digits. The reason for this name can be explained as follows.

We have from Eqs. 7.102 and 7.103

$$\sum_{j=1}^{\nu} a_{ij}\, \xi_j \oplus \xi_{\nu+i} = 0 \quad ; \quad 1 \leq i \leq n-\nu \qquad (7.104)$$

This suggests defining, for $j > \nu$,

$$a_{ij} \equiv \begin{cases} 1 \quad ; \quad \nu < j = \nu + i \\ 0 \quad ; \quad \nu < j \neq \nu + i \end{cases} \qquad (7.105)$$

so that the entire matrix of the coefficients a_{ij} becomes

$$\mathscr{A} \equiv \begin{bmatrix} a_{11} & a_{12} & \ldots & a_{1\nu} & 1 & 0 & \ldots & 0 \\ a_{21} & a_{22} & \ldots & a_{2\nu} & 0 & 1 & \ldots & 0 \\ \cdot & \cdot & \cdot & \cdot & \cdot & \cdot & \cdot & \cdot \\ \cdot & \cdot & \cdot & \cdot & \cdot & \cdot & \cdot & \cdot \\ a_{(n-\nu)1} & a_{(n-\nu)2} & \ldots & a_{(n-\nu)\nu} & 0 & 0 & \ldots & 1 \end{bmatrix} \qquad (7.106)$$

In other words, the first ν columns of $\mathscr{A}$ consist of arbitrary binary digits, while the remaining $n - \nu$ columns form a unitary matrix. Then, Eq. 7.104 can be rewritten in the form

$$\sum_{j=1}^{n} a_{ij}\, \xi_j = 0 \quad ; \quad 1 \leq i \leq n - \nu \qquad (7.107)$$

The values of the integer j for which $a_{ij} = 1$ for each i (that is, in each row of the matrix) are said to form a check-set. Then, Eq. 7.107 states that the weight of the sequence formed by the digits ξ_j associated with each check-set must be even. This evenness (or parity) is established, for each integer i, by the digit corresponding to $j = \nu + i$, because all the other digits associated with the same check-set are equal to message digits. This is the reason why the digits ξ_j corresponding to $\nu < j \leq n$ are called parity-check digits.

For parity-check codes, maximum-likelihood decoding of the channel output can be performed as follows. Let

$$v \equiv \eta_1 \eta_2 \cdots \eta_n \tag{7.108}$$

be the output sequence and define a new sequence

$$g \equiv \gamma_1 \gamma_2 \cdots \gamma_{n-\nu} \tag{7.109}$$

where

$$\sum_{j=1}^{n}{}^{\oplus}\, a_{ij}\eta_j \equiv \gamma_i \quad ; \quad 1 \leq i \leq n-\nu \tag{7.110}$$

The sequence g is known as the check sequence associated with the output sequence v. Modulo-2 addition of Eqs. 7.107 and 7.110 yields

$$\sum_{j=1}^{n}{}^{\oplus}\, a_{ij}(\xi_j \oplus \eta_j) = \gamma_i \quad ; \quad 1 \leq i \leq n-\nu \tag{7.111}$$

We observe, on the other hand, that

$$\zeta_j \equiv \xi_j \oplus \eta_j = \begin{cases} 0 \; ; & \eta_j = \xi_j \\ 1 \; ; & \eta_j \neq \xi_j \end{cases} \tag{7.112}$$

In other words, $\zeta_j = 0$ when the corresponding input digit has not been changed by the channel noise, and $\zeta = 1$ when it has been changed. Thus the sequence

$$s = \zeta_1 \zeta_2 \cdots \zeta_n \tag{7.113}$$

represents the channel noise; its weight k is the number of input digits that have been changed by noise. Finally, substituting ζ_j for $\xi_j \oplus \eta_j$ in Eq. 7.111 yields

$$\sum_{j=1}^{n}{}^{\oplus}\, a_{ij}\zeta_j = \gamma_i \quad ; \quad 1 \leq i \leq n-\nu \tag{7.114}$$

The digits γ_i of the check sequence g can be computed from the channel output according to Eq. 7.110. The digits of the noise sequence s must satisfy the set of $n - \nu$ linear equations represented by Eq. 7.114. Since there are n digits ζ_j and $n - \nu$ equations, there are at least 2^{ν} distinct sequences s that satisfy the set of equations. Maximum likelihood decoding corresponds to selecting among these possible noise sequences the one with minimum weight; in fact, the probability of occurrence of any particular noise sequence s of weight k is

$$P(s) = p^{k}(1 - p)^{n-k} \tag{7.115}$$

Then, modulo-2 addition of the first ν digits of the selected noise sequence to the corresponding digits of the received sequence yields the most likely message. When the messages are equiprobable, this decoding operation minimizes the probability of error.

The above decoding procedure results in an error whenever there exists a noise sequence satisfying Eq. 7.114 whose weight is smaller than that of the noise sequence that has actually occurred. According to Eq. 7.114 the digits γ_i of the check sequence g are specified by the elements of the matrix $\mathscr{A}$ and by the noise sequence that has actually occurred. Thus the probability of error is independent of the message transmitted. This is an important property of parity-check codes.

Another important property of parity-check codes is that the set of M input sequences u representing messages form a group under the operation of modulo-2 addition digit by digit. An up-to-date treatment of the group properties of parity-check codes is presented in Ref. [3] .

It is clear from Eq. 7.106 that a parity-check code is uniquely specified by $\nu(n - \nu)$ binary digits, namely, the elements of the first ν columns of the matrix $\mathscr{A}$. Of course these digits must be stored by the encoder and by the decoder. We shall describe below parity-check codes that are uniquely specified by $n-1$ binary digits, and evaluate an upper bound to their average probability of error when the $n-1$ binary digits are selected independently at random. We shall refer to this special class of parity-check codes as convolution codes.

Let $b_1, b_2, \ldots, b_{n-1}$ be a set of $n - 1$ binary digits. A convolution code is a parity-check code for which the elements of the first ν columns of the matrix $\mathscr{A}$ are given by

$$a_{ij} = b_{n-\nu+j-i} \quad ; \quad 1 \leq j \leq \nu \;, \; 1 \leq i \leq n-\nu \tag{7.116}$$

For instance, the matrix $\mathscr{A}$ of a convolution code with $\nu = 4$ and $n = 7$ has the form

$$\mathscr{A} = \begin{bmatrix} b_3 & b_4 & b_5 & b_6 & 1 & 0 & 0 \\ b_2 & b_3 & b_4 & b_5 & 0 & 1 & 0 \\ b_1 & b_2 & b_3 & b_4 & 0 & 0 & 1 \end{bmatrix} \qquad (7.117)$$

Then, Eq. 7.103 becomes

$$\xi_{\nu+i} = \sum_{j=1}^{\nu} b_{n-\nu+j-i}\, a_j \quad ; \quad 1 \leq i \leq n-\nu \qquad (7.118)$$

It is clear from Eq. 7.118 that in the case of a convolution code, the last $n-\nu$ digits of the input sequence u are obtained by convolving the message sequence m defined by Eq. 7.99 with the sequence $b_1 b_2 \ldots b_{n-1}$. The whole encoding operation could then be instrumented as indicated schematically in Fig. 7.5

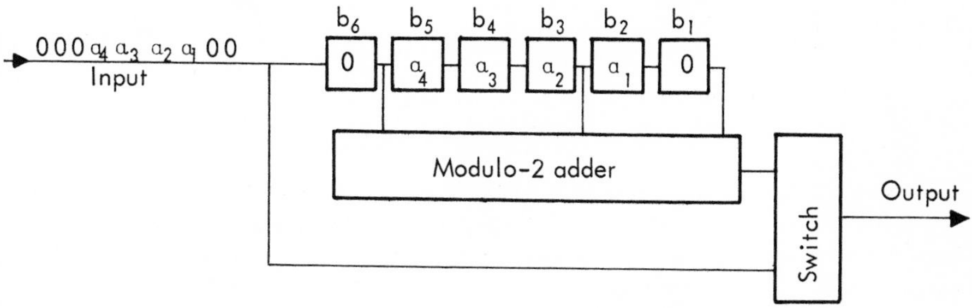

Fig. 7.5. Convolution encoder

for $n = 7$ and $\nu = 4$. The input to the encoder of Fig. 7.5 consists of a sequence of binary digits in which groups of ν message digits, $a_1\, a_2 \ldots a_\nu$, alternate with groups of $n-\nu$ digits 0 . The main part of the encoder consists of a shift register (binary delay line) with $n-1$ stages. The output of the ith stage is fed to the modulo-2 adder if and only if $b_i = 1$. In Fig. 7.5, $b_1 = b_3 = b_6 = 1$ and $b_2 = b_4 = b_5 = 0$. The switch connects the modulo-2 adder to the output when the shift register contains all the digits $a_1\, a_2 \ldots a_\nu$ of a particular message, and connects the input directly to the output otherwise. It is clear that the encoder of Fig. 7.5 generates in succession the digits ξ_j specified by Eqs. 7.102 and 7.118.

Next, we shall derive an upper bound to the average probability of error for the ensemble of convolution codes generated by selecting the digits b_1 , b_2 , ..., b_{n-1} independently at random with equal probabilities. It is clear from the definition of the ensemble that the 2^{n-1} distinct convolution codes have the same ensemble probability.

Theorem. Let us consider the ensemble of convolution codes generated by selecting independently at random with equal probabilities the $n-1$ binary digits that define a particular code, where n is the number of channel digits in which ν message digits are encoded. If p is the noise probability of the binary symmetric channel, and maximum-likelihood decoding is employed, the average probability of error $\overline{P}(e)$ for such an ensemble of convolution codes satisfies

$$\overline{P}(e) \leq 2^{-(n-\nu)} \sum_{k=0}^{r} b_k N_k + \sum_{k=r+1}^{n} b_k \tag{7.119}$$

where

$$b_k \equiv \binom{n}{k} p^k (1-p)^{n-k} \tag{7.120}$$

$$N_k \equiv \sum_{i=0}^{k} \binom{n}{i} \tag{7.121}$$

and r is an arbitrary integer in the range $0 \leq r \leq n$.

Proof. We saw above that a decoding error occurs whenever there exists a noise sequence s' whose digits ζ'_j satisfy Eq. 7.114 and whose weight is smaller than the weight of the noise sequence s that has actually occurred. In addition, an error may occur when there exists a noise sequence s' satisfying Eq. 7.114 whose weight is equal to that of s. There are no other situations in which a decoding error may occur. Thus an upper bound to the average probability of error can be obtained by evaluating an upper bound to the probability of existence of a noise sequence s' satisfying Eq. 7.114 with weight smaller than or equal to that of s.

If both s and s' satisfy Eq. 7.114, their corresponding digits ζ_j and ζ'_j must satisfy

$$\sum_{j=1}^{n} a_{ij} (\zeta_j \oplus \zeta'_j) = 0 \tag{7.122}$$

We observe, first of all, that this equation cannot be satisfied for all integers i if s and s' differ only in the last $n-\nu$ digits. In fact, of the digits for which $j > \nu$, only the pair corresponding to $j = \nu + i$ contributes to the summation, as evidenced by the last $n-\nu$ columns of the matrix $\mathscr{A}$ given by Eq. 7.106. Next, let us suppose that s and s' differ in one or more of the digits corresponding to $j \leq \nu$, and indicate with h the smallest value of $j \leq \nu$ for which ζ'_j differs from ζ_j, that is,

$$\zeta_j \oplus \zeta'_j = \begin{cases} 0 \; ; & 1 \leq j < h \\ 1 \; ; & j = h \leq \nu \end{cases} \tag{7.123}$$

Regardless of the values assumed by the terms on the lefthand side of Eq. 7.122 for $j \neq h$, the probability over the ensemble of convolution codes that Eq. 7.122 is satisfied for any one particular integer i is equal to 1/2. In fact, we have from Eq. 7.116

$$a_{ih} = b_{n-\nu+h-i} \tag{7.124}$$

and, by assumption,

$$\Pr(b_{n-\nu+h-i} = 0) = \Pr(b_{n-\nu+h-i} = 1) = \frac{1}{2} \tag{7.125}$$

Furthermore, as shown below, the probability that Eq. 7.122 is satisfied for any particular i is independent of whether or not the same equation is satisfied for any $i' < i$. In fact, it follows from Eq. 7.116 that for any $i' < i$, the digit $a_{i'j} \equiv b_{n-\nu+j-i'}$ can be identical to the digit $a_{ih} \equiv b_{n-\nu+h-i}$ only for $j < h$. Then, because of Eq. 7.123, any digit $a_{i'j} \equiv a_{ih}$ is multiplied by 0 in Eq. 7.122, and therefore its actual value is immaterial. The statistical independence stated above is then insured by the assumed statistical independence of the digits $b_{n-\nu+h-i}$. We can conclude that the probability that Eq. 7.122 is simultaneously satisfied for all values of i is equal to $2^{-(n-\nu)}$.

Let k be the weight of the noise sequence s that has actually occurred, and indicate with N_k the number of sequences of n digits with weight not exceeding k, given by Eq. 7.121. The probability that any one of these sequences, together with s, will satisfy Eq. 7.122 is, by the above arguments, equal to either 0 or $2^{-(n-\nu)}$. On the other hand, the probability that out of N_k different events one or more will actually occur cannot exceed the sum of the probabilities of the individual events. Thus the probability P_k that there exists a sequence s' satisfying Eq. 7.122 of weight not exceeding k satisfies

$$P_k \leq N_k \, 2^{-(n-\nu)} \tag{7.126}$$

The righthand side of Eq. 7.126 increases with the integer k and eventually becomes larger than 1. Thus since P_k is a probability, a more satisfactory upper bound is given by

$$P_k \leq \begin{cases} N_k\, 2^{-(n-\nu)} & ; \quad 0 \leq k \leq r \\ 1 & ; \quad r < k \leq n \end{cases} \tag{7.127}$$

where r is an arbitrary integer in the range $0 \leq r \leq n$. Then, indicating with b_k the probability of occurrence of noise sequences of weight k , given by Eq. 7.120, we obtain for the average probability of error over the ensemble of convolution codes

$$\overline{P}(e) \leq \sum_{k=0}^{n} b_r P_k \leq \sum_{k=0}^{r} b_k N_k\, 2^{-(n-\nu)} + \sum_{k=r+1}^{n} b_k \tag{7.128}$$

which coincides with Eq. 7.119.

QED

It is most important to note that Eq. 7.119 becomes identical to Eq. 7.80 when 2^ν , the number of distinct sequences of ν binary digits, is identified with M , the number of distinct messages. It follows that if we indicate with ρ a parameter related to the transmission rate

$$R \equiv \frac{\log_2 M}{n} = \frac{\nu}{n} \tag{7.129}$$

by Eq. 7.70, the average probability of error over the ensemble of convolution codes satisfies

$$\overline{P}(e) < K\, 2^{-n\alpha_U} \tag{7.130}$$

where K and α_U are given as functions of ρ by Eqs. 7.73 and 7.74. In other words, the upper bound to the average probability of error for convolution codes coincides with the upper bound to the average probability of error for the more general ensemble of binary codes discussed in the preceding section. This result is of great importance because it implies that a randomly selected convolution code can be expected to yield approximately the same probability of error as a code constructed by selecting independently at random the digits of the input sequences assigned to the messages. Thus no demonstrable loss of performance results from the use of convolution codes, which are by far more convenient from a practical standpoint.

Corollary. Let us consider the ensemble of parity-check codes obtained by selecting independently at random the digits in the first ν columns of the matrix defined by Eq. 7.106. When maximum-likelihood decoding is employed, the average probability of error satisfies Eq. 7.119 in the statement of the preceding theorem.

Proof. The arguments used in proving the preceding theorem hold all the more when all the digits a_{ij}, with $j \leq \nu$, are statistically independent as in the ensemble of parity-check codes contemplated in the corollary.

QED

7.5. Summary and Conclusions

We have discussed in this chapter the encoding of messages for transmission through a binary symmetric channel, the simplest channel for which the input is never uniquely specified by the output. The probability of error that can be achieved for this channel was estimated by means of upper and lower bounds. For any fixed transmission rate smaller than the channel capacity, both of these bounds were found to decrease exponentially with increasing n, the number of channel digits per message. For rates greater than a critical rate R_c, depending on the noise probability p, the magnitudes of the exponential coefficients by which n is multiplied in the two bounds turned out to be equal, so that the two bounds provide a rather accurate estimate of the probability of error that can be achieved. However, the magnitudes of the exponential coefficients in the two bounds are different for transmission rates smaller than R_c. The upper bound, in particular, permitted us to conclude that the probability of error can be made as small as desired for any fixed transmission rate smaller than the channel capacity.

We turned our attention next to parity-check codes and, in particular, to the special class of parity-check codes known as convolution codes. Convolution codes are of particular interest because they are uniquely specified by n-1 binary digits, where n is the number of channel digits per message. This implies that a relatively small amount of storage is required to provide the encoder and the decoder with the necessary information about the encoding scheme employed. We were able to derive, for convolution codes, an upper bound to the probability of error identical to the upper bound previously obtained for arbitrary binary codes. Thus the advantages of convolution codes can be obtained with no demonstrable loss of performance.

No specific way of constructing binary codes has been discussed because no procedure is known that will guarantee a probability of error smaller than the upper bound given by Eq. 7.119 for all values of n and ν for which ν/n is smaller than the channel capacity. Various parity-check codes that yield a satisfactory probability of error for values of n and ν within limited ranges are discussed in Ref. [3]. In view of the lack of any satisfactory general encoding procedure, it is very important that, because of the theorem embodying Eq. 7.89, a randomly selected convolution code is very likely to yield a probability of error in the neighborhood of the upper bound given by Eq. 7.119.

The schematic diagram, shown in Fig. 7.5, of a convolution encoder clearly indicates that the complexity of such an encoder increases in proportion to the number of channel digits per message, for any fixed transmission rate. Thus the complexity of the encoder should not present any serious practical problem. On the other hand, the complexity of a decoder instrumented according to the decoding procedure outlined in Sec. 7.4 would increase roughly exponentially with n. Three different decoding procedures whose complexities grow only slightly faster than linearly with n have been suggested in recent years. The first one, developed by J.M. Wozencraft is based on a sequential encoding procedure of the convolution type. It is discussed in Ref. [4] together with experimental results obtained by simulating the entire communication process on a digital computer. The second procedure, recently suggested by R. Gallager [5], is restricted to parity-check codes with very small check-sets. The third procedure, developed also very recently by W. Peterson [3], is strictly limited to a special class of parity-check codes which yield an acceptable probability of error only for values of n and ν within limited ranges. Since excellent presentations of these decoding procedures are available elsewhere, they will not be discussed in this text.

All the results presented in this chapter, including those pertaining to convolution codes, can be readily generalized to channels of the type defined by Eq. 5.23. Some, but not all, of them will be extended in Chapter 9 to arbitrary, discrete, constant channels.

7.6. Selected References

1. P. Elias, "Coding for Two Noisy Channels," in Information Theory (C. Cherry, Editor), Butterworth, London (1956), p. 61.

2. W. Feller, An Introduction to Probability Theory and its Applications, 2nd Ed., John Wiley and Sons, Inc., New York (1957). The binomial distribution is discussed in Secs. 1 to 4 of Chap. VI. The bounds to the factorial given in Eq. 7.5 are derived in Sec. 9 of Chap. II.

3. W.W. Peterson, Error-Correcting Codes, The Technology Press and John Wiley and Sons, Inc., New York (1961).

4. J.M. Wozencraft, and B. Reiffen, Sequential Decoding, The Technology Press and John Wiley and Sons, Inc., New York (1961).

5. R.G. Gallager, "Low-Density Parity-Check Codes," Doctoral Thesis, Department of Electrical Engineering, M.I.T. (1960).

*Chapter 8

MULTINOMIAL DISTRIBUTIONS

The extension of the results of the preceding chapter to arbitrary, discrete, constant channels requires the evaluation of bounds to multinomial probability distributions, analogous to those derived in Sec. 7.1 for binomial distributions. Such bounds will be obtained with the help of a mathematical technique which has become known as the "tilting of probability distributions." This technique was first introduced by F. Esscher in 1932 and has since been extended by various authors, including W. Feller [1] and H. Chernov [2]. The material to be presented in this chapter originated mostly from informal seminar notes prepared by C. E. Shannon [3]. We shall confine our discussion to multinomial probability distributions, although the same mathematical techniques can be used in connection with a much broader class of probability distributions.

8.1. Moment-Generating Functions

Moment-generating functions play a key role in the mathematical techniques discussed here. Let A be a discrete ensemble consisting of points a_1, a_2, ..., a_L, and indicate with $P(a)$ the probability distribution of such an ensemble. A random variable $\phi(a)$ is defined at each of the points of the ensemble. The moment-generating function of this random variable is, by definition,

$$g(s) \equiv \sum_A e^{s\phi(a)} P(a) \tag{8.1}$$

where s is a real-valued parameter.

The name "moment-generating function" stems from the properties of the successive derivatives of $g(s)$ with respect to s. We have for the first derivative

$$g'(s) \equiv \frac{dg(s)}{ds} = \sum_A \phi(a)\, e^{s\phi(a)} P(a) \tag{8.2}$$

and for the second derivative

$$g''(s) \equiv \frac{d^2 g(s)}{ds^2} = \sum_{A} \phi(a)^2 \, e^{s\phi(a)} \, P(a) \tag{8.3}$$

Similar expressions are obtained for the higher-order derivatives, involving the corresponding higher powers of the random variable.

Setting $s = 0$ in Eq. 8.2 yields

$$g'(0) = \sum_{A} \phi(a) \, P(a) \equiv \overline{\phi} \tag{8.4}$$

where $\overline{\phi}$ is the average value, or first moment, of the random variable. Similarly, setting $s = 0$ in Eq. 8.3 yields

$$g''(0) = \sum_{A} \phi(a)^2 \, P(a) \equiv \overline{\phi^2} \tag{8.5}$$

where $\overline{\phi^2}$ is the mean-square value, or second moment, of the random variable. Clearly, the values of the higher-order derivatives of $g(s)$ evaluated for $s = 0$ yield the higher-order moments of the random variable.

The logarithm of the moment-generating function, namely

$$\gamma(s) \equiv \ln g(s) \tag{8.6}$$

turns out to be more useful for our purposes than the function itself. The successive derivatives of $\gamma(s)$ with respect to s, known as the semi-invariants of the probability distribution, have properties similar to those of $g(s)$. It is convenient, in interpreting these derivatives, to define the family of auxiliary probability distributions

$$Q(a) \equiv \frac{e^{s\phi(a)} \, P(a)}{g(s)} = e^{s\phi(a) - \gamma(s)} \, P(a) \tag{8.7}$$

in which each member corresponds to a particular value of the parameter s. It is clear from the form of Eq. 8.7 that

$$[Q(a)]_{s=0} = P(a) \tag{8.8}$$

and that the probabilities of the points corresponding to relatively larger values of $\phi(a)$ are enhanced for $s > 0$ and reduced for $s < 0$.

We obtain for the first derivative of $\gamma(s)$, with the help of Eq. 8.2,

$$\gamma'(s) \equiv \frac{d\gamma(s)}{ds} = \frac{g'(s)}{g(s)} = \sum_A \phi(a)\, Q(a) \equiv \bar{\bar{\phi}} \tag{8.9}$$

where $\bar{\bar{\phi}}$ indicates the average value of the random variable with respect to the auxiliary probability distribution Q(a) defined by Eq. 8.7. Similarly, we obtain for the second derivative, with the help of Eq. 8.3,

$$\gamma''(s) \equiv \frac{d^2\gamma(s)}{ds^2} = \frac{g''(s)}{g(s)} - \left(\frac{g'(s)}{g(s)}\right)^2$$

$$= \sum_A \phi(a)^2\, Q(a) - \left[\sum \phi(a)\, Q(a)\right]^2 = \overline{\overline{\phi^2}} - [\bar{\bar{\phi}}]^2 \tag{8.10}$$

where $\overline{\overline{\phi^2}}$ indicates the mean-square value of the random variable with respect to Q(a) . Thus $\gamma''(s)$ is the variance of the random variable with respect to Q(a) , and therefore it is a non-negative quantity. It follows, in view of Eq. 8.8, that

$$\bar{\bar{\phi}} \equiv \gamma'(s) \begin{cases} > \bar{\phi}\,; & s > 0 \\ = \bar{\phi}\,; & s = 0 \\ < \bar{\phi}\,; & s < 0 \end{cases} \tag{8.11}$$

In words, this equation means that the average value of the random variable with respect to Q(a) increases monotonically with s , and it is greater than $\bar{\phi}$ for $s > 0$ and smaller than $\bar{\phi}$ for $s < 0$. For this reason, Q(a) is said to be a tilted probability distribution. The amount of tilting increases with the magnitude of s , while its direction depends on the sign of s .

A very important property of moment-generating functions is that the moment-generating function of the sum of two statistically independent random variables is equal to the product of the moment-generating functions of the two separate random variables. More precisely, let B be a second discrete ensemble consisting of points b_1 , b_2 , . . . , b_L with probability distribution P(b) . Let us indicate with $\phi_a(a)$ the random variable defined for the ensemble of points A and with $\phi_b(b)$ the random variable defined for the ensemble B . Since the two random variables are, by assumption, statistically independent, the moment-generating function for the probability distribution of their sum is

$$g_{ab}(s) \equiv \sum_{A}\sum_{B} e^{s[\phi_a(a) + \phi_b(b)]} P(a)\, P(b)$$

$$= \sum_{A} e^{s\,\phi_a(a)} P(a) \sum_{B} e^{s\phi_b(b)} P(b) = g_a(s)\, g_b(s) \qquad (8.12)$$

where $g_a(s)$ and $g_b(s)$ are the moment-generating functions of the two separate random variables.

8.2. Tilting of Probability Distributions

We shall be concerned primarily with sequences of n statistically independent events

$$a^n \equiv a_1\, a_2\, \ldots\, a_i\, \ldots\, a_n \qquad (8.13)$$

where each event a_i can be any one of the points a of the ensemble A, and each event is governed by the same probability distribution $P(a)$, that is,

$$P(a_i) \equiv \Pr(a_i = a) \equiv P(a) \;;\quad 1 \leq i \leq n \qquad (8.14)$$

If identical random variables $\phi(a_i)$ are defined for each of the n events, that is,

$$[\phi(a_i)]_{a_i = a} \equiv \phi(a) \;;\quad 1 \leq i \leq n \qquad (8.15)$$

such random variables are statistically independent and equally distributed, in view of the fact that the events themselves are statistically independent and equally distributed.

Let us indicate with A^n the product ensemble formed by all the possible sequences a^n, and with

$$\Phi(a^n) \equiv \sum_{i=1}^{n} \phi(a_i) \qquad (8.16)$$

the sum of the values assumed by the n random variables for the events of a particular sequence a^n. The moment-generating function of the random variable $\Phi(a^n)$ defined over the product ensemble A^n can be obtained from the moment-generating functions associated with the individual events a_i. Since the random variables $\phi(a_i)$ are statistically independent and equally distributed, successive application of Eq. 8.12 yields for the desired moment-generating function

$$G(s) \equiv \sum_{A^n} e^{s\Phi(a^n)} P(a^n) = g^n(s) \tag{8.17}$$

and for its logarithm

$$\Gamma(s) \equiv \ln G(s) = n\,\gamma(s) \tag{8.18}$$

where $g(s)$ and $\gamma(s)$ are defined by Eqs. 8.1 and 8.6.

The first and second derivatives of $\Gamma(s)$ with respect to s can be obtained directly from Eqs. 8.9, and 8.10, with the help of Eq. 8.18.

$$\Gamma'(s) \equiv \frac{d\Gamma(s)}{ds} = n\,\gamma'(s) = n\bar{\bar{\phi}} \tag{8.19}$$

$$\Gamma''(s) \equiv \frac{d^2\Gamma(s)}{ds^2} = n\,\gamma''(s) = n\left\{\overline{\overline{\phi^2}} - [\bar{\bar{\phi}}]^2\right\} \tag{8.20}$$

Again, these derivatives represent the average value and the variance of $\Phi(a^n)$ with respect to the tilted probability distribution

$$Q(a^n) \equiv e^{s\Phi(a^n) - \Gamma(s)} P(a^n) = \prod_{i=1}^{n} Q(a_i) \tag{8.21}$$

where

$$[Q(a_i)]_{a_i=a} \equiv Q(a) \tag{8.22}$$

and $Q(a)$ is defined by Eq. 8.7.

The probability distribution of the random variable $\Phi(a^n)$ with respect to $Q(a^n)$ is tilted relatively to the probability distribution of the same random variable with respect to $P(a^n)$ in the same sense that the probability distribution of $\phi(a)$ with respect to $Q(a)$ is tilted relatively to that with respect to $P(a)$. Again, the amount of tilting increases with the magnitude of s, and its direction depends on the sign of s. This fact can be exploited in evaluating the tails of the probability distribution of $\Phi(a^n)$ with respect to $P(a^n)$ as follows.

Let A^n_ϕ be the set of sequences a^n for which $\Phi(a^n) \leq n\phi$, where ϕ is an arbitrary number. The distribution function of the random variable $\Phi(a^n)$ with respect to $P(a^n)$ is, by definition,

$$F(n\phi) \equiv \Pr[\Phi(a^n) \leq n\phi] = \sum_{A^n_\phi} P(a^n) \tag{8.23}$$

Similarly, the distribution function of the same random variable with respect to $Q(a^n)$ is

$$F_Q(n\phi) \equiv \sum_{A_\phi^n} Q(a^n) \tag{8.24}$$

Then it follows from Eq. 8.21 that the increments of the two distribution functions are related by

$$dF(n\phi) = e^{-n[s\phi - \gamma(s)]}\, dF_Q(n\phi) \tag{8.25}$$

If $\Phi(a^n)$ is the sum of n statistically independent random variables with finite first and second moments, its probability distribution, according to the central-limit theorem, becomes gaussian in the limit of n approaching infinity. The convergence with increasing n, however, is not fast enough to provide asymptotically correct estimates of the actual probability distribution for deviations from the mean proportional to n. These are just the types of estimates that we shall need. On the other hand, good estimates can be obtained for deviations proportional to $\sqrt{n}$, that is, proportional to the standard deviation of the distribution. This limitation of estimates based simply on the central-limit theorem can be circumvented by tilting the probability distribution as follows.

The probability distribution of $\Phi(a^n)$ with respect to $Q(a^n)$, as well as that with respect to $P(a^n)$, converges toward a gaussian distribution with increasing n. On the other hand, the difference between the mean values of the two distributions is given by

$$\Gamma'(s) - \Gamma'(0) = n[\gamma'(s) - \gamma'(0)] = n[\bar{\bar{\phi}} - \bar{\phi}] \tag{8.26}$$

and therefore it increases linearly with n for a fixed value of s. In other words, the deviation of the mean of the tilted distribution from the mean of the untilted distribution increases linearly with n. Thus since good estimates of the tilted distribution near its mean can be obtained in a variety of ways with the help of the central-limit theorem, correspondingly good estimates of the untilted distribution can be obtained with the help of Eq. 8.25. Simple estimates of the distribution function defined by Eq. 8.23 are derived in the following sections in the form of upper and lower bounds. More precise estimates are given in [1].

8.3. Upper Bounds to Multinomial Distribution Functions

We shall now evaluate upper bounds to the tails of multinomial distributions with the help of the tilting technique discussed in the preceding section. For the sake of emphasis, these bounds are stated as theorems.

Let us consider again a discrete ensemble A consisting of a finite number of points, and indicate with $P(a)$ the probability distribution characterizing the ensemble, and with $\phi(a)$ a random variable defined for the points of the ensemble. We shall assume that $\gamma(s)$, the logarithm of the moment-generating function of this random variable defined by Eq. 8.6, together with its first and second derivatives with respect to s are finite for values of s in an interval $s_1 < s < s_2$ including $s = 0$. We shall be concerned again with sequences a^n of n statistically independent events a_i, each of which can be any one of the points a of the ensemble A, and with the sum $\Phi(a^n)$ of the random variables $\phi(a_i)$ associated with the events. In particular, we shall be concerned with the distribution function $F(n\phi)$ of the random variable $\Phi(a^n)$ defined by Eq. 8.23.

Theorem. The multinomial distribution function $F(n\phi)$ satisfies the inequality

$$F(n\phi) \leq e^{-n[s\gamma'(s)-\gamma(s)]} \quad ; \quad s_1 < s \leq 0 \tag{8.27}$$

where

$$\phi = \gamma'(s) \leq \overline{\phi} \quad ; \quad s_1 < s \leq 0 \tag{8.28}$$

The exponential coefficient in Eq. 8.27 is given by

$$s\gamma'(s) - \gamma(s) = \sum_{A} Q(a) \ln \frac{Q(a)}{P(a)} \geq 0 \tag{8.29}$$

where $Q(a)$ is the auxiliary probability distribution defined by Eq. 8.7.

Proof. Let A^n_ϕ be the set of sequences a^n for which $\Phi(a^n) \leq n\phi$. We have from Eqs. 8.18, 8.21, and 8.23 for $s \leq 0$

$$F(n\phi) = e^{n\gamma(s)} \sum_{A^n_\phi} e^{-s\Phi(a^n)} Q(a^n) \leq e^{n[\gamma(s)-s\phi]} \sum_{A^n_\phi} Q(a^n) \tag{8.30}$$

On the other hand, since $Q(a^n)$ is a probability distribution over the product space A^n,

$$\sum_{A^n_\phi} Q(a^n) \leq 1 \tag{8.31}$$

It follows that

$$F(n\phi) \leq e^{-n[s\phi-\gamma(s)]} \quad ; \quad s_1 < s \leq 0 \tag{8.32}$$

The last inequality is satisfied for $s_1 < s \leq 0$. Thus we are free to select the value s within this interval that minimizes the righthand side of Eq. 8.32. Equating to zero the derivative with respect to s of the exponential coefficient yields

$$\frac{d}{ds}[s\phi-\gamma(s)] = \phi - \gamma'(s) = 0 \tag{8.33}$$

from which we obtain

$$\gamma'(s) = \phi \tag{8.34}$$

Furthermore, in view of Eq. 8.10,

$$\frac{d^2}{ds^2}[s\phi-\gamma(s)] = -\gamma''(s) \leq 0 \tag{8.35}$$

It follows that the value of s for which Eq. 8.34 is satisfied maximizes the exponential coefficient $s\phi - \gamma(s)$, and therefore minimizes the righthand side of Eq. 8.32. Then substituting $\gamma'(s)$ for ϕ in Eq. 8.32 yields Eq. 8.27. The fact that ϕ is smaller than $\overline{\phi}$, the average value of the random variable $\phi(a)$, follows immediately from Eq. 8.11.

The exponential coefficient can be evaluated as follows. We have from Eq. 8.9

$$s\gamma'(s) - \gamma(s) = s\sum_A \phi(a)\,Q(a) - \gamma(s) = \sum_A Q(a)\,[s\phi(a) - \gamma(s)] \tag{8.36}$$

On the other hand, we have from Eq. 8.7

$$\ln\frac{Q(a)}{P(a)} = s\phi(a) - \gamma(s) \tag{8.37}$$

Substituting the lefthand side of this equation in the righthand side of Eq. 8.36 yields Eq. 8.29. Finally the non-negative character of the summation in Eq. 8.29 can be readily proved with the help of Eq. 2.91. We obtain

$$-\sum_A Q(a)\ln\frac{Q(a)}{P(a)} \leq \sum_A Q(a)\left[\frac{P(a)}{Q(a)} - 1\right] = 0 \tag{8.38}$$

QED

The approximations involved in obtaining Eq. 8.27 deserve further discussion. We observe, first of all, that Eq. 8.34 implies that the probability distribution of the random variable $\phi(a)$

with respect to $Q(a)$ is tilted in such a way as to make its mean $\overline{\overline{\phi}} = \gamma'(s)$ coincide with the value ϕ in the argument of the distribution function. This implies, in turn, that the mean value of $\Phi(a^n)$ with respect to $Q(a^n)$ coincides with $n\phi$. It follows that the summation on the lefthand side of Eq. 8.31 includes all sequences a^n for which $\Phi(a^n)$ is smaller than, or equal to, its mean value with respect to the auxiliary distribution $Q(a^n)$. Thus the approximation in Eq. 8.31 should increase the upper bound only by a factor in the neighborhood of 2.

The approximation involved in Eq. 8.30, however, has a much greater effect. The approximation results from setting the value of $\Phi(a^n)$ equal to the largest value that this random variable assumes for any sequence a^n in the set A_ϕ^n, namely $n\phi$. A more precise evaluation of the lefthand side of Eq. 8.30 [3], with the help of the central-limit theorem, introduces on the righthand side of Eq. 8.27 a factor roughly inversely proportional to the magnitude of s and to $\sqrt{n}$. The exponential coefficient, however, remains unchanged. It is most important to note that the inequality in Eq. 8.30 is valid only for $s \leq 0$. This implies, in turn, that the probability distribution of $\Phi(a^n)$ is tilted toward smaller values of the random variable; the mean value of $\Phi(a^n)$ with respect to $Q(a^n)$ becomes equal to its mean value with respect to $P(a^n)$ for $s = 0$. In other words, Eq. 8.27 is valid only for the lower tail of the probability distribution. A similar upper bound for the upper tail of the probability distribution is given by the following theorem.

Theorem. The complement of the distribution function $F(n\phi)$ satisfies the inequality

$$1-F(n\phi) \equiv \Pr[\phi(a^n) > n\gamma'(s)] \leq e^{-n[s\gamma'(s)-\gamma(s)]} \; ; \quad 0 \leq s < s_2 \tag{8.39}$$

where

$$\phi = \gamma'(s) \geq \overline{\Phi} \; ; \quad 0 \leq s < s_2 \tag{8.40}$$

The exponential coefficient in Eq. 8.39 is given by

$$s\gamma'(s) - \gamma(s) = \sum_A Q(a) \ln \frac{Q(a)}{P(a)} \geq 0 \tag{8.41}$$

Proof. The proof of this theorem is identical to the proof of the preceding theorem except for the fact that s is positive and the set A_ϕ^n is replaced by its complement, namely the set of sequences a^n for which $\Phi(a^n) > n\phi$. QED

The interpretation of this second theorem is also identical to that of the first one, except for the fact that the probability distributions of the random variables $\phi(a)$ and $\Phi(a^n)$ with respect to $Q(a)$ and $Q(a^n)$ are tilted toward larger values of the random variables rather than toward smaller values.

We shall turn our attention next to two important generalizations of the preceding theorems. Let us define a second random variable $\theta(a)$ for the points of the ensemble A. The joint moment-generating function of the two random variables $\phi(a)$ and $\theta(a)$ is, by definition,

$$g(s, t) \equiv \sum_A e^{s\phi(a)+t\theta(a)} P(a) \tag{8.42}$$

where t is a new parameter playing a role similar to that of s. Let

$$\gamma(s, t) \equiv \ln g(s, t) \tag{8.43}$$

and define the family of auxiliary probability distributions

$$Q(a) \equiv e^{s\phi(a)+t\theta(a)-\gamma(s,t)} P(a) \tag{8.44}$$

We have for the first partial derivatives of $\gamma(s, t)$ with respect to s and t

$$\gamma_s'(s, t) \equiv \frac{\partial\gamma(s, t)}{\partial s} = \sum_A \phi(a)\, Q(a) = \bar{\bar{\phi}} \tag{8.45}$$

$$\gamma_t'(s, t) \equiv \frac{\partial\gamma(s, t)}{\partial t} = \sum_A \theta(a)\, Q(a) = \bar{\bar{\theta}} \tag{8.46}$$

These two partial derivatives represent again the mean values of the two random variables with respect to the auxiliary probability distribution $Q(a)$.

Returning now to the sequence of events a^n, we associate with each event a_i a second random variable $\theta(a_i)$, and indicate with

$$\Theta(a^n) \equiv \sum_{i=1}^{n} \theta(a_i) \tag{8.47}$$

the sum of the values assumed by these n independent random variables. The logarithm of the joint moment-generating function of the two random variables $\Phi(a^n)$ and $\Theta(a^n)$ is

$$\Gamma(s,t) \equiv \ln \sum_{A^n} e^{s\Phi(a^n) + t\Theta(a^n)} P(a^n) = n\gamma(s,t) \qquad (8.48)$$

and the corresponding auxiliary probability distribution is

$$Q(a^n) \equiv e^{s\Phi(a^n) + t\Theta(a^n) - \Gamma(s,t)} P(a^n) = \prod_{i=1}^{n} Q(a_i) \qquad (8.49)$$

Let $A^n_{\phi\theta}$ be the set of sequences a^n for which, simultaneously, $\Phi(a^n) \le n\phi$ and $\Theta(a^n) \le n\theta$. The joint distribution function of the random variables $\Phi(a^n)$ and $\Theta(a^n)$ is, by definition,

$$F(n\phi, n\theta) \equiv \Pr(\Phi \le n\phi\,,\ \Theta \le n\theta) = \sum_{A^n_{\phi\theta}} P(a^n) \qquad (8.50)$$

We shall assume in what follows that $\gamma(s,t)$ and its first and second partial derivatives with respect to s and t are finite for values of s and t in the two intervals $s_1 < s < s_2$, and $t_1 < t < t_2$ including $s = 0$ and $t = 0$.

Theorem. The joint multinomial distribution function of the pair of random variables $\Phi(a^n)$ and $\Theta(a^n)$ satisfies the inequality

$$F(n\phi, n\theta) \le e^{-n[s\gamma_s'(s,t) + t\gamma_t'(s,t) - \gamma(s,t)]} \quad ; \ s_1 < s \le 0\,,\ t_1 < t \le 0 \qquad (8.51)$$

where

$$\left.\begin{aligned} \phi &= \gamma_s'(s,t) \qquad ; \qquad & s_1 < s \le 0 \\ \theta &= \gamma_t'(s,t) & t_1 < t \le 0 \end{aligned}\right\} \qquad (8.52)$$

The exponential coefficient in Eq. 8.51 is given by

$$s\gamma_s'(s,t) + t\gamma_t'(s,t) - \gamma(s,t) = \sum_A Q(a) \ln \frac{Q(a)}{P(a)} \ge 0 \qquad (8.53)$$

Proof. This proof is very similar to that of the preceding theorem. Since, by definition, $\Phi(a^n)$ does not exceed $n\phi$, and $\Theta(a^n)$ does not exceed $n\theta$ for any of the sequences in the set $A^n_{\phi\theta}$, we obtain from Eqs. 8.48, 8.49, and 8.50, for $s \le 0$ and $t \le 0$,

$$F(n\phi, n\theta) = e^{n\gamma(s,t)} \sum_{A^n_{\phi\theta}} e^{-[s\Phi(a^n) + t\Theta(a^n)]} Q(a^n)$$

$$\leq e^{n[\gamma(s,t) - s\phi - t\theta]} \sum_{A^n_{\phi\theta}} Q(a^n) \leq e^{-n[s\phi + t\theta - \gamma(s,t)]} \tag{8.54}$$

Again, this inequality is satisfied for $s_1 < s \leq 0$ and $t_1 < t \leq 0$. Thus we can select the particular values of s and t within these intervals that minimize the righthand side of Eq. 8.54. Equating to zero the partial derivative of the exponential coefficient with respect to s yields

$$\frac{\partial}{\partial s}[s\phi + t\theta - \gamma(s,t)] = \phi - \gamma'_s(s,t) = 0 \tag{8.55}$$

from which we obtain

$$\phi = \gamma'_s(s,t) \tag{8.56}$$

Similarly, equating to zero the derivative with respect to t yields

$$\theta = \gamma'_s(s,t) \tag{8.57}$$

We can readily check, by evaluating the second partial derivatives of $\gamma(s,t)$, that the values of s and t that satisfy Eqs. 8.56 and 8.57 maximize the exponential coefficient and therefore minimize the righthand side of Eq. 8.54.

Finally, evaluating the exponential coefficient as in the proofs of preceding theorems yields Eq. 8.53. QED

It is clear that similar upper bounds to joint distribution functions can be obtained for an arbitrary number of random variables defined over the same ensemble.

The distribution function for two random variables has, so to speak, four different tails, corresponding to the four possible combinations

$$\begin{array}{ll} s \leq 0, \ t \leq 0; & s \leq 0, \ t \geq 0 \\ s \geq 0, \ t \leq 0; & s \geq 0, \ t \geq 0 \end{array} \tag{8.58}$$

It should be clear by now that the same expression provides an upper bound to all four tails, although of course for values of s and t in different ranges. More precisely, we have

$$e^{-n\sum_{A} Q(a)\ln\frac{Q(a)}{P(a)}} \geq \begin{cases} \Pr[\Phi(a^n) \leq n\phi, \Theta(a^n) \leq n\theta]\,; & s_1 < s \leq 0,\ t_1 < t \leq 0 \\ \Pr[\Phi(a^n) \leq n\phi, \Theta(a^n) > n\theta]\,; & s_1 < s \leq 0,\ 0 \leq t < t_2 \\ \Pr[\Phi(a^n) > n\phi, \Theta(a^n) \leq n\theta]\,; & 0 \leq s < s_2, t_1 < t \leq 0 \\ \Pr[\Phi(a^n) > n\phi, \Theta(a^n) > n\theta]\,; & 0 \leq s < s_2, 0 \leq t < t_2 \end{cases} \tag{8.59}$$

where the summation on the righthand side of Eq. 8.53 has been substituted for the exponential coefficient in Eq. 8.51.

The second generalization of the upper bounds derived above concerns sequences of events which are statistically independent but not necessarily governed by the same probability distribution. Let us suppose that the first n_1 events of a sequence a^n are governed by a probability distribution $P_1(a)$, the next n_2 events by a probability distribution $P_2(a)$, etc.; that is,

$$[P(a_i)]_{a_i=a} \equiv \begin{cases} P_1(a) & ; \quad 0 < i \leq n_1 \\ P_2(a) & ; \quad n_1 < i \leq n_1 + n_2 \\ \cdots\cdots & \cdots\cdots\cdots \\ P_k(a) & ; \quad \sum_{j=1}^{k-1} n_j < i \leq \sum_{j=1}^{k} n_j \\ \cdots\cdots & \cdots\cdots\cdots \\ P_K(a) & ; \quad n - n_K < i \leq n \end{cases} \tag{8.60}$$

where K is the number of distinct probability distributions. Correspondingly, different random variables may be associated with the different events of the sequence. We shall assume, however, that the same random variable is associated with all the events that are governed by the same probability distribution, that is,

$$[\phi(a_i)]_{a_i=a} \equiv \phi_k(a)\ ; \quad \sum_{j=1}^{k-1} n_j < i \leq \sum_{j=1}^{k} n_j \tag{8.61}$$

For each particular probability distribution and corresponding random variable, the logarithm of the moment-generating function is, by definition,

$$\gamma_k(s) \equiv \ln \sum_{A} e^{s\phi_k(a)} P_k(a) \tag{8.62}$$

The corresponding family of auxiliary probability distributions is

$$Q_k(a) \equiv e^{s\phi_k(a) - \gamma_k(s)} P_k(a) = [Q(a_i)]_{a_i = a}; \quad \sum_{j=1}^{k-1} n_j < i \leq \sum_{j=1}^{k} n_j \tag{8.63}$$

The first and second derivatives of $\gamma_k(s)$ can be readily evaluated with the help of Eqs. 8.9 and 8.10 and can be interpreted again as the mean value and the variance of $\phi_k(a)$ with respect to $Q_k(a)$.

Let

$$\Phi(a^n) \equiv \sum_{i=1}^{n} \phi(a_i) \tag{8.64}$$

be the sum of the values assumed by the random variables associated with the events of a particular sequence a^n. The logarithm of the moment-generating function of $\Phi(a^n)$ can be readily evaluated by repeated application of Eq. 8.12, in view of the fact that the individual random variables are statistically independent. We obtain

$$\Gamma(s) \equiv \ln \sum_{A^n} e^{s\Phi(a^n)} P(a^n) = \sum_{k=1}^{K} n_k \gamma_k(s) = n\gamma(s) \tag{8.65}$$

where

$$\gamma(s) \equiv \sum_{k=1}^{K} \frac{n_k}{n} \gamma_k(s) \tag{8.66}$$

Correspondingly, we can define the family of auxiliary probability distributions

$$Q(a^n) \equiv e^{s\Phi(a^n) - \Gamma(s)} P(a^n) = \prod_{i=1}^{n} Q(a_i) \tag{8.67}$$

for the points of the ensemble A^n representing the sequences a^n. We shall assume in what follows that all $\gamma_k(s)$ together with their first and second derivatives with respect to s are finite for values of s in some interval $s_1 < s < s_2$ including $s = 0$.

Theorem. The distribution function $F(n\phi)$ of the random variable $\Phi(\alpha^n)$ satisfies the two inequalities

$$F(n\phi) \leq e^{-n[s\gamma'(s) - \gamma(s)]} \quad ; \quad s_1 < s \leq 0 \tag{8.68}$$

$$1 - F(n\phi) \leq e^{-n[s\gamma'(s) - \gamma(s)]} \quad ; \quad 0 \leq s < s_2 \tag{8.69}$$

where

$$\phi = \gamma'(s) \begin{cases} \leq \gamma'(0) \; ; & s_1 < s \leq 0 \\ \geq \gamma'(0) \; ; & 0 \leq s < s_2 \end{cases} \tag{8.70}$$

The exponential coefficient in Eqs. 8.68 and 8.69 is given by

$$s\gamma'(s) - \gamma(s) = \sum_{k=1}^{K} \frac{n_k}{n} \sum_{A} Q_k(a) \ln \frac{Q_k(a)}{P_k(a)} \geq 0 \tag{8.71}$$

Proof. The proof of this theorem is very similar to the proofs of the preceding theorems. Let A_ϕ^n be the set of sequences α^n for which $\Phi(\alpha^n) \leq n\phi$. We have from Eqs. 8.65 and 8.67

$$\begin{aligned} F(n\phi) &\equiv \sum_{A_\phi^n} P(\alpha^n) = e^{n\gamma(s)} \sum_{A_\phi^n} e^{-s\Phi(\alpha^n)} Q(\alpha^n) \\ &\leq e^{-n[s\phi - \gamma(s)]} \sum_{A_\phi^n} Q(\alpha^n) \leq e^{-n[s\phi - \gamma(s)]} ; \quad s_1 < s \leq 0 \end{aligned} \tag{8.72}$$

This inequality is valid for all negative values of s within the specified interval. Thus the righthand side can be minimized by equating to zero the derivative with respect to s of the exponential coefficient, that is,

$$\frac{d}{ds} [s\phi - \gamma(s)] = \phi - \gamma'(s) = 0 \tag{8.73}$$

from which we obtain

$$\phi = \gamma'(s) = \sum_{k=1}^{K} \frac{n_k}{n} \gamma_k'(s) \tag{8.74}$$

The value of s that satisfies Eq. 8.74 maximizes the exponential coefficient because

$$\frac{d^2}{ds^2}[s\phi - \gamma(s)] = -\gamma''(s) = -\sum_{k=1}^{K} \frac{n}{n_k}\gamma''_k(s) \qquad (8.75)$$

and $\gamma''_k(s)$ represents the variance of $\phi_k(a)$, as indicated by Eq. 8.10, and therefore its value is non-negative. Substitution of $\gamma'(s)$ for ϕ in Eq. 8.72 yields Eq. 8.68. A similar derivation yields Eq. 8.69.

The fact that $\gamma'(s)$ satisfies Eq. 8.70 follows immediately from the fact that its derivative, namely $\gamma''(s)$, is non-negative. Since $n\gamma'(0)$ is the mean value of the random variable $\Phi(a^n)$ with respect to $P(a^n)$, Eq. 8.70 implies that the probability distribution of $\Phi(a^n)$ with respect to $Q(a^n)$ is tilted toward smaller values of the random variable for $s < 0$, and toward larger values of the random variable for $s > 0$.

Finally, following the same procedure as in Eqs. 8.36, 8.37, and 8.38 for each integer k, we obtain

$$s\gamma'_k(s) - \gamma_k(s) = \sum_{A} Q_k(s) \ln \frac{Q_k(a)}{P_k(a)} \geq 0 \qquad (8.76)$$

from which Eq. 8.71 follows immediately, with the help of Eq. 8.66. QED

This theorem can be readily extended to situations in which two or more random variables are associated with each event. Upper bounds to the four tails of the resulting joint distribution function of the two random variables $\Phi(a^n)$ and $\Theta(a^n)$ can be obtained from Eq. 8.59. For this purpose, the summation at the exponent must be replaced by the righthand side of Eq. 8.71 with each auxiliary probability distribution $Q_k(a)$ defined as in Eq. 8.44.

8.4. Lower Bounds to Multinomial Terms

Let us indicate again with A a discrete ensemble consisting of points $a_1, a_2, \ldots, a_j, \ldots, a_L$, with $P(a)$ the corresponding probability distribution, and with $\phi(a)$ a random variable defined for the points of the ensemble. We shall consider, as in the preceding sections, the ensemble A^n of the sequences

$$a^n \equiv a_1 \, a_2 \ldots a_i \ldots a_n \qquad (8.77)$$

consisting of n statistically independent and equally distributed events belonging to the ensemble A. In other words, the probability distribution of each event a_i is given by

$$[P(a_i)]_{a_i = a_j} \equiv P(a_j) \qquad (8.78)$$

Again, we associate with each event a_i a random variable $\phi(a_i)$ given by

$$[\phi(a_i)]_{a_i=a_j} \equiv \phi(a_j) \tag{8.79}$$

Since the events of the sequence a^n are statistically independent and equally distributed, the corresponding random variables are also statistically independent and equally distributed.

Let us indicate again with

$$\Phi(a^n) \equiv \sum_{i=1}^{n} \phi(a_i) \tag{8.80}$$

the sum of the random variables associated with the events of the sequence a^n. Our ultimate objective is to obtain convenient lower bounds to the distribution function

$$F(n\phi) \equiv \sum_{A_\phi^n} P(a^n) = \sum_{A_\phi^n} \prod_{i=1}^{n} P(a_i) \tag{8.81}$$

and to its complement $1 - F(n\phi)$, where A_ϕ^n is the set of sequences a^n for which $\Phi(a^n) \leq n\phi$. The general procedure for obtaining these lower bounds is to disregard all the terms on the righthand side of Eq. 8.81 except for the largest ones. For this reason, we must study in greater detail than we did before the structure of the multinomial probability distribution associated with the ensemble of sequences A^n.

Let us indicate with n_j the number of events in a particular sequence for which $a_i = a_j$. We shall refer to the set of integers $n_1, n_2, \ldots, n_L$, associated with each sequence as the composition of the sequence. Clearly,

$$n = \sum_{j=1}^{L} n_j \tag{8.82}$$

The value of the random variable $\Phi(a^n)$ for a particular sequence is

$$\Phi(a^n) \equiv \Phi(n_1, n_2, \ldots, n_L) \equiv \sum_{j=1}^{L} n_j \phi(a_j) \tag{8.83}$$

and therefore it depends only on the composition of the sequences.

The number of distinct sequences with the same composition, and therefore with the same value of $\Phi(a^n)$, is given by the multinomial coefficient

$$N(n_1, n_2, \ldots, n_L) = \frac{n!}{\prod_{j=1}^{L} n_j!} \tag{8.84}$$

The probability of occurrence of a particular sequence is similarly a function only of the composition, being the product of the probabilities of the particular events constituting the sequence. Thus all the sequences that have the same composition are equiprobable, and the sum of their probabilities is given by

$$Pr(n_1, n_2, \ldots, n_L) = N(n_1, n_2, \ldots, n_L) \prod_{j=1}^{L} P(a_j)^{n_j} \tag{8.85}$$

We may regard this sum as the probability of the composition consisting of the set of integers $n_1, n_2, \ldots, n_L$.

Theorem. The number of distinct sequences with the same composition satisfies the inequality

$$N(n_1, n_2, \ldots, n_L) \geq (2\pi n)^{-\frac{L-1}{2}} e^{-\frac{L}{12}} e^{\sum_{j=1}^{L} n_j \ln \frac{n}{n_j}} \tag{8.86}$$

Proof. The righthand side of Eq. 8.86 is obtained by substituting for the factorial in the numerator of Eq. 8.84 the lower bound given by Eq. 7.5, and for each factorial in the denominator the upper bound given also by Eq. 7.5. These substitutions yield

$$N(n_1, n_2, \ldots, n_L) \geq \sqrt{2\pi n}\; e^{\sum_{j=1}^{L} n_j \ln \frac{n}{n_j}} \prod_{j=1}^{L} \frac{1}{\sqrt{2\pi n_j}} e^{-\frac{1}{12 n_j}} \tag{8.87}$$

Clearly, this inequality is still valid if we substitute n for each n_j in the denominator. Furthermore, if all the integers n_j differ from zero, the inequality remains valid when we substitute the integer 1 for each n_j in the exponent of the last factor on the righthand side of Eq. 8.87. These substitutions immediately yield Eq. 8.86. If only $L' \leq L$ of the integers n_j are different from zero, the number of factorials in the denominator of Eq. 8.84 is equal to L', and therefore L' must be substituted for L in Eq. 8.86. Since $L \geq L'$, however, Eq. 8.86 remains valid with L, regardless of the value of L'. QED

Our next objective is to find a convenient lower bound to the probability of a particular composition given by Eq. 8.85 when the corresponding value of the random variable $\Phi(\alpha^n)$ is approximately equal to its mean value over the ensemble of sequences, that is,

$$\sum_{j=1}^{L} n_j\, \phi(a_j) \simeq \sum_{j=1}^{L} nP(a_j)\, \phi(a_j) \tag{8.88}$$

we shall need for this purpose the following lemma.

Lemma. Let us label the points of the ensemble A in order of increasing value of the associated random variable, that is,

$$\phi(a_i) \geq \phi(a_j) \quad ; \quad i > j \tag{8.89}$$

and define

$$\Delta \equiv \operatorname*{Max}_{j}\, [\phi(a_{j+1}) - \phi(a_j)] \tag{8.90}$$

There exists a set of integers $n_1, n_2, \ldots, n_j, \ldots, n_L$, and a particular value i of the integer j, $1 \leq j \leq L$, for which

$$\sum_{j=1}^{L} n_j = n \tag{8.91}$$

$$|n_j - n\,P(a_j)| \leq 1 \tag{8.92}$$

$$0 \leq \sum_{j=1}^{L} [n_j - n\,P(a_j)]\; \phi(a_j) < \Delta \tag{8.93}$$

and

$$-\Delta \leq \sum_{j=1}^{L} [n_j - n\,P(a_j)]\; \phi(a_j) - [\phi(a_{i+1}) - \phi(a_i)] < 0 \tag{8.94}$$

Proof. Let us define the set of L integers m_j

$$n\,P(a_j) < m_j \leq n\,P(a_j) + 1 \tag{8.95}$$

It follows from this definition that

$$n < \sum_{j=1}^{L} m_j = n + h \leq n + L \tag{8.96}$$

where h is a positive integer not exceeding L . Clearly, Eqs. 8.91 and 8.92 can be satisfied by making L - h of the integers n_j equal to the corresponding integers m_j and the remaining h integers n_j equal to the corresponding $m_j - 1$. The value of the difference between the two sides of Eq. 8.88, namely

$$\sum_{j=1}^{L} [n_j - n\,P(a_j)]\,\phi(a_j) \tag{8.97}$$

depends of course on the particular L - h integers n_j that are equal to the corresponding m_j . Its largest value is obtained for the set of integers n_j' defined by

$$\begin{aligned} nP(a_j) &< n_j' = m_j \leq nP(a_j) + 1 \quad ; \quad h < j \leq L \\ nP(a_j) - 1 &< n_j' = m_j - 1 \leq nP(a_j) \quad ; \quad 1 \leq j \leq h \end{aligned} \tag{8.98}$$

Correspondingly, the smallest value is obtained for the set of integers n_j'' defined by

$$\begin{aligned} nP(a_j) - 1 &< n_j'' = m_j - 1 \leq nP(a_j) \quad ; \quad L - h < j \leq L \\ nP(a_j) &< n_j'' = m_j \leq n\,P(a_j) + 1 \quad ; \quad 1 \leq j \leq L - h \end{aligned} \tag{8.99}$$

We shall now show that the quantity in Eq. 8.97 is positive for the set of integers n_j' and negative for the set of integers n_j'' .

We observe, for this purpose, that since the integers n_j' satisfy Eq. 8.91,

$$\sum_{j=1}^{h} [n_j' - n\,P(a_j)] + \sum_{j=h+1}^{L} [n_j' - n\,P(a_j)] = 0 \tag{8.100}$$

It follows, in view of Eq. 8.98, that

$$\sum_{j=h+1}^{L} [n_j' - n\,P(a_j)] = -\sum_{j=1}^{h} [n_j' - n\,P(a_j)] > 0 \qquad (8.101)$$

We have then

$$\sum_{j=1}^{L} [n_j' - n\,P(a_j)]\,\phi(a_j) \geq \phi(a_h) \sum_{j=1}^{h} [n_j' - n\,P(a_j)] + \phi(a_{h+1}) \sum_{j=h+1}^{L} [n_j' - n\,P(a_j)] \qquad (8.102)$$

$$= [\phi(a_{h+1}) - \phi(a_h)] \sum_{j=h+1}^{L} [n_j' - n\,P(a_j)] \geq 0$$

A similar procedure yields for the set of integers n_j''

$$\sum_{j=1}^{L} [n_j'' - n\,P(a_j)]\,\phi(a_j) \leq [\phi(a_{h+1}) - \phi(a_h)] \sum_{j=L-h+1}^{L} [n_j'' - n\,P(a_j)] \leq 0 \qquad (8.103)$$

The final step in the proof consists of showing that the set of integers n_j' can be transformed into the set of integers n_j'' in successive steps, one of which must yield a set of integer n_j that satisfies Eqs. 8.93 and 8.94. According to Eq. 8.98, h is the largest value of j for which $n_j' \leq n\,P(a_j)$. Let $n_h = n_h' + 1$, $n_{h+1} = n_{h+1}' - 1$, and $n_j = n_j'$ for all other values of j. For this new set of integers, still satisfying Eqs. 8.91 and 8.92, the value of the quantity in Eq. 8.97 is reduced by

$$\phi(a_{h+1}) - \phi(a_h) \leq \Delta \qquad (8.104)$$

from the value it assumes for the set n_j'. The largest value of j in this new set of integers for which $n_j < n\,P(a_j)$ is $h+1$. Let us then increase n_{h+1} by one unit and decrease n_{h+2} by one unit. The sum of the n_j remains invariant to this operation, but the quantity of Eq. 8.97 decreases by

$$\phi(a_{h+2}) - \phi(a_{h+1}) \leq \Delta \qquad (8.105)$$

In general, let us increase successively by one unit the integer n_g and decrease by one unit the integer n_{g+1}, where g is the largest value of j for which $n_j \leq n\,P(a_j)$ and $n_{j+1} > n\,P(a_{j+1})$. Each successive operation of this type decreases the value of the quantity in Eq. 8.97 by an amount smaller than or equal to Δ. Eventually, the resulting set of integers will become equal to the set n_j''.

We can conclude that, in view of Eqs. 8.102 and 8.103, the above procedure changes the value of the quantity in Eq. 8.97 from positive to negative in successive steps of magnitude not exceeding the maximum difference Δ given by Eq. 8.90. It follows that there must exist a set of integers n_j that satisfies both Eq. 8.93 and Eq. 8.94.

QED

We are now ready to derive a lower bound to the probability of a particular composition when the corresponding value of the random variable $\Phi(a^n)$ is approximately equal to the mean value given by the righthand side of Eq. 8.88.

Theorem. Let

$$\bar{\phi} = \sum_{j=1}^{L} P(a_j)\ \phi(a_j) \tag{8.106}$$

be the average value of the random variable $\phi(a)$. There exists a set of L integers n_j and a particular value i of j such that the random variable defined by Eq. 8.83 satisfies the two inequalities

$$n\bar{\phi} \leq \Phi(n_1, \ldots, n_i, n_{i+1}, \ldots, n_L) < n\bar{\phi} + \Delta \tag{8.107}$$

$$n\bar{\phi} - \Delta \leq \Phi(n_1, \ldots, n_i + 1, n_{i+1} - 1, \ldots, n_L) < n\bar{\phi} \tag{8.108}$$

where Δ is given by Eq. 8.90, and the probability of the corresponding composition, given by Eq. 8.85, satisfies the inequality

$$\left.\begin{array}{l} \ln \Pr(n_1, \ldots, n_i, n_{i+1}, \ldots, n_L) \\ \\ \ln \Pr(n_1, \ldots, n_i+1, n_{i+1}-1, \ldots, n_L) \end{array}\right\} \geq - \left[\frac{L-1}{2} \ln(2\pi n) + \frac{L}{12} + \sum_{j=1}^{L} \frac{1}{nP(a_j)}\right] \tag{8.109}$$

Proof. We have from Eqs. 8.85 and 8.86

$$\ln \Pr(n_1, n_2, \ldots, n_L) \geq - \left[\frac{L-1}{2} \ln(2\pi n) + \frac{L}{12} + \sum_{j=1}^{L} n_j \ln \frac{n_j}{n P(a_j)}\right] \tag{8.110}$$

We must find an upper bound to the summation on the righthand side of this equation. For this purpose, let

$$\delta_j \equiv n_j - n P(a_j) \tag{8.111}$$

We know from the preceding theorem that there exists a set of L integers n_j for which Eqs. 8.107 and 8.108 are satisfied. This set of integers as well as that obtained by increasing n_i and decreasing n_{i+1} by one unit satisfy Eqs. 8.91 and 8.92, and therefore for both of them

$$|\delta_j| \leq 1 \; ; \quad 1 \leq j \leq L \tag{8.112}$$

We have then, with the help of Eq. 2.91,

$$\sum_{j=1}^{L} n_j \ln \frac{n_j}{n P(a_j)} \leq \sum_{j=1}^{L} n_j \left[\frac{n_j}{n P(a_j)} - 1 \right] = \sum_{j=1}^{L} [n P(a_j) + \delta_j] \frac{\delta_j}{n P(a_j)}$$

$$= \sum_{j=1}^{L} \delta_j + \sum_{j=1}^{L} \frac{\delta_j^2}{n P(a_j)} \tag{8.113}$$

On the other hand, Eq. 8.91 implies that

$$\sum_{j=1}^{L} \delta_j = 0 \tag{8.114}$$

and the value 1 can be substituted for each δ_j^2 in view of Eq. 8.112. It follows that

$$\sum_{j=1}^{L} n_j \ln \frac{n_j}{n P(a_j)} \leq \frac{1}{n} \sum_{j=1}^{L} \frac{1}{P(a_j)} \tag{8.115}$$

Substituting the righthand side of this inequality for the summation in Eq. 8.110 yields Eq. 8.109 for the set of integers $n_1, \ldots, n_i, n_{i+1}, \ldots, n_L$. The same result is obtained for the set of integers $n_1, \ldots, n_i + 1, n_{i+1} - 1, \ldots, n_L$ in view of the fact that Eqs. 8.112 and 8.114 are satisfied also by the second set of integers.

QED

8.5. Lower Bounds to Multinomial Distribution Functions

The last theorem of the preceding section can be used to derive a lower bound to the distribution function defined by Eq. 8.81 and to its complement. We shall use for this purpose the tilting technique discussed in Sec. 8.2, and assume that $\gamma(s)$, the logarithm of the moment-generating function of the random variable $\phi(a)$, together with its first and second derivatives are finite within the interval $s_1 < s < s_2$ including $s = 0$.

Theorem. The distribution function defined by Eq. 8.81 for the random variable $\Phi(a^n)$ defined by Eq. 8.80 and its complement satisfy the inequality

$$-\left\{\left[\frac{L-1}{2}\ln(2\pi n) + |s|\,\Delta + \frac{L}{12} + \frac{1}{n}\sum_{A}\frac{1}{Q(a)}\right] + n[s\gamma'(s) - \gamma(s)]\right\}$$

$$\leq \begin{cases} \ln F(n\phi) \quad ; \quad s_1 < s \leq 0 \\ \\ \ln[1 - F(n\phi)]; \; 0 \leq s < s_2 \end{cases} \tag{8.116}$$

where

$$s\gamma'(s) - \gamma(s) = \sum_{A} Q(a)\ln\frac{Q(a)}{P(a)} \geq 0 \tag{8.117}$$

and

$$\Delta \equiv \max_{j}\,[\phi(a_{j+1}) - \phi(a_j)] \tag{8.118}$$

The auxiliary probability distribution $Q(a)$, $\gamma(s)$, and $\gamma'(s)$ are defined by Eqs. 8.7, 8.6, and 8.9.

Proof. Let A^n_ϕ be the set of sequences a^n for which $\Phi(a^n) \leq n\phi$. We have from Eqs. 8.18, 8.21, and 8.81

$$F(n\phi) = \sum_{A^n_\phi} P(a^n) = e^{n\gamma(s)}\sum_{A^n_\phi} e^{-s\Phi(a^n)}\,Q(a^n)$$

$$\geq e^{n\gamma(s) - s\Phi(n_1, n_2, \ldots, n_L)}\,Pr_Q(n_1, n_2, \ldots, n_L) \tag{8.119}$$

where $n_1, n_2, \ldots, n_L$ is a sequence composition for which

$$\Phi(n_1, n_2, \ldots, n_L) \leq n\phi \tag{8.120}$$

and the last factor on the righthand side of Eq. 8.20 is the probability of such a composition evaluated with respect to the tilted probability distribution $Q(a^n)$.

Let us select the negative value of the parameter s for which

$$\phi = \gamma'(s) = \sum_{A} Q(a)\ \phi(a) \le \bar{\phi} \tag{8.121}$$

Since $\gamma'(s)$ is the mean value of the random variable $\phi(a)$ with respect to the probability distribution $Q(a)$, the theorem incorporating Eq. 8.109 with $Q(a)$ substituted for $P(a)$, states that there exists a set of L integers $n_1, n_2, \ldots, n_L$ for which

$$n\gamma'(s) - \Delta \le \Phi(n_1, n_2, \ldots, n_L) < n\gamma'(s) \tag{8.122}$$

$$\ln \Pr_Q(n_1, n_2, \ldots, n_L) \ge -\left[\frac{L-1}{2}\ln(2\pi n) + \frac{L}{12} + \frac{1}{n}\sum \frac{1}{Q(a)}\right] \tag{8.123}$$

Then substituting the lefthand side of Eq. 8.122 and the righthand side of Eq. 8.123 in Eq. 8.119 yields

$$\ln F(n\phi) \ge -\left\{\left[\frac{L-1}{2}\ln(2\pi n) + |s|\Delta + \frac{L}{12} + \frac{1}{n}\sum_{A}\frac{1}{Q(a)}\right] + n[s\gamma'(s) - \gamma(s)]\right\}$$

$$; \quad s_1 < s \le 0 \tag{8.124}$$

which coincides with the part of Eq. 8.116 corresponding to $F(n\phi)$. The part of the same equation corresponding to $1 - F(n\phi)$ is obtained in a similar manner for positive values of s. Also, Eq. 8.117 follows from Eqs. 8.36, 8.37, and 8.38. QED

It is most important to note that the asymptotic behavior of the lower bounds given by Eq. 8.116 and the upper bounds given by Eqs. 8.27 and 8.39 have the same asymptotic behavior for large n. Thus this asymptotic behavior, specified by the exponential coefficient given by Eq. 8.117, is the correct asymptotic behavior of $F(n\phi)$ and $1 - F(n\phi)$.

The lower bounds given by Eq. 8.116 can be extended to situations in which different probability distributions and different random variables are associated with the events constituting the sequences a^n. Upper bounds for the two tails of the probability distribution of $\Phi(a^n)$ in this more general case are given by the theorem incorporating Eqs. 8.68 and 8.69. Let us consider K different probability distributions $P_k(a)$, $1 \le k \le K$, and K corresponding random variables $\phi_k(a)$, and indicate with n_k the number of events governed by the same probability distribution $P_k(a)$ and with which the same random variable $\phi_k(a)$ is associated. We shall assume again that $\gamma_k(s)$, the logarithm of moment-generating function of the random variable $\phi_k(a)$, together with its first and second derivatives with respect to s are finite for $s_1 < s < s_2$, and $1 \le k \le K$.

<u>Theorem.</u> Let $\Phi(a^n)$ be the sum of the values assumed by the random variables associated with the events of a sequence of a^n. The distribution function $F(n\phi)$ of $\Phi(a^n)$ and its

complement $1 - F(n\phi)$ satisfy the inequality

$$-\left[\frac{K(L-1)}{2}\ln(2\pi n) + |s|\Delta + \frac{KL}{12} + \sum_{k=1}^{K}\sum_{A}\frac{1}{n_k Q_k(a)}\right]$$

$$- n[s\gamma'(s) - \gamma(s)] \le \begin{cases} \ln F(n\phi) & ; \quad s_1 < s \le 0 \\ \ln[1 - F(n\phi)] & ; \quad 0 \le s < s_2 \end{cases} \tag{8.125}$$

where

$$s\gamma'(s) - \gamma(s) = \sum_{k=1}^{K}\frac{n_k}{n}\sum_{A} Q_k(a)\ln\frac{Q_k(a)}{P_k(a)} \ge 0 \tag{8.126}$$

and

$$\gamma_k(s) \equiv \ln\sum_{A} e^{s\,\phi_k(a)} P_k(a) \tag{8.127}$$

$$Q_k(a) \equiv e^{s\,\phi_k(a) - \gamma_k(s)} P_k(s) \tag{8.128}$$

$$\gamma(s) \equiv \sum_{k=1}^{K}\frac{n_k}{n}\gamma_k(s) \tag{8.129}$$

$$\Delta \equiv \max_{k,\,j}\,[\phi_k(a_{j+1}) - \phi_k(a_j)] \tag{8.130}$$

Proof. Let us indicate with n_{kj} the number of events governed by the probability distribution $P_k(a)$ that are equal to a_j in a particular sequence α^n, and with

$$\Phi_k(n_{k1}, n_{k2}, \ldots, n_{kL}) \equiv \sum_{j=1}^{L} n_{kj}\,\phi_k(a_j) \tag{8.131}$$

the sum of the values assumed by the random variables associated with the events governed by the same probability distribution $P_k(a)$. Using the same terminology as in Sec. 8.3, we have from Eqs. 8.65, 8.66, and 8.67

$$F(n\phi) \equiv \sum_{A_\phi^n} P(a^n) = e^{n\gamma(s)} \sum_{A_\phi^n} e^{-s\Phi(a^n)} Q(a^n) \qquad (8.132)$$

where A_ϕ^n is the set of sequences a^n for which

$$\Phi(a^n) = \sum_{k=1}^{K} \Phi_k(n_{k1}, n_{k2}, \ldots, n_{kL}) \leq n\phi \qquad (8.133)$$

The tilted probability distribution for the sequence a^n is given by

$$Q(a^n) = \prod_{k=1}^{K} \prod_{j=1}^{L} Q_k(a_j)^{n_{kj}} \qquad (8.134)$$

Let us label the values of each random variable $\phi_k(a_j)$ in order of increasing value, that is,

$$\phi_k(a_i) \geq \phi_k(a_j) \quad ; \quad i > j \qquad (8.135)$$

The average value of the random variable $\phi_k(a)$ with respect to the tilted probability distribution $Q_k(a)$ is given by

$$\sum_A Q_k(a)\, \phi_k(a) = \gamma_k'(s) \qquad (8.136)$$

Then the theorem incorporating Eq. 8.109 with $Q_k(a_j)$ substituted for $P(a_j)$ states that there exists a set of L integers n_{kj} satisfying Eq. 8.137 for which

$$\sum_{j=1}^{L} n_{kj} = n_k \qquad (8.137)$$

$$\left.\begin{array}{l} \ln \Pr_Q(n_{k1}, \ldots, n_{ki}, n_{k(i+1)}, \ldots, n_{kL}) \\ \\ \ln \Pr_Q(n_{k1}, \ldots, n_{ki}+1, n_{k(i+1)}-1, \ldots, n_{kL}) \end{array}\right\}$$

$$\geq -\left[\frac{L-1}{2} \ln(2\pi n) + \frac{L}{12} + \sum_A \frac{1}{n_k Q_k(a)}\right] \qquad (8.138)$$

$$n\gamma_k'(s) \le \Phi_k(n_{k1}, \ldots, n_{ki}, n_{k(i+1)}, \ldots, n_{kL}) < n_k\gamma_k'(s) + \Delta_k \tag{8.139}$$

$$-\Delta_k \le \Phi_k(n_{k1}, \ldots, n_{ki} + 1, n_{k(i+1)} - 1, \ldots, n_{kL}) < n_k\gamma_k'(s) \tag{8.140}$$

where

$$\Delta_k \equiv \max_j \, [\phi_k(a_{j+1}) - \phi_k(a_j)] \tag{8.141}$$

Then adding the inequalities given by Eq. 8.138 for $1 \le k \le K$ yields a lower bound to the probability of occurrence of the set of sequences whose composition is specified by the set of KL integers n_{kj},

$$\sum_{k=1}^{K} \ln Pr_Q(n_{k1}, n_{k2}, \ldots, n_{kL}) \ge -\sum_{k=1}^{K}\left[\frac{L-1}{2}\ln(2\pi n_k) + \frac{L}{12} + \sum_A \frac{1}{n_k Q_k(a)}\right]$$

$$\ge -\left[\frac{K(L-1)}{2}\ln(2\pi n) + \frac{KL}{12} + \sum_{k=1}^{K}\sum_A \frac{1}{n_k Q_k(a)}\right] \tag{8.142}$$

This inequality is satisfied regardless of whether we select, for any particular k, the set of integers in the upper part of Eq. 8.138 or the set of integers in the lower part of the same equation. The value of the random variable $\Phi(\alpha^n)$, however, depends on which of the two sets of integers is selected for each particular k. If the upper set is selected for all k, we have from Eq. 8.139

$$\Phi(\alpha^n) = \sum_{k=1}^{K} \Phi_k(n_{k1}, \ldots, n_{ki}, n_{k(i+1)}, \ldots, n_{kL}) \ge n\gamma'(s) \tag{8.143}$$

Conversely, if the lower set of integers in Eq. 8.138 is used for all k, we have from Eq. 8.140

$$\Phi(\alpha^n) = \sum_{k=1}^{K} \Phi_k(n_{k1}, \ldots, n_{ki}+1, n_{k(i+1)} - 1, \ldots, n_{kL}) \le n\gamma'(s) \tag{8.144}$$

Intermediate values of $\Phi(\alpha^n)$ can be obtained by selecting the upper integers in Eq. 8.138 for some values of k and the lower integers for the remaining values. Clearly, successive intermediate values differ at most by the amount Δ defined by Eq. 8.130.

We can conclude therefore that there exists a set of KL integers n_{kj} satisfying Eq. 8.137 and Eq. 8.142 for which

$$n\gamma'(s) - \Delta \leq \Phi(a^n) < n\gamma'(s) \qquad (8.145)$$

Finally, a lower bound for $F(n\phi)$ is obtained by selecting the negative value of s for which

$$\gamma'(s) = \phi \leq \bar{\phi} \qquad (8.146)$$

and disregarding all the terms in the summation on the righthand side of Eq. 8.132 except for the sequences a^n for which Eq. 8.145 is satisfied. Then substituting for $\Phi(a^n)$ the lower bound given by Eq. 8.145 and for $Q(a^n)$ the lower bound given by Eq. 8.142 yields for $s_1 < s \leq 0$

$$\ln F(n\Phi) \geq n\left[\gamma(s) - s\gamma'(s)\right] - |s|\Delta - \left[\frac{K(L-1)}{2}\ln(2\pi n) + \frac{KL}{12} + \sum_{k=1}^{K}\sum_{A}\frac{1}{n_k Q_k(a)}\right] \qquad (8.147)$$

The upper part of Eq. 8.26 follows immediately from this inequality. The lower part can be obtained in a similar manner for positive values of s. Also, Eq. 8.126 follows from Eq. 8.76. QED

Again, the asymptotic behavior for large n of the lower bounds given by Eq. 8.125 is identical to the asymptotic behavior of the corresponding upper bounds given by Eq. 8.68 and 8.69.

8.6. Summary and Conclusions

This chapter has been devoted to the development of the mathematical tools needed in the next chapter for our study of the coding of messages for discrete, constant channels These tools, however, are of considerable importance in their own right because of their usefulness in a wide variety of statistical problems. For instance, they can be used in connection with the encoding of a fixed-rate source, discussed in Chapter 4, to obtain close estimates of the probability of ambiguous encoding.

The usefulness of the bounds derived in Secs. 8.3 and 8.4 stems from the fact that they provide simple, yet asymptotically correct, estimates of multinomial distribution functions. Two important concepts are involved in the derivation of these bounds. The first one is that the moment-generating function of the sum of independent random variables is equal to the product of the moment-generating functions of the individual random variables. The second concept is that each term of a multinomial distribution is equal to the corresponding term of a tilted distribution multiplied by an exponential factor, whose exponent is a linear function of the number of random variables and of the sum of the values assumed by the random variables for the term in question. Then if the mean of the tilted distribution is adjusted to coincide with the value of this sum, the exponential factor, by itself, yields the correct asymptotic behavior of the term when the number of random variables approaches infinity.

The versatility of this mathematical technique for estimating multinomial distributions will be amply demonstrated in the next chapter. We shall see there that, if the random variables are properly chosen, this technique can be effectively employed even in some situations in which the random variables are not statistically independent. Furthermore, it should be stressed again that our discussion of this technique has been restricted to multinomial distributions only for the sake of conceptual simplicity. It can be readily extended to a much broader class of distributions of sums of independent random variables.

8.7. Selected References

1. W. Feller, "Generalization of a Probability Limit Theorem of Cramer," Trans. Am. Math. Soc., 54 361 (1943).

2. H. Chernov, "A Measure of Asymptotic Efficiency for Tests of an Hypothesis Based on the Sum of Observations," Ann. of Math. Stat., 23, 493 (1952).

3. C. E. Shannon, Notes for Seminar held at the Massachusetts Institute of Technology (1956).

*Chapter 9

ENCODING FOR DISCRETE, CONSTANT CHANNELS

We shall discuss in this chapter the encoding and decoding of messages for transmission through discrete, constant channels. In particular, we shall derive upper and lower bounds to the probability that a message will be erroneously decoded, similar to those obtained in Chapter 7 for binary symmetric channels. These bounds will show that if ν is the number of binary digits represented by each message, the probability of error can be made to decrease exponentially with increasing ν for any transmission rate smaller than the channel capacity.

We owe to C. E. Shannon the discovery that the probability of error can be made to vanish for any transmission rate smaller than the channel capacity. His basic theorems to this effect, published in 1948 [1, 2], pertain to a limited class of discrete channels with memory, including discrete, constant channels, and to continuous channels disturbed by additive, white, gaussian noise with limited average input power. The first proof that the probability of error can be made to vanish exponentially with ν, the number of binary digits represented by each message, was published by A. Feinstein in 1954 [3]. The vanishing of the probability of error for various classes of channels has since been investigated in a number of papers by Blackwell et al., Elias, Feinstein, Khinchin, Shannon, Wolfowitz, and others. Of particular engineering importance are the bounds to the probability of error obtained by Shannon for discrete channels [4], for two-way discrete, constant channels [5], and for time-discrete, constant gaussian channels [6]. Also of practical importance is the recent proof by J. Kelly [7] that no demonstrable loss of performance results from the use, in connection with time-discrete gaussian channels, of a class of additive codes, somewhat similar to those discussed in Sec. 7.4, in which the signals representing messages can be constructed as sums of $\nu + 1$ generators, where ν is the number of binary digits constituting each message.

Most of the material in this chapter was developed very recently by the author, and it is presented here for the first time. The error bounds of Secs. 9.2 and 9.5, however, were first obtained by C. E. Shannon in 1957 following a different procedure. This part of Shannon's work, which includes several other interesting results, is still unpublished.

9.1. Discrete, Constant Channels

A discrete, constant channel is characterized by its input space X, consisting of K distinct letters $x_1, x_2, \ldots, x_k, \ldots, x_K$, its output space Y, consisting of L distinct letters $y_1, y_2, \ldots, y_j, \ldots, y_L$, and the fixed conditional probability distribution $P(y|x)$, relating the output letters to the input letters. The evaluation of the capacity C of such channels is discussed in Sec. 5.5. We saw there that the average mutual information between input and output letters reaches its maximum value, C, when the input probability distribution $P(x)$ is such that

$$I(x_k ; Y) = \sum_{j=1}^{L} P(y_j|x_k) \log \frac{P(y_j|x_k)}{P(y_j)} = C \; ; \; k = 1, 2, \ldots, K \tag{9.1}$$

This set of K equations, together with the set of L equations

$$P(y_j) = \sum_{k=1}^{K} P(x_k)\, P(y_j|x_k) \; ; \; j = 1, 2, \ldots, L \tag{9.2}$$

form a set of $K + L$ equations in the $L + K$ unknowns $P(y_j)$ and $P(x_k)$. The desired set of $P(x_k)$ is the solution that yields the largest value of C under the constraint $P(x_k) \geq 0$. It can be readily checked that in the special case of doubly uniform channels discussed in Sec. 5.3, the maximizing probability distribution $P(x)$ is uniform.

Important special cases arise when some of the conditional probabilities $P(y_j|x_k)$ are equal to zero. Two input letters x_k and x_i are said to be adjacent if there is at least one output letter y_j for which $P(y_j|x_k) \neq 0$ and $P(y_j|x_i) \neq 0$. This definition implies that non-adjacent letters can always be distinguished by the decoder. Thus if a channel has m_0 mutually non-adjacent letters, $\log_2 m_0$ bits per letter can be transmitted through the channel with probability of error identically equal to zero, by encoding messages into sequences of non-adjacent letters. Furthermore, C. E. Shannon has shown [8] that it is possible in many cases to transmit with zero probability of error at a rate larger than $\log_2 m_0$, by encoding messages into sequences consisting of adjacent as well as non-adjacent letters. The least upper bound to the transmission rate for which zero probability of error can be obtained is known has the "zero-error capacity" of the channel. Unfortunately, no general procedure has yet been found for evaluating the zero-error capacity of a channel. It can be closely estimated, however, in many cases with the help of upper and lower bounds developed by Shannon [8]. A simple

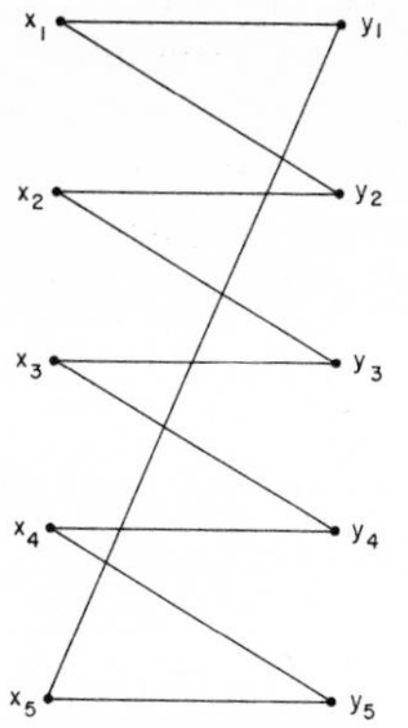

Fig. 9.1. Channel with positive zero-error capacity

example given by Shannon of a channel for which the largest number of mutually non-adjacent letters is 2, but with a zero-error capacity greater than one bit per letter, is shown in Fig. 9.1. It can be readily checked that, while there are several pairs of non-adjacent input letters, no three letters are mutually non-adjacent. On the other hand, the five sequences of two letters

$$x_1x_1, \; x_2x_3, \; x_3x_5, \; x_4x_2, \; x_5x_4$$

are non-adjacent in the sense that there exists no output sequence of two letters that can result from more than one of these input sequences. It follows that the zero-error capacity of the channel is at least $\frac{1}{2}\log 5$.

9.2. A Lower Bound to the Probability of Error

We shall develop first a lower bound to the probability of error for a set of M equiprobable messages. By lower bound to the probability of error we shall mean a function $P_L(e)$ of the number n of channel events per message and of a rate parameter R_L such that, for any transmission rate

$$R \equiv \frac{\ln M}{n} \geq R_L \tag{9.3}$$

any assignment of channel input sequences to messages, and any decoding criterion, the probability of a decoding error satisfies the inequality

$$P(e) \geq P_L(e) \tag{9.4}$$

The derivation of the expressions for R_L and $P_L(e)$ involves several successive steps which will be presented below as a sequence of theorems.

We saw in Sec. 6.1 that the operation of encoding may be regarded as a mapping of the message space, consisting of the points $m_1, m_2, \ldots, m_M$, into the input-sequence space U, consisting of all possible sequences u of n events belonging to the space X. We shall indicate with u_i the input sequence into which the message m_i is mapped. Correspondingly, the decoding operation may be regarded as a partitioning of the output-sequence space V consisting of all possible sequences v of n events belonging to the space Y, into M subsets $w_1, w_2, \ldots, w_M$. Each subset w_i consists of all the sequences v that are to be decoded into the message m_i.

The conditional probability $P(v|u)$ depends on the letter composition of the two sequences u and v. We shall indicate with $n(x_k)$ the number of letters x_k in a particular sequence u, and with $n(y_j)$ the number of letters y_j in a particular sequence v. Similarly, we shall indicate with $n(x_k y_j)$ the number of corresponding letter pairs $x_k\, y_j$ in the two sequences, regarded as a single sequence of letter pairs. Clearly, we have for any particular pair of sequences

$$\sum_{X} n(xy) = n(y) \quad ; \quad \sum_{Y} n(xy) = n(x) \qquad (9.5)$$

and

$$\sum_{XY} n(xy) = n \qquad (9.6)$$

We shall refer to the set of integers $n(x)$ associated with a particular input sequence u as the composition of u, and to the set of integers $n(y)$ associated with a particular output sequence v as the composition of v. Similarly, we shall refer to the set of integers $n(xy)$ associated with a particular sequence pair uv as the composition of uv.

Since the channel is, by assumption, constant, the conditional probability $P(v|u)$ is equal to the product of the values assumed by the conditional probability $P(y|x)$ for the letter pairs constituting uv. Thus

$$P(v|u) = \prod_{XY} P(y|x)^{n(xy)} \qquad (9.7)$$

We saw in Sec. 7.2 that for a set of M equiprobable messages, the probability that the message transmitted will be correctly decoded is given by Eq. 7.40, which is reproduced below for convenience of reference,

$$1 - P(e) = \frac{1}{M} \sum_{i=1}^{M} \sum_{w_i} P(v|u_i) \qquad (9.8)$$

where $P(v|u_i)$ is the conditional probability that the sequence v is the channel output when the sequence u_i, representing the message m_i, is the channel input. We saw, also in the same section, that the probability of correct decoding is a maximum, for any particular assignment of input sequences to messages, when and only when

$$P(v|u_i) \geq P(v|u_j) \text{ for every } v \text{ in } w_i\,,\ i \leq j \leq M\,,\ 1 \leq i \leq M \tag{9.9}$$

This condition, which corresponds to maximum-likelihood decoding, maximizes the a posteriori probability because the messages are equiprobable.

Let us consider the distance

$$D(xy) \equiv \ln \frac{f(y)}{P(y|x)} \tag{9.10}$$

where $P(y|x)$ is the conditional probability distribution characterizing the channel, and $f(y)$ is an arbitrary, positive function of y for which

$$\sum_{Y} f(y) = 1 \tag{9.11}$$

Then the distance between any two particular sequences u and v is defined as

$$D(uv) \equiv \sum_{XY} n(xy)\, D(xy) = \ln \frac{F(v)}{P(v|u)} \tag{9.12}$$

where

$$F(v) = \prod_{Y} f(y)^{n(y)} \tag{9.13}$$

is the probability of v if its letters are selected independently at random with probability $f(y)$.

Theorem. Let us consider a particular assignment of channel input sequences u_i to M messages m_i, and a partitioning of the space V of the channel output sequences v into M disjoint decoding subsets w_i in one-to-one correspondence to the messages, for which the following condition is satisfied for some constant D_0: Each subset w_i contains all sequences v for which $D(u_i v) < D_0$ and no sequence v for which $D(u_i v) > D_0$. For the given assignment of channel input sequences to messages and for all partitionings of the output space V into decoding subsets w_i , the probability of error satisfies the inequality

$$P(e) \geq \frac{1}{M} \sum_{i=1}^{M} \Pr\,[D(u_i v) > D_0] \tag{9.14}$$

Proof. Let us indicate with W a partitioning consisting of subsets w_i that satisfy the condition stated in the theorem, and with W' a partitioning consisting of subsets w_i' that do not satisfy such a condition. Every sequence v_h belonging to a subset w_i' for which $D(u_i v_h) > D_0$ must belong, in the partitioning W, to some subset w_j associated with some other input sequence u_j for which $D(u_j v_h) \leq D_0$. This implies that the summation on the righthand side of Eq. 9.8 includes, in the case of W, a term $P(v_h|u_j)$, while, in the case of W', it includes in its place a term $P(v_h|u_i) < P(v_h|u_j)$. Thus the probability of correct decoding for W' is smaller than that for W. Conversely, every sequence v_h that does not belong to the subset w_i' associated with an input sequence u_i for which $D(u_i v_h) < D_0$ must belong to the subset w_j' associated with a u_j for which $D(u_j v_h) \geq D_0$. Then the term in Eq. 9.8 for v_h is smaller for W' than for W.

For any partitioning W that satisfies the condition of the theorem, a decoding error will occur whenever the distance $D(u_i v)$ of the output sequence v from the input sequence u_i exceeds D_0. A decoding error may or may not occur when $D(u_i v) = D_0$. It follows that the probability of error must satisfy Eq. 9.14.

QED

Each $\Pr[D(u_i v) > D_0]$ on the righthand side of Eq. 9.14 is the sum of the conditional probabilities $P(v|u_i)$ of the sequences v for which $D(u_i v) > D_0$. On the other hand, both $P(v|u_i)$ and $D(u_i v)$ depend on the pair $u_i v$ only through its composition $n(xy)$, as indicated by Eqs. 9.7, 9.12, and 9.13. It follows, in view of Eq. 9.5, that $\Pr[D(u_i v) > D_0]$ depends on u_i only through its composition $n(x)$; that is, it has the same value for all sequences u_i with the same composition.

Theorem. Let us consider the block encoding of a set of M equiprobable messages into input sequences consisting of n events, under the constraint that all such input sequences must have the same composition, characterized by a prescribed set of integers $n(x)$. Let us further indicate with V_0 the set of sequences v for which $D(u_0 v) \leq D_0$ for any particular sequence u_0 having the prescribed composition. Then, if

$$M \geq \frac{1}{\sum_{V_0} F(v)} \tag{9.15}$$

All assignments of sequences with the prescribed composition to messages yields a probability of error satisfying the inequality

$$P(e) \geq \sum_{V_0^*} P(v|u_0) \tag{9.16}$$

where V_0^* is the complement of V_0, that is, the set of sequences v for which $D(u_0v) > D_0$.

Proof. Let us consider any particular assignment of sequences with the specified composition to the M messages, and a partitioning of the output sequence space V into decoding subsets w_i satisfying the conditions stated in the theorem incorporating Eq. 9.14. Then the same theorem states that the probability of error for any realizable partitioning of V must satisfy Eq. 9.14. On the other hand, each term in the summation on the righthand side of Eq. 9.14 depends only on the value D_0 and on the composition of the input sequence u_i. It follows that Eq. 9.14 reduces to Eq. 9.16.

Let us consider next the relation between the value D_0 and the value of the integer M. We observe, for this purpose, that the functions $f(y)$ and $F(v)$ may be regarded as probability distributions over the space Y, and the output-sequence space V. Then, if we label with the subscript F the probability of any particular occurrence with respect to the probability distribution $F(v)$, the denominator in Eq. 9.15 can be written in the form

$$\sum_{V_0} F(v) = \Pr_F[D(u_0v) \leq D_0] \tag{9.17}$$

Again the righthand side of this equation assumes the same value for all sequences u_0 having the same composition. We observe further that each w_i satisfying the conditions of the theorem incorporating Eq. 9.14 includes all the sequences for which $D(u_iv) < D_0$, but not necessarily all the sequences for which $D(u_iv) = D_0$. It follows that

$$\sum_{w_i} F(v) \leq \sum_{V_0} F(v) \tag{9.18}$$

On the other hand, the decoding subsets w_i are disjoint and, together, must include all the sequences of the space V. Thus we obtain from Eq. 9.18

$$\sum_{i=1}^{M} \sum_{w_i} F(v) = 1 \leq M \sum_{V_0} F(v) \tag{9.19}$$

which yields immediately Eq. 9.15. In other words, the condition that every sequence v of V must be included in some subset w_i implies that the value of D_0 and the corresponding set V_0 must be large enough to satisfy Eq. 9.15. Of course, any larger value of D_0 implies a correspondingly larger set V_0, which in turn implies a smaller set V_0^* and therefore a smaller lower bound to the probability of error in Eq. 9.16.

QED

The next step in our derivation consists of finding lower-bound estimates of the summations in Eqs. 9.15 and 9.16. These estimates yield the following fundamental theorem.

Theorem. Let us consider a discrete, constant channel characterized by a conditional probability distribution $P(y|x)$, and the block encoding of M equiprobable messages into channel input sequences with the same composition specified by a set of integers $n(x)$, and define

$$\gamma(s) \equiv \sum_X P(x) \ln \sum_Y P(y|x)^{1-s} Q(y)^s \tag{9.20}$$

$$\gamma'(s) \equiv \left[\frac{\partial \gamma(s)}{\partial s}\right]_{Q(y)=\text{const}} \tag{9.21}$$

where

$$P(x) \equiv \frac{n(x)}{n} \tag{9.22}$$

and

$$Q(y|x) \equiv \frac{P(y|x)^{1-s} Q(y)^s}{\sum_Y P(y|x)^{1-s} Q(y)^s} \tag{9.23}$$

$$Q(y) \equiv \sum_X P(x) Q(y|x) = \sum_X \frac{P(x) P(y|x)^{1-s} Q(y)^s}{\sum_Y P(y|x)^{1-s} Q(y)^s} \tag{9.24}$$

For any transmission rate R, in nats per letter, satisfying the inequality

$$R \equiv \frac{\ln M}{n} \geq \frac{\beta}{n} + I \quad ; \quad 0 \leq s < 1 \tag{9.25}$$

and any assignment of channel input sequences to messages, the probability of error satisfies the inequality

$$P(e) \geq e^{-\beta - n\alpha} \quad ; \quad 0 \leq s < 1 \tag{9.26}$$

where

$$\beta \equiv \frac{1}{2} KL \ln(2\pi n) - \ln p_m + \frac{KL}{12} + \frac{1}{n} \sum_{XY} \frac{1}{P(x)\, Q(y|x)} \tag{9.27}$$

p_m is the smallest value of $P(y|x)$, K is the number of input letters, L the number of output letters, and

$$I \equiv (s-1)\gamma'(s) - \gamma(s) = \sum_{XY} P(x)\, Q(y|x) \ln \frac{Q(y|x)}{Q(y)} \geq 0 \tag{9.28}$$

$$\alpha \equiv s\gamma'(s) - \gamma(s) = \sum_{XY} P(x)\, Q(y|x) \ln \frac{Q(y|x)}{P(y|x)} \geq 0 \tag{9.29}$$

Proof. The theorem incorporating Eqs. 9.15 and 9.16 states that for any transmission rate per channel event

$$R \equiv \frac{\ln M}{n} \geq -\frac{1}{n} \ln \sum_{V_0} F(v) \tag{9.30}$$

the probability of error must satisfy the inequality

$$P(e) \geq \sum_{V_0^*} P(v|u_0) \tag{9.31}$$

where u_0 is any particular input sequence with the specified composition, $P(v|u_0)$ is defined by Eq. 9.7, and $F(v)$ is defined by Eq. 9.13. The output sets V_0 and V_0^* are the complementary subsets of the output-sequence space V for which

$$D(u_0 v) \leq D_0 \quad \text{for } v \text{ in } V_0 \tag{9.32}$$

$$D(u_0 v) > D_0 \quad \text{for } v \text{ in } V_0^* \tag{9.33}$$

where $D(u_0 v)$ is the distance defined by Eq. 9.12 and D_0 is an independent parameter. Our objective then is to obtain lower bounds to the summations over V_0 and V_0^* in Eqs. 9.30 and 9.31.

A lower bound to the summation on the righthand side of Eq. 9.31 can be obtained with the help of the theorem incorporating Eq. 8.125. Let us identify the points y of the channel output space Y with the points a of the space A, the conditional probability distribution $P(y|x_k)$ with the probability distribution $P_k(a)$, the integers $n(x_k)$ with the integers n_k, the random variable

$D(x_k y)$ with $\phi_k(a)$, D_0 with $n\phi$. Let us further indicate with $Q(y|x_k)$ the tilted conditional-probability distribution corresponding to $Q_k(a)$, and with Y_k the set of output letters for which $P(y|x_k) \neq 0$. Then substituting L for L - 1 in Eq. 8.125 yields

$$\ln \sum_{V_0^*} P(v \mid u_0) \geq -\left[\frac{KL}{2} \ln(2\pi n) + |s|\Delta + \frac{KL}{12} + \frac{1}{n} \sum_{k=1}^{K} \sum_{Y_k} \frac{1}{P(x_k)\, Q(y \mid x_k)}\right]$$

$$- n[s\gamma'(s) - \gamma(s)] \quad ; \quad 0 \leq s \qquad (9.34)$$

where, in view of Eq. 8.130,

$$\Delta \leq \max_{x_k, y} \ln \frac{f(y)}{P(y|x_k)} \leq - \ln p_m \quad ; \quad y \text{ in } Y_k \qquad (9.35)$$

and

$$\gamma(s) = \sum_{k=1}^{K} P(x_k) \ln \sum_{Y_k} e^{sD(x_k y)} P(y|x_k) = \sum_{k=1}^{K} P(x_k) \ln \sum_{Y_k} P(y|x_k)^{1-s} f(y)^s \qquad (9.36)$$

$$\gamma'(s) = \frac{\partial \gamma(s)}{\partial s} = \sum_{k=1}^{K} \sum_{Y_k} P(x_k)\, Q(y|x_k) \ln \frac{f(y)}{P(y|x_k)} = \frac{D_0}{n} \qquad (9.37)$$

$$Q(y|x_k) = \frac{P(y|\, x_k)^{1-s} f(y)^s}{\sum_{Y} P(y|x_k)^{1-s} f(y)^s} \quad ; \quad y \text{ in } Y_k \qquad (9.38)$$

It is important to note for future reference that, for $s < 1$, Y can be substituted for Y_k in the above equations because all the terms for which $P(y|x_k) = 0$ vanish anyway. This substitution cannot be made, however, for other values of s , because the same terms become infinite for $s \geq 1$.

A lower bound to the summation on the righthand side of Eq. 9.30 can be obtained with the help of the same theorem. Let us make the same identifications as above, except for the probability distributions $P_k(a)$, which are now identified with f(y) for all values of k . We obtain then

$$\ln \sum_{V_0} F(v) \geq -\left[\frac{KL}{2} \ln(2\pi n) + |t|\Delta + \frac{KL}{12} + \frac{1}{n} \sum_{XY} \frac{1}{P(x)\, Q_0(y|x)}\right]$$

$$- n[t\gamma_0'(t) - \gamma_0(t)] \quad ; \quad t < 0 \qquad (9.39)$$

where t has been substituted for the parameter s in Eq. 8.125 to distinguish it from the parameter used in Eq. 9.34 , Δ satisfies Eq. 9.35, and

$$\gamma_0(t) \equiv \sum_X P(x) \ln \sum_Y e^{tD(xy)} f(y) = \sum_X P(x) \ln \sum_Y P(y|x)^{-t} f(y)^{1+t} \tag{9.40}$$

$$\gamma_0'(t) = \frac{\partial \gamma_0(t)}{\partial t} = \sum_{XY} P(x)\, Q_0(y|x) \ln \frac{f(y)}{P(y|x)} = \frac{D_0}{n} \tag{9.41}$$

$$Q_0(y|x) = \frac{P(y|x)^{-t} f(y)^{1+t}}{\sum_Y P(y|x)^{-t} f(y)^{1+t}} \tag{9.42}$$

The summations in these equations extend over the entire output space Y rather than over Y_k because f(y) does not vanish for any output letter. The terms corresponding to $P(y|x) = 0$ vanish for $t < 0$ but become infinite for $t \geq 0$. For this reason, Eq. 9.39 is valid only for $t < 0$ rather than for $t \leq 0$.

Since both $\gamma'(s)$ and $\gamma_0'(t)$ are set equal to D_0/n in Eqs. 9.37 and 9.41, the parameters s and t must be so related that

$$\gamma_0'(t) = \gamma'(s) \tag{9.43}$$

or equivalently,

$$\sum_{XY} P(x)\, Q(y|x) \ln \frac{f(y)}{P(y|x)} = \sum_{XY} P(x)\, Q_0(y|x) \ln \frac{f(y)}{P(y|x)} \quad ; \quad t < 0 ,\ s \geq 0 \tag{9.44}$$

This condition, in turn, is implied by the more stringent requirement

$$Q(y|x) = \frac{P(y|x)^{1-s} f(y)^s}{\sum_Y P(y|x)^{1-s} f(y)^s} = \frac{P(y|x)^{-t} f(y)^{1+t}}{\sum_Y P(y|x)^{-t} f(y)^{1+t}} = Q_0(y|x) \ ; \ t < 0 ,\ s \geq 0 \tag{9.45}$$

which can be satisfied by setting

$$t = s - 1 \ ; \quad 0 \leq s < 1 \tag{9.46}$$

Then since $s < 1$, we obtain from Eqs. 9.34 and 9.35

$$\frac{1}{n} \ln P(e) \geq -\frac{\beta}{n} - [s\gamma'(s) - \gamma(s)] \ ; \quad 0 \leq s < 1 \tag{9.47}$$

where β is defined by Eq. 9.27 and Y can be substituted for Y_k in the expressions for $\gamma(s)$ and $\gamma'(s)$. Furthermore, since the magnitude of t cannot exceed unity, we obtain from Eqs. 9.35 and 9.39

$$-\frac{1}{n} \ln \sum_{V_0} F(v) \leq \frac{\beta}{n} + [(s-1)\gamma'(s) - \gamma(s)] \quad ; \quad 0 \leq s < 1 \tag{9.48}$$

It follows that Eq. 9.30 is satisfied whenever the transmission rate R satisfies

$$R \geq \frac{\beta}{n} + [(s-1)\gamma'(s) - \gamma(s)] \quad ; \quad 0 \leq s < 1 \tag{9.49}$$

We can conclude that the probability of error must satisfy Eq. 9.47 whenever R satisfies Eq. 9.49

We observe next that Eqs. 9.47 and 9.49 are valid for any positive function $f(y)$ satisfying Eq. 9.11. In particular, they are valid for

$$f(y) = \sum_{X} P(x)\, Q(y|x) \equiv Q(y) \quad ; \quad 0 \leq s < 1 \tag{9.50}$$

It can be shown that such a choice of $f(y)$ minimizes

$$a \equiv s\gamma'(s) - \gamma(s) = \sum_{XY} P(x)\, Q(y|x) \ln \frac{Q(y|x)}{P(y|x)} \quad ; \quad 0 \leq s < 1 \tag{9.51}$$

for any fixed value of

$$I \equiv (s-1)\gamma'(s) - \gamma(s) = \sum_{XY} P(x)\, Q(y|x) \ln \frac{Q(y|x)}{f(y)} \quad ; \quad 0 \leq s < 1 \tag{9.52}$$

so that it approximately maximizes the righthand side of Eq. 9.47 for any fixed value of the righthand side of Eq. 9.49. This fact is immaterial, however, as far as the proof of the theorem is concerned.

Finally, substituting $Q(y)$ for $f(y)$ in Eqs. 9.47 and 9.49 yields Eqs. 9.26 and 9.25 in the statement of the theorem. The non-negative character of the quantities I and a can be readily proved with the help of Eq. 2.91:

$$-a \equiv \sum_{XY} P(x)\, Q(y|x) \ln \frac{Q(y)}{Q(y|x)} \leq \sum_{XY} P(x)\,[Q(y) - Q(y|x)] = 0 \tag{9.53}$$

$$- I \equiv \sum_{XY} P(x)\, Q(y|x) \ln \frac{P(y|x)}{Q(y|x)} \leq \sum_{XY} P(x)\, [P(y|x) - Q(y|x)] = 0 \quad (9.54)$$

QED

9.3. Asymptotic Behavior of Lower Bound

The righthand sides of Eqs. 9.25 and 9.26 are primarily controlled, for large n, by I and α, respectively. More precisely, we have

$$\left.\begin{aligned} &\lim_{n\to\infty} R \geq I \\ &\lim_{n\to\infty} \frac{1}{n} \ln P(e) \geq -\alpha \end{aligned}\right\} \; ; \; 0 \leq s < 1 \quad (9.55)$$

Thus we may confine our discussion of the above theorem to a study of the relation between the quantities I and α, given by Eqs. 9.28 and 9.29 in terms of the parameter s.

We have, for $s = 0$,

$$[I]_{s=0} = \sum_{XY} P(x)\, P(y|x) \ln \frac{P(y|x)}{P(y)} = I(X\,;\,Y) \; ; \; [\alpha]_{s=0} = 0 \quad (9.56)$$

where $I(X\,;\,Y)$ is the average mutual information between input and output letters when the input probability distribution coincides with the composition $P(x)$ of the input sequences assigned to messages. The behavior of I and α for $0 \leq s < 1$ is best investigated by evaluating their derivatives with respect to s. We shall use for this purpose the following theorem.

Theorem. The function $\gamma(s)$ has the following properties:

$$\gamma'(s) \equiv \left[\frac{\partial \gamma(s)}{\partial s}\right]_{Q(y) = \text{const.}} = \frac{d\gamma(s)}{ds} \quad (9.57)$$

$$\gamma''(s) \equiv \frac{d^2\gamma(s)}{ds^2} = \frac{\partial^2\gamma(s)}{\partial s^2} + \sum_X P(x) \left\{ s^2 \left[\sum_Y Q(y|x) \frac{d \ln Q(y)}{ds} \right]^2 \right.$$

$$\left. + s(1-s) \sum_Y Q(y|x) \left[\frac{d \ln Q(y)}{ds}\right]^2 \right\} \geq 0 \; ; \; 0 \leq s < 1 \quad (9.58)$$

$$\left[\frac{\partial^2 \gamma(s)}{\partial s^2}\right]_{Q(y) = \text{const.}} = \sum_X P(x) \sum_Y Q(y|x) \left[D(xy) - \sum_Y Q(y|x)\, D(xy) \right]^2 \geq 0$$

(9.59)

where $D(xy)$ is defined by Eqs. 9.10 and 9.50.

Proof. We observe from Eqs. 9.20 and 9.24 that $\gamma(s)$ is a function of s and of the variables $Q(y)$, each of which is in turn a function of s. Indicating with $Q_s'(y)$ the derivative of $Q(y)$ with respect to s, we have,

$$\frac{d\gamma(s)}{ds} = \frac{\partial\gamma(s)}{\partial s} + \sum_Y Q_s'(y) \frac{\partial\gamma(s)}{\partial Q(y)} \tag{9.60}$$

On the other hand, differentiating $\gamma(s)$ with respect to $Q(y)$ yields, with the help of Eq. 9.23,

$$\frac{\partial\gamma(s)}{\partial Q(y)} = s\sum_X P(x) \frac{P(y|x)^{1-s} Q(y)^{s-1}}{\sum_Y P(y|x)^{1-s} Q(y)^s} = s \sum_X P(x) \frac{Q(y|x)}{Q(y)} = s \tag{9.61}$$

$$\sum_Y Q_s'(y) \frac{\partial\gamma(s)}{\partial Q(y)} = s \frac{d}{ds} \sum_Y Q(y) = 0 \tag{9.62}$$

We have for the second total derivative

$$\frac{d^2\gamma(s)}{ds^2} = \frac{\partial^2\gamma(s)}{\partial s^2} + 2\sum_Y Q_s'(y) \frac{\partial^2\gamma(s)}{\partial s \partial Q(y)} + \sum_{YY^*} Q_s'(y)\, Q_s'(y^*) \frac{\partial^2\gamma(s)}{\partial Q(y)\, \partial Q(y^*)} \tag{9.63}$$

However, in view of Eq. 9.57,

$$\frac{d^2\gamma(s)}{ds^2} = \frac{d}{ds}\frac{\partial\gamma(s)}{\partial s} = \frac{\partial^2\gamma(s)}{\partial s^2} + \sum_Y Q_s'(y) \frac{\partial^2\gamma(s)}{\partial s \partial Q(y)} \tag{9.64}$$

so that

$$\sum_Y Q_s'(y) \frac{\partial^2\gamma(s)}{\partial s \partial Q(y)} = -\sum_{YY^*} Q_s'(y)\, Q_s'(y^*) \frac{\partial^2\gamma(s)}{Q(y) \partial Q(y^*)} \tag{9.65}$$

Then, evaluating the righthand side of this equation with the help of Eq. 9.23 yields

$$\sum_X P(x) \left\{ s^2 \left[\sum_Y Q_s'(y) \frac{P(y|x)^{1-s} Q(y)^{s-1}}{\sum_Y P(y|x)^{1-s} Q(y)^s} \right]^2 + s(1-s) \sum_Y [Q_s'(y)]^2 \frac{P(y|x)^{1-s} Q(y)^{s-2}}{\sum_Y P(y|x)^{1-s} Q(y)^s} \right\}$$

$$= \sum_X P(x) \left\{ s^2 \left[\sum_Y Q(y|x) \frac{d \ln Q(y)}{ds} \right]^2 + s(1-s) \sum_Y Q(y|x) \left[\frac{d \ln Q(y)}{ds} \right]^2 \right\} \tag{9.66}$$

Finally, substituting this expression for the last term on the right-hand side of Eq. 9.64 yields Eq. 9.58 in the statement of the theorem.

Differentiating Eq. 9.10 yields,

$$\frac{\partial^2 \gamma(s)}{\partial s^2} = \frac{\partial^2}{\partial s^2} \sum_X P(x) \ln \sum_Y e^{sD(xy)} P(y|x)$$

$$= \sum_X P(x) \left\{ \sum_Y Q(y|x)\, D(xy)^2 - \left[\sum_Y Q(y|x)\, D(xy) \right]^2 \right\} \qquad (9.67)$$

from which Eq. 9.59 is readily obtained by rearranging terms. The righthand side of this equation is the average over X of the variance of $D(xy)$ with respect to $Q(y|x)$.

QED

We are now ready to evaluate the derivatives of I and α with respect to s. We obtain from Eqs. 9.28 and 9.29, with the help of the last theorem,

$$\frac{dI}{ds} = (s - 1)\, \gamma''(s) \leq 0 \; ; \quad \frac{d\alpha}{ds} = s\gamma''(s) \geq 0 \; ; \quad 0 \leq s < 1 \qquad (9.68)$$

We can conclude that α increases monotonically with increasing s, while I decreases monotonically. Furthermore, if we regard α as a function of I, we obtain from Eq. 9.68,

$$\frac{d\alpha}{dI} = \frac{d\alpha/ds}{dI/ds} = -\frac{s}{1 - s} \leq 0 \; ; \quad 0 \leq s < 1 \qquad (9.69)$$

and

$$\frac{d^2\alpha}{dI^2} = \left[\frac{d}{ds}\frac{d\alpha}{dI}\right] \Big/ \frac{dI}{ds} = \frac{1}{(1 - s)^3\, \gamma''(s)} \geq 0 \; ; \quad 0 \leq s < 1 \qquad (9.70)$$

The curves of Fig. 9.2 illustrate typical relations between α and I. The slope is negative and vanishes for s = 0, that is,

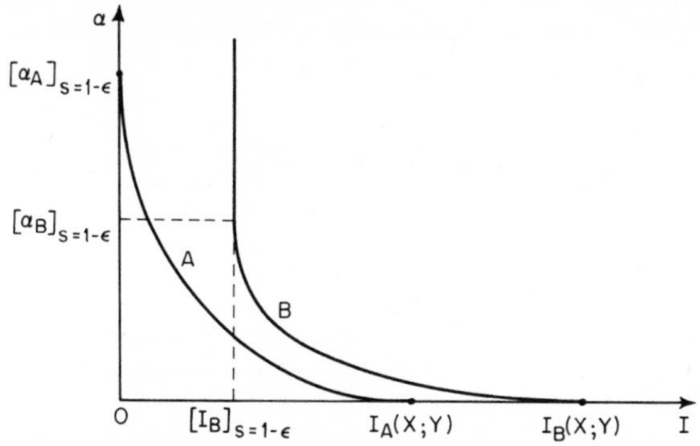

Figure 9.2. Typical behavior of α as a function of I

$I = I(X;Y)$. Its magnitude increases with increasing s and decreasing I and approaches infinity for s approaching unity. However, I may or may not vanish when s approaches unity, depending on the particular channel, as discussed below.

We observe, first of all, that the theorem incorporating Eqs. 9.25 and 9.26 is valid for $0 \leq s < 1$, but not for $s = 1$. We shall label with $s = 1 - \epsilon$ the value approached by any quantity when s approaches unity, but $s < 1$.

We have from Eq. 9.23

$$Q(y|x) = \begin{cases} \dfrac{Q(y)}{\sum_{Y_x} Q(y)} & ; \quad P(y|x) \neq 0 \\ 0 & ; \quad P(y|x) = 0 \end{cases} \quad ; \quad s = 1 - \epsilon \qquad (9.71)$$

where Y_x is the set of output letters y for which $P(y|x) \neq 0$. Then we obtain from Eq. 9.24

$$Q(y) = Q(y) \sum_{X_y} \frac{P(x)}{\sum_{Y_x} Q(y)} \quad ; \quad s = 1 - \epsilon \qquad (9.72)$$

where X_y is the set of input letters x for which $P(y|x) \neq 0$. In order for this last equation to be satisfied, it must be

$$\text{either} \quad \sum_{X_y} \frac{P(x)}{\sum_{Y_x} Q(y)} = 1 \quad , \quad \text{or} \quad Q(y) = 0 \quad ; \quad s = 1 - \epsilon \qquad (9.73)$$

from which $Q(y)$ can be evaluated. The corresponding values of α and I are then, from Eqs. 9.28 and 9.29,

$$\alpha = \sum_X P(x) \sum_{Y_x} \frac{Q(y)}{\sum_{Y_x} Q(y)} \ln \frac{Q(y)}{P(y|x) \sum_{Y_x} Q(y)} \quad ; \quad s = 1 - \epsilon \qquad (9.74)$$

$$I = \sum_X P(x) \ln \frac{1}{\sum_{Y_x} Q(y)} \quad ; \quad s = 1 - \epsilon \qquad (9.75)$$

We can conclude that $[I]_{s=1-\epsilon}$ vanishes if and only if each Y_x includes all output letters y for which $Q(y) \neq 0$, that is, if $P(y|x) \neq 0$ for all pairs xy for which $P(x) \neq 0$ and $Q(y) \neq 0$.

Theorem. The value of I vanishes for s approaching unity if and only if there exists one or more output letters y for which $P(y|x) \neq 0$ for every input letter x for which $P(x) \neq 0$.

Proof. It is evident from Eq. 9.75 that the righthand side can vanish only if the condition of the theorem is met, because otherwise at least one of the subsets Y_x would not contain all the output letters y for which $Q(y) \neq 0$. On the other hand, if the condition of the theorem is met, Eq. 9.72 can be satisfied by making $Q(y) = 0$ for all output letters y for which $P(y|x) = 0$ for at least one input letter x with $P(x) \neq 0$.

QED

The curves shown in Fig. 9.2 do not actually terminate at the points $[\alpha]_{s=1-\epsilon}$ but, as we shall see, rise vertically to infinity. The restriction $s < 1$ in Eqs. 9.25 and 9.26 results from the restriction $t < 0$ in Eq. 9.39 and the relation between t and s imposed by Eq. 9.46. This relation, in turn, results from setting both $\gamma'(s)$ and $\gamma_0'(t)$ equal to D_0/n in Eqs. 9.37 and 9.41. Thus Eq. 9.26 is valid also for $s \geq 1$, that is, for $D_0/n = \gamma'(s) \geq \gamma'(1)$, but Eq. 9.25 is not. We observe, on the other hand, that the lefthand side of Eq. 9.39 increases with increasing D_0, that is, with increasing size of the set V_0. Thus the righthand side of Eq. 9.37 remains valid for $t < 0$ and $D_0/n \geq \gamma_0'(t)$. It follows that for

$$\lim_{n\to\infty} R \geq [I]_{s=1-\epsilon} \tag{9.76}$$

the corresponding probability of error must satisfy

$$\lim_{n\to\infty} -\frac{1}{n} \ln P(e) \leq [s\gamma'(s) - \gamma(s)] \quad ; \quad s \geq 1 \tag{9.77}$$

where $\gamma(s)$ and $\gamma'(s)$ are given by Eqs. 9.36 and 9.37. Then since the righthand side of Eq. 9.77 approaches infinity with s, the curves of Fig. 9.2 must become vertical lines for $I = [I]_{s=1-\epsilon}$. In other words, the lower bound to the probability of error vanishes for $I \leq [I]_{s=1-\epsilon}$. The vanishing of the lower bound for nonzero values of I will be further discussed in the following section.

9.4. Optimization of Lower Bound

The lower bound to the probability of error given by Eqs. 9.25 and 9.26 was derived on the assumption that all input sequences assigned to messages have the same composition. The composition, in turn, can be optimized to yield the smallest lower bound to the probability of error corresponding to any particular transmission rate. On the other hand, while it is reasonable to expect, from symmetry considerations, that the smallest lower bound will be obtained with input sequences having the same composition, the proof that this is actually the case is not trivial.

Theorem. The smallest lower bound to the probability of error is obtained, for any given transmission rate, when the input sequences assigned to messages have the same optimum composition.

Proof. Let us indicate with

$$P_i(x) \equiv \frac{n_i(x)}{n} \tag{9.78}$$

the composition of the input sequence assigned to the ith message, and with

$$p_i \equiv \Pr[D(u_i v) > D_0] \tag{9.79}$$

the probability that the distance from u_i of the output sequence v resulting from it exceeds D_0. Similarly, let us indicate with

$$q_i \equiv \Pr_F[D(u_i v) \leq D_0] \tag{9.80}$$

the probability that the distance from u_i of a sequence v constructed by selecting its letters independently at random with probability $f(y)$ does not exceed D_0

Since the messages are assumed to be equiprobable, the theorem incorporating Eq. 9.14 yields, for any number M of messages,

$$P(e) \geq \frac{1}{M} \sum_{i=1}^{M} p_i \tag{9.81}$$

where D_0 is the largest distance from each u_i of any output sequence belonging to the corresponding decoding subset w_i. Furthermore, since the M decoding subsets must contain all output sequences, the argument employed in deriving Eq. 9.15 yields now

$$\sum_{i=1}^{M} q_i \geq 1 \quad ; \quad R \equiv \frac{\ln M}{n} \tag{9.82}$$

For each input sequence u_i, lower bounds to the probabilities p_i and q_i can be evaluated by the same method employed in deriving Eqs. 9.47 and 9.48. We obtain

$$\frac{1}{n} \ln p_i \geq -\frac{\beta_i}{n} - [s\gamma_i'(s) - \gamma_i(s)] \quad ; \quad 0 \leq s < 1 \qquad (9.83)$$

$$\frac{1}{n} \ln q_i \geq -\frac{\beta_i}{n} - [(s-1)\gamma_i'(s) - \gamma_i(s)] \quad ; \quad 0 \leq s < 1 \qquad (9.84)$$

where

$$\gamma_i'(s) = \frac{D_0}{n} \qquad (9.85)$$

and β_i , $\gamma_i(s)$, and $\gamma_i'(s)$ are the quantities defined by Eqs. 9.27, 9.36, and 9.37 with $P_i(x)$ substituted for $P(x)$.

We observe next that the righthand side of Eq. 9.83 differs from the righthand side of Eq. 9.84 by $\gamma_i'(s)$. Thus for any fixed value of D_0 , the righthand sides of Eqs. 9.83 and 9.84 are simultaneously minimized by the same $P_i(x)$. Furthermore, since D_0 has the same value for all sequences u_i. assigned to messages, the righthand side of Eq. 9.81 is minimized, and the lower bound to R given by Eq. 9.82 is maximized by the same $P_i(x)$ for all input sequences u_i. We can conclude that the smallest lower bound to the probability of error and the greatest lower bound to the corresponding transmission rate are obtained when all the input sequences assigned to messages have the same composition.

QED

After proving that the smallest lower bound is obtained by employing input sequences with the same optimum composition, we must determine this optimum composition. The solid lines in Fig. 9.3 illustrate the relations between α and I for two different

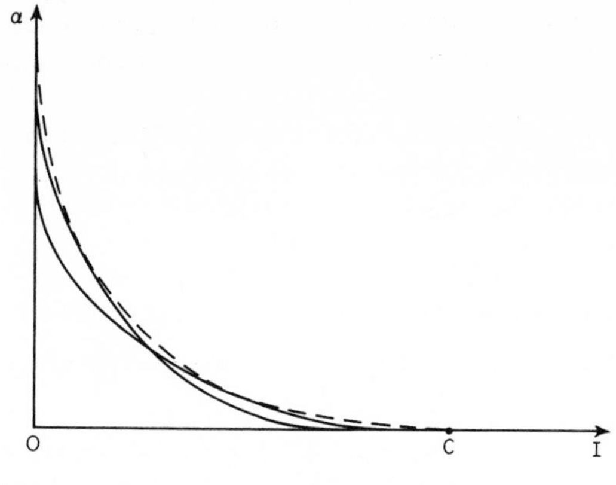

Figure 9.3. Optimum relation between α and I obtained as the envelope of constant – P(x) curves

compositions which maximize α for two different values of I. The broken line in the same figure illustrates the relation between α and I that results when the maximizing composition is used for each value of I. Clearly, this line is the upper envelope of the curves for all possible compositions and all value of s in the range $0 \leq s < 1$. Thus it must be tangent at each point to the curve corresponding to the composition which maximizes α for that particular value of I.

We observe, on the other hand, that the derivative of α with respect to I depends only on s, and is negative or zero for $0 \leq s < 1$ as indicated by Eq. 9.69. It follows that for any given s in the range of interest, the tangents to the curves corresponding to different compositions are all parallel, and each of them intersects the I-axis at some point $I_0 \geq 0$. This suggests that the optimum composition, for any given value of s, can be obtained by maximizing I_0, that is, by determining the composition which yields the uppermost tangent.

Theorem. The value of the intercept I_0 is maximized by the input-sequence composition $P_m(x)$ for which

$$\left.\begin{aligned} \gamma_k(s) &\equiv \ln \sum_Y P(y|x_k)^{1-s}\, Q(y)^s = \gamma_m(s) \;; \quad 0 < s < 1 \\ \gamma_k'(0) &\equiv \sum_Y P(y|x_k) \ln \frac{P(y)}{P(y|x_k)} = \gamma_m'(0) \;; \quad s = 0 \end{aligned}\right\} ; \; k = 1, 2, \ldots, K \tag{9.86}$$

for all x_k for which $P_m(x_k) \neq 0$ where $\gamma_m(s)$ is independent of k. In other words, the moment-generating function of $D(x_k y)$ is independent of k for the optimum input-sequence composition.

Proof. We have for the intercept I_0, with the help of Eq. 9.69,

$$I_0 = I + \frac{1-s}{s}\,\alpha = -\frac{1}{s}\,\gamma(s) \tag{9.87}$$

Thus for $s \neq 0$, we must minimize $\gamma(s)$ with respect to $P(x)$, under the constraint $\sum_X P(x) = 1$. Following Lagrange's procedure, $\gamma(s)$ is stationary with respect to variations of $P(x)$ when

$$\frac{\partial}{\partial P(x_k)}\left[\gamma(s) + \lambda \sum_X P(x)\right] = \frac{\partial \gamma(s)}{\partial P(x_k)} + \lambda = 0 \;; \quad k = 1, 2, \ldots, K \tag{9.88}$$

where λ is independent of k. We observe, on the other hand, that $\gamma(s)$ depends on $P(x_k)$ through $Q(y)$ as well as directly. Thus we obtain from Eq. 9.20, with the help of Eq. 9.61,

$$\frac{\partial\gamma(s)}{\partial P(x_k)} = \gamma_k(s) + \sum_Y \frac{\partial Q(y)}{\partial P(x_k)} \frac{\partial\gamma(s)}{\partial Q(y)}$$

$$= \gamma_k(s) + s \frac{\partial}{\partial P(x_k)} \sum_Y Q(y) = \gamma_k(s) \qquad (9.89)$$

Then substituting the righthand side of this equation in Eq. 9.88 yields

$$\gamma_k(s) = -\lambda \quad ; \quad k = 1, 2, \ldots, K \qquad (9.90)$$

which coincides with the upper part of Eq. 9.86 when $-\lambda$ is identified with $\gamma_m(s)$.

In the special case of $s = 0$, we must minimize the limit of $\gamma(s)/s$ when s approaches zero. We obtain

$$\frac{\partial}{\partial P(x_k)} \lim_{s\to 0} \frac{\gamma(s)}{s} = \frac{\partial\gamma'(0)}{\partial P(x_k)} = \gamma_k'(0) = -\lambda \qquad (9.91)$$

which coincides with the lower part of Eq. 9.86 when $-\lambda$ is identified with $\gamma_m'(0)$. Incidentally, the lower part of Eq. 9.86 coincides with the condition, expressed by Eq. 5.60, which must be satisfied by the input-probability distribution corresponding to channel capacity.

It remains to show that the input-sequence composition $P_m(x)$ satisfying Eq. 9.86 corresponds to a maximum of I_0. We observe, for this purpose, that if $P(x)$ vanishes for all input letters except x_h, $Q(y)$ becomes equal to $Q(y|x_h)$, which in turn becomes equal to $P(y|x_h)$. Under these conditions, both α and I vanish, and therefore I_0 vanishes. It follows that if there is only one composition that satisfied Eq. 9.86, that composition must correspond to a maximum of I_0. If there are several compositions that satisfy Eq. 9.86, the one corresponding to the largest value of I_0 must be selected.

QED

Let us indicate with α_m and I_m the values of α and I for the optimum composition, that is, the coordinates of the broken line in Fig. 9.3. We have from Eq. 9.69

$$\frac{d\alpha_m}{dI_m} = -\frac{s}{1-s} \quad ; \quad 0 \leq s < 1 \qquad (9.92)$$

Thus the broken line of Fig. 9.3 is tangent to the I-axis for $s = 0$. The corresponding value of I_m is

$$[I_m]_{s=0} = \max_{P(x)} I(X; Y) = C \tag{9.93}$$

where C is the channel capacity. We have in the vicinity of $I_m = C$, with the help of Eqs. 9.70 and 9.86,

$$a_m \simeq \frac{1}{2}\left[\frac{d^2 a_m}{dI_m^2}\right]_{s=0}(C - I_m)^2 = \frac{1}{2}\,\frac{(C-I_m)^2}{\gamma_m''(0)} \tag{9.94}$$

where

$$\gamma_m''(0) = \sum_{XY} P_m(x)\,P(y|x)\,[I(x;y) - C]^2 \tag{9.95}$$

For $s \neq 0$, we have from Eqs. 9.24 and 9.86.

$$\sum_X P_m(x)\,P(y_j|x)^{1-s} = g_m(s)\,Q(y_j)^{1-s}\ ; \quad j = 1, 2, \ldots, L \tag{9.96}$$

$$\sum_Y P(y|x_k)^{1-s}\,Q(y)^s = g_m(s) = e^{\gamma_m(s)}\ ; \quad k = 1, 2, \ldots, K \tag{9.97}$$

These two conditions form a set of $L + K$ equations in K variables $P_m(x)$ and L variables $Q(y_j)$. This set of equations breaks into two sets of linear equations in $Q(y)^s$ and $P_m(x)$ when $K = L$. Their solution becomes trivially simple in the special case of a channel which is uniform both from the output and from the input. If the channel is uniform from the input, Eq. 9.97 is satisfied when the $Q(y_j)$ are all identical. Then if the channel is uniform from the output, Eq. 9.96 is satisfied when the $P_m(x_k)$ are also all identical. Thus the optimum input-sequence composition is uniform for all values of s. Let us indicate with p_j for $1 \leq j \leq L = K$ the set of values assumed by the $P(y|x)$. Then we obtain in this simple case

$$a_m = \sum_j \frac{p_j^{1-s}}{\sum_j p_j^{1-s}} \ln \frac{p_j^{1-s}}{p_j \sum_j p_j^{1-s}} \tag{9.98}$$

$$I_m = \sum_j \frac{p_j^{1-s}}{\sum_j p_j^{1-s}} \ln \frac{p_j^{1-s}}{\sum_j p_j^{1-s}} + \ln L \qquad (9.99)$$

In the special case of a binary symmetric channel, these equations yield the expressions for α_L and $C(\rho)$, given by Eqs. 7.58 and 7.57, respectively. For s approaching unity, Eqs. 9.96 and 9.97 yield

$$\sum_{Y_k} Q(y_j) = g_m(1-\epsilon) \quad ; \quad k = 1, 2, \ldots, K \qquad (9.100)$$

$$\sum_{X_j} P(x_k) = g_m(1-\epsilon) \quad ; \quad j = 1, 2, \ldots, L \qquad (9.101)$$

where Y_k is the set of output letters y_j for which $P(y_j|x_k) \neq 0$, X_j is the set of input letters x_k for which $P(y_j|x_k) \neq 0$, and $g_m(1-\epsilon)$ is the limit of $g_m(s)$. Then we obtain from Eq. 9.75

$$[I]_{s=1-\epsilon} = \ln \frac{1}{g_m(1-\epsilon)} \begin{cases} = 0 \quad ; & g_m(1-\epsilon) = 1 \\ \neq 0 \quad ; & \text{otherwise} \end{cases} \qquad (9.102)$$

We can conclude, as in the preceding section, that the vertical part of the optimum relation between α and I lies on the α-axis if and only if there exists one or more output letters y for which $P(y|x) \neq 0$ for all input letters x. Furthermore, if this condition is not satisfied, the value given by the righthand side of Eq. 9.102 must be an upper bound to the zero-error capacity of the channel. As a matter of fact, Eqs. 9.100, 9.101, and 9.102 are identical to those obtained by Shannon [8] for his upper bound to the zero-error capacity of a discrete channel. It must be stressed, however, that $[I]_{s=1-\epsilon} > 0$ does not necessarily imply that the zero-error capacity is also different from zero.

A last comment is in order regarding the evaluation of the optimum input-sequence composition. The solution of Eqs. 9.96 and 9.97 may yield negative values for some of the $P(x)$. In such a case, the desired maximum of I_0 is located on the boundary of the region defined by $P(x) \geq 0$. Then Eqs. 9.96 and 9.97 must be solved again with one of the variables $P(x)$ set equal to zero. If the solution still yields negative values for some of the other $P(x)$, one additional $P(x)$ must be set equal to zero. This process is continued until an acceptable solution is obtained. If, for a given number of variables $P(x)$ set equal to zero, more than one acceptable solution exists, the one must be selected that corresponds to the largest intercept I_0 .

9.5. Random Encoding for Discrete, Constant Channels

We shall discuss in this section a general technique for evaluating upper bounds to the probability of occurrence of a decoding error when a set of M equiprobable messages are encoded into sequences of n channel-input events for transmission through a discrete, constant channel. By an upper bound to the probability of error we mean a value $P_U(e)$ depending on the integer n and on the transmission rate

$$R \equiv \frac{\ln M}{n} < C \tag{9.103}$$

such that for any n and R there exists a set of M input sequences and a decoding procedure for which the probability of error is smaller than or equal to $P_U(e)$. This technique, known as "random coding," is a generalization of that employed in Sec. 7.3 in connection with binary symmetric channels, and it is based on the same argument used by Shannon in his original proof that the probability of error can be made to vanish for any $R < C$ in the limit of n approaching infinity.

Let us consider a constant channel with input events represented by the points x of a discrete space X , and output events represented by the points y of a similarly discrete space Y . The conditional-probability distribution $P(y|x)$ is, by assumption, independent of the past of the transmission. The nth power of this channel has been defined in Sec. 6.1 as the channel with input space U consisting of all possible sequences u of n events belonging to X , and with output space V consisting of all possible sequences of n events belonging to Y . The ith event of the sequence u will be indicated, as in Sec. 6.1, with ξ_i and the corresponding output event of the sequence v will be indicated with η_i . Thus

$$u \equiv \xi_1 \xi_2 \dots \xi_n \quad , \quad v \equiv \eta_1 \eta_2 \dots \eta_n \tag{9.104}$$

where ξ_i may be any point of the input space X , and η_i any point of the output space Y .

Since the channel is constant, the conditional-probability distribution $P(v|u)$ for the nth power channel is given by

$$P(v|u) = \prod_{i=1}^{n} P(\eta_i|\xi_i) \tag{9.105}$$

where

$$P(\eta_i|\xi_i) \equiv P(y|x) \quad ; \quad \eta_i = y \text{ , } \xi_i = x \tag{9.106}$$

We shall assume in what follows that the message space consists of M equiprobable messages $m_1, m_2, \ldots, m_M$. The symbol M will be used to indicate the message space as well as the number of messages in it. With reference to the general discussion of block encoding in Sec. 6.1, and in particular to Fig. 6.1, block encoding may be regarded as a mapping of the message space M into the input space U of the nth power channel. The mapping, of course, should be selected in such a way as to enable the decoder to recognize the message transmitted with as small a probability of error as possible. Unfortunately, no general way has yet been found to construct an optimum mapping, or even a reasonably good mapping. Very useful upper bounds to the probability of error, however, can be obtained by evaluating the average probability of error over the ensemble of mappings generated by a random assignment of input sequences to messages. In fact, if $\overline{P}(e)$ is the average probability of error, there must exist some particular mapping for which the probability of error does not exceed $\overline{P}(e)$. Furthermore, the theorem embodying Eq. 7.89 states that, for any number $A > 1$, the probability is smaller than $1/A$ that a random assignment of input sequences to messages will yield a probability of error exceeding $A\overline{P}(e)$.

Let $P(u)$ be a probability distribution over the input space U of the nth power channel. The input sequences assigned to messages are selected independently at random with probability $P(u)$. Thus if we indicate with m_k a particular message and with u_j a particular input sequence, the probability that the message m_k is represented for transmission by the input sequence u_j is $P(u_j)$ independently of the particular input sequences employed to represent the other messages. Then the transmission probability of any particular input sequence u over the ensemble of mappings so generated is equal to $P(u)$. It is most important to note, however, that this is true only over the ensemble of mappings, and not for any particular mapping of the ensemble. In fact, the M input sequences assigned to the messages by a particular mapping are transmitted with equal probabilities when that particular mapping is employed, while all other input sequences are never transmitted.

The average probability of error corresponding to any such random assignment of input sequences to messages depends, of course, on the probability distribution $P(u)$ employed in selecting the input sequences, which defines the ensemble of mappings over which the probability of error is averaged. The mathematically simplest class of probability distributions is obtained by setting

$$P(u) = \prod_{i=1}^{n} P(\xi_i) \tag{9.107}$$

where

$$P(\xi_i) \equiv P(x) \quad ; \quad \xi_i = x \tag{9.108}$$

and $P(x)$ is an arbitrary probability distribution over the channel input space X. For this class of $P(u)$ the ensemble of input sequences U becomes the product ensemble of n statistically independent ensemble X_i governed by the same probability distribution $P(x)$. This is equivalent to saying that the input sequence corresponding to each particular message is constructed by selecting its successive events independently at random with probability $P(x)$. The average probability of error for such an ensemble of mappings will be evaluated in Sec. 9.7.

The above class of probability distributions $P(u)$ assigns the same probability to all the sequences u that have the same composition, that is, to all the sequences that differ from one another by a permutation of their events. The selection probability of an input sequence, however, depends on its composition, and sequences of all compositions have a non-zero probability of being selected. Another important class of mapping ensembles can be defined by restricting the input sequences employed to represent messages to those having a particular composition, that is, by assigning equal probabilities to the sequences of a particular composition, and zero probability to all other sequences. We shall refer to this type of encoding as "fixed-composition encoding." The average probability of error for fixed-composition encoding will be evaluated in Sec. 9.6.

The evaluation of the average probability of error can be formulated independently of the particular probability distribution $P(u)$ employed. We shall assume in this connection that the channel output is decoded according to the maximum-likelihood criterion, that is, that any particular output sequence v is decoded into the message m that maximizes the conditional probability $P(v|m)$. Since the messages are, by assumption, equiprobable, this decoding criterion is equivalent to maximizing the a posteriori probability $P(m|v)$, which in turn results in the minimization of the probability of error. It is hardly necessary to point out that the decoder knows the particular mapping used by the encoder; in other words, the mapping is random only in the sense that the probability of error is averaged over an ensemble of mappings.

Let us suppose that a particular message has been transmitted, and indicate with u the corresponding input sequence, and with v the resulting channel output. According to the specified decoding criterion, an error may be committed only when one of the other $M - 1$ messages is represented by an input sequence u' for which

$$P(v|u') \geq P(v|u) \tag{9.109}$$

As in Sec. 9.2, let F(v) be an arbitrary, positive function of v satisfying the condition

$$\sum_{V} F(v) = 1 \tag{9.110}$$

and

$$D(uv) \equiv \ln \frac{F(v)}{P(v|u)} \tag{9.111}$$

be the distance between u and v. In terms of this measure of distance the condition expressed by Eq. 9.109 becomes

$$D(u'v) \leq D(uv) \tag{9.112}$$

It is clear that Eq. 9.109 implies Eq. 9.112 and vice versa, regardless of the particular function F(v) employed in the definition of the measure of distance.

We shall be concerned, in evaluating the average probability of error, with the product ensemble UVU' consisting of the triplets of sequences uvu' and characterized by the joint-probability distribution

$$P(u, v, u') = P(u)\, P(v \mid u)\, P(u') \tag{9.113}$$

The ensemble U' is identical to the ensemble U; the only difference between the two ensembles is that u represents the input sequence corresponding to the message actually transmitted, while u' represents the input sequence corresponding to some other message. Since the same probability distribution P(u) is used for all messages in assigning input sequences to messages, the probability distribution P(u') is identical to P(u).

<u>Theorem.</u> Let D_0 be an arbitrary constant, and indicate with U'_{uv} the set of sequences u' which satisfy Eq. 9.112 for any particular pair uv, with $(UV)_0$ the set of sequence pairs uv for which $D(uv) \leq D_0$, and with $(UV)_0^*$ the complementary set for which $D(uv) > D_0$. The average probability of error over the ensemble of mappings characterized by the probability distribution P(u) satisfies the inequality

$$\overline{P}(e) \leq M\, P_1 + P_2 \tag{9.114}$$

where

$$P_1 \equiv \Pr\,[D(uv) \leq D_0\,,\ D(u'v) \leq D(uv)] \equiv \sum_{(UV)_0} P(u)\, P(v|u) \sum_{U'_{uv}} P(u') \tag{9.115}$$

$$P_2 \equiv \Pr[D(uv) > D_0] \equiv \sum_{(UV)_0^*} P(u)\, P(v|u) \qquad (9.116)$$

Proof. Suppose that a particular message represented by the input sequence u has been transmitted, and that the resulting channel output is a particular sequence v. The probability that some other particular message is represented by a sequence u' that does not belong to the set U'_{uv} is

$$1 - \Pr(U'_{uv}) = 1 - \sum_{U'_{uv}} P(u') \qquad (9.117)$$

Since input sequences are assigned to messages at random, independently of one another, the probability that all the sequences u' assigned to the other M - 1 messages do not belong to the set U'_{uv} is given by the $(M - 1)^{th}$ power of the righthand side of Eq. 9.117. It follows that the conditional average probability of error for a given pair uv is

$$\overline{P}(e|uv) \le 1 - [1 - \Pr(U'_{uv})]^{M-1} \qquad (9.118)$$

An upper bound to the righthand side of Eq. 9.118 can be obtained by retaining only the first two terms of the binomial expansion of the $(M - 1)^{th}$ power,

$$\overline{P}(e|uv) \le 1 - [1 - (M - 1) \Pr(U'_{uv})] \le M \Pr(U'_{uv}) \qquad (9.119)$$

On the other hand, the righthand side of this equation increases with the size of the set U'_{uv}, and therefore with the distance D(uv), and eventually exceeds unity. Thus a more satisfactory upper bound to $\overline{P}(e|uv)$ is given by

$$\overline{P}(e|uv) \le \begin{cases} M \Pr(U'_{uv}) & ; \quad D(uv) \le D_0 \\ 1 & ; \quad D(uv) > D_0 \end{cases} \qquad (9.120)$$

where D_0 is an arbitrary constant whose value will be selected later on.

The average probability of error over the entire ensemble of mappings is obtained by averaging $\overline{P}(e|uv)$ over the product ensemble UV, that is,

$$\overline{P}(e) = \sum_{UV} P(u)\, P(v|u)\, \overline{P}(e|uv) \qquad (9.121)$$

Then substituting for $\overline{P}(e|uv)$ the righthand side of Eq. 9.120 yields Eqs. 9.114, 9.115 and 9.116.

QED

The evaluation of the two probabilities P_1 and P_2 given by Eqs. 9.115 and 9.116 requires the specification of the particular probability distribution P(u) that defines the ensemble of mappings. We shall evaluate in the next section these two probabilities in the case of fixed-composition encoding. The evaluation of P_1 and P_2 for a probability distribution P(u) belonging to the class defined by Eqs. 9.107 and 9.108 will be carried out in Sec. 9.7.

9.6. Probability of Error for Fixed-Composition, Random Codes

We shall develop in this section an upper-bound estimate of the average probability of error when the input sequences assigned to messages have the same letter composition and are selected at random with equal probabilities from the set of sequences having such composition. As in Sec. 9.2, we shall indicate with $n(x_k)$ the number of letters x_k in a particular sequence u, and with $n(y_j)$ the number of letters y_j in a particular output sequence v. Similarly, we shall indicate with $n(x_k y_j)$ the number of corresponding letter pairs $x_k y_j$ in the two sequences. Clearly, these integers are related by Eqs. 9.5 and 9.6. We shall refer to the set of integers n(x) associated with a particular sequence u as the composition of the sequence u, and we shall indicate this set of integers with c(u). Similarly, we shall refer to the set of integers n(y) associated with a sequence v as the composition c(v) of the sequence v, and to the set of integers n(xy) associated with a pair of sequences uv as the composition c(uv) of the pair of sequences uv.

Let f(y) be a positive function of y for which

$$\sum_{Y} f(y) = 1 \tag{9.122}$$

and define

$$F(v) \equiv \prod_{Y} f(y)^{n(y)} \tag{9.123}$$

Then the distance defined by Eq. 9.111 becomes

$$D(uv) = \sum_{XY} n(xy) \ln \frac{f(y)}{P(y|x)} = \sum_{XY} n(xy)\, D(xy) \tag{9.124}$$

Clearly, this distance depends on the sequence pair only through its composition represented by the set of integers $n(xy)$. We shall be concerned in our derivation with the probability of selecting, from the set of sequences u having a prescribed composition, a sequence u' whose distance from some sequence v is $D(u'v) \leq D_1$, where D_1 is a constant. Similarly, we shall be concerned with the probability of selecting, from the set of sequences v with a given composition, a sequence v' whose distance from a particular u is $D(uv') \leq D_1$. These two probabilities are related by the following lemma.

Lemma. Let u and v be two particular sequences, and select equiprobably at random a sequence u' having the same composition as u, and a sequence v' having the same composition as v. Then

$$\Pr[D(u'v) \leq D(uv) | c(u') = c(u)] = [\Pr D(uv') \leq D(uv) | c(v') = c(v)] \tag{9.125}$$

Proof. Let us indicate with C_{uv} the set of sequence-pair compositions for which

$$\sum_{XY} n(xy) \ln \frac{f(y)}{P(y|x)} \leq D(uv) \tag{9.126}$$

and the corresponding sets of integers $n(x)$ and $n(y)$ coincide with the compositions $c(u)$ and $c(v)$, respectively. The number of sequences u' for which $D(u'v) \leq D(uv)$ and $c(u') = c(u)$ is

$$\sum_{C_{uv}} \frac{\prod_{Y} n(y)!}{\prod_{XY} n(xy)!} = \prod_{Y} n(y)! \sum_{C_{uv}} \left[\prod_{XY} n(xy)!\right]^{-1} \tag{9.127}$$

Similarly, the number of sequence v' for which $D(uv') \leq D(uv)$, and $c(v') = c(v)$ is

$$\sum_{C_{uv}} \frac{\prod_{X} n(x)!}{\prod_{XY} n(xy)!} = \prod_{X} n(x)! \sum_{C_{uv}} \left[\prod_{XY} n(xy)!\right]^{-1} \tag{9.128}$$

The total number of sequences u' for which $c(u') = c(u)$ is

$$\frac{n!}{\prod_X n(x)!} \tag{9.129}$$

and the number of sequences v' for which c(v') = c(v) is

$$\frac{n!}{\prod_Y n(y)!} \tag{9.130}$$

Since the sequence u' is selected equiprobably at random from the set of sequences for which c(u') = c(u) , dividing Eq. 9.127 by Eq. 9.129 yields

$$Pr[D(u'v) \leq D(uv) \,|\, c(u') = c(u)]$$

$$= \frac{1}{n!}\left[\prod_X n(x)!\right]\left[\prod_Y n(y)!\right]\sum_{C_{uv}}\left[\prod_{XY} n(xy)!\right]^{-1} \tag{9.131}$$

Similarly, dividing Eq. 9.128 by Eq. 9.130 yields

$$Pr[D(uv') \leq D(uv) \,|\, c(v') = c(v)]$$

$$= \frac{1}{n!}\left[\prod_X n(x)!\right]\left[\prod_Y n(y)!\right]\sum_{C_{uv}}\left[\prod_{XY} n(xy)!\right]^{-1} \tag{9.132}$$

Since the righthand sides of Eqs. 9.131 and 9.132 are equal, they yield Eq. 9.125 in the statement of the lemma.

QED

We are now ready to state and prove the main result of this section.

Theorem. Let us consider a discrete, constant channel characterized by a conditional-probability distribution P(y|x) , and a particular input-sequence composition characterized by integers n(x) , and define the ensemble of mappings of messages into channel-input sequences obtained by assigning to each message an input sequence selected at random with replacement from those having the given composition. In addition, let

$$P(x) \equiv \frac{n(x)}{n} \tag{9.133}$$

and define the tilted conditional-probability distribution

$$Q(y|x) \equiv \frac{P(y|x)^{1-s}\, Q(y)^s}{\sum_Y P(y|x)^{1-s}\, Q(y)^s} \quad ; \quad 0 \leq s \leq \frac{1}{2} \tag{9.134}$$

where the tilted probability distribution $Q(y)$ satisfies the set of simultaneous equations

$$Q(y) \equiv \sum_X P(x)\, Q(y|x) = \sum_X \frac{P(x)\, P(y|x)^{1-s}\, Q(y)^s}{\sum_Y P(y|x)^{1-s}\, Q(y)^s} \; ; \; 0 \leq s \leq \frac{1}{2} \tag{9.135}$$

Indicating with K the number of points in the channel-input space X, the average probability of error over the ensemble of mappings satisfies the inequality

$$\overline{P}(e) \leq \begin{cases} [1 + (2\pi n)^{K/2}\, e^{K/12}]\, e^{-n\alpha} & ; \; R_c < R < I(X;Y) \\ (2\pi n)^{K/2}\, e^{K/12}\, e^{-n[\alpha_c + R_c - R]} & ; \; 0 \leq R \leq R_c \end{cases} \tag{9.136}$$

where the exponential coefficient α is related parametrically to the transmission rate per event R, for $R_c < R \leq I(X;Y)$,

$$0 \leq \alpha \equiv \sum_{XY} P(x)\, Q(y|x) \ln \frac{Q(y|x)}{P(y|x)} \leq \alpha_c \quad ; \quad 0 \leq s \leq \frac{1}{2} \tag{9.137}$$

$$I(X;Y) \geq R \equiv \sum_{XY} P(x)\, Q(y|x) \ln \frac{Q(y|x)}{Q(y)} \geq R_c \; ; \quad 0 \leq s \leq \frac{1}{2} \tag{9.138}$$

and

$$\alpha_c = [\alpha]_{s=1/2} \; ; \; R_c = [R]_{s=1/2} \tag{9.139}$$

$$[\alpha]_{s=0} = 0 \; ; \; [R]_{s=0} = I(X;Y) \equiv \sum_{XY} P(x)\, P(y|x) \ln \frac{P(y|x)}{P(y)} \tag{9.139}$$

Proof. An upper bound to the average probability of error is given by the theorem incorporating Eq. 9.114 when each of the ensembles U and U' consist of the channel-input sequences with the prescribed composition taken with equal probabilities. An upper bound to the probability P_2 given by Eq. 9.116 can be readily obtained with the help of the theorem incorporating Eq. 8.69. For this purpose, let us identify the points y of the channel-output space Y with the points a of the space A of the theorem, the conditional-probability distribution $P(y|x_k)$ with the probability distribution $P_k(a)$, the integers n_k with the integers $n(x_k)$, the random variable $D(x_k y)$ with $\phi_k(a)$, and D_0 with $n\phi$. Then we obtain from Eq. 8.69, with the help of Eqs. 8.62, 8.63, 8.71, and 8.74,

$$P_2 < e^{-n[s\gamma'(s) - \gamma(s)]} \quad ; \quad 0 \leq s \tag{9.141}$$

where

$$\gamma'(s) = \sum_{XY} P(x)\, Q(y|x)\, D(xy) = \frac{D_0}{n} > \sum_{XY} P(x)\, P(y|x)\, D(xy) \tag{9.142}$$

$$s\gamma'(s) - \gamma(s) = \sum_{XY} P(x)\, Q(y|x) \ln \frac{Q(y|x)}{P(y|x)} \tag{9.143}$$

and

$$Q(y|x) \equiv \frac{e^{sD(xy)}\, P(y|x)}{\sum_{Y} e^{sD(xy)}\, P(y|x)} = \frac{P(y|x)^{1-s}\, f(y)^s}{\sum_{Y} P(y|x)^{1-s}\, f(y)^s} \tag{9.144}$$

The value of the parameter s is specified by Eq. 9.142 for any particular value of D_0 satisfying the righthand inequality.

Next let us derive an upper bound to the probability P_1 given by Eq. 9.115. We observe, first of all, that since the sequence u is selected equiprobably from the set of channel-input sequences with the specified composition, the probability that $D(u'v) \leq D(uv) \leq D_0$ is independent of the particular u input to the channel. Thus indicating with u_0 any particular input sequence with the specified composition

$$P_1 = \sum_{V_0} P(v|u_0)\, \Pr[D(u'v) \leq D(u_0 v)|\, c(u') = c(u_0)] \tag{9.145}$$

where V_0 is the set of sequences v for which $D(u_0 v) \leq D_0$. Then it follows from the lemma incorporating Eq. 9.125 that

$$P_1 = \sum_{V_0} P(v|u_0)\, \Pr[D(u_0 v') \leq D(u_0 v)|\, c(v') = c(v)] \tag{9.146}$$

The second factor on the righthand side of Eq. 9.146 is the conditional probability for a given pair u_0v that, if we select equiprobably at random a sequence v' having the same composition as v, $D(u_0v') \leq D(u_0v)$. An upper bound to this conditional probability can be obtained as follows.

Let us consider, for each point x_k of the input space, the product ensemble formed by selecting two points y and y' of the output space with the joint probability $P(y|x_k)\, f(y')$, and define for this product ensemble the two random variables

$$D(x_ky) \equiv \ln \frac{f(y)}{P(y|x_k)} \;;\quad D(x_ky') \equiv \ln \frac{f(y')}{P(y'|x_k)} \tag{9.147}$$

Then if u_0 is a particular input sequence, the conditional-probability distribution of the pair of sequences vv' obtained by selecting independently n pairs yy' is

$$P(v|u_0)\, F(v) = \prod_{k=1}^{K} \prod_{Y} P(y|x_k)^{n(x_ky)} \prod_{Y'} f(y')^{n(y')} \tag{9.148}$$

where the set of integers $n(x_ky)$ is the composition of the pair of sequences u_0v, the set of integers $n(y')$ is the composition of the sequence v', and K is the number of points in the channel input space X. Clearly, since the channel is constant, $P(v|u)$ is the conditional-probability distribution of the nth power channel. The probability $P(v')$ is the same for all sequences v' having the same composition. Over the ensemble VV' of the sequence pairs vv', the distances $D(u_0v)$ and $D(u_0v')$, defined by Eq. 9.124 are both sums of independent random variables $D(x_ky)$ and $D(x_ky')$, respectively. Then proceeding as in Sec. 8.3, we define for each x_k the logarithm of the moment-generating function

$$\gamma_k(t, r) \equiv \ln \sum_{YY'} e^{t\,D(x_ky)+r[D(x_ky')-D(x_ky)]} f(y')\, P(y|x_k) \tag{9.149}$$

where t and r are parameters associated with the random variables $D(x_ky)$ and $D(x_ky') - D(x_ky)$, respectively. Correspondingly, the logarithm of the moment-generating function for the random variables $D(u_0v)$ and $D(u_0v') - D(u_0v)$ is given by

$$\Gamma_0(t, r) \equiv \ln \sum_{VV'} e^{t\,D(u_0v)+r[D(u_0v')-D(u_0v)]} F(v')\, P(v|u_0)$$

$$= \sum_{k=1}^{K} n(x_k)\, \gamma_k(t, r) = n\, \gamma_0(t, r) \tag{9.150}$$

where

$$\gamma_0(t, r) \equiv \sum_{k=1}^{K} P(x_k)\, \gamma_k(t, r) \tag{9.151}$$

and

$$P(x) \equiv \frac{n(x)}{n} \tag{9.152}$$

Next we define the tilted probability distributions

$$Q_0(y, y'|\, x_k) \equiv e^{t\, D(x_k y) + r[D(x_k y') - D(x_k y)] - \gamma_k(t, r)}\, f(y')\, P(y|\, x_k)$$

$$= \frac{P(y|\, x_k)^{1-t+r}\, f(y)^{t-r}\, f(y')^{1+r}\, P(y'|\, x_k)^{-r}}{\sum_{Y} P(y|x_k)^{1-t+r}\, f(y)^{t-r} \sum_{Y'} P(y'|\, x_k)^{-r}\, f(y')^{1+r}} \tag{9.153}$$

$$Q_0(v, v'|\, u_0) \equiv e^{t\, D(u_0 v) + r[D(u_0 v') - D(u_0 v)] - n\gamma_0(t, r)}\, F(v')\, P(v|\, u_0) \tag{9.154}$$

We shall now proceed to the evaluation of an upper-bound estimate of the probability P_1 given by Eq. 9.146.

Expressing the conditional probability on the righthand side of Eq. 9.146 as the ratio of the corresponding joint probability and the probability of the condition yields

$$P_1 = \sum_{V_0} P(v|\, u_0)\, \frac{\Pr[D(u_0 v') \leq D(u_0 v)\,,\ c(v') = c(v)]}{\Pr[c(v') = c(v)]} \tag{9.155}$$

where V_0 is the set of sequences v for which $D(u_0 v) \leq D_0$. Let V'_v be the set of sequences v' that have the same composition as v, and let V'_{0v} be the subset of V'_v for which $D(u_0 v') \leq D(u_0 v)$ Then Eq. 9.155 can be rewritten in the form

$$P_1 = \sum_{V_0} \frac{\sum_{V'_{0v}} P(v|\, u_0)\, F(v')}{\sum_{V'_v} F(v')} \tag{9.156}$$

It is important to note that since the sequences of the set V'_v have the same composition, $F(v')$ has the same value for all the sequences of such a set. It follows that the ratio of the summations in Eq. 9.156 is the conditional probability, for a given pair uv, that if we select equiprobably at random a sequence v' from the set of sequences that have the same composition as v, its distance from u_0 satisfies the inequality $D(u_0v') \leq D(u_0v)$.

An upper bound to the summation in the numerator of Eq. 9.156 can be obtained as follows, with the help of the tilted probability distribution defined by Eq. 9.154. Since all the sequences v' of the subset V'_{0v} have a distance from u_0 not exceeding $D(u_0v)$, we have

$$\sum_{V'_{0v}} P(v|u_0)\, F(v') = e^{n\gamma_0(t,\, r) - t\, D(u_0v)} \sum_{V'_{0v}} e^{-r[D(u_0v') - D(u_0v)]}\, Q_0(v, v'|u_0)$$

$$\leq e^{n\gamma_0(t,\, r) - t\, D(u_0v)} \sum_{V'_{0v}} Q_0(v, v'|u_0)\ ; \quad r \leq 0 \qquad (9.157)$$

The exponent on the righthand side of this equation is minimized, as usual, by equating to zero its partial derivative with respect to r, that is,

$$\gamma'_r(r, t) = \frac{\partial}{\partial r}\gamma_0(r, t) = \sum_X P(x) \sum_{XY'} Q_0(y, y'|x)[D(xy') - D(xy)] = 0 \qquad (9.158)$$

This condition is satisfied if $Q_0(y, y'|x)$ is a symmetrical function of y and y'. Inspection of Eq. 9.153 shows that such a symmetry can be obtained by setting

$$r = \frac{t-1}{2}\ ; \quad t \leq 1 \qquad (9.159)$$

Under these conditions, we have

$$Q_0(y, y'|x_k) = Q_0(y|x_k)\, Q_0(y'|x_k) \qquad (9.160)$$

where

$$Q_0(y|x_k) = \frac{P(y|x_k)^{(1-t)/2}\, f(y)^{(1+t)/2}}{\sum_Y P(y|x_k)^{(1-t)/2}\, f(y)^{(1+t)/2}} \qquad (9.161)$$

In words, $Q_0(y, y'|x_k)$ is the product of two identical conditional-probability distributions. Then substituting the righthand side of Eq. 9.160 in Eq. 9.157 and extending the summation from V'_{0v} to V'_v yield

$$\sum_{V'_{0v}} P(v|u_0)\, F(v') \leq e^{n\gamma_0(t,r) - t\, D(uv_0)}\, Q_0(v|u_0) \sum_{V'_{0v}} Q(v'|u_0)$$

$$\leq e^{n\gamma_0(t,r) - t\, D(u_0 v)}\, Q_0(v|u_0) \sum_{V'_v} Q(v'|u_0) \quad ; \quad t \leq 1 \tag{9.162}$$

This is the desired upper bound to the numerator in Eq. 9.156.

Let us consider next the denominator in Eq. 9.156. It is convenient, in this connection, to define a conditional-probability distribution $f(y'|x)$ for which

$$f(y') = \sum_{X} P(x)\, f(y'|x) \tag{9.163}$$

This conditional-probability distribution defines, in turn, the conditional-probability distribution $F(v'|u)$ obtained as the product of the values of $f(y'|x)$ for each corresponding pair of events of the sequences v' and u_0. Then if we indicate with U_0 the subset of U consisting of all the sequences u having the specified composition $nP(x)$, we have

$$F(v') = \sum_{U} P(u)\ F(v'|u) \geq \sum_{U_0} P(u)\, F(v'|u) \tag{9.164}$$

It follows that

$$\sum_{V'_v} F(v') \geq \sum_{U_0} P(u) \sum_{V'_v} F(v'|u) \tag{9.165}$$

The summation over V'_v in this equation depends only on the composition of u, and not on the particular u among those having the same composition. This follows from the fact that V'_v contains all the permutations of any sequence v' with the same composition as v, and therefore the terms in the summations for different u's with the same composition are simply permutations of the same set of numbers. Under these conditions, the summation over U_0 in Eq. 9.166 can be evaluated independently of the summation over V'_v.

The values of the probabilities $P(u)$ in the summation over U_0 are all identical because they correspond to sequences having the same composition. More precisely, the summation U_0 is simply the term of the multinomial probability distribution corresponding to sequences u having the prescribed composition $n(x) = nP(x)$.

We obtain then, with the help of the theorem incorporating Eq. 8.86, with K identified with L and nP(x) with n_j,

$$\sum_{U_0} P(u) = \frac{n!}{\prod_X [n\, P(x)]!} \prod_X P(x)^{nP(x)} \geq (2\pi n)^{-K/2} e^{-K/12} \tag{9.166}$$

Finally, substituting the righthand side of this equation in Eq. 9.165 yields

$$\sum_{V'_v} F(v') \geq (2\pi n)^{-K/2} e^{-K/12} \sum_{V'_v} F(v'|u_0) \tag{9.167}$$

where u_0 is any particular u having the specified composition.

Our next objective is to find an upper bound to the ratio in Eq. 9.156. For this purpose, we must bound the ratio of the summations over V'_v in Eqs. 9.162 and 9.167. This ratio can be made equal to one by setting

$$f(y') = \sum_X P(x)\, Q_0(y'|x) = Q_0(y') \tag{9.168}$$

which implies that

$$f(y'|x) = Q_0(y'|x) \quad ; \quad F(v'|u) = Q_0(v'|u) \tag{9.169}$$

Then substituting the righthand sides of Eqs. 9.162 and 9.167 in Eq. 9.156 yields

$$P_1 \leq (2\pi n)^{K/2} e^{K/12} e^{n\gamma_0(t,r)} \sum_{V_0} e^{-t\, D(uv)} Q_0(v|u) \tag{9.170}$$

Finally, since all the sequences v belonging to V_0 have a distance from u not exceeding D_0, we obtain

$$P_1 \leq (2\pi n)^{K/2} e^{K/12} e^{n\gamma_0(t,r) - t\, D_0} \quad ; \quad t \leq 0 \tag{9.171}$$

The righthand side of Eq. 9.171 can be minimized, as before, by equating to zero the partial derivative of $\gamma_0(t, r)$ with respect to t, which yields

$$\gamma'_t(t,r) \equiv \frac{\partial\gamma_0(t,r)}{\partial t} = \sum_{XY} P(x)\, Q_0(y|x)\, D(xy) = \frac{D_0}{n} \tag{9.172}$$

We observe, on the other hand, that $\gamma'(s)$ has already been set equal to D_0/n in Eq. 9.142. It follows that $\gamma'(s) = \gamma_t'(t, r)$, which implies in turn that

$$\sum_Y Q(y|x_k)\, D(x_k y) = \sum_Y Q_0(y|x_k)\, D(x_k y) \tag{9.173}$$

This condition is met if

$$Q(y|x_k) = Q_0(y|x_k) \tag{9.174}$$

which is satisfied, in turn, if

$$s = (1 + t)/2 \ ; \quad 0 \leq s \leq 1/2 \tag{9.175}$$

as evident by inspection of Eqs. 9.144 and 9.161.

We obtain, under these conditions,

$$\gamma_0(t, r) = 2 \sum_X P(x) \ln \sum_Y P(y|x)^{1-s}\, Q(y)^s = 2\gamma(s) \tag{9.176}$$

from which it follows that

$$t\gamma_t'(t, r) - \gamma_0(t, r) = (2s - 1)\gamma'(s) - 2\gamma(s) \tag{9.177}$$

Finally, substituting the righthand side of Eq. 9.177 for the exponent in Eq. 9.171 yields

$$P_1 \leq (2\pi n)^{K/2}\, e^{K/12}\, e^{-n\{[(s-1)\gamma'(s)-\gamma(s)]+[s\gamma'(s)-\gamma(s)]\}} \ ; \quad 0 \leq s \leq 1/2 \tag{9.178}$$

This is the desired upper bound to the probability P_1 defined by Eq. 9.146. The first term in the exponent is given by

$$(s - 1)\,\gamma'(s) - \gamma(s) = \sum_{XY} P(x)\, Q(y|x) \ln \frac{Q(y|x)}{Q(y)} \tag{9.179}$$

while the second term is given by Eq. 9.143.

Next let

$$R \equiv \frac{\ln M}{n} \ \text{nats/event} \tag{9.180}$$

be the transmission rate per channel event. Substituting the right-hand sides of Eqs. 9.141 and 9.178 in Eq. 9.114 yields

$$\overline{P}(e) \leq (2\pi n)^{K/2}\, e^{K/12}\, e^{-n\{[(s-1)\gamma'(s)-\gamma(s)] + [s\gamma'(s)-\gamma(s)] - R\}} + e^{-n[s\gamma'(s)-\gamma(s)]} \ ; \quad 0 \leq s \leq \frac{1}{2} \tag{9.181}$$

This equation is valid for all values of s in the specified range. Thus we are free to select, for each rate R, the value of s which minimizes the righthand side of Eq. 9.181. On the other hand, since $\gamma(s)$ and $\gamma'(s)$ are defined exactly as in Eqs. 9.20 and 9.21, we have from Eq. 9.68

$$\frac{d}{ds}[(s-1)\gamma'(s)-\gamma(s)] = (s-1)\gamma''(s) \leq 0 \quad ; \quad 0 \leq s < 1 \tag{9.182}$$

$$\frac{d}{ds}[s\gamma'(s)-\gamma(s)] = s\gamma''(s) \geq 0 \quad ; \quad 0 \leq s < 1 \tag{9.183}$$

from which it follows that

$$\frac{d}{ds}\{[(s-1)\gamma'(s)-\gamma(s)]+[s\gamma'(s)-\gamma(s)]\} = (2s-1)\gamma''(s) \leq 0 \; ; \; 0 \leq s \leq \frac{1}{2} \tag{9.184}$$

Thus the two exponential coefficients in Eq. 9.181 vary monotonically with s in opposite directions. Under these conditions, the righthand side of Eq. 9.181 can be approximately minimized by setting, in view of Eq. 9.179,

$$R = \sum_{XY} P(x)\, Q(y|x) \ln \frac{Q(y|x)}{Q(y)} \quad ; \quad 0 \leq s \leq \frac{1}{2} \tag{9.185}$$

from which we obtain

$$\overline{P}(e) \leq [1 + (2\pi n)^{K/2}\, e^{K/12}]\; e^{-n\alpha} \quad ; \quad 0 \leq s \leq \frac{1}{2} \tag{9.186}$$

where

$$\alpha \equiv \sum_{XY} P(x)\, Q(y|x) \ln \frac{Q(y|x)}{P(y|x)} \quad ; \quad 0 \leq s \leq \frac{1}{2} \tag{9.187}$$

These last two equations coincide with the upper part of Eq. 9.136 and with Eq. 9.137 in the statement of the theorem.

It is important to note that Eq. 9.185 fixes the value of the parameter s as a function of R, and therefore it establishes a parametric relation between the transmission rate R and the exponential coefficient α given by Eq. 9.187. On the other hand, Eq. 9.185 can be satisfied only for $s \leq 1/2$ and therefore for transmission rates $R \geq R_c$, where R_c is the critical rate defined by Eq. 9.139, corresponding to the exponential coefficient α_c defined also in the same equation.

We observe next that the righthand side of Eq. 9.184 vanishes for $s = 1/2$, so that $\alpha_c + R_c$ is the maximum value assumed by the exponential coefficient by which n is multiplied in Eq. 9.178.

Furthermore, $s = 1/2$ corresponds to $t = 0$ in Eq. 9.171, and therefore to $D_0 = n\gamma_t'(0, -\frac{1}{2}) = n\gamma'(\frac{1}{2})$ in Eq. 9.172. Thus, for $D_0 > n\gamma'(\frac{1}{2})$, we can substitute V for V_0 in Eq. 9.155 without unduly weakening the resulting upper-bound approximation. This is equivalent to setting $D_0 = \infty$, so that the expressions for P_1 and P_2 given by Eqs. 9.115 and 9.116 reduce to

$$P_1 = \sum_V P(v|u_0) \Pr[D(u_0v') \leq D(u_0v) | c(v') = c(v)] \quad ; \quad P_2 = 0 \qquad (9.188)$$

The evaluation of an upper bound to the expression for P_1 given by Eq. 9.188 proceeds exactly as before, except for the fact that the condtion $D(u_0v) \leq D_0$ is eliminated by setting $t = 0$ in Eq. 9.153. The desired upper bound to P_1 under these conditions is given by Eq. 9.178 for $s = 1/2$, as indicated by Eq. 9.175. Then substituting in Eq. 9.114 $P_2 = 0$ and the upper bound given by Eq. 9.178 for $s = 1/2$ yields

$$\overline{P}(e) \leq (2\pi n)^{K/2} e^{K/12} e^{-n[a_c + R_c - R]} \quad ; \quad 0 \leq R \leq R_c \qquad (9.189)$$

which coincides with the lower part of Eq. 9.136 in the statement of the theorem.

Finally, it follows from Eqs. 9.182 and 9.183 that R decreases monotonically with increasing s, while a increases monotonically with increasing s. Both R and a are non-negative, as shown by Eqs. 9.53 and 9.54.

QED

The upper bound to the average probability of error given by Eq. 9.136 is governed primarily by the exponential coefficient by which n is multiplied. More precisely,

$$\lim_{n\to\infty} \frac{1}{n} \ln \overline{P}(e) = -a_U \qquad (9.190)$$

where

$$a_U \equiv \begin{cases} [s\gamma'(s) - \gamma(s)] = \sum_{XY} P(x)\,Q(y|x) \ln \dfrac{Q(y|x)}{P(y|x)} \; ; & R_c \leq R \leq I(X;Y) \\ a_c + R_c - R = -2\gamma(\frac{1}{2}) - R \; ; & 0 \leq R \leq R_c \end{cases} \qquad (9.191)$$

and

$$R = [(s-1)\gamma'(s) - \gamma(s)] = \sum_{XY} P(x)\,Q(y|x) \ln \frac{Q(y|x)}{Q(y)} \quad ; \quad R_c \leq R \leq I(X;Y) \qquad (9.192)$$

Comparison of Eqs. 9.191 and 9.192 with Eqs. 9.29 and 9.28 shows that the expressions for α_U and R coincide, for $R_c \leq R$, with the expressions for the quantities α and I that control the asymptotic behavior of the lower bound to the probability of error for fixed-composition codes. Thus the upper part of Eq. 9.191 in conjunction with Eq. 9.192 gives the correct asymptotic behavior of the smallest probability of error that can be achieved for a given rate R and a given input-sequence composition. The asymptotic behavior of the upper bound, however, diverges from that of the lower bound for $0 \leq R < R_c$.

The behavior of α_U as a function of R is illustrated by the solid line in Fig. 9.4 for a fixed input-sequence composition.

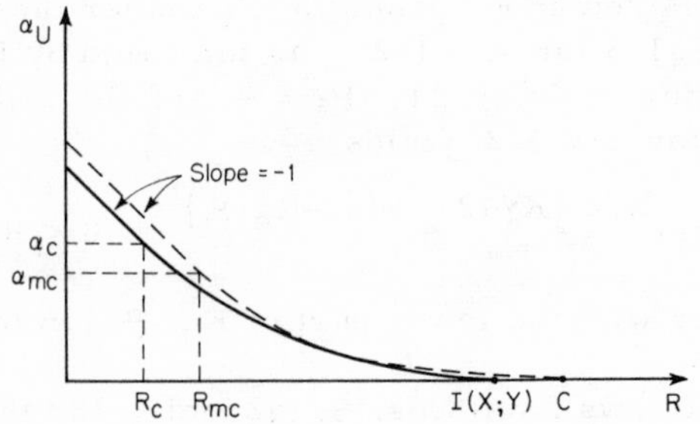

Figure 9.4. Relations between α_U and R for fixed composition (solid line) and optimum composition (broken line)

The part of the curve corresponding to $R < R_c$ is a straight line of slope equal to -1, as evident from the lower part of Eq. 9.191. Since the curve coincides, for $R_c \leq R$, with the corresponding curve of α as a function of I shown in Fig. 9.3, its slope is given by

$$\frac{d\alpha_U}{dR} = -\frac{s}{1-s} \; ; \quad 0 \leq s \leq \tfrac{1}{2} \, , \quad I(X;Y) \geq R \geq R_c \qquad (9.193)$$

Thus the slope is continuous for $R = R_c$, that is, for $s = 1/2$.

Let us consider next the optimization of the input-sequence composition, that is, the evaluation of the composition $P_m(x)$ which yields the largest value of α_U for any given rate R. Since, for $0 \leq s \leq 1/2$, the upper-bound exponential coefficient α_U coincides with the lower-bound exponential coefficient α given by Eq. 9.29 when R is identified with the quantity I given by Eq. 9.28, the maximizing input-sequence composition for this range of values of s is given by the theorem incorporating Eq. 9.86. Furthermore, since the slope of the straight-line portion of the relation between α_U and R is independent of P(x), the optimum composition for smaller values of R is that given by the same theorem for $s = 1/2$.

We obtain from Eqs. 9.96 and 9.97 for $s = 1/2$

$$\sum_X P_m(x)\sqrt{P(y_j|x)} = g_m(\tfrac{1}{2})\sqrt{Q(y_j)} \; ; \quad j = 1, 2, \ldots, L \qquad (9.194)$$

and

$$\sum_Y \sqrt{P(y|x_k)\,Q(y)} = g_m(\tfrac{1}{2}) \; ; \quad k = 1, 2, \ldots, K \qquad (9.195)$$

which yield in turn

$$\sum_X P_m(x)\sum_Y \sqrt{P(y|x_k)\,P(y|x)} = [g_m(\tfrac{1}{2})]^2 \; ; \quad k = 1, 2, \ldots, K \qquad (9.196)$$

Thus the maximizing composition $P_m(x)$ for $R = R_c$ can be evaluated as the solution of a set of K linear equations in K unknowns. The value of $g_m(\frac{1}{2})$ is set by the requirement that the sum of the $P_m(x)$ be equal to unity. Finally, the maximum value of α_U for $R = 0$ is

$$\max\,[\alpha_U]_{R=0} = \alpha_{mc} + R_{mc} = -2\gamma_m(\tfrac{1}{2}) = -\ln\,[g_m(\tfrac{1}{2})]^2 \qquad (9.197)$$

We can conclude that the optimum relation between α_U and R , shown in Fig. 9.4 as a broken line, coincides with the optimum lower-bound relation between α and I from the end point $R = C$ to the critical point $R = R_{mc}$ where the slope becomes equal to -1 . The optimum relation is a straight line of slope equal to -1 for $R < R_{mc}$. Thus we have proved the following fundamental theorem.

> Theorem. For any discrete, constant channel, it is possible to encode messages into sequences of n input events and to decode the corresponding sequences of output events in such a way that, for any transmission rate smaller than the channel capacity, the probability of error will vanish exponentially with increasing n .

9.7. Probability of Error for Randomly Constructed Codes

The upper bound to the probability or error obtained in the preceding section for fixed-composition codes coincides asymptotically with the corresponding lower-bound derived in Secs. 9.2, and 9.3 for rates greater than or equal to the critical rate R_c. Thus no asymptotically better upper bound can be obtained by changing the ensemble of mappings over which the average probability of error is evaluated. On the other hand, since the random construction of mappings is of practical as well as of theoretical interest, it is important to determine whether or not the same average probability of error is obtained when the fixed-composition constraint on the input sequences assigned to messages is relaxed into the corresponding constraint on the average composition. More precisely, our objective in this section is to obtain an upper-bound estimate of the righthand side of Eq. 9.114 when the probability distribution employed in assigning input sequences to messages is of the type given by Eqs. 9.107 and 9.108, and to compare this estimate with that obtained in the preceding section.

It was pointed out in Sec. 9.5 that, for the probability distributions $P(u)$ defined by Eqs. 9.107 and 9.108, the ensemble of input sequences U becomes the product ensemble of n statistically independent ensembles X_i described by the same probability distribution $P(x)$. Thus the input sequence corresponding to each particular message may be thought of as having been constructed by selecting each successive event independently at random with probability $P(x)$.

Theorem. Let us consider a discrete, constant channel characterized by a conditional-probability distribution $P(y|x)$, and the ensemble of mappings of messages into channel-input sequences obtained by assigning to each message a sequence of n channel input events selected independently at random with probability $P(x)$ from a discrete ensemble X, and define for the product space XY the tilted probability distribution

$$Q(x, y) \equiv Q(y)\, Q(x|y) \tag{9.198}$$

where

$$Q(y) \equiv \frac{\left[\sum_{X} P(x)\, P(y|x)^{1-s}\right]^{1/(1-s)}}{\sum_{Y}\left[\sum_{X} P(x)\, P(y|x)^{1-s}\right]^{1/(1-s)}} \quad ; \quad 0 \le s \le \tfrac{1}{2} \tag{9.199}$$

$$Q(x|y) \equiv \frac{P(x)\, P(y|x)^{1-s}}{\sum_{X} P(x)\, P(y|x)^{1-s}} \quad ; \quad 0 \le s \le \tfrac{1}{2} \tag{9.200}$$

The average probability of error over the ensemble of mappings satisfies the inequality

$$\overline{P}(e) \leq \begin{cases} 2e^{-n\alpha} & ; \quad R_c \leq R \leq I(X;Y) \\ e^{-n[\alpha_c + R_c - R]} & ; \quad 0 \leq R \leq R_c \end{cases} \tag{9.201}$$

where the exponential coefficient α is related parametrically to the transmission rate per event R, for $R_c < R \leq R_0$, by

$$0 \leq \alpha \equiv \sum_{XY} Q(x,y) \ln \frac{Q(x,y)}{P(x)\, P(y|x)} \leq \alpha_c \quad ; \quad 0 \leq s \leq \tfrac{1}{2} \tag{9.202}$$

$$I(X;Y) \geq R \equiv \sum_{XY} Q(x,y) \ln \frac{Q(x|y)}{P(x)} \geq R_c \quad ; \quad 0 \leq s \leq \tfrac{1}{2} \tag{9.203}$$

and

$$\alpha_c \equiv [\alpha]_{s=1/2} \quad ; \quad R_c \equiv [R]_{s=1/2} \tag{9.204}$$

$$[\alpha]_{s=0} = 0 \quad ; \quad [R]_{s=0} = I(X;Y) \equiv \sum_{XY} P(x)\, P(y|x) \ln \frac{P(y|x)}{P(y)} \tag{9.205}$$

Proof. Let $F(v)$ in Eq. 9.111 be of the form

$$F(v) = \prod_{i=1}^{n} f(\eta_i) \tag{9.206}$$

where

$$[f(\eta_i)]_{\eta_i = y} \equiv f(y) \quad ; \quad \sum_{Y} f(y) = 1 \tag{9.207}$$

and $f(y)$ is a positive function of y. Since the n events constituting the sequence u assigned to a particular message are selected independently at random with the same probability $P(x)$, it follows from Eqs. 9.105, 9.106, and 9.206 that the random variable $D(uv)$ defined by Eq. 9.111 is the sum of n statistically independent, equally distributed random variables

$$D(\xi_i \eta_i) \equiv D(xy) \equiv \ln \frac{f(y)}{P(y|x)} \quad ; \quad \xi_i = x\,, \; \eta_i = y \tag{9.208}$$

An upper bound to the probability P_2 given by Eq. 9.116 can be obtained with the help of the theorem incorporating Eq. 8.39. For this purpose, let us identify the points xy of the product ensemble XY with the points a of the ensemble A of the theorem, the probability distribution $P(x, y) = P(x) P(y|x)$ with the probability distribution $P(a)$, the random variable $D(xy)$ with the random variable $\phi(a)$, and D_0 with $n\phi$. We obtain then

$$P_2 \leq e^{-n[s\gamma'(s)-\gamma(s)]} \quad ; \quad 0 \leq s \tag{9.209}$$

where

$$\gamma(s) \equiv \ln \sum_{XY} e^{s\,D(xy)} P(x) P(y|x) = \ln \sum_{XY} P(x) P(y|x)^{1-s} f(y)^{s} \tag{9.210}$$

$$\gamma'(s) \equiv \sum_{XY} Q(x, y) D(xy) = \sum_{XY} Q(x, y) \ln \frac{f(y)}{P(y|x)} = \frac{D_0}{n} \tag{9.211}$$

$$Q(x, y) \equiv \frac{e^{s\,D(xy)} P(x) P(y|x)}{\sum_{XY} e^{s\,D(xy)} P(x) P(y|x)} = \frac{P(x) P(y|x)^{1-s} f(y)^{s}}{\sum_{XY} P(x) P(y|x)^{1-s} f(y)^{s}} \tag{9.212}$$

An upper bound to the probability P_1 given by Eq. 9.115 can be obtained, in a similar manner, with the help of the theorem incorporating Eq. 8.51. For this purpose, let us identify the points xyx' of the product space XYX' with the points a of the ensemble A of the theorem, the probability distribution $P(x, y, x')$ with the probability distribution $P(a)$, the random variable $D(xy)$ with $\phi(a)$, the random variable $D(x'y) - D(xy)$ with the random variable $\theta(a)$, and D_0 with $n\phi$. Furthermore, since $D(u'v) - D(uv) \leq 0$, we have

$$D(x'y) - D(xy) \leq \gamma_t'(r, t) = 0 \tag{9.213}$$

where r has been substituted for s to avoid confusion with the parameter used in the upper bound to P_2. Then we obtain from Eq. 8.51, again substituting r for s,

$$P_1 \leq e^{-n[r\gamma_r'(r, t)+t\gamma_t'(r, t)-\gamma_0(r, t)]} \quad ; \quad r \leq 0 \, , \, t \leq 0 \tag{9.214}$$

$$\gamma_0(r,t) \equiv \ln \sum_{XYX'} e^{r\,D(xy)+t[D(x'y)-D(xy)]}\, P(x)\, P(y|x)\, P(x')$$

$$= \ln \sum_{XYX'} P(x)\, P(y|x)^{1-r+t}\, f(y)^{r}\, P(x')\, P(y|x')^{-t} \qquad (9.215)$$

$$\gamma_r'(r,t) = \sum_{XY} Q_0(x,y)\, D(xy) = \frac{D_0}{n} \qquad (9.216)$$

$$\gamma_t'(r,t) = \sum_{XYX'} Q_0(x,y,x')[D(x'y) - D(xy)] = 0 \qquad (9.217)$$

and, with the help of Eq. 8.44,

$$Q_0(x,y,x') \equiv \frac{e^{r\,D(xy)+t[D(x'y)-D(xy)]}\, P(x)\, P(y|x)\, P(x')}{\sum_{XYX'} e^{rD(xy)+t[D(x'y)-D(xy)]}\, P(x)\, P(y|x)\, P(x')} \qquad (9.218)$$

$$= \frac{P(x)\, P(y|x)^{1-r+t}\, f(y)^{r}\, P(x')\, P(y|x')^{-t}}{\sum_{XYX'} P(x)\, P(y|x)^{1-r+t}\, f(y)^{r}\, P(x')\, P(y|x')^{-t}}$$

$$Q_0(x,y) \equiv \sum_{X'} Q_0(x,y,x') \qquad (9.219)$$

The values of the two parameters r and t must satisfy Eqs. 9.216 and 9.217. Clearly, Eq. 9.217 is satisfied if the tilted probability distribution $Q_0(x,y,x')$, is a symmetrical function of x and x'. Such a symmetry can be achieved by setting

$$1 - r + t = -t \qquad (9.220)$$

from which we obtain, in view of the condition on r in Eq. 9.214,

$$r = 1 + 2t \quad ; \quad t \leq -\tfrac{1}{2} \qquad (9.221)$$

Then substituting for r the value given by this equation yields

$$Q_0(x, y, x') = \frac{P(x)\, P(y|x)^{-t}\, f(y)^{1+2t}\, P(x')\, P(y|x')^{-t}}{\sum_{XYX'} P(x)\, P(y|x)^{-t}\, f(y)^{1+2t}\, P(x')\, P(y|x')^{-t}} \tag{9.222}$$

The value of t must satisfy Eq. 9.216. Although the value of D_0 has not yet been fixed, this value also appears in Eq. 9.211, which must be satisfied by the parameter s on which the exponent in Eq. 9.209 depends. These conditions expressed by Eqs. 9.211 and 9.216 imply that

$$\gamma'(s) = \gamma_r'(r, t) \tag{9.223}$$

which can be satisfied by requiring that

$$Q(x, y) = Q_0(x, y) \tag{9.224}$$

that is,

$$\frac{P(x)\, P(y|x)^{1-s}\, f(y)^{s}}{\sum_{XY} P(x)\, P(y|x)^{1-s}\, f(y)^{s}} = \frac{P(x)\, P(y|x)^{-t}\, f(y)^{1+2t} \sum_{X'} P(x')\, P(y|x')^{-t}}{\sum_{XY} P(x)\, P(y|x)^{-t}\, f(y)^{1+2t} \sum_{X'} P(x')\, P(y|x')^{-t}} \tag{9.225}$$

Let

$$1 - s = -t \tag{9.226}$$

which implies, in view of the conditions on s and t in Eqs. 9.209 and 9.221, that

$$t = s - 1 \quad ; \quad 0 \leq s \leq \tfrac{1}{2} \tag{9.227}$$

Then Eq. 9.225 can be satisfied by setting

$$K\, f(y)^{s} = f(y)^{1+2t} \sum_{X'} P(x')P(y|x')^{-t} \tag{9.228}$$

that is,

$$K\, f(y)^{1-s} = \sum_{X'} P(x')\, P(y|x')^{1-s} = \sum_{X} P(x)\, P(y|x)^{1-s} \tag{9.229}$$

where K is a normalizing factor to be determined with the help of Eq. 9.207. Thus the arbitrary function f(y) must be

$$f(y) = \frac{\left[\sum_X P(x)\, P(y|x)^{1-s}\right]^{1/(1-s)}}{\sum_Y \left[\sum_X P(x)\, P(y|x)^{1-s}\right]^{1/(1-s)}} \qquad (9.230)$$

Also, multiplying both sides of Eq. 9.229 by $f(y)^s$ and adding over Y yields, with the help of Eq. 9.210,

$$K = \sum_{XY} P(x)\, P(y|x)^{1-s} f(y)^s = e^{\gamma(s)} = \left\{\sum_Y \left[\sum_X P(x)\, P(y|x)^{1-s}\right]^{1/1-s}\right\}^{1-s} \qquad (9.231)$$

We are now in a position to evaluate the final expressions for the tilted probability distributions. We obtain from Eq. 9.212, with the help of Eqs. 9.207 and 9.229,

$$Q(y) = \sum_X Q(x, y) = \frac{Kf(y)}{\sum_Y Kf(y)} = f(y) \qquad (9.232)$$

and therefore

$$Q(x|y) = \frac{Q(x, y)}{Q(y)} = \frac{P(x)\, P(y|x)^{1-s}}{K\, f(y)^{1-s}} = \frac{P(x)\, P(y|x)^{1-s}}{\sum_X P(x)\, P(y|x)^{1-s}} \qquad (9.233)$$

These two equations coincide with Eqs. 9.199 and 9.200 in the statement of the theorem. Finally, we obtain from Eqs. 9.222 and 9.215 with the help of Eqs. 9.210, 9.226, 9.229, 9.232, and 9.233,

$$Q_0(x, y, x') = Q(y)\, Q(x|y)\, Q(x'|y) \qquad (9.234)$$

$$\gamma_0(r, t) = 2\gamma(s)\ ; \qquad s = 1 + t = \frac{1+r}{2} \qquad (9.235)$$

and, with the help of Eqs. 9.217 and 9.223,

$$r\gamma_r'(r, t) + t\gamma_t'(r, t) - \gamma_0(r, t) = [s\gamma'(s) - \gamma(s)] + [(s-1)\gamma'(s) - \gamma(s)] \qquad (9.236)$$

This is the exponential coefficient in Eq. 9.214. We are now ready to substitute the righthand sides of Eqs. 9.209 and 9.214 in Eq. 9.114.

Let

$$R \equiv \frac{\ln M}{n} \text{ nats/event} \tag{9.237}$$

be the transmission rate per event. We obtain, with the help of Eq. 9.236,

$$\overline{P}(e) \leq e^{-n\{[s\gamma'(s)-\gamma(s)]+[(s-1)\gamma'(s)-\gamma(s)]-R\}} + e^{-n[s\gamma'(s)-\gamma(s)]}; \quad 0 \leq s \leq \tfrac{1}{2} \tag{9.238}$$

where

$$\gamma(s) \equiv \ln \sum_{XY} P(x)\, P(y|x)^{1-s}\, Q(y)^{s} \tag{9.239}$$

$$\gamma'(s) \equiv \left[\frac{\partial \gamma(s)}{\partial s}\right]_{Q(y) = \text{const.}} = \sum_{XY} Q(x, y) \ln \frac{Q(y)}{P(y|x)} \tag{9.240}$$

This equation is valid for all values of s in the range $0 \leq s \leq \frac{1}{2}$, so that we are free to use the value of s in this range which minimizes its righthand side. Let us consider, in this regard, the behavior of the two exponential coefficients as functions of s. The quantity $\gamma(s)$ depends on s through $Q(y)$ as well as directly. On the other hand, we shall show below on p. 332 that

$$\left.\begin{aligned} \gamma'(s) &\equiv \left[\frac{\partial \gamma(s)}{\partial s}\right]_{Q(y) = \text{const.}} = \frac{d\gamma(s)}{ds} \\ \gamma''(s) &\equiv \frac{d^2\gamma(s)}{ds^2} \geq \left[\frac{d^2\gamma(s)}{ds^2}\right]_{Q(y) = \text{const.}} \geq 0 \quad ; \quad 0 \leq s < 1 \end{aligned}\right\} \tag{9.241}$$

Thus,

$$\frac{d}{ds}\{[s\gamma'(s) - \gamma(s)] + [(s-1)\gamma'(s) - \gamma(s)]\} = (2s-1)\gamma''(s) \leq 0 \quad ; \quad 0 \leq s \leq \tfrac{1}{2} \tag{9.242}$$

$$\left.\begin{aligned} \frac{d}{ds}[s\gamma'(s) - \gamma(s)] &= s\gamma''(s) \geq 0 \\ \frac{d}{ds}[(s-1)\gamma'(s) - \gamma(s)] &= (s-1)\gamma''(s) \leq 0 \end{aligned}\right\}; \quad 0 \leq s < 1 \tag{9.243}$$

Since the two exponential coefficients in Eq. 9.238 vary monotonically with s in opposite directions, the righthand side of the equation is approximately minimized by the value of s for which

$$R = (s - 1)\,\gamma'(s) - \gamma(s) \quad ; \quad 0 \leq s \leq \tfrac{1}{2} \tag{9.244}$$

Furthermore, we obtain, with the help of Eqs. 9.212, 9.232, 9.233, 9.239 and 9.240,

$$R = (s - 1)\,\gamma'(s) - \gamma(s) = \sum_{XY} Q(x, y) \ln \frac{Q(x|y)}{P(x)} \tag{9.245}$$

$$a = s\gamma'(s) - \gamma(s) = \sum_{XY} Q(x, y) \ln \frac{Q(x, y)}{P(x, y)} \tag{9.246}$$

Then substituting the righthand sides of Eqs. 9.245 and 9.246 in Eq. 9.238 yields the upper part of Eq. 9.201 in the statement of the theorem. A proof that $R \geq 0$ and $a \geq 0$ can be readily obtained with the help of Eq. 2.91.

The lower part of Eq. 9.201 can be obtained as follows. We observe, first of all, that the exponential coefficient of the first term on the righthand side of Eq. 9.238 reaches its maximum value, for a fixed R, when $s = \frac{1}{2}$, as indicated by Eq. 9.242. Next we note that the restriction $s \leq \frac{1}{2}$ originates from the restriction $r \leq 0$ in Eq. 9.214. Both of these facts imply that P_1, defined by Eq. 9.115, increases only slightly when D_0 is increased beyond the value given by Eq. 9.216 for $r = 0$. Thus for $D_0 \geq n\gamma_r'(0, -\frac{1}{2})$, we can set $D_0 = \infty$ without unduly degrading our upper-bound estimate of $\overline{P}(e)$. This is equivalent to setting

$$P_1 = \Pr[D(u'v) \leq D(uv)] \quad ; \quad P_2 = 0 \tag{9.247}$$

The evaluation of P_1 under these conditions proceeds as before, except for setting $r = 0$ in Eqs. 9.215 and 9.218. Then $f(y)$ disappears from these two equations, and the requirement imposed by Eq. 9.217 is satisfied for $t = -\frac{1}{2}$. It follows that,

$$P_1 \leq e^{n\gamma_0(0, -\frac{1}{2})} \tag{9.248}$$

where

$$\gamma_0(0, -\tfrac{1}{2}) = \ln \sum_{Y} \left[\sum_{X} P(x) \sqrt{P(y|x)} \right]^2 \tag{9.249}$$

and, with the help of Eqs. 9.235, 9.245, and 9.246,

$$\gamma_0(0, -\tfrac{1}{2}) = 2\gamma(\tfrac{1}{2}) = -[a_c + R_c] \tag{9.250}$$

Finally, substituting the righthand side of Eq. 9.248 and $P_2 = 0$ in Eq. 9.114 yields the lower part of Eq. 9.201 in the statement of the theorem.

QED

9.8. Optimization of Input Probability Distribution

The upper bound to the average probability of error given by Eq. 9.201 depends on n and the exponential coefficient

$$a_U \equiv \begin{cases} a \equiv s\gamma'(s) - \gamma(s) & ; \quad R_c \le R \le I(X;Y) \\ a_c + R_c - R = -2\gamma(\tfrac{1}{2}) - R ; & 0 \le R \le R_c \end{cases} \tag{9.251}$$

where the value of s, for $0 \le s \le \frac{1}{2}$, is given by

$$R = (s-1)\,\gamma'(s) - \gamma(s) \quad ; \quad R_c \le R \le I(X;Y) \tag{9.252}$$

and

$$R_c = -\tfrac{1}{2}\gamma'(\tfrac{1}{2}) - \gamma(\tfrac{1}{2}) \quad ; \quad I(X;Y) = \sum_{XY} P(x)\,P(y|x)\ln\frac{P(y|x)}{P(y)} \tag{9.253}$$

The behavior of a_U as a function of R can be investigated by evaluating the derivatives of these quantities with respect to s with the help of the following theorem.

Theorem. The function $\gamma(s)$ has the following properties:

$$\gamma'(s) \equiv \left[\frac{\partial\gamma(s)}{\partial s}\right]_{Q(y)\,=\,\text{const.}} = \frac{d\gamma(s)}{ds} \tag{9.254}$$

$$\left.\begin{aligned} \gamma''(s) \equiv \frac{d^2\gamma(s)}{ds^2} &= \left[\frac{\partial^2\gamma(s)}{\partial s^2}\right]_{Q(y)\,=\,\text{const.}} + s(1-s)\sum_{Y} Q(y)\left[\frac{d\ln Q(y)}{ds}\right]^2 \\ &\ge 0 \quad ; \quad 0 \le s < 1 \\ \left[\frac{\partial^2\gamma(s)}{\partial s^2}\right]_{Q(y)\,=\,\text{const.}} &= \sum_{XY} Q(x,y)\left[D(xy) - \sum_{XY} Q(x,y)\,D(xy)\right]^2 \ge 0 \end{aligned}\right\} \tag{9.255}$$

where D(xy) is defined by Eqs. 9.208 and 9.232.

Proof. We observe from Eq. 9.239 that $\gamma(s)$ is a function of s and of the variables Q(y), each of which is in turn a function of s. Indicating with $Q'_s(y)$ the derivative of Q(y) with respect to s, we have,

$$\frac{d\gamma(s)}{ds} = \frac{\partial\gamma(s)}{\partial s} + \sum_{Y} Q'_s(y)\,\frac{\partial\gamma(s)}{\partial Q(y)}$$

On the other hand, differentiating $\gamma(s)$ with respect to Q(y) yields, with the help of Eqs. 9.229, 9.231, and 9.232,

$$\frac{\partial \gamma(s)}{\partial Q(y)} = s \sum_X e^{-\gamma(s)} P(x)\, P(y|x)^{1-s}\, Q(y)^{s-1} = s \qquad (9.256)$$

$$\sum_Y Q_s'(y) \frac{\partial \gamma(s)}{\partial Q(y)} = s \frac{d}{ds} \sum_Y Q(y) = 0 \qquad (9.257)$$

We have for the second total derivative

$$\frac{d^2\gamma(s)}{ds^2} = \frac{\partial^2\gamma(s)}{\partial s^2} + 2\sum_Y Q_s'(y) \frac{\partial^2\gamma(s)}{\partial s \partial Q(y)} + \sum_{YY^*} Q_s'(y)\, Q_s'(y^*) \frac{\partial^2 \gamma(s)}{\partial Q(y)\, \partial Q(y^*)}$$

However, in view of Eq. 9.254,

$$\frac{d^2\gamma(s)}{ds^2} = \frac{d}{ds}\frac{\partial\gamma(s)}{\partial s} = \frac{\partial^2\gamma(s)}{\partial s^2} + \sum_Y Q_s'(y) \frac{\partial^2\gamma(s)}{\partial s\, \partial Q(y)} \qquad (9.258)$$

so that

$$\sum_Y Q_s'(y) \frac{\partial^2\gamma(s)}{\partial s \partial Q(y)} = - \sum_{YY^*} Q_s'(y)\, Q_s'(y^*) \frac{\partial^2\gamma(s)}{\partial Q(y)\, \partial Q(y^*)} \qquad (9.259)$$

The righthand side of this equation is then evaluated with the help of Eqs. 9.229, 9.231, and 9.232, and substituted for the last term on the righthand side of Eq. 9.258. The first part of Eq. 9.255 follows after rearrangement and cancellation of terms. The second part of the same equation is readily obtained by differentiating Eq. 9.210.

QED

We have, with the help of this theorem,

$$\left.\begin{aligned} \frac{da}{ds} &= s\gamma''(s) \geq 0 \\ \frac{dR}{ds} &= (s-1)\,\gamma''(s) \leq 0 \end{aligned}\right\} ; \quad 0 \leq s \leq \tfrac{1}{2} \qquad (9.260)$$

where $\gamma''(s)$ is given by Eq. 9.255 and

$$\left.\begin{aligned} \frac{da}{dR} &= \frac{da/ds}{dR/ds} = -\frac{s}{1-s} \leq 0 \\ \frac{d^2a}{dR^2} &= \left[\frac{d}{ds}\frac{da}{dR}\right] \Big/ \frac{dR}{ds} = \frac{1}{(1-s)^3\,\gamma''(s)} \geq 0 \end{aligned}\right\} ; \; 0 \leq s \leq \tfrac{1}{2} \qquad (9.261)$$

A typical relation between a_U and R is illustrated in Fig. 9.5. The slope of the curve vanishes together with a_U for $s = 0$, $R = I(X; Y)$. Its magnitude increases with s and becomes unity for $s = \frac{1}{2}$, corresponding to $R = R_c$. The magnitude of the slope remains equal to unity for $0 \leq R \leq R_c$. The end point at $R = 0$ is, with the help of Eqs. 9.249 and 9.250,

$$[a_U]_{R=0} = a_c + R_c = -2\gamma(\tfrac{1}{2}) = -\ln \sum_Y \left[\sum_X P(x)\sqrt{P(y|x)}\right]^2 \qquad (9.262)$$

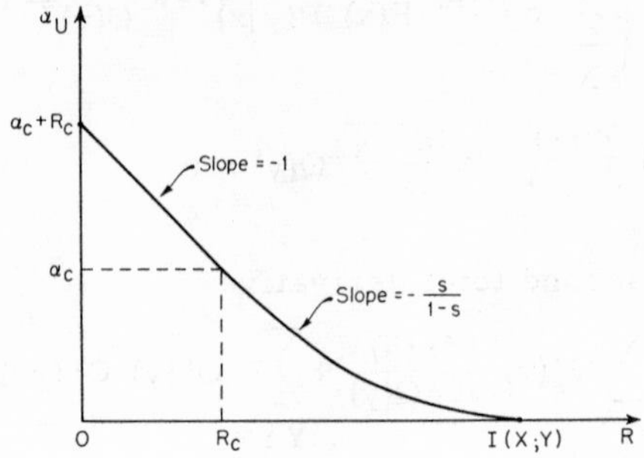

Fig. 9.5. Typical relation between α_U and R

Next let us turn our attention to the optimization of the input-probability distribution P(x) . We wish to maximize α_U with respect to P(x) for any fixed value of R . We shall use for this purpose the same argument employed in Sec. 9.4, in conjunction with the theorem incorporating Eq. 9.86. The optimum relation between α_U and R is the upper envelope of the curves for all possible probability distributions P(x) . Then since the derivative of α_U with respect to R depends only on s , the tangents to the curves corresponding to different P(x) are all parallel for any given value of s . Thus if we indicate with R_0 the intercept of any such tangent with the R-axis, the optimum P(x) for any particular value of s is the one which maximizes R_0 .

Theorem. The value of the intercept R_0 is maximized by the probability distribution $P_m(x)$ for which

$$\left.\begin{aligned} &\sum_Y P(y|x_k)^{1-s}\, Q(y)^s = g_m(s) \quad ; \quad 0 < s \le \tfrac{1}{2} \\ &\sum_Y P(y|x_k) \ln \frac{P(y)}{P(y|x_k)} = \gamma_m'(0) \quad ; \quad s = 0 \end{aligned}\right\} k = 1, 2, \ldots, K \tag{9.263}$$

for all x_k for which $P_m(x_k) \neq 0$, where

$$g_m(s) = \sum_{XY} P(x)\, P(y|x)^{1-s}\, Q(y)^s = e^{\gamma_m(s)} \tag{9.264}$$

and $\gamma_m(s)$ is the value assumed by $\gamma(s)$ for $P(x) = P_m(x)$

Proof. We have for the intercept R_0 , with the help of Eq. 9.261,

$$R_0 = R + \frac{1-s}{s}\alpha = -\frac{1}{s}\gamma(s) \tag{9.265}$$

Thus for $s \neq 0$, we must minimize $\gamma(s)$ with respect to $P(x)$, under the constraint $\sum_X P(x) = 1$. Following Lagrange's procedure, $\gamma(s)$ is stationary with respect to variations of $P(x)$ when

$$\frac{\partial}{\partial P(x_k)}\left[\gamma(s) + \lambda \sum_X P(x)\right] = \frac{\partial \gamma(s)}{\partial P(x_k)} + \lambda = 0 \ ; \quad k = 1, 2, \ldots, K \tag{9.266}$$

where λ is independent of k. We observe, on the other hand, that $\gamma(s)$ depends on $P(x_k)$ through $Q(y)$ as well as directly. Thus we obtain from Eq. 9.239, with the help of Eq. 9.256,

$$\frac{\partial \gamma(s)}{\partial P(x_k)} = \frac{1}{g_m(s)} \sum_Y P(y|x_k)^{1-s}\, Q(y)^s + s \frac{\partial}{\partial P(x_k)} \sum_Y Q(y)$$

$$= \frac{1}{g_m(s)} \sum_Y P(y|x_k)^{1-s}\, Q(y)^s \tag{9.267}$$

where $g_m(s)$ is given by Eq. 9.264. Then substituting the righthand side of this equation in Eq. 9.266 yields

$$\sum_Y P(y|x_k)^{1-s}\, Q(y)^s = -\lambda\, g_m(s) \ ; \quad 0 < s \leq \tfrac{1}{2} \tag{9.268}$$

Finally, multiplying both sides of this equation by $P_m(x)$ and adding over X yields $\lambda = -1$, and Eq. 9.268 coincides with the upper part of Eq. 9.263 in the statement of the theorem.

In the special case of $s = 0$, we must minimize the limit of $\gamma(s)/s$ when s approaches zero. We obtain

$$\frac{\partial}{\partial P(x_k)} \lim_{s \to 0} \frac{\gamma(s)}{s} = \frac{\partial \gamma'(0)}{\partial P(x_k)} = \frac{\partial}{\partial P(x_k)} \sum_{XY} P(x)\, P(y|x) \ln \frac{P(y)}{P(y|x)}$$

$$= \sum_Y P(y|x_k) \ln \frac{P(y)}{P(y|x_k)} = -\lambda \tag{9.269}$$

Then, multiplying both sides of this equation by $P_m(x)$ and adding over X yields $-\lambda = \gamma'_m(0)$, so that Eq. 9.269 becomes identical to the lower part of Eq. 9.263.

It remains to show that the probability distribution $P_m(x)$ that satisfies Eq. 9.263 corresponds to a maximum of R_0. We observe for this purpose that if $P(x)$ vanishes for all input letters except x_h, $Q(y) = P(y|x_h)$, $Q(x_h|y) = 1$, and $Q(x_k|y) = 0$ for $k \neq h$. Under these conditions both R and α vanish, as evident from Eqs. 9.245 and 9.246, and therefore R_0 vanishes. It follows that if there is only one probability distribution $P(x)$ that satisfies Eq. 9.263, it must correspond to a maximum of R_0. If there are several distributions that satisfy Eq. 9.263, the one corresponding to the largest value of R_0 must be selected.

QED

For $s = 0$, Eq. 9.263 is the same as the condition, given by Eq. 5.60, that must be satisfied by the input-probability distribution corresponding to channel capacity. For $0 < s \leq \frac{1}{2}$, we obtain from Eqs. 9.229, 9.231, 9.232, and 9.263,

$$\sum_{X} P_m(x)\, P(y_j|x)^{1-s} = g_m(s)\, Q(y_j)^{1-s} \quad ; \quad j = 1, 2, \ldots, L \tag{9.270}$$

$$\sum_{Y} P(y|x_k)^{1-s}\, Q(y)^{s} = g_m(s) \quad ; \quad k = 1, 2, \ldots, K \tag{9.271}$$

These two conditions form a set of $L + K$ equations in K variables $P_m(x)$ and L variables $Q(y_j)$, which are identical to the set formed by Eqs. 9.96 and 9.97 for fixed-composition codes. Furthermore, we have, with the help of Eq. 9.271,

$$Q(x) = \sum_{Y} Q(x, y) = \sum_{Y} \frac{P_m(x)\, P(y|x)^{1-s}\, Q(y)^{s}}{g_m(s)} = P_m(x) \tag{9.272}$$

so that

$$Q(y|x) = \frac{P(y|x)^{1-s}\, Q(y)^{s}}{\sum_{Y} P(y|x)^{1-s}\, Q(y)^{s}} \tag{9.273}$$

which coincides with the definition of $Q(y|x)$, given by Eq. 9.23, for fixed-composition codes. Then with the help of Eqs. 9.272 and 9.273, we obtain for the optimum α and R from Eqs. 9.245 and 9.246

$$\alpha_m = \sum_{XY} P_m(x)\, Q(y|x) \ln \frac{Q(y|x)}{P(y|x)} \tag{9.274}$$

$$R_m = \sum_{XY} P_m(x)\, Q(y|x) \ln \frac{Q(y|x)}{Q(y)} \tag{9.275}$$

which coincide with the corresponding quantities for fixed-composition codes, given by Eqs. 9.137 and 9.138, with $P_m(x)$ substituted for $P(x)$. Thus we have proved the following important theorem.

> Theorem. The optimum relation between the exponential coefficient α_U in the upper-bound estimate of the average probability of error and the transmission rate R is the same regardless of whether the input sequences assigned to messages are selected at random from those having the composition $P_m(x)$ or are constructed by selecting their letters independently at random with probability $P_m(x)$.

It must be stressed, however, that this theorem applies only to the optimum relation between α_U and R . In general, if $P(x)$ is not optimum, the coefficient α_U for fixed-composition codes is greater than that for codes constructed by selecting the input-sequence letters at random with probability $P(x)$. This follows from the fact that the two coefficients are different and the one corresponding to fixed-composition codes always coincides with the exponential coefficient in the lower bound to the probability of error.

In view of the above theorem, no further discussion is required of the optimum relation between α_U and R .

9.9. Summary and Conclusions

We have discussed in this final chapter the encoding and decoding of messages for transmission through discrete, constant channels. We began by evaluating a lower bound to the probability of error when the input sequences assigned to messages have the same composition. This lower bound was found to be of the form

$$P(e) \geq e^{-(\beta+n\alpha)} \tag{9.276}$$

for any transmission rate

$$R \geq \frac{\beta}{n} + I \tag{9.277}$$

where β is a slowly varying function of n , and α and I are independent of n . Thus the bound could be described asymptotically in terms of the functional relation between α and I , in the range in which these two quantities are positive.

Next the composition was optimized to yield the smallest lower bound to the probability of error for any given transmission rate. We found that the optimum composition is that for which the moment-generating function of the random variable $\ln [Q(y)/P(y|x_k)]$ is the same for all input letters x_k. This condition led to a set of $K + L$ equations in the K variables describing the input-sequence composition and the L variables $Q(y)$ describing the tilted output probability distribution. These equations are similar to those obtained in Chapter 5 in connection with the evaluation of the channel capacity, and actually become identical to them when the transmission rate coincides with the channel capacity. The curve marked "lower-bound" in Fig. 9.6 illustrates a typical

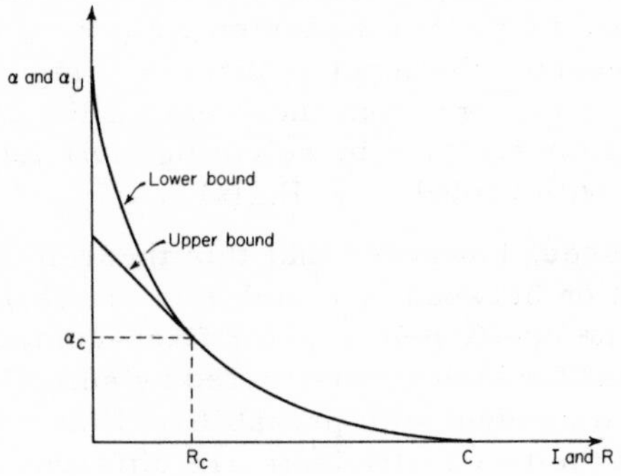

Fig. 9.6. Optimum asymptotic behavior of upper and lower bounds to the probability of error

optimum relation between α and I. The end point C is the capacity of the channel, and the corresponding optimum composition coincides with the input probability distribution for which the average mutual information between input and output letters becomes equal to C.

For the lower-bound curve of Fig. 9.6 the exponential coefficient becomes infinite when I approaches zero. There are channels, however, for which α becomes infinite for a positive value of I. Such channels are characterized by the fact that no output letter can result from all input letters with non-zero probability. The value of I for which the optimum α becomes infinite coincides with the upper bound to the zero-error capacity obtained by Shannon.

Next we evaluated an upper bound to the average probability of error when the input sequences assigned to messages are selected independently and equiprobably from those having a specified composition. This upper bound was found to be of the form

$$\overline{P}(e) \leq A\, e^{-n\alpha_U} \tag{9.278}$$

where A is a slowly varying function of n , and α_U is independent of n and a function of the transmission rate R . For R larger than a critical value R_c , depending on the channel and on the input-sequence composition, the relation between α_U and R is identical to the relation between the quantities α and I associated with the lower bound. Thus over this range of transmission rates, the upper bound and the lower bound have the same asymptotic behavior. For transmission rates smaller than R_c , $\alpha_U - \alpha_c = R_c - R$, where α_c is the critical value of α corresponding to R_c . Therefore, the upper and lower bounds diverge exponentially for $R \leq R_c$. The optimum relation between α_U and R is illustrated in Fig. 9.6 by the curve marked "upper bound." The slope of the straight-line part is equal to -1 .

The last topic discussed in the chapter concerned the effect on the average probability of error of relaxing the constraint on the input sequences assigned to messages from strictly fixed composition to independent selection of the sequence letters according to a prescribed probability distribution. The upper bound to the average probability of error for the latter type of random encoding was found to be also of the form given by Eq. 9.278. The value of α_U is, in general, smaller than that obtained with fixed-composition encoding for the same transmission rate, and composition formally identical to the selection probability distribution. But the optimum values of α_U for any given $R < C$ turn out to be identical in the two cases. In the special case of channels that are uniform from both the input and the output, the optimum input-sequence composition is uniform for all transmission rates, and so is the optimum probability distribution to be employed in the random construction of the input sequences.

The bounds to the probability of error obtained in this chapter provide a proof that it is possible to transmit through a discrete, constant channel at any rate smaller than the channel capacity with an arbitrarily small probability of error. Although no general procedure is known for constructing codes with this property, the random assignment of input sequences to messages envisioned in the derivation of the upper bounds can be successfully employed in practice. In other words, the construction of satisfactory codes does not constitute a serious problem in practice. Instead, the instrumentation of the encoding and decoding operations is the major limitation to the development of communication systems that are both accurate and efficient.

The class of channels discussed in this chapter provides a satisfactory model for many physical communication channels. Channel models including memory are required, however, to represent dispersive physical channels and channels disturbed by noise with appreciable dependence on its own past. While results as sharp as those presented in this chapter are not available for channels with memory and would be very difficult to obtain, much can be done in practice in connection with such channels through judicious heuristic extrapolation of results derived for constant channels. Judicious heuristic extrapolations are often the main bridge linking theory to engineering practice.

In closing this last chapter, the author would like to express his personal belief that communication engineering is at the threshold of a major technical revolution. Much remains to be done before the transmission performance that has been proved to be possible in principle becomes a widespread practical reality, but the road in this direction seems clear of major stumbling blocks. The main requirement for fast progress is imaginative experimental work based on a deep appreciation of the theoretical foundations already established.

9.10. Selected References

1. C. E. Shannon, "A Mathematical Theory of Communication," Bell System Tech. J., 27, 379, 623 (1948).
2. C. E. Shannon, "Communication in the Presence of Noise," Proc. I. R. E., 37, 10 (1949).
3. A. Feinstein, "A New Basic Theorem of Information Theory," I. R. E. Trans. I. T. - 4, 2 (1954).
4. C. E. Shannon, "Certain Results in Coding Theory for Noisy Channels," Information and Control, 1, 6 (1957).
5. C. E. Shannon, "Two-Way Communication Channels," Proc. of the Fourth Berkeley Symposium on Mathematical Statistics and Probability (to be published).
6. C. E. Shannon, "Probability of Error for Optimal Codes in a Gaussian Channel," Bell System Tech. J., 38, 611 (1959).
7. J. L. Kelly, "A Class of Codes for Signaling on a Noisy Continuous Channel," I. R. E. Trans. I. T.-6, 22 (1960).
8. C. E. Shannon, "Zero-Error Capacity of Noisy Channels," I. R. E. Trans. I. T.-2, 8 (1956).

APPENDIXES

Appendix A

PROBLEMS

Problems for Chapter 1

1.1. The messages u_0, u_1, u_2, u_3 occur with probabilities 1/2, 1/4, 1/8, 1/8, and are represented for transmission purposes by the four binary codewords 00, 01, 10, 11. Indicating with x the first digit of these codewords, and with y the second digit, find

a. the probability of $x = 1$.

b. the conditional probability of $y = 0$ given $x = 1$, and of $y = 0$ given $x = 0$.

c. the conditional probability of u_2 given $x = 1$.

1.2. The messages u_0, u_1, u_2, u_3 occur with probabilities 1/2, 1/4, 1/8, 1/8, and are represented for transmission purposes by the four binary codewords 0, 10, 110, 111.

a. Show that if successive messages are statistically independent, the digits 0 and 1 occur with equal probabilities in the resulting sequence of codewords, and that each digit in such a sequence is statistically independent of all others.

b. Find the average value (expectation) of the number of binary digits per message.

1.3. A physical channel disturbed by thermal-agitation noise can often be represented by the following model. The channel input events are voltage pulses of width T and amplitude x, and the channel output voltage is measured by an instrument which indicates its average value over each time interval T corresponding to an input pulse. The indication of the instrument is $y = x + z$, where the noise z is gaussianly distributed with zero mean and variance equal to N,

$$p(z) = \frac{1}{\sqrt{2\pi N}} e^{-z^2/2N}$$

If the input pulses have fixed magnitude $|x| = \sqrt{S}$, but either positive or negative polarity,

a. plot, as a function of S/N, the probability that the polarity of the output indication is opposite to that of the corresponding input pulse.

b. show that the probability of part (a) is equal to $\frac{1}{2} - \sqrt{\frac{S}{2\pi N}}$

for $\frac{S}{N} << 1$, and to $\sqrt{\frac{N}{2\pi S}}\ e^{-S/2N}$ for $\frac{S}{N} >> 1$.

c. find an expression for the conditional probability that the polarity of the input pulse is positive given any particular value of the output indication, when the a priori probability of a positive input polarity is q .

1.4. Two identical channels, representable by the model described in Problem 1.3, are connected in cascade in such a way that $x' = y\sqrt{\frac{S}{S+N}}$ where x' is the amplitude of the input pulse of the second channel and y is the output indication of the first channel. If the input pulse of the first channel has fixed magnitude $|x| = \sqrt{S}$, but either positive or negative polarity, find expressions for the probability that the polarity of the output indication of the second channel is different from that of the input pulse of the first channel for $\frac{S}{N} << 1$ and $\frac{S}{N} >> 1$.

1.5. Repeat Problem 1.4 when the two channels are cascaded in such a way that $x' = \sqrt{S}\,\frac{y}{|y|}$. Show that if only the polarities of the input pulses and of the output indications are of interest, the two individual channels and their cascade combination are equivalent to binary symmetric channels.

Problems for Chapter 2

2.1. Consider the message ensemble shown in Fig. 1.2. Message 3 is fed to the encoder. Evaluate the additional information provided about it by each of the successive digits output from the encoder when

a. the code words shown in the second column are used.

b. the code words shown in the fourth column are used.

2.2. An urn contains 5 black balls and 10 white balls. Three balls are selected at random from the urn without replacement, and the result of this experiment is transmitted through a communication system. Suppose that the balls selected are, in order, black, black, white.

a. What is the total amount of information to be transmitted if only the number of black balls and of white balls is of interest?

b. What is the total amount of information to be transmitted if also the order in which the balls are selected is of interest?

c. In case (b), if the color of the three balls is transmitted by means of three successive binary digits in order of selection, what is the information provided by the first, second, and third digit?

d. Repeat part (c) if it had been agreed that the colors were to be transmitted in order opposite to that of selection.

2.3. In a female population X, consisting of 1/4 blondes, 1/2 brunettes, and 1/4 redheads, blondes are always on time for engagements, redheads are always late, and each brunette always flips an unbiased coin for each engagement to decide whether to be prompt or tardy.

a. How much information is given by the statement "x, a member of X, arrived on time" about each of the following propositions?

i. x is a blonde

ii. x is a brunette

iii. x is a redhead

b. How much information is given by the statement "x, a member of X, arrived on time for three engagements in a row" about the proposition "x is a brunette?"

2.4. A binary communication system is disturbed by noise in such a way that each input digit has a probability p of being changed by the channel noise. Eight messages may be transmitted with equal probabilities; they are represented by the following code words:

$u_1 \equiv 0\ 0\ 0\ 0$	$u_5 \equiv 1\ 0\ 0\ 1$
$u_2 \equiv 0\ 0\ 1\ 1$	$u_6 \equiv 1\ 0\ 1\ 0$
$u_3 \equiv 0\ 1\ 0\ 1$	$u_7 \equiv 1\ 1\ 0\ 0$
$u_4 \equiv 0\ 1\ 1\ 0$	$u_8 \equiv 1\ 1\ 1\ 1$

If the sequence of digits $v \equiv 0\ 0\ 0\ 0$ is received, determine

a. the amount of information provided about u_1 by the first digit received.

b. the additional amounts of information about u_1 provided by the second digit received, the third digit, and the fourth digit.

2.5. In a mythical engineering college, the student body X has the following characteristics:

i. Half of the students are in the Electrical Engineering Department.

ii. One-quarter of the students are women, none of whom are in the Electrical Engineering Department.

iii. Two-thirds of the men in every department have crew cuts. None of the women in any department have crew cuts.

Given that x is a member of this student body,

a. how much additional information is given to you about the proposition "x has a crew cut" by the statement "x is not an Electrical Engineer?"

b. how would the answers to (a) change if the statement "x is not an Electrical Engineer" were replaced by the statement "x is an Electrical Engineer"?

2.6. A discrete channel has input letters x_1 , x_2 and output letters y_0 , y_1 , y_2 . The two input letters occur with equal probabilities and successive letters are statistically independent. The conditional probabilities $P(y|x)$ are given in the following table:

	y_0	y_1	y_2
x_1	1/32	61/64	1/64
x_2	1/32	1/64	61/64

a. Compute and plot the distribution function for the random variable $I(x; y)$.
b. Evaluate the expectation and the variance of $I(x; y)$.

2.7. A source generates statistically independent binary digits with probabilities 1/4 and 3/4. Find the expectation and variance of the self-information of a sequence of 100 binary digits.

2.8. The digits input to a binary symmetric channel are equiprobable and statistically independent. Each input digit has probability 1/10 of being changed by the channel noise. Find the expectation and the variance of the mutual information between a sequence of 100 input digits and the corresponding sequence of 100 output digits.

2.9. A discrete source generates in succession and independently letters belonging to a ternary alphabet. The three letters x_1 , x_2 , x_3 have, respectively, durations 1, 2, 3 seconds, and probabilities 6/11, 3/11, and 2/11. If the instantaneous self-information of the source is defined as the self-information of the letters it is generating divided by the duration of the letter,
a. plot the probability that the instantaneous self-information be equal to I at a time selected at random.
b. compute the average value of the self-information in bits per second.
c. supposing that it were possible to change the letter probabilities but not their durations, compute the maximum average value of the self-information in bits per second, and the corresponding letter probabilities.

2.10. Consider a check board with eight rows and eight columns represented respectively by the discrete variables x and y . Two objects, A and B , are located on the board, their positions being represented by x_A , y_A , x_B , y_B . A and B can occupy any two squares on the board with equal probability but cannot occupy the same square. Determine:

a. the average information provided by x_A and y_A about the position of A .
b. the average information provided by x_A and y_A about the position of B .
c. the average information provided by x_B and y_B about the position of B when the position of A is known.

If the two objects are indistinguishable, determine:

d. the average information provided about the positions of the two objects by the coordinates of either one of them.
e. the average amount of information provided by x_A , y_A , x_B , y_B about the positions of both objects.
f. suppose the values of x_A , x_B , y_A , y_B were given without reference to the corresponding subscripts; that is, suppose that the rows and columns occupied by the pair of objects were indicated without stating the correspondence between rows and columns, what would be the average amount of information provided by such indications about the positions of the two identical objects?

2.11. Consider a set of twelve boxes, each of which is occupied by an object with probability $p = 1/4$, and is empty with probability $q = 3/4$, independently of the other boxes. It is desired to determine which boxes are occupied and which are empty.

a. A measurement performed on the set of boxes indicates that four of the twelve boxes are occupied. How much information does this measurement provide on the average about the occupancy of the boxes?
b. Repeat part (a) if the measurement indicates only that the number of boxes is even.

2.12. Consider a discrete product ensemble XYZ characterized by a probability distribution $P(x, y, z)$. Show by means of suitable examples that the following inequalities are incorrect:

$$I(X; Y) \leq I(X; Y|Z) \quad ; \quad I(X; Y) \geq I(X; Y|Z)$$

2.13. Given a discrete probability distribution $P(x, y, z)$ over the product ensemble XYZ , show that

a. $I(XYZ) = I(XZ) + I(Y|X) - I(Z; Y|X)$
b. $I(X; Y|Z) - I(X; Y) = I(Y; Z|X) - I(Y; Z) = I(Z; X|Y) - I(Z; X)$

2.14. The entropy of a discrete ensemble is regarded as a measure of uncertainty. Substantiate this interpretation by proving that any change of the probabilities of the ensemble that amounts to increasing the probability of a member at the expense of the probability of a more probable member will increase the entropy of the ensemble.

2.15. Two discrete sets of symbols X and Y are related by a joint probability distribution $P(x, y)$. Consider the quantity

$$H(X) - H(X|y) .$$

Can this quantity be positive? Can it be negative? Interpret your answers in terms of a communication process.

2.16. The following three probability distributions are defined over the product space XY :

$$P_1(x) \quad ; \quad P_2(x) \quad ; \quad P_0(x) = \tfrac{1}{2}[P_1(x) + P_2(x)]$$

with $P(y|x)$ being the same for all three distributions. Labeling the corresponding entropies and mutual informations with the same subscripts, show that

$$H_0(Y) \geq \tfrac{1}{2}[H_1(Y) + H_2(Y)]$$

$$I_0(X;Y) \geq \tfrac{1}{2}[I_1(X;Y) + I_2(X;Y)]$$

2.17. Let Y be an ensemble consisting of L points y_j with probability distribution $P(y)$, and let

$$q_j = P(y_j) - P(y_{j+1}) \geq 0$$

Show that

$$H(Y) \geq \sum_{j=1}^{L} j\, q_j \log j$$

Hint: Consider the product ensemble XY consisting of L^2 pairs xy , and let

$$P(x_k) = k\, q_k \quad ; \quad P(y_j|x_k) = \begin{cases} 0 & ; \quad j > k \\ 1/k & ; \quad j \leq k \end{cases}$$

where k and j are positive integers in the ranges $1 \leq k \leq L$, $1 \leq j \leq L$.

2.18. The input of a channel over a time interval T is given by

$$u(t) = x_1 \cos \frac{2\pi m}{T} t + x_2 \sin \frac{2\pi m}{T} t \quad ; \quad 0 < t < T$$

where m is a positive integer. The coefficients x_1 and x_2 are gaussianly distributed with zero mean and variance equal to S and are statistically independent of each other. The channel output is a similar function of time

$$v(t) = y_1 \cos \frac{2\pi m}{T} t + y_2 \sin \frac{2\pi m}{T} t \quad ; \quad 0 < t < T$$

where

$$y_1 = x_1 + z_1 \quad , \quad y_2 = y_2 + z_2$$

and z_1 and z_2 are gaussianly distributed with zero mean and variance equal to N and are statistically independent of each other and of x_1 and x_2. Determine the average value of the mutual information between input and output time functions.

2.19. The input to a channel and the corresponding output are represented by the phases ϕ and θ of two sinusoidal time functions. The probability density of ϕ is uniform, and that of the phase difference $\theta - \phi$ is

$$p(\theta - \phi) = \frac{1}{\pi} \cos^2 \frac{\theta - \phi}{2} \; ; \quad -\pi \leq \theta - \phi \leq \pi$$

The phase difference $\theta - \phi$ is statistically independent of ϕ. Evaluate the average value of the mutual information between input and output phases.

2.20. Let x and y be random variables with joint probability density p(xy), assumed to be finite and continuous.

a. Prove that

$$I(X; Y) = \int_{-\infty}^{\infty} \int_{-\infty}^{\infty} p(x)\, p(y|x) \ln \frac{p(y|x)}{p(y)}\, dx\, dy \geq 0$$

b. Show, by means of a suitable example, that the inequality

$$H(X) = -\int_{-\infty}^{\infty} p(x) \ln p(x)\, dx \geq 0$$

is incorrect. Compare these results with the corresponding results for discrete ensembles, and explain their similarities and differences.

2.21. Consider two random variables x and y and their sum

$$z = x + y \; .$$

a. Show that if x and y are statistically independent, the entropies H(X), H(Y), H(Z) satisfy the inequalities

$$H(Z) \geq H(X) \quad ; \quad H(Z) \geq H(Y)$$

b. Show through an example that the above inequalities are not necessarily satisfied when x and y are not statistically independent.

Problems for Chapter 3

3.1. A number M of pennies are given of which M - 1 are known to have the same weight. The Mth penny may have the same weight as the others, may be heavier, or may be lighter. A scale is available on which two groups of pennies may be compared. It is desired to find the odd penny, if there is one, and to determine whether it is heavier or lighter than the others. Find the maximum value of M for which the problem may be solved with n weighing operations, and describe in detail the procedure required if:

a. a standard penny is available for comparison, in addition to the M pennies.

b. a standard penny is not available.

Suggestion: Consider the $2M + 1$ possible answers as forming a set of equiprobable alternatives, and assign to each alternative a code word representing the results of successive weighing operations.

3.2. A set of M messages $u_1, u_2, \ldots, u_M$ are to be encoded into binary digits. The message probabilities are given by

$$P(u_k) = 2^{-k}, \text{ for } 1 \le k \le M-1 \; ; \; P(u_M) = 2^{-(M-1)}$$

a. What is the minimum average number of digits per message?

b. What is the code efficiency corresponding to the answer of part (a)?

c. Indicate how the code words corresponding to the answer of part (a) might be constructed.

d. What is the limit of the value found in part (a) when M approaches infinity?

3.3. It is desired to construct an unambiguous set of seven code words consisting respectively of $n_1, n_2, \ldots, n_7$ binary digits.

a. What condition must be satisfied by the integers $n_1, n_2, \ldots, n_7$ in order for the desired set to be realizable?

b. Construct a set for $n_1 = n_2 = 2$, $n_3 = n_4 = n_5 = 3$, $n_6 = n_7 = 4$.

c. With what probabilities should the code words of part (b) be transmitted in order for the code efficiency to be a maximum? What is this maximum value?

3.4. Consider the following method [Ch. 3, Ref. 1] of constructing binary code words for a message ensemble U with probability distribution P(u). Let $P(u_k) \le P(u_j)$ for $k > j \ge 1$, and define

$$Q_i = \sum_{k=1}^{i-1} P(u_k) \text{ for } i > 1 \; ; \; Q_1 = 0$$

The code word assigned to message u_i is the number $Q_i < 1$, written in the binary number system, and approximated to the first n_i digits, where n_i is the integer equal to or just larger than $I(u_i)$.

a. Construct binary code words for a set of eight messages occurring with probabilities 1/4, 1/4, 1/8, 1/8, 1/16, 1/16, 1/16, 1/16.
b. State the conditions that must be satisfied by a set of code words in order to provide an unambiguous representation of the corresponding messages.
c. Prove that the method described above yields in all cases a set of code words satisfying the conditions of part (b), and whose average length $\overline{n}$ satisfies the inequality

$$H(U) \leq \overline{n} < H(U) + 1$$

3.5. Given an ensemble of eight messages with probabilities 1/2, 1/4, 1/8, 1/16, 1/64, 1/64, 1/64, 1/64, find three assignments of binary code words to messages for which, respectively,
a. the average code word length is minimized
b. the maximum code word length is minimized.
c. no code word length is larger than four, and the average code word length is minimized, subject to this constraint.

Compute the efficiency of the three sets of code words. For each set, draw the probability distribution of the code word length, and compute its mean value and its variance.

3.6. A source generates statistically independent letters with entropy equal to 2 bits per letter. It is desired to construct binary code words for all possible sequences of 10 letters.
a. Estimate the required average number of binary digits per letter in terms of upper and lower bounds.
b. Under what conditions can unity efficiency be obtained?

3.7. Find an optimum set of binary code words for a message ensemble with probability distribution $P(u_1) = 0.3$, $P(u_2) = 0.25$, $P(u_3) = 0.2$, $P(u_4) = 0.15$, $P(u_5) = 0.1$. Determine the amount of information provided about u_5 by each digit of the corresponding binary word. Compute the code efficiency for the optimum set of code words.

3.8. Consider an ensemble of messages with probabilities 0.3, 0.2, 0.2, 0.1, 0.1, 0.05, 0.05. Find two optimum sets of binary code words of lengths 2, 2, 2, 3, 4, 5, 5 and 2, 2, 3, 3, 3, 4, 4. Transform one set into the other by means of operations that do not change the average number of digits per message.

3.9. A source generates a sequence of statistically independent binary digits occurring with probabilities 1/3 and 2/3. Construct optimum ternary code words for messages consisting of three successive digits. Compute the resulting code efficiency. Can the coding tree be complete for a ternary alphabet when the messages are sequences of binary digits of the same length?

Problems for Chapter 4

4.1. A stochastic source generates a sequence of events $a_1, a_2, \ldots, a_i, \ldots$, each event being one of the four letter a_1, a_2, a_3, a_4 of the set A . The source is described by the following probability distributions:

$$P(a_i) = \frac{1}{4} \; ; \quad a_i = a_1, a_2, a_3, a_4$$

$P(a_i | a_{i-1}) =$

a_{i-1} \ a_i	a_1	a_2	a_3	a_4
a_1	1/2	1/4	1/8	1/8
a_2	1/4	1/8	1/8	1/2
a_3	1/8	1/8	1/2	1/4
a_4	1/8	1/2	1/4	1/8

$$P(a_i | a_{i-1}, a_{i-2}, \ldots, a_1) = P(a_i | a_{i-1})$$

a. Evaluate the entropies $H(A)$, $H(A|A^1)$, $H(A|A^2)$, $H(A|A^\infty)$.

b. Subdivide the sequence of events into messages consisting of two successive events, and construct optimum binary code words for the resulting ensemble of messages. Evaluate the resulting average number of binary digits per event, $\overline{n}$, and the corresponding code efficiency $H(A|A^\infty)/\overline{n}$.

c. For each letter of A , construct an optimum set of four code words representing the four possible letters following it in the sequence. Evaluate the resulting code efficiency.

4.2. Consider a stationary source of letters A, B, C, for which the probability of each letter depends only on the preceding letter. The probabilities of the possible ordered letter pairs are given by the following matrix, in which the rows correspond to the first letter and the columns to the second letter:

	A	B	C
A	0.2	0.05	0.15
B	0.15	0.05	0.1
C	0.05	0.2	0.05

It is desired to represent the source output by means of binary digits. Determine the optimum code words and the resulting code efficiency for the following encoding schemes:

a. The sequence is divided into successive pairs of letters and each pair is represented by a binary code word.

b. Each letter is represented by a binary word, but the set of words used depends on the preceding letter.
c. Each letter is represented by a binary word. Only one set of three words is used, but the correspondence between binary words and letters depends on the preceding letter.

4.3. A fixed-rate source generates statistically independent binary events A and B, with probabilities $P(A) = p < \frac{1}{2}$, $P(B) = 1 - p$. The source output is segmented into messages consisting of ν successive events, and each message is represented for transmission by a code word consisting of $n_\nu < \nu$ binary digits. The messages containing $k \leq r$ events A are represented by different code words, while one and the same code word is assigned to the remaining messages. Show that if

$$\frac{n_\nu}{\nu} \geq \frac{1}{\nu} \log_2 \left[1 + \sum_{k=0}^{r} \frac{\nu!}{k!(\nu-k)!} \right]$$

the probability of occurrence of an ambiguously encoded message satisfies the inequality

$$P_a \leq \sum_{k=r+1}^{\nu} \frac{\nu!}{k!(\nu-k)!} p^k (1-p)^{\nu-k}$$

4.4. Using the results of Sec. 7.1, show that the two inequalities of Problem 4.3 can be replaced by

$$\frac{n_\nu}{\nu} \geq \frac{1}{\nu} \left[1 + \log_2 \frac{1-\rho}{1-2\rho} - \tfrac{1}{2} \log_2 [2\pi\nu\rho(1-\rho)] \right] - [\rho \log_2 \rho + (1-\rho) \log_2 (1-\rho)]$$

$$P_a \leq \frac{p(1-\rho)}{\rho - p} \frac{1}{\sqrt{2\pi\nu\rho(1-\rho)}} 2^{-\nu\left[\rho \log_2 \frac{\rho}{p} + (1-\rho) \log_2 \frac{1-\rho}{1-p}\right]}$$

for $\rho \equiv \frac{r}{\nu}$ in the range $p < \rho < 1/2$. Conclude that for large values of ν, P_a approaches zero exponentially with increasing ν whenever n_ν/ν exceeds the source entropy per event.

4.5. A fixed-rate source generates statistically independent events belonging to a discrete ensemble A of letters $a_1, a_2, \ldots, a_L$ with probability distribution $P(a)$. The source output is segmented into messages consisting of ν successive events, and each message is represented for transmission by a code word consisting of n_ν binary digits. The messages whose self-information does not exceed some value $I > \nu H(A)$ are represented by different code words, while one and the same code word is assigned to the messages whose self-information exceeds I .

Using the results of Sec. 8. 3 (see also Problems 8. 4 and 8. 5) show that if

$$\frac{n_\nu}{\nu} \geq \frac{1}{\nu} - \sum_A Q(a) \log_2 Q(a) \geq H(A)$$

where

$$Q(a) = \frac{P(a)^{1-s}}{\sum_A P(a)^{1-s}} \quad ; \quad 0 \leq s \leq 1$$

the probability of occurrence of an ambiguously encoded message satisfies the inequality

$$P_a \leq 2^{-\nu\alpha}$$

where

$$\alpha = \sum_A Q(a) \log_2 \frac{Q(a)}{P(a)} \geq 0$$

4. 6. It is desired to re-encode more efficiently by means of binary digits the output of the Markov source illustrated here:

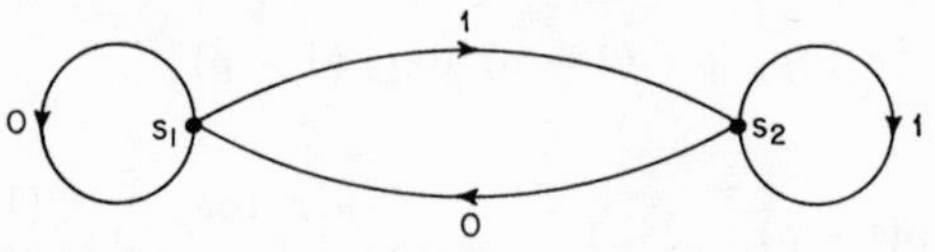

$P(0|s_1) = 0.8$ $P(0|s_2) = 0.6$

$P(1|s_1) = 0.2$ $P(1|s_2) = 0.4$

a. Find the stationary value of the entropy per digit for the source.
b. Construct the Markov diagram for pairs of digits.
c. Construct optimum binary code words for all pairs of digits, taking into account the state of the source, and evaluate the resulting code efficiency.

4.7. The state diagram of a Markov source and the letter probabilities for each state are given below. The initial state is s_0 .

	s_0	s_1	s_2	s_3	s_4
a_1	0.3	0.7	0.3	0.5	0.3
a_2	0	0.125	0.5	0.1	0.5
a_3	0.7	0.075	0	0.1	0
a_4	0	0.1	0.2	0.3	0.2

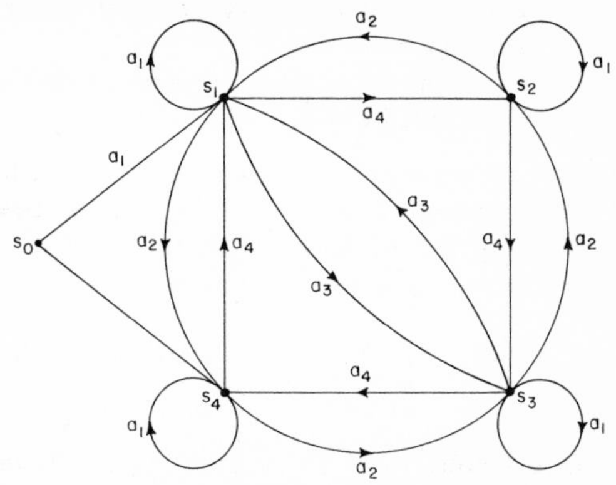

a. Show that the asymptotic state probabilities are $P(s_0) = 0$, $P(s_1) = 0.4$, $P(s_2) = 0.1$, $P(s_3) = 0.3$, $P(s_4) = 0.2$

b. Evaluate the source entropy per letter.

c. Construct an optimum set of four binary code words for each state, and evaluate the resulting code efficiency.

d. Construct a single optimum set of code words to be used for all states, and evaluate the resulting code efficiency.

4.8. The Markov source shown below generates sequences of binary digits. The source is initially in state s_0 .

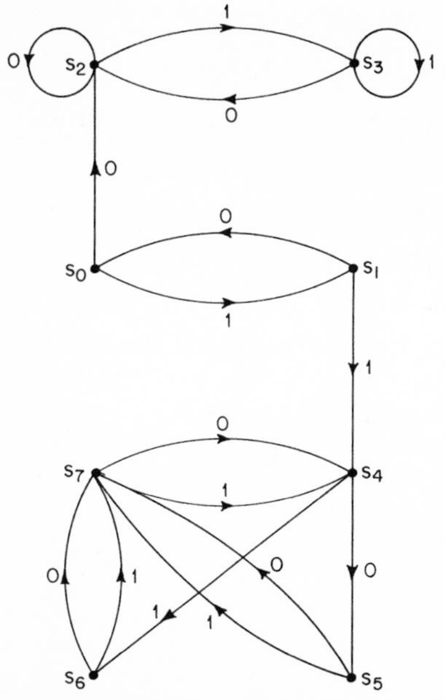

	$P(0\|s_i)$	$P(1\|s_i)$
s_0	1/2	1/2
s_1	1/2	1/2
s_2	1/2	1/2
s_3	1/4	3/4
s_4	1/4	3/4
s_5	1/4	3/4
s_6	1/2	1/2
s_7	1/2	1/2

a. Indicate which states are transient and which are recurrent.
b. Identify any irreducible subchains that might be present, and determine the period of any periodic subchain.
c. Find the probability of eventually reaching each irreducible subchain.
d. Find the asymptotic value of the entropy per digit for each irreducible subchain.

4.9. For an aperiodic Markov source with L letters, let P(r) be the rank probability defined by Eq. 4.144, and $q_r = P(r) - P(r+1)$. Show [Ch. 4, Ref. 7] that

$$\sum_{r=1}^{L} r q_r \log r \leq H(A|A^{\infty}) \leq - \sum_{r=1}^{L} P(r) \log P(r)$$

Use Problem 2.16 in proving the lower bound.

4.10. Consider a discrete, stationary, aperiodic stochastic source for which each output event depends only on the preceding ν events, and represent the source by means of a Markov diagram with L^{ν} states, where L is the number of letters in the source alphabet. Consider also the reduced Markov diagram obtained by merging into a single state the L states for which the preceding $\nu - 1$ output events form identical sequences. This reduced diagram takes into account the dependence on only $\nu - 1$ preceding output events. Show that if P(r) is the rank probability defined by Eq. 4.144, and P'(r) is the corresponding probability for the reduced diagram,

$$\sum_{r=1}^{t} P(r) \geq \sum_{r=1}^{t} P'(r) \quad ; \quad 1 \leq t \leq L$$

and that the two bounds in Problem 4.9 satisfy the inequalities [Ch. 4, Ref. 7]

$$- \sum_{r=1}^{L} P(r) \log P(r) \leq \sum_{r=1}^{L} P'(r) \log P'(r)$$

$$\sum_{r=1}^{L} r\, q_r \log r \leq \sum_{r=1}^{L} r\, q'_r \log r$$

Problems for Chapter 5

5.1. The input digits of two identical binary channels have independently a probability p of being changed by the channel noise.

a. The two channels are connected in cascade; that is, the digit received through one channel is transmitted through the other channel. What is the capacity of the resulting channel?

b. The two channels are connected in parallel; that is, the same digit is transmitted through both channels, although the two digits received are not necessarily equal. What is the capacity of the resulting channel?

5.2.† Evaluate the capacities of the three channels

$$\begin{bmatrix} 1-p & p & 0 \\ 0 & 1-p & p \\ p & 0 & 1-p \end{bmatrix} \qquad \begin{bmatrix} \frac{1-p}{2} & \frac{1-p}{2} & \frac{p}{2} & \frac{p}{2} \\ \frac{p}{2} & \frac{p}{2} & \frac{1-p}{2} & \frac{1-p}{2} \end{bmatrix} \qquad \begin{bmatrix} 1-p_1-p_2 & p_1 & p_2 \\ p_2 & 1-p_1-p_2 & p_1 \\ p_1 & p_2 & 1-p_1-p_2 \end{bmatrix}$$

(a) (b) (c)

Show that channel (b) is equivalent to a binary symmetric channel.

5.3. Evaluate the capacity of the binary channel

$$\begin{bmatrix} 1-p_1 & p_1 \\ p_2 & 1-p_2 \end{bmatrix}$$

5.4. Evaluate the capacities of the two channels

$$\begin{bmatrix} 1-p & p & 0 & 0 \\ p & 1-p & 0 & 0 \\ 0 & 0 & 1-p & p \\ 0 & 0 & p & 1-p \end{bmatrix} \qquad \begin{bmatrix} 1-p & p & 0 \\ p & 1-p & 0 \\ 0 & 0 & 1 \end{bmatrix}$$

(a) (b)

5.5. Let C_1, C_2, ..., C_n be the capacities of n discrete, constant channels. The sum channel of these n channels is defined as a channel whose input and output spaces are the unions of the corresponding spaces of the n channels. In other words, the sum channel is equivalent to having all n channels available but using

† Channels are defined in the following problems by $\mathscr{P}$-matrices in which the rows correspond to input letters and the column to output letters.

only one of them at any given time [channel (a) in Problem 5.4 is the sum of two identical binary symmetric channels]. Show [Ch. 5, Ref. 2] that the capacity of the sum channel is given by

$$C = \log_2 \sum_{k=1}^{n} 2^{C_k}$$

5.6. Show that the capacity of the channel

$$\begin{bmatrix} 3/4 & 1/4 & 1/4 \\ 1/4 & 3/4 & 1/4 \\ 1/3 & 1/3 & 1/3 \end{bmatrix}$$

is obtained by setting equal to zero the probability of one of the input letters. Evaluate the channel capacity.

5.7. The channel defined in Problem 1.3 may be regarded as a time-discrete, constant, continuous channel with input events x occurring at intervals equal to T seconds, and output events $y = x + z$. The noise z is gaussianly distributed with zero mean and variance equal to N, and is statistically independent of x. Let $\overline{x^2} \leq S$ and $N = N_0/2T$ where S and N_0 are constants.

a. Plot the channel capacity in nats/sec. as a function of T.

b. Find the asymptotic value C_∞ of the channel capacity when $2ST/N_0 << 1$.

5.8. The input x of the channel defined in Problem 5.7 can assume only the two values $\sqrt{S}$ and $-\sqrt{S}$, and only the polarity of the channel output is observed.

a. Show that the resulting channel can be represented by a binary symmetric channel.

b. Show that the capacity per second of the equivalent binary channel is equal to $2/\pi \; C_\infty$ for $2ST/N_0 << 1$, where C_∞ is the answer to part (b) of Problem 5.7.

5.9. Let x_1 and x_2 be the input events and y_1 and y_2 be the corresponding output events of two identical channels of the type described in Problem 5.7. The mean-square values of the input events are limited by $\overline{x_1^2} \leq S$, $\overline{x_2^2} \leq S$ where S is a constant. The additive noises z_1 and z_2 are gaussianly distributed with zero mean and variance N, and are statistically independent of each other and of both input events.

a. Evaluate the capacity of the two channels connected in cascade, that is, the capacity of the channel with input x_c and output y_c when

$$x_c = x_1 \quad , \quad x_2 = Ky_1 \quad , \quad y_c = y_2$$

where K is an appropriate constant.

b. Evaluate the capacity of the two channels connected in parallel, that is, the capacity of the channel with input x_p and output y_p when

$$x_p = x_1 = x_2 \quad , \quad y_p = y_1 + y_2$$

c. Show that the sum of the answers to parts (a) and (b) is equal to $\log(1 + S/N)$.

5.10. The input of a channel disturbed by additive, white, gaussian noise of density N_0 is restricted as follows. The input time function $u(t)$ over any time interval $0 < t < T$ consists of a sequence of m rectangular pulses of the form

$$f_k(t) = \begin{cases} a_k \cos q t + b_k \sin q t \quad , & (k-1)\frac{T}{m} < t < k\frac{T}{m} \\ 0 \quad , & \text{otherwise} \end{cases}$$

where $q = \nu \; 2\pi m/T$, ν is a fixed positive integer, and k is an integer in the range $1 \leq k \leq m$. Furthermore, the joint-probability distribution of the coefficients a_k and b_k for $1 \leq k \leq m$ must be such that the ensemble average of the power

$\frac{1}{T}\int_0^T u^2(t)\, dt$ does not exceed a given value S . Evaluate the capacity of this channel.

5.11. The coefficients a_k and b_k in Problem 5.10 are restricted to the values $\sqrt{S}$ and $-\sqrt{S}$, and the channel output consists of two sequences of m binary digits indicating the polarities of

$$\int_{(k-1)T/m}^{kT/m} [u(t) + n(t)] \cos q t \, dt \quad ; \quad \int_{(k-1)T/m}^{kT/m} [u(t) + n(t)] \sin q t \, dt$$

where $n(t)$ is the channel noise. Evaluate the capacity of this channel when

$$\frac{ST}{mN_0} << 1$$

where N_0 is the spectral density of the white noise.

5.12. Consider the problem of telemetering data from a spaceship in the vicinity of Mars. Assume that distance = 10^8 km, gain of transmitting antenna = 10 db, effective area of receiving antenna = 300 m^2 . The noise may be assumed to be additive, stationary, gaussian, and white with density corresponding to an effective receiver temperature of 50°K. Find the minimum antenna energy required per bit of information.

5.13. The attenuation of a transmission channel is equal to 0.001 f db, where f is the frequency in c.p.s. The noise at the output terminals is additive, stationary, gaussian, and white with spectral density N_0. Find the channel capacity and the corresponding signal-power spectrum as a function of the average input power S. Hint: Assume that the output signal (noise included) is amplified in such a way as to eliminate the frequency dependence of the attenuation over an appropriate frequency band.

Problems for Chapter 6

6.1. Two equiprobable messages, m_1 and m_2, are encoded for transmission through a binary symmetric channel into the sequences 0 0 0 and 1 1 1, respectively. Each digit has probability 0.1 of being changed by the channel noise. Find

a. the channel capacity.
b. the minimum probability of error and the corresponding decoding subsets w_1 and w_2.
c. the equivocation $H(M|W)$ and the average mutual information between output sequences and messages.

Compare the value of $H(M|W)$ with the upper bound given by Eq. 6.16.

6.2. The following eight sequences are employed to represent a set of eight equiprobable messages for transmission through a binary symmetric channel:

$$u_1 = 0\ 0\ 0\ 0\ 0\ 0 \qquad u_5 = 1\ 0\ 0\ 1\ 1\ 1$$
$$u_2 = 0\ 0\ 1\ 1\ 0\ 1 \qquad u_6 = 1\ 0\ 1\ 0\ 1\ 0$$
$$u_3 = 0\ 1\ 0\ 1\ 1\ 0 \qquad u_7 = 1\ 1\ 0\ 0\ 0\ 1$$
$$u_4 = 0\ 1\ 1\ 0\ 1\ 1 \qquad u_8 = 1\ 1\ 1\ 1\ 0\ 0$$

Find the minimum probability of error as a function of the noise probability p of the channel.

6.3. A time-continuous channel disturbed by additive, stationary, white, gaussian noise with spectral density N_0 is employed as follows. The channel input in each successive time interval of length T is either $u_1(t) = f(t)$ or $u_2(t) = -f(t)$, where $f(t)$ is a specified time function with mean-square value equal to S. The channel output in each corresponding time interval T is decoded into either $u_1(t)$ or $u_2(t)$ according to the maximum-likelihood criterion.

a. Show that the time-continuous channel, when employed in the above manner, is equivalent to a binary symmetric channel.
b. Plot the capacity of the equivalent binary symmetric channel as a function of $2ST/N_0$.

c. Show that for $2\,ST/N_0 << 1$, the capacity (in nats/sec.) of the equivalent binary symmetric channel is equal to $2/\pi\ C_\infty$. where C_∞ is the infinite-bandwidth capacity of the original time-continuous channel.

6.4. Consider a time-continuous channel disturbed by additive, stationary, white, gaussian noise of spectral density N_0, whose input is constrained to be a sequence of sinusoidal pulses of width T of the form

$$\sqrt{2S}\ \sin\left(2\pi \frac{k}{T} t + \phi\right) \quad ; \quad 0 < t < T$$

where ϕ can assume the values 0, $\pi/2$, π, $3\pi/2$, S is a constant, and k is a fixed positive integer. The corresponding channel output is decoded into one of the four possible values of ϕ according to the maximum likelihood criterion

a. Show that the resulting quaternary channel is equivalent to two independent binary symmetric channels in parallel.

b. Plot the capacity of the resulting channel as a function of $2\,ST/N_0$.

c. Find asymptotic expressions for the capacity per second of the resulting channel when $2\,ST/N_0 << 1$ and when $2\,ST/N_0 >> 1$.

6.5. A communication system is designed to transmit binary digits in the form of two sinusoidal signals of frequencies $f_1 = 1,000$ kilocycles and $f_2 = 1,001$ kilocycles, lasting 10^{-3} sec. These signals are received in the presence of additive, stationary, white, gaussian noise. Let S be the average signal power at the receiver and N_0 the noise power per unit bandwidth.

a. Compute the value of S/N_0 required to insure a probability of error smaller than 10^{-5}.

b. For the ratio S/N_0 found in part (a) and the same probability of error per digit, compute a lower bound to the transmission rate (bits per second) that can be achieved by transmitting each sequence of six binary digits in the form of one out of 64 sinusoidal signals of frequency $f_k = 1,000 + k$ kilocycles $(0 \leq k \leq 63)$.

c. How many different signal frequencies must be used, for the same probability of error and the same value of S/N_0, to achieve a transmission rate equal at least to one-half the capacity C_∞ defined by Eq. 5.164?

6.6. Describe the pulse-position modulation systems equivalent to the frequency-modulation systems of Problem 6.5, and show in detail why they are equivalent.

Problems for Chapter 7

7.1. Let N_k be the number of sequences of n binary digits that differ from a given one in k or less places. Show that there exist at least $2^n/N_{2r}$ sequences that differ from one another in more than r places. See E. N. Gilbert, B.S.T.J., 31, 504, (1952).

7.2. Consider a binary symmetric channel with a noise probability $p < 1/4$. Show, with the help of Problem 7.1, that it is possible to transmit through such a channel at any rate per channel event

$$R \leq \frac{1}{n}\left\{\frac{1}{2}\log_2\left[4\pi n\rho(1-2\rho)\right] - \log_2\frac{1-2\rho}{1-4\rho}\right\} + \left[1 + 2\rho\log_2 2\rho + (1-2\rho)\log_2(1-2\rho)\right]$$

with a probability of error

$$P(e) \leq \frac{1}{\sqrt{2\pi n\rho(1-\rho)}}\;\frac{p(1-\rho)}{\rho - p}\;2^{-n\left[\rho\log_2\frac{\rho}{p} + (1-\rho)\log_2\frac{1-\rho}{1-p}\right]}$$

where $p \leq \rho = \frac{r}{n} \leq \frac{1}{4}$

7.3. Consider a binary symmetric channel with noise probability p. Show that for any rate R smaller than, but very close to, the channel capacity C, the exponential coefficient a_U defined by Eq. 7.74 is given approximately by

$$a_U \simeq \frac{1}{2}(C - R)^2\;\frac{\log_2 e}{p(1-p)\left[\log_2\frac{p}{1-p}\right]^2}$$

7.4. Let $p = \frac{1}{2} - \delta$ be the noise probability of a binary symmetric channel. Show that when δ approaches zero, the exponential coefficient a_U defined by Eq. 7.74 becomes

$$a_U = \begin{cases} C\left[1 - \sqrt{\frac{R}{C}}\right]^2 & ; \quad \frac{1}{4} < \frac{R}{C} \leq 1 \\ \frac{C}{2}\left[1 - \frac{2R}{C}\right] & ; \quad 0 \leq \frac{R}{C} \leq \frac{1}{4} \end{cases}$$

where $C = 2\delta^2\log_2 e$ is the channel capacity and R is the transmission rate.

7.5. Consider the binary symmetric channel defined in Problem 6.3 for $\frac{2ST}{N_0} << 1$. Compare, with the help of Problem 7.4, the exponential coefficient a_U defined by Eq. 7.74 with the exponential coefficient a defined by Eq. 6.92. Show that when $\frac{2ST}{N_0} << 1$, reducing the time-continuous channel to a binary symmetric channel has the same effect as multiplying S by $2/\pi$.

7.6. Consider a binary symmetric channel with noise probability $p = 0.05$. Compute upper and lower bounds to the probability of error for a rate $R = 1/2$ bit per digit, and input-sequence length $n = 100$ and $n = 600$.

7.7. Consider a binary erasure channel with erasure probability p, and the encoding of a set of M equiprobable messages into sequences of n input digits [Ch. 7, Ref. 1].

a. Show that if

$$M \geq 2^{n-r}$$

the probability of error satisfies the inequality

$$P(e) \geq \tfrac{1}{2} \sum_{k=r+1}^{n} \binom{n}{k} p^k (1-p)^{n-k}$$

b. Show that if the digits of the input sequences assigned to messages are selected equiprobably and independently at random, the average probability of error satisfies the inequality

$$\overline{P}(e) \leq 1 - \sum_{k=0}^{n} \left[1 - 2^{-(n-k)}\right]^{M-1} \binom{n}{k} p^k (1-p)^{n-k}$$

Problems for Chapter 8

8.1. A die is thrown n times. Find upper and lower bounds to the probability that the sum of the numbers obtained does not exceed $3n$.

8.2. Each of two gamblers, A and B, throws a die n times. Find an upper bound to the probability that the sum of the numbers obtained by A does not exceed $3n$ but exceeds the sum of the numbers obtained by B.

8.3. A source generates statistically independent letters A and B with probability $P(A) = p$, $P(B) = 1 - p$. Using the methods discussed in Chapter 8, find upper and lower bounds to the probability that the number of A's in a sequence of n letters exceeds $r > np$. Compare these bounds with those given in Sec. 7.1.

8.4. A positive function $\phi(a)$ is defined for the alphabet A consisting of the L letters $a_1, a_2, \ldots, a_L$. Find upper and lower bounds to the number M of sequences of n letters for which the sum of the corresponding values assumed by $\phi(a)$ does not exceed a specified value $n\phi$, where ϕ is smaller than the arithmetic mean of $\phi(a)$. Hint: Regard the sequences as formed by selecting n letters independently and equiprobably at random [Ch. 8, Ref. 3].

8.5. A source generates statistically independent letters belonging to an ensemble A (consisting of L letters a_1, a_2, ..., a_L) with probability distribution P(a) and entropy H(A).

a. Show that $1 - F(I)$, the probability of occurrence of a sequence of n letters whose self-information exceeds $I \geq n\,H(A)$, satisfies the inequality

$$1 - F(I) \leq e^{-\alpha n}$$

where

$$\alpha = \sum_A Q(a) \ln \frac{Q(a)}{P(a)} \geq 0$$

$$Q(a) = \frac{P(a)^{1-s}}{\sum_A P(a)^{1-s}} \quad ; \quad s \geq 0$$

and

$$-\sum_A Q(a) \ln P(a) = \frac{I}{n}$$

b. Show, with the help of Problem 8.4, that the number M of sequences of n letters whose self-information does not exceed I satisfies the inequality

$$M \leq e^{nR}$$

where

$$R = -\sum_A Q(a) \ln Q(a) \geq 0 \quad ; \quad s \leq 1$$

c. Plot α as a function of R for a ternary alphabet with

$$P(a_1) = 0.6, \; P(a_2) = 0.3, \; P(a_3) = 0.1.$$

d. Find $\frac{d\alpha}{dR}$ and $\frac{d^2\alpha}{dR^2}$. <u>Hint:</u> Differentiate with respect to s.

e. Find an approximate expression for $\alpha(R)$ when R is very close to H(A)

Problems for Chapter 9

9.1. Find optimum upper and lower bounds to the probability of error in the special case of a binary symmetric channel, and compare them with those obtained in Chapter 7.

9.2. Consider a binary channel (Z channel) in which a 0 has probability $p = 1/2$ of being changed into a 1, while a 1 has zero probability of being changed into a 0.

a. Find the channel capacity.

b. Plot the optimum input composition as a function of s.

c. Find expressions for the optimum $Q(y|x)$ as a function of s.

d. Plot the curves of Fig. 9.6 for the optimum upper and lower bounds to the probability of error.

9.3. Consider a binary channel with the noise-probability matrix

$$\begin{bmatrix} 3/4 & 1/4 \\ 1/8 & 7/8 \end{bmatrix}$$

a. Plot the optimum input composition as a function of the transmission-rate parameter I defined by Eq. 9.28.

b. Find an approximate expression for the exponential coefficient α_U as a function of the transmission rate R, for R very close to the channel capacity.

9.4. Find an upper bound to the zero-error capacity of the channel shown in Fig. 9.1 [Ch. 9, Ref. 8].

Appendix B

Entropy Tables

(Courtesy of Professor W. W. Peterson)

$$q = 1 - p \; ; \; H = -p \log_2 p - q \log_2 q$$

p	$-\log_2 p$	$-p \log_2 p$	H	$-q \log_2 q$	$-\log q$	q
.0001	13.287712	0.001329	0.001473	0.000144	0.000144	0.9999
.0002	12.287712	0.002458	0.002746	0.000289	0.000289	0.9998
.0003	11.702750	0.003511	0.003944	0.000433	0.000433	0.9997
.0004	11.287712	0.004515	0.005092	0.000577	0.000577	0.9996
.0005	10.965784	0.005483	0.006204	0.000721	0.000722	0.9995
.0006	10.702750	0.006422	0.007287	0.000865	0.000866	0.9994
.0007	10.480357	0.007336	0.008346	0.001010	0.001010	0.9993
.0008	10.287712	0.008230	0.009384	0.001154	0.001155	0.9992
.0009	10.117787	0.009106	0.010404	0.001298	0.001299	0.9991
.0010	9.965784	0.009966	0.011408	0.001442	0.001443	0.9990
.0011	9.828281	0.010811	0.012397	0.001586	0.001588	0.9989
.0012	9.702750	0.011643	0.013373	0.001730	0.001732	0.9988
.0013	9.587273	0.012463	0.014338	0.001874	0.001877	0.9987
.0014	9.480357	0.013273	0.015291	0.002018	0.002021	0.9986
.0015	9.380822	0.014071	0.016234	0.002162	0.002166	0.9985
.0016	9.287712	0.014860	0.017167	0.002306	0.002310	0.9984
.0017	9.200249	0.015640	0.018091	0.002450	0.002455	0.9983
.0018	9.117787	0.016412	0.019007	0.002595	0.002599	0.9982
.0019	9.039785	0.017176	0.019914	0.002739	0.002744	0.9981
.0020	8.965784	0.017932	0.020814	0.002882	0.002888	0.9980
.0021	8.895395	0.018680	0.021707	0.003026	0.003033	0.9979
.0022	8.828281	0.019422	0.022593	0.003170	0.003177	0.9978
.0023	8.764150	0.020158	0.023472	0.003314	0.003322	0.9977
.0024	8.702750	0.020887	0.024345	0.003458	0.003467	0.9976
.0025	8.643856	0.021610	0.025212	0.003602	0.003611	0.9975
.0026	8.587273	0.022327	0.026073	0.003746	0.003756	0.9974
.0027	8.532825	0.023039	0.026929	0.003890	0.003901	0.9973
.0028	8.480357	0.023745	0.027779	0.004034	0.004045	0.9972
.0029	8.429731	0.024446	0.028624	0.004178	0.004190	0.9971
.0030	8.380822	0.025142	0.029464	0.004322	0.004335	0.9970
.0031	8.333516	0.025834	0.030299	0.004465	0.004479	0.9969
.0032	8.287712	0.026521	0.031130	0.004609	0.004624	0.9968
.0033	8.243318	0.027203	0.031956	0.004753	0.004769	0.9967
.0034	8.200249	0.027881	0.032778	0.004897	0.004914	0.9966
.0035	8.158429	0.028555	0.033595	0.005041	0.005058	0.9965
.0036	8.117787	0.029224	0.034408	0.005184	0.005203	0.9964
.0037	8.078259	0.029890	0.035218	0.005328	0.005348	0.9963
.0038	8.039785	0.030551	0.036023	0.005472	0.005493	0.9962
.0039	8.002310	0.031209	0.036825	0.005616	0.005638	0.9961
.0040	7.965784	0.031863	0.037622	0.005759	0.005782	0.9960
.0041	7.930160	0.032514	0.038417	0.005903	0.005927	0.9959
.0042	7.895395	0.033161	0.039207	0.006047	0.006072	0.9958
.0043	7.861448	0.033804	0.039994	0.006190	0.006217	0.9957
.0044	7.828281	0.034444	0.040778	0.006334	0.006362	0.9956
.0045	7.795859	0.035081	0.041559	0.006477	0.006507	0.9955
.0046	7.764150	0.035715	0.042336	0.006621	0.006652	0.9954
.0047	7.733123	0.036346	0.043110	0.006765	0.006797	0.9953
.0048	7.702750	0.036973	0.043881	0.006908	0.006942	0.9952
.0049	7.673002	0.037598	0.044650	0.007052	0.007087	0.9951
.0050	7.643856	0.038219	0.045415	0.007195	0.007232	0.9950
.0051	7.615287	0.038838	0.046177	0.007339	0.007377	0.9949
.0052	7.587273	0.039454	0.046936	0.007482	0.007522	0.9948
.0053	7.559792	0.040067	0.047693	0.007626	0.007667	0.9947
.0054	7.532825	0.040677	0.048447	0.007769	0.007812	0.9946
.0055	7.506353	0.041285	0.049198	0.007913	0.007957	0.9945

p	$-\log_2 p$	$-p\log_2 p$	H	$-q\log_2 q$	$-\log q$	q
.0056	7.480357	0.041890	0.049946	0.008056	0.008102	0.9944
.0057	7.454822	0.042492	0.050692	0.008200	0.008247	0.9943
.0058	7.429731	0.043092	0.051436	0.008343	0.008392	0.9942
.0059	7.405069	0.043690	0.052177	0.008487	0.008537	0.9941
.0060	7.380822	0.044285	0.052915	0.008630	0.008682	0.9940
.0061	7.356975	0.044878	0.053651	0.008774	0.008827	0.9939
.0062	7.333516	0.045468	0.054385	0.008917	0.008973	0.9938
.0063	7.310432	0.046056	0.055116	0.009060	0.009118	0.9937
.0064	7.287712	0.046641	0.055845	0.009204	0.009263	0.9936
.0065	7.265345	0.047225	0.056572	0.009347	0.009408	0.9935
.0066	7.243318	0.047806	0.057296	0.009490	0.009553	0.9934
.0067	7.221623	0.048385	0.058018	0.009634	0.009699	0.9933
.0068	7.200249	0.048962	0.058739	0.009777	0.009844	0.9932
.0069	7.179188	0.049536	0.059457	0.009920	0.009989	0.9931
.0070	7.158429	0.050109	0.060172	0.010063	0.010134	0.9930
.0071	7.137965	0.050680	0.060886	0.010207	0.010280	0.9929
.0072	7.117787	0.051248	0.061598	0.010350	0.010425	0.9928
.0073	7.097888	0.051815	0.062308	0.010493	0.010570	0.9927
.0074	7.078259	0.052379	0.063015	0.010636	0.010716	0.9926
.0075	7.058894	0.052942	0.063721	0.010780	0.010861	0.9925
.0076	7.039785	0.053502	0.064425	0.010923	0.011006	0.9924
.0077	7.020926	0.054061	0.065127	0.011066	0.011152	0.9923
.0078	7.002310	0.054618	0.065827	0.011209	0.011297	0.9922
.0079	6.983932	0.055173	0.066525	0.011352	0.011443	0.9921
.0080	6.965784	0.055726	0.067222	0.011495	0.011588	0.9920
.0081	6.947862	0.056278	0.067916	0.011638	0.011733	0.9919
.0082	6.930160	0.056827	0.068609	0.011781	0.011879	0.9918
.0083	6.912673	0.057375	0.069300	0.011925	0.012024	0.9917
.0084	6.895395	0.057921	0.069989	0.012068	0.012170	0.9916
.0085	6.878321	0.058466	0.070676	0.012211	0.012315	0.9915
.0086	6.861448	0.059008	0.071362	0.012354	0.012461	0.9914
.0087	6.844769	0.059549	0.072046	0.012497	0.012606	0.9913
.0088	6.828281	0.060089	0.072729	0.012640	0.012752	0.9912
.0089	6.811979	0.060627	0.073409	0.012783	0.012897	0.9911
.0090	6.795859	0.061163	0.074088	0.012926	0.013043	0.9910
.0091	6.779918	0.061697	0.074766	0.013069	0.013189	0.9909
.0092	6.764150	0.062230	0.075442	0.013212	0.013334	0.9908
.0093	6.748554	0.062762	0.076116	0.013354	0.013480	0.9907
.0094	6.733123	0.063291	0.076789	0.013497	0.013625	0.9906
.0095	6.717857	0.063820	0.077460	0.013640	0.013771	0.9905
.0096	6.702750	0.064346	0.078130	0.013783	0.013917	0.9904
.0097	6.687800	0.064872	0.078798	0.013926	0.014062	0.9903
.0098	6.673002	0.065395	0.079464	0.014069	0.014208	0.9902
.0099	6.658356	0.065918	0.080129	0.014212	0.014354	0.9901
.0100	6.643856	0.066439	0.080793	0.014355	0.014500	0.9900
.0102	6.615287	0.067476	0.082116	0.014640	0.014791	0.9898
.0104	6.587273	0.068508	0.083433	0.014926	0.015083	0.9896
.0106	6.559792	0.069534	0.084745	0.015211	0.015374	0.9894
.0108	6.532825	0.070555	0.086051	0.015497	0.015666	0.9892
.0110	6.506353	0.071570	0.087352	0.015782	0.015958	0.9890
.0112	6.480357	0.072580	0.088647	0.016067	0.016249	0.9888
.0114	6.454822	0.073585	0.089938	0.016353	0.016541	0.9886
.0116	6.429731	0.074585	0.091223	0.016638	0.016833	0.9884
.0118	6.405069	0.075580	0.092503	0.016923	0.017125	0.9882
.0120	6.380822	0.076570	0.093778	0.017208	0.017417	0.9880

p	$-\log_2 p$	$-p\log_2 p$	H	$-q\log_2 q$	$-\log q$	q
.0122	6.356975	0.077555	0.095048	0.017493	0.017709	0.9878
.0124	6.333516	0.078536	0.096314	0.017778	0.018001	0.9876
.0126	6.310432	0.079511	0.097574	0.018063	0.018293	0.9874
.0128	6.287712	0.080483	0.098831	0.018348	0.018586	0.9872
.0130	6.265345	0.081449	0.100082	0.018633	0.018878	0.9870
.0132	6.243318	0.082412	0.101329	0.018917	0.019170	0.9868
.0134	6.221623	0.083370	0.102572	0.019202	0.019463	0.9866
.0136	6.200249	0.084323	0.103810	0.019487	0.019755	0.9864
.0138	6.179188	0.085273	0.105044	0.019771	0.020048	0.9862
.0140	6.158429	0.086218	0.106274	0.020056	0.020340	0.9860
.0142	6.137965	0.087159	0.107499	0.020340	0.020633	0.9858
.0144	6.117787	0.088096	0.108721	0.020625	0.020926	0.9856
.0146	6.097888	0.089029	0.109938	0.020909	0.021219	0.9854
.0148	6.078259	0.089958	0.111151	0.021193	0.021511	0.9852
.0150	6.058894	0.090883	0.112361	0.021477	0.021804	0.9850
.0152	6.039785	0.091805	0.113566	0.021761	0.022097	0.9848
.0154	6.020926	0.092722	0.114768	0.022046	0.022390	0.9846
.0156	6.002310	0.093636	0.115966	0.022330	0.022683	0.9844
.0158	5.983932	0.094546	0.117160	0.022614	0.022977	0.9842
.0160	5.965784	0.095453	0.118350	0.022897	0.023270	0.9840
.0162	5.947862	0.096355	0.119537	0.023181	0.023563	0.9838
.0164	5.930160	0.097255	0.120720	0.023465	0.023856	0.9836
.0166	5.912673	0.098150	0.121899	0.023749	0.024150	0.9834
.0168	5.895395	0.099043	0.123075	0.024033	0.024443	0.9832
.0170	5.878321	0.099931	0.124248	0.024316	0.024737	0.9830
.0172	5.861448	0.100817	0.125417	0.024600	0.025030	0.9828
.0174	5.844769	0.101699	0.126582	0.024883	0.025324	0.9826
.0176	5.828281	0.102578	0.127744	0.025167	0.025618	0.9824
.0178	5.811979	0.103453	0.128903	0.025450	0.025911	0.9822
.0180	5.795859	0.104325	0.130059	0.025733	0.026205	0.9820
.0182	5.779918	0.105195	0.131211	0.026017	0.026499	0.9818
.0184	5.764150	0.106060	0.132360	0.026300	0.026793	0.9816
.0186	5.748554	0.106923	0.133506	0.026583	0.027087	0.9814
.0188	5.733123	0.107783	0.134649	0.026866	0.027381	0.9812
.0190	5.717857	0.108639	0.135788	0.027149	0.027675	0.9810
.0192	5.702750	0.109493	0.136925	0.027432	0.027969	0.9808
.0194	5.687800	0.110343	0.138058	0.027715	0.028263	0.9806
.0196	5.673002	0.111191	0.139189	0.027998	0.028558	0.9804
.0198	5.658356	0.112035	0.140316	0.028281	0.028852	0.9802
.0200	5.643856	0.112877	0.141441	0.028563	0.029146	0.9800
.0202	5.629501	0.113716	0.142562	0.028846	0.029441	0.9798
.0204	5.615287	0.114552	0.143681	0.029129	0.029735	0.9796
.0206	5.601212	0.115385	0.144796	0.029411	0.030030	0.9794
.0208	5.587273	0.116215	0.145909	0.029694	0.030325	0.9792
.0210	5.573467	0.117043	0.147019	0.029976	0.030619	0.9790
.0212	5.559792	0.117868	0.148126	0.030259	0.030914	0.9788
.0214	5.546245	0.118690	0.149231	0.030541	0.031209	0.9786
.0216	5.532825	0.119509	0.150332	0.030823	0.031504	0.9784
.0218	5.519528	0.120326	0.151431	0.031105	0.031799	0.9782
.0220	5.506353	0.121140	0.152527	0.031388	0.032094	0.9780
.0222	5.493297	0.121951	0.153621	0.031670	0.032389	0.9778
.0224	5.480357	0.122760	0.154712	0.031952	0.032684	0.9776
.0226	5.467533	0.123566	0.155800	0.032234	0.032979	0.9774
.0228	5.454822	0.124370	0.156886	0.032516	0.033274	0.9772
.0230	5.442222	0.125171	0.157969	0.032797	0.033570	0.9770

p	$-\log_2 p$	$-p\log_2 p$	H	$-q\log_2 q$	$-\log q$	q
.0232	5.429731	0.125970	0.159049	0.033079	0.033865	0.9768
.0234	5.417348	0.126766	0.160127	0.033361	0.034160	0.9766
.0236	5.405069	0.127560	0.161202	0.033643	0.034456	0.9764
.0238	5.392895	0.128351	0.162275	0.033924	0.034751	0.9762
.0240	5.380822	0.129140	0.163346	0.034206	0.035047	0.9760
.0242	5.368849	0.129926	0.164413	0.034487	0.035343	0.9758
.0244	5.356975	0.130710	0.165479	0.034769	0.035638	0.9756
.0246	5.345198	0.131492	0.166542	0.035050	0.035934	0.9754
.0248	5.333516	0.132271	0.167603	0.035331	0.036230	0.9752
.0250	5.321928	0.133048	0.168661	0.035613	0.036526	0.9750
.0252	5.310432	0.133823	0.169717	0.035894	0.036822	0.9748
.0254	5.299028	0.134595	0.170770	0.036175	0.037118	0.9746
.0256	5.287712	0.135365	0.171822	0.036456	0.037414	0.9744
.0258	5.276485	0.136133	0.172870	0.036737	0.037710	0.9742
.0260	5.265345	0.136899	0.173917	0.037018	0.038006	0.9740
.0262	5.254289	0.137662	0.174961	0.037299	0.038303	0.9738
.0264	5.243318	0.138424	0.176004	0.037580	0.038599	0.9736
.0266	5.232430	0.139183	0.177043	0.037861	0.038895	0.9734
.0268	5.221623	0.139939	0.178081	0.038141	0.039192	0.9732
.0270	5.210897	0.140694	0.179116	0.038422	0.039488	0.9730
.0272	5.200249	0.141447	0.180149	0.038703	0.039785	0.9728
.0274	5.189680	0.142197	0.181180	0.038983	0.040081	0.9726
.0276	5.179188	0.142946	0.182209	0.039264	0.040378	0.9724
.0278	5.168771	0.143692	0.183236	0.039544	0.040675	0.9722
.0280	5.158429	0.144436	0.184261	0.039825	0.040972	0.9720
.0282	5.148161	0.145178	0.185283	0.040105	0.041269	0.9718
.0284	5.137965	0.145918	0.186303	0.040385	0.041566	0.9716
.0286	5.127841	0.146656	0.187322	0.040665	0.041863	0.9714
.0288	5.117787	0.147392	0.188338	0.040945	0.042160	0.9712
.0290	5.107803	0.148126	0.189352	0.041226	0.042457	0.9710
.0292	5.097888	0.148858	0.190364	0.041506	0.042754	0.9708
.0294	5.088040	0.149588	0.191374	0.041786	0.043051	0.9706
.0296	5.078259	0.150316	0.192382	0.042065	0.043349	0.9704
.0298	5.068544	0.151043	0.193388	0.042345	0.043646	0.9702
.0300	5.058894	0.151767	0.194392	0.042625	0.043943	0.9700
.0302	5.049308	0.152489	0.195394	0.042905	0.044241	0.9698
.0304	5.039785	0.153209	0.196394	0.043184	0.044538	0.9696
.0306	5.030325	0.153928	0.197392	0.043464	0.044836	0.9694
.0308	5.020926	0.154645	0.198388	0.043744	0.045134	0.9692
.0310	5.011588	0.155359	0.199382	0.044023	0.045431	0.9690
.0312	5.002310	0.156072	0.200375	0.044302	0.045729	0.9688
.0314	4.993092	0.156783	0.201365	0.044582	0.046027	0.9686
.0316	4.983932	0.157492	0.202353	0.044861	0.046325	0.9684
.0318	4.974829	0.158200	0.203340	0.045140	0.046623	0.9682
.0320	4.965784	0.158905	0.204325	0.045420	0.046921	0.9680
.0322	4.956795	0.159609	0.205307	0.045699	0.047219	0.9678
.0324	4.947862	0.160311	0.206288	0.045978	0.047517	0.9676
.0326	4.938984	0.161011	0.207268	0.046257	0.047816	0.9674
.0328	4.930160	0.161709	0.208245	0.046536	0.048114	0.9672
.0330	4.921390	0.162406	0.209220	0.046815	0.048412	0.9670
.0332	4.912673	0.163101	0.210194	0.047093	0.048711	0.9668
.0334	4.904008	0.163794	0.211166	0.047372	0.049009	0.9666
.0336	4.895395	0.164485	0.212136	0.047651	0.049308	0.9664
.0338	4.886833	0.165175	0.213104	0.047930	0.049606	0.9662
.0340	4.878321	0.165863	0.214071	0.048208	0.049905	0.9660

p	$-\log_2 p$	$-p\log_2 p$	H	$-q\log_2 q$	$-\log q$	q
.0342	4.869860	0.166549	0.215036	0.048487	0.050204	0.9658
.0344	4.861448	0.167234	0.215999	0.048765	0.050502	0.9656
.0346	4.853084	0.167917	0.216960	0.049044	0.050801	0.9654
.0348	4.844769	0.168598	0.217920	0.049322	0.051100	0.9652
.0350	4.836501	0.169278	0.218878	0.049600	0.051399	0.9650
.0352	4.828281	0.169955	0.219834	0.049878	0.051698	0.9648
.0354	4.820107	0.170632	0.220788	0.050157	0.051997	0.9646
.0356	4.811979	0.171306	0.221741	0.050435	0.052296	0.9644
.0358	4.803897	0.171979	0.222692	0.050713	0.052596	0.9642
.0360	4.795859	0.172651	0.223642	0.050991	0.052895	0.9640
.0362	4.787866	0.173321	0.224589	0.051269	0.053194	0.9638
.0364	4.779918	0.173989	0.225536	0.051547	0.053494	0.9636
.0366	4.772013	0.174656	0.226480	0.051824	0.053793	0.9634
.0368	4.764150	0.175321	0.227423	0.052102	0.054093	0.9632
.0370	4.756331	0.175984	0.228364	0.052380	0.054392	0.9630
.0372	4.748554	0.176646	0.229304	0.052657	0.054692	0.9628
.0374	4.740818	0.177307	0.230242	0.052935	0.054992	0.9626
.0376	4.733123	0.177965	0.231178	0.053212	0.055291	0.9624
.0378	4.725470	0.178623	0.232113	0.053490	0.055591	0.9622
.0380	4.717857	0.179279	0.233046	0.053767	0.055891	0.9620
.0382	4.710284	0.179933	0.233977	0.054045	0.056191	0.9618
.0384	4.702750	0.180586	0.234908	0.054322	0.056491	0.9616
.0386	4.695255	0.181237	0.235836	0.054599	0.056791	0.9614
.0388	4.687800	0.181887	0.236763	0.054876	0.057091	0.9612
.0390	4.680382	0.182535	0.237688	0.055153	0.057392	0.9610
.0392	4.673002	0.183182	0.238612	0.055430	0.057692	0.9608
.0394	4.665661	0.183827	0.239534	0.055707	0.057992	0.9606
.0396	4.658356	0.184471	0.240455	0.055984	0.058293	0.9604
.0398	4.651088	0.185113	0.241374	0.056261	0.058593	0.9602
.0400	4.643856	0.185754	0.242292	0.056538	0.058894	0.9600
.0402	4.636661	0.186394	0.243208	0.056815	0.059194	0.9598
.0404	4.629501	0.187032	0.244123	0.057091	0.059495	0.9596
.0406	4.622376	0.187668	0.245036	0.057368	0.059796	0.9594
.0408	4.615287	0.188304	0.245948	0.057644	0.060096	0.9592
.0410	4.608232	0.188938	0.246858	0.057921	0.060397	0.9590
.0412	4.601212	0.189570	0.247767	0.058197	0.060698	0.9588
.0414	4.594225	0.190201	0.248675	0.058474	0.060999	0.9586
.0416	4.587273	0.190831	0.249581	0.058750	0.061300	0.9584
.0418	4.580353	0.191459	0.250485	0.059026	0.061601	0.9582
.0420	4.573467	0.192086	0.251388	0.059303	0.061902	0.9580
.0422	4.566613	0.192711	0.252290	0.059579	0.062204	0.9578
.0424	4.559792	0.193335	0.253190	0.059855	0.062505	0.9576
.0426	4.553003	0.193958	0.254089	0.060131	0.062806	0.9574
.0428	4.546245	0.194579	0.254986	0.060407	0.063108	0.9572
.0430	4.539519	0.195199	0.255882	0.060683	0.063409	0.9570
.0432	4.532825	0.195818	0.256776	0.060958	0.063711	0.9568
.0434	4.526161	0.196435	0.257670	0.061234	0.064012	0.9566
.0436	4.519528	0.197051	0.258561	0.061510	0.064314	0.9564
.0438	4.512925	0.197666	0.259452	0.061786	0.064616	0.9562
.0440	4.506353	0.198280	0.260341	0.062061	0.064917	0.9560
.0442	4.499810	0.198892	0.261228	0.062337	0.065219	0.9558
.0444	4.493297	0.199502	0.262114	0.062612	0.065521	0.9556
.0446	4.486812	0.200112	0.262999	0.062887	0.065823	0.9554
.0448	4.480357	0.200720	0.263883	0.063163	0.066125	0.9552
.0450	4.473931	0.201327	0.264765	0.063438	0.066427	0.9550

p	$-\log_2 p$	$-p\log_2 p$	H	$-q\log_2 q$	$-\log q$	q
.0452	4.467533	0.201933	0.265646	0.063713	0.066730	0.9548
.0454	4.461164	0.202537	0.266525	0.063989	0.067032	0.9546
.0456	4.454822	0.203140	0.267404	0.064264	0.067334	0.9544
.0458	4.448509	0.203742	0.268280	0.064539	0.067636	0.9542
.0460	4.442222	0.204342	0.269156	0.064814	0.067939	0.9540
.0462	4.435963	0.204942	0.270030	0.065089	0.068241	0.9538
.0464	4.429731	0.205540	0.270903	0.065363	0.068544	0.9536
.0466	4.423526	0.206136	0.271775	0.065638	0.068846	0.9534
.0468	4.417348	0.206732	0.272645	0.065913	0.069149	0.9532
.0470	4.411195	0.207326	0.273514	0.066188	0.069452	0.9530
.0472	4.405069	0.207919	0.274382	0.066462	0.069755	0.9528
.0474	4.398969	0.208511	0.275248	0.066737	0.070058	0.9526
.0476	4.392895	0.209102	0.276113	0.067011	0.070360	0.9524
.0478	4.386846	0.209691	0.276977	0.067286	0.070663	0.9522
.0480	4.380822	0.210279	0.277840	0.067560	0.070967	0.9520
.0482	4.374823	0.210866	0.278701	0.067834	0.071270	0.9518
.0484	4.368849	0.211452	0.279561	0.068109	0.071573	0.9516
.0486	4.362900	0.212037	0.280420	0.068383	0.071876	0.9514
.0488	4.356975	0.212620	0.281277	0.068657	0.072179	0.9512
.0490	4.351074	0.213203	0.282134	0.068931	0.072483	0.9510
.0492	4.345198	0.213784	0.282989	0.069205	0.072786	0.9508
.0494	4.339345	0.214364	0.283843	0.069479	0.073090	0.9506
.0496	4.333516	0.214942	0.284695	0.069753	0.073393	0.9504
.0498	4.327710	0.215520	0.285547	0.070027	0.073697	0.9502
.0500	4.321928	0.216096	0.286397	0.070301	0.074001	0.9500
.0502	4.316169	0.216672	0.287246	0.070574	0.074304	0.9498
.0504	4.310432	0.217246	0.288094	0.070848	0.074608	0.9496
.0506	4.304719	0.217819	0.288940	0.071121	0.074912	0.9494
.0508	4.299028	0.218391	0.289786	0.071395	0.075216	0.9492
.0510	4.293359	0.218961	0.290630	0.071668	0.075520	0.9490
.0512	4.287712	0.219531	0.291473	0.071942	0.075824	0.9488
.0514	4.282088	0.220099	0.292315	0.072215	0.076128	0.9486
.0516	4.276485	0.220667	0.293155	0.072489	0.076432	0.9484
.0518	4.270904	0.221233	0.293995	0.072762	0.076737	0.9482
.0520	4.265345	0.221798	0.294833	0.073035	0.077041	0.9480
.0522	4.259806	0.222362	0.295670	0.073308	0.077345	0.9478
.0524	4.254289	0.222925	0.296506	0.073581	0.077650	0.9476
.0526	4.248793	0.223487	0.297341	0.073854	0.077954	0.9474
.0528	4.243318	0.224047	0.298174	0.074127	0.078259	0.9472
.0530	4.237864	0.224607	0.299007	0.074400	0.078564	0.9470
.0532	4.232430	0.225165	0.299838	0.074673	0.078868	0.9468
.0534	4.227016	0.225723	0.300668	0.074945	0.079173	0.9466
.0536	4.221623	0.226279	0.301497	0.075218	0.079478	0.9464
.0538	4.216250	0.226834	0.302325	0.075491	0.079783	0.9462
.0540	4.210897	0.227388	0.303152	0.075763	0.080088	0.9460
.0542	4.205563	0.227942	0.303977	0.076036	0.080393	0.9458
.0544	4.200249	0.228494	0.304802	0.076308	0.080698	0.9456
.0546	4.194955	0.229045	0.305625	0.076580	0.081003	0.9454
.0548	4.189680	0.229594	0.306447	0.076853	0.081308	0.9452
.0550	4.184425	0.230143	0.307268	0.077125	0.081614	0.9450
.0552	4.179188	0.230691	0.308088	0.077397	0.081919	0.9448
.0554	4.173970	0.231238	0.308907	0.077669	0.082225	0.9446
.0556	4.168771	0.231784	0.309725	0.077941	0.082530	0.9444
.0558	4.163591	0.232328	0.310542	0.078213	0.082836	0.9442
.0560	4.158429	0.232872	0.311357	0.078485	0.083141	0.9440

p	$-\log_2 p$	$-p\log_2 p$	H	$-q\log_2 q$	$-\log q$	q
.0562	4.153286	0.233415	0.312172	0.078757	0.083447	0.9438
.0564	4.148161	0.233956	0.312985	0.079029	0.083753	0.9436
.0566	4.143054	0.234497	0.313798	0.079301	0.084058	0.9434
.0568	4.137965	0.235036	0.314609	0.079572	0.084364	0.9432
.0570	4.132894	0.235575	0.315419	0.079844	0.084670	0.9430
.0572	4.127841	0.236113	0.316228	0.080116	0.084976	0.9428
.0574	4.122805	0.236649	0.317036	0.080387	0.085282	0.9426
.0576	4.117787	0.237185	0.317843	0.080659	0.085589	0.9424
.0578	4.112787	0.237719	0.318649	0.080930	0.085895	0.9422
.0580	4.107803	0.238253	0.319454	0.081201	0.086201	0.9420
.0582	4.102837	0.238785	0.320258	0.081473	0.086507	0.9418
.0584	4.097888	0.239317	0.321060	0.081744	0.086814	0.9416
.0586	4.092956	0.239847	0.321862	0.082015	0.087120	0.9414
.0588	4.088040	0.240377	0.322663	0.082286	0.087427	0.9412
.0590	4.083141	0.240905	0.323462	0.082557	0.087733	0.9410
.0592	4.078259	0.241433	0.324261	0.082828	0.088040	0.9408
.0594	4.073393	0.241960	0.325059	0.083099	0.088347	0.9406
.0596	4.068544	0.242485	0.325855	0.083370	0.088654	0.9404
.0598	4.063711	0.243010	0.326650	0.083641	0.088960	0.9402
.0600	4.058894	0.243534	0.327445	0.083911	0.089267	0.9400
.0605	4.046921	0.244839	0.329427	0.084588	0.090035	0.9395
.0610	4.035047	0.246138	0.331402	0.085264	0.090803	0.9390
.0615	4.023270	0.247431	0.333371	0.085940	0.091571	0.9385
.0620	4.011588	0.248718	0.335334	0.086615	0.092340	0.9380
.0625	4.000000	0.250000	0.337290	0.087290	0.093109	0.9375
.0630	3.988504	0.251276	0.339240	0.087965	0.093879	0.9370
.0635	3.977100	0.252546	0.341185	0.088639	0.094649	0.9365
.0640	3.965784	0.253810	0.343123	0.089313	0.095420	0.9360
.0645	3.954557	0.255069	0.345055	0.089986	0.096190	0.9355
.0650	3.943416	0.256322	0.346981	0.090659	0.096962	0.9350
.0655	3.932361	0.257570	0.348902	0.091332	0.097733	0.9345
.0660	3.921390	0.258812	0.350816	0.092004	0.098506	0.9340
.0665	3.910502	0.260048	0.352724	0.092676	0.099278	0.9335
.0670	3.899695	0.261280	0.354627	0.093348	0.100051	0.9330
.0675	3.888969	0.262505	0.356524	0.094019	0.100824	0.9325
.0680	3.878321	0.263726	0.358415	0.094689	0.101598	0.9320
.0685	3.867752	0.264941	0.360301	0.095360	0.102372	0.9315
.0690	3.857260	0.266151	0.362181	0.096030	0.103147	0.9310
.0695	3.846843	0.267356	0.364055	0.096699	0.103922	0.9305
.0700	3.836501	0.268555	0.365924	0.097369	0.104697	0.9300
.0705	3.826233	0.269749	0.367787	0.098037	0.105473	0.9295
.0710	3.816037	0.270939	0.369644	0.098706	0.106249	0.9290
.0715	3.805913	0.272123	0.371497	0.099374	0.107026	0.9285
.0720	3.795859	0.273302	0.373343	0.100041	0.107803	0.9280
.0725	3.785875	0.274476	0.375185	0.100709	0.108581	0.9275
.0730	3.775960	0.275645	0.377021	0.101376	0.109359	0.9270
.0735	3.766112	0.276809	0.378851	0.102042	0.110137	0.9265
.0740	3.756331	0.277968	0.380677	0.102708	0.110916	0.9260
.0745	3.746616	0.279123	0.382497	0.103374	0.111695	0.9255
.0750	3.736966	0.280272	0.384312	0.104039	0.112475	0.9250
.0755	3.727380	0.281417	0.386121	0.104704	0.113255	0.9245
.0760	3.717857	0.282557	0.387926	0.105369	0.114035	0.9240
.0765	3.708396	0.283692	0.389725	0.106033	0.114816	0.9235
.0770	3.698998	0.284823	0.391519	0.106696	0.115597	0.9230
.0775	3.689660	0.285949	0.393308	0.107360	0.116379	0.9225

p	$-\log_2 p$	$-p \log_2 p$	H	$-q \log_2 q$	$-\log q$	q
.0780	3.680382	0.287070	0.395093	0.108023	0.117161	0.9220
.0785	3.671164	0.288186	0.396872	0.108685	0.117944	0.9215
.0790	3.662004	0.289298	0.398646	0.109348	0.118727	0.9210
.0795	3.652901	0.290406	0.400415	0.110009	0.119510	0.9205
.0800	3.643856	0.291508	0.402179	0.110671	0.120294	0.9200
.0805	3.634867	0.292607	0.403939	0.111332	0.121079	0.9195
.0810	3.625934	0.293701	0.405693	0.111992	0.121863	0.9190
.0815	3.617056	0.294790	0.407443	0.112653	0.122648	0.9185
.0820	3.608232	0.295875	0.409187	0.113312	0.123434	0.9180
.0825	3.599462	0.296956	0.410927	0.113972	0.124220	0.9175
.0830	3.590745	0.298032	0.412663	0.114631	0.125006	0.9170
.0835	3.582080	0.299104	0.414393	0.115289	0.125793	0.9165
.0840	3.573467	0.300171	0.416119	0.115948	0.126580	0.9160
.0845	3.564905	0.301234	0.417840	0.116606	0.127368	0.9155
.0850	3.556393	0.302293	0.419556	0.117263	0.128156	0.9150
.0855	3.547932	0.303348	0.421268	0.117920	0.128945	0.9145
.0860	3.539520	0.304399	0.422975	0.118577	0.129734	0.9140
.0865	3.531156	0.305445	0.424678	0.119233	0.130523	0.9135
.0870	3.522841	0.306487	0.426376	0.119889	0.131313	0.9130
.0875	3.514573	0.307525	0.428070	0.120544	0.132104	0.9125
.0880	3.506353	0.308559	0.429759	0.121200	0.132894	0.9120
.0885	3.498179	0.309589	0.431443	0.121854	0.133685	0.9115
.0890	3.490051	0.310615	0.433123	0.122509	0.134477	0.9110
.0895	3.481968	0.311636	0.434799	0.123162	0.135269	0.9105
.0900	3.473931	0.312654	0.436470	0.123816	0.136062	0.9100
.0905	3.465938	0.313667	0.438137	0.124469	0.136854	0.9095
.0910	3.457990	0.314677	0.439799	0.125122	0.137648	0.9090
.0915	3.450084	0.315683	0.441457	0.125774	0.138442	0.9085
.0920	3.442222	0.316684	0.443111	0.126426	0.139236	0.9080
.0925	3.434403	0.317682	0.444760	0.127078	0.140030	0.9075
.0930	3.426625	0.318676	0.446405	0.127729	0.140826	0.9070
.0935	3.418890	0.319666	0.448046	0.128379	0.141621	0.9065
.0940	3.411195	0.320652	0.449682	0.129030	0.142417	0.9060
.0945	3.403542	0.321635	0.451314	0.129680	0.143213	0.9055
.0950	3.395929	0.322613	0.452943	0.130329	0.144010	0.9050
.0955	3.388355	0.323588	0.454566	0.130978	0.144808	0.9045
.0960	3.380822	0.324559	0.456186	0.131627	0.145605	0.9040
.0965	3.373327	0.325526	0.457802	0.132276	0.146403	0.9035
.0970	3.365871	0.326490	0.459413	0.132923	0.147202	0.9030
.0975	3.358454	0.327449	0.461020	0.133571	0.148001	0.9025
.0980	3.351074	0.328405	0.462623	0.134218	0.148801	0.9020
.0985	3.343732	0.329358	0.464223	0.134865	0.149601	0.9015
.0990	3.336428	0.330306	0.465818	0.135511	0.150401	0.9010
.0995	3.329160	0.331251	0.467409	0.136157	0.151202	0.9005
.1000	3.321928	0.332193	0.468996	0.136803	0.152003	0.9000
.1005	3.314733	0.333131	0.470579	0.137448	0.152805	0.8995
.1010	3.307573	0.334065	0.472158	0.138093	0.153607	0.8990
.1015	3.300448	0.334996	0.473733	0.138737	0.154410	0.8985
.1020	3.293359	0.335923	0.475304	0.139381	0.155213	0.8980
.1025	3.286304	0.336846	0.476871	0.140024	0.156016	0.8975
.1030	3.279284	0.337766	0.478434	0.140668	0.156820	0.8970
.1035	3.272297	0.338683	0.479993	0.141310	0.157624	0.8965
.1040	3.265345	0.339596	0.481549	0.141953	0.158429	0.8960
.1045	3.258425	0.340505	0.483100	0.142595	0.159235	0.8955
.1050	3.251539	0.341412	0.484648	0.143236	0.160040	0.8950

p	$-\log_2 p$	$-p\log_2 p$	H	$-q\log_2 q$	$-\log q$	q
.1055	3.244685	0.342314	0.486192	0.143877	0.160847	0.8945
.1060	3.237864	0.343214	0.487732	0.144518	0.161653	0.8940
.1065	3.231075	0.344109	0.489268	0.145158	0.162460	0.8935
.1070	3.224317	0.345002	0.490800	0.145798	0.163268	0.8930
.1075	3.217591	0.345891	0.492329	0.146438	0.164076	0.8925
.1080	3.210897	0.346777	0.493854	0.147077	0.164884	0.8920
.1085	3.204233	0.347659	0.495375	0.147716	0.165693	0.8915
.1090	3.197600	0.348538	0.496892	0.148354	0.166503	0.8910
.1095	3.190997	0.349414	0.498406	0.148992	0.167312	0.8905
.1100	3.184425	0.350287	0.499916	0.149629	0.168123	0.8900
.1105	3.177882	0.351156	0.501422	0.150266	0.168933	0.8895
.1110	3.171368	0.352022	0.502925	0.150903	0.169745	0.8890
.1115	3.164884	0.352885	0.504424	0.151539	0.170556	0.8885
.1120	3.158429	0.353744	0.505919	0.152175	0.171368	0.8880
.1125	3.152003	0.354600	0.507411	0.152811	0.172181	0.8875
.1130	3.145605	0.355453	0.508899	0.153446	0.172994	0.8870
.1135	3.139236	0.356303	0.510384	0.154080	0.173807	0.8865
.1140	3.132894	0.357150	0.511864	0.154715	0.174621	0.8860
.1145	3.126580	0.357993	0.513342	0.155348	0.175436	0.8855
.1150	3.120294	0.358834	0.514816	0.155982	0.176251	0.8850
.1155	3.114035	0.359671	0.516286	0.156615	0.177066	0.8845
.1160	3.107803	0.360505	0.517753	0.157247	0.177882	0.8840
.1165	3.101598	0.361336	0.519216	0.157880	0.178698	0.8835
.1170	3.095420	0.362164	0.520676	0.158511	0.179515	0.8830
.1175	3.089267	0.362989	0.522132	0.159143	0.180332	0.8825
.1180	3.083141	0.363811	0.523584	0.159774	0.181149	0.8820
.1185	3.077041	0.364629	0.525034	0.160404	0.181968	0.8815
.1190	3.070967	0.365445	0.526480	0.161035	0.182786	0.8810
.1195	3.064917	0.366258	0.527922	0.161664	0.183605	0.8805
.1200	3.058894	0.367067	0.529361	0.162294	0.184425	0.8800
.1205	3.052895	0.367874	0.530796	0.162923	0.185245	0.8795
.1210	3.046921	0.368677	0.532228	0.163551	0.186065	0.8790
.1215	3.040972	0.369478	0.533657	0.164179	0.186886	0.8785
.1220	3.035047	0.370276	0.535083	0.164807	0.187707	0.8780
.1225	3.029146	0.371070	0.536505	0.165434	0.188529	0.8775
.1230	3.023270	0.371862	0.537923	0.166061	0.189351	0.8770
.1235	3.017417	0.372651	0.539339	0.166688	0.190174	0.8765
.1240	3.011588	0.373437	0.540750	0.167314	0.190997	0.8760
.1245	3.005782	0.374220	0.542159	0.167939	0.191821	0.8755
.1250	3.000000	0.375000	0.543564	0.168564	0.192645	0.8750
.1255	2.994241	0.375777	0.544966	0.169189	0.193470	0.8745
.1260	2.988504	0.376552	0.546365	0.169814	0.194295	0.8740
.1265	2.982791	0.377323	0.547761	0.170438	0.195120	0.8735
.1270	2.977100	0.378092	0.549153	0.171061	0.195946	0.8730
.1275	2.971431	0.378857	0.550542	0.171684	0.196773	0.8725
.1280	2.965784	0.379620	0.551928	0.172307	0.197600	0.8720
.1285	2.960160	0.380381	0.553310	0.172929	0.198427	0.8715
.1290	2.954557	0.381138	0.554689	0.173551	0.199255	0.8710
.1295	2.948976	0.381892	0.556065	0.174173	0.200084	0.8705
.1300	2.943416	0.382644	0.557438	0.174794	0.200913	0.8700
.1305	2.937878	0.383393	0.558808	0.175415	0.201742	0.8695
.1310	2.932361	0.384139	0.560174	0.176035	0.202572	0.8690
.1315	2.926865	0.384883	0.561538	0.176655	0.203402	0.8685
.1320	2.921390	0.385623	0.562898	0.177274	0.204233	0.8680
.1325	2.915936	0.386361	0.564255	0.177893	0.205064	0.8675

p	$-\log_2 p$	$-p\log_2 p$	H	$-q\log_2 q$	$-\log q$	q
.1330	2.910502	0.387097	0.565609	0.178512	0.205896	0.8670
.1335	2.905088	0.387829	0.566959	0.179130	0.206728	0.8665
.1340	2.899695	0.388559	0.568307	0.179748	0.207561	0.8660
.1345	2.894322	0.389286	0.569652	0.180365	0.208394	0.8655
.1350	2.888969	0.390011	0.570993	0.180982	0.209228	0.8650
.1355	2.883635	0.390733	0.572331	0.181599	0.210062	0.8645
.1360	2.878321	0.391452	0.573667	0.182215	0.210897	0.8640
.1365	2.873027	0.392168	0.574999	0.182830	0.211732	0.8635
.1370	2.867752	0.392882	0.576328	0.183446	0.212568	0.8630
.1375	2.862496	0.393593	0.577654	0.184061	0.213404	0.8625
.1380	2.857260	0.394302	0.578977	0.184675	0.214240	0.8620
.1385	2.852042	0.395008	0.580297	0.185289	0.215077	0.8615
.1390	2.846843	0.395711	0.581614	0.185903	0.215915	0.8610
.1395	2.841663	0.396412	0.582928	0.186516	0.216753	0.8605
.1400	2.836501	0.397110	0.584239	0.187129	0.217591	0.8600
.1405	2.831358	0.397806	0.585547	0.187741	0.218430	0.8595
.1410	2.826233	0.398499	0.586852	0.188353	0.219270	0.8590
.1415	2.821126	0.399189	0.588154	0.188964	0.220110	0.8585
.1420	2.816037	0.399877	0.589453	0.189575	0.220950	0.8580
.1425	2.810966	0.400563	0.590749	0.190186	0.221791	0.8575
.1430	2.805913	0.401246	0.592042	0.190796	0.222633	0.8570
.1435	2.800877	0.401926	0.593332	0.191406	0.223475	0.8565
.1440	2.795859	0.402604	0.594619	0.192016	0.224317	0.8560
.1445	2.790859	0.403279	0.595904	0.192625	0.225160	0.8555
.1450	2.785875	0.403952	0.597185	0.193233	0.226004	0.8550
.1455	2.780909	0.404622	0.598464	0.193841	0.226848	0.8545
.1460	2.775960	0.405290	0.599739	0.194449	0.227692	0.8540
.1465	2.771027	0.405956	0.601012	0.195056	0.228537	0.8535
.1470	2.766112	0.406618	0.602282	0.195663	0.229382	0.8530
.1475	2.761213	0.407279	0.603549	0.196270	0.230228	0.8525
.1480	2.756331	0.407937	0.604813	0.196876	0.231075	0.8520
.1485	2.751465	0.408593	0.606074	0.197481	0.231922	0.8515
.1490	2.746616	0.409246	0.607332	0.198086	0.232769	0.8510
.1495	2.741783	0.409896	0.608588	0.198691	0.233617	0.8505
.1500	2.736966	0.410545	0.609840	0.199295	0.234465	0.8500
.1505	2.732165	0.411191	0.611090	0.199899	0.235314	0.8495
.1510	2.727380	0.411834	0.612337	0.200503	0.236164	0.8490
.1515	2.722610	0.412475	0.613581	0.201106	0.237013	0.8485
.1520	2.717857	0.413114	0.614823	0.201709	0.237864	0.8480
.1525	2.713119	0.413751	0.616061	0.202311	0.238715	0.8475
.1530	2.708396	0.414385	0.617297	0.202913	0.239566	0.8470
.1535	2.703689	0.415016	0.618530	0.203514	0.240418	0.8465
.1540	2.698998	0.415646	0.619760	0.204115	0.241270	0.8460
.1545	2.694321	0.416273	0.620988	0.204715	0.242123	0.8455
.1550	2.689660	0.416897	0.622213	0.205315	0.242977	0.8450
.1555	2.685014	0.417520	0.623435	0.205915	0.243831	0.8445
.1560	2.680382	0.418140	0.624654	0.206514	0.244685	0.8440
.1565	2.675765	0.418757	0.625870	0.207113	0.245540	0.8435
.1570	2.671164	0.419373	0.627084	0.207711	0.246395	0.8430
.1575	2.666576	0.419986	0.628295	0.208309	0.247251	0.8425
.1580	2.662004	0.420597	0.629503	0.208907	0.248108	0.8420
.1585	2.657445	0.421205	0.630709	0.209504	0.248965	0.8415
.1590	2.652901	0.421811	0.631912	0.210101	0.249822	0.8410
.1595	2.648372	0.422415	0.633112	0.210697	0.250680	0.8405
.1600	2.643856	0.423017	0.634310	0.211293	0.251539	0.8400

p	$-\log_2 p$	$-p\log_2 p$	H	$-q\log_2 q$	$-\log q$	q
.1605	2.639355	0.423616	0.635504	0.211888	0.252398	0.8395
.1610	2.634867	0.424214	0.636696	0.212483	0.253257	0.8390
.1615	2.630394	0.424809	0.637886	0.213077	0.254117	0.8385
.1620	2.625934	0.425401	0.639073	0.213671	0.254978	0.8380
.1625	2.621488	0.425992	0.640257	0.214265	0.255839	0.8375
.1630	2.617056	0.426580	0.641438	0.214858	0.256700	0.8370
.1635	2.612637	0.427166	0.642617	0.215451	0.257563	0.8365
.1640	2.608232	0.427750	0.643794	0.216043	0.258425	0.8360
.1645	2.603841	0.428332	0.644967	0.216635	0.259288	0.8355
.1650	2.599462	0.428911	0.646138	0.217227	0.260152	0.8350
.1655	2.595097	0.429489	0.647306	0.217818	0.261016	0.8345
.1660	2.590745	0.430064	0.648472	0.218409	0.261881	0.8340
.1665	2.586406	0.430637	0.649635	0.218999	0.262746	0.8335
.1670	2.582080	0.431207	0.650796	0.219588	0.263612	0.8330
.1675	2.577767	0.431776	0.651954	0.220178	0.264478	0.8325
.1680	2.573467	0.432342	0.653109	0.220767	0.265345	0.8320
.1685	2.569180	0.432907	0.654262	0.221355	0.266212	0.8315
.1690	2.564905	0.433469	0.655412	0.221943	0.267080	0.8310
.1695	2.560643	0.434029	0.656560	0.222531	0.267948	0.8305
.1700	2.556393	0.434587	0.657705	0.223118	0.268817	0.8300
.1705	2.552156	0.435143	0.658847	0.223705	0.269686	0.8295
.1710	2.547932	0.435696	0.659987	0.224291	0.270556	0.8290
.1715	2.543720	0.436248	0.661125	0.224877	0.271426	0.8285
.1720	2.539520	0.436797	0.662260	0.225462	0.272297	0.8280
.1725	2.535332	0.437345	0.663392	0.226047	0.273169	0.8275
.1730	2.531156	0.437890	0.664522	0.226632	0.274041	0.8270
.1735	2.526992	0.438433	0.665649	0.227216	0.274913	0.8265
.1740	2.522841	0.438974	0.666774	0.227799	0.275786	0.8260
.1745	2.518701	0.439513	0.667896	0.228383	0.276660	0.8255
.1750	2.514573	0.440050	0.669016	0.228966	0.277534	0.8250
.1755	2.510457	0.440585	0.670133	0.229548	0.278409	0.8245
.1760	2.506353	0.441118	0.671248	0.230130	0.279284	0.8240
.1765	2.502260	0.441649	0.672360	0.230711	0.280159	0.8235
.1770	2.498179	0.442178	0.673470	0.231292	0.281036	0.8230
.1775	2.494109	0.442704	0.674577	0.231873	0.281912	0.8225
.1780	2.490051	0.443229	0.675682	0.232453	0.282790	0.8220
.1785	2.486004	0.443752	0.676785	0.233033	0.283668	0.8215
.1790	2.481968	0.444272	0.677885	0.233612	0.284546	0.8210
.1795	2.477944	0.444791	0.678982	0.234191	0.285425	0.8205
.1800	2.473931	0.445308	0.680077	0.234769	0.286304	0.8200
.1805	2.469929	0.445822	0.681170	0.235347	0.287184	0.8195
.1810	2.465938	0.446335	0.682260	0.235925	0.288065	0.8190
.1815	2.461959	0.446845	0.683347	0.236502	0.288946	0.8185
.1820	2.457990	0.447354	0.684433	0.237079	0.289827	0.8180
.1825	2.454032	0.447861	0.685516	0.237655	0.290709	0.8175
.1830	2.450084	0.448365	0.686596	0.238231	0.291592	0.8170
.1835	2.446148	0.448868	0.687674	0.238806	0.292475	0.8165
.1840	2.442222	0.449369	0.688750	0.239381	0.293359	0.8160
.1845	2.438307	0.449868	0.689823	0.239955	0.294243	0.8155
.1850	2.434403	0.450365	0.690894	0.240529	0.295128	0.8150
.1855	2.430509	0.450859	0.691962	0.241103	0.296013	0.8145
.1860	2.426625	0.451352	0.693028	0.241676	0.296899	0.8140
.1865	2.422752	0.451843	0.694092	0.242249	0.297786	0.8135
.1870	2.418890	0.452332	0.695153	0.242821	0.298673	0.8130
.1875	2.415037	0.452820	0.696212	0.243393	0.299560	0.8125

p	$-\log_2 p$	$-p\log_2 p$	H	$-q\log_2 q$	$-\log q$	q
.1880	2.411195	0.453305	0.697269	0.243964	0.300448	0.8120
.1885	2.407364	0.453788	0.698323	0.244535	0.301337	0.8115
.1890	2.403542	0.454269	0.699375	0.245105	0.302226	0.8110
.1895	2.399730	0.454749	0.700424	0.245675	0.303116	0.8105
.1900	2.395929	0.455226	0.701471	0.246245	0.304006	0.8100
.1905	2.392137	0.455702	0.702516	0.246814	0.304897	0.8095
.1910	2.388355	0.456176	0.703559	0.247383	0.305788	0.8090
.1915	2.384584	0.456648	0.704599	0.247951	0.306680	0.8085
.1920	2.380822	0.457118	0.705637	0.248519	0.307573	0.8080
.1925	2.377070	0.457586	0.706672	0.249086	0.308466	0.8075
.1930	2.373327	0.458052	0.707705	0.249653	0.309359	0.8070
.1935	2.369595	0.458517	0.708736	0.250219	0.310254	0.8065
.1940	2.365871	0.458979	0.709765	0.250785	0.311148	0.8060
.1945	2.362158	0.459440	0.710791	0.251351	0.312044	0.8055
.1950	2.358454	0.459899	0.711815	0.251916	0.312939	0.8050
.1955	2.354759	0.460355	0.712836	0.252481	0.313836	0.8045
.1960	2.351074	0.460811	0.713856	0.253045	0.314733	0.8040
.1965	2.347399	0.461264	0.714873	0.253609	0.315630	0.8035
.1970	2.343732	0.461715	0.715887	0.254172	0.316528	0.8030
.1975	2.340075	0.462165	0.716900	0.254735	0.317427	0.8025
.1980	2.336428	0.462613	0.717910	0.255297	0.318326	0.8020
.1985	2.332789	0.463059	0.718918	0.255859	0.319226	0.8015
.1990	2.329160	0.463503	0.719924	0.256421	0.320126	0.8010
.1995	2.325539	0.463945	0.720927	0.256982	0.321027	0.8005
.2000	2.321928	0.464386	0.721928	0.257542	0.321928	0.8000
.2010	2.314733	0.465261	0.723924	0.258662	0.323733	0.7990
.2020	2.307573	0.466130	0.725910	0.259780	0.325539	0.7980
.2030	2.300448	0.466991	0.727888	0.260897	0.327348	0.7970
.2040	2.293359	0.467845	0.729856	0.262011	0.329160	0.7960
.2050	2.286304	0.468692	0.731816	0.263124	0.330973	0.7950
.2060	2.279284	0.469532	0.733767	0.264235	0.332789	0.7940
.2070	2.272297	0.470366	0.735709	0.265344	0.334607	0.7930
.2080	2.265345	0.471192	0.737642	0.266451	0.336428	0.7920
.2090	2.258425	0.472011	0.739567	0.267556	0.338250	0.7910
.2100	2.251539	0.472823	0.741483	0.268660	0.340075	0.7900
.2110	2.244685	0.473629	0.743390	0.269761	0.341903	0.7890
.2120	2.237864	0.474427	0.745288	0.270861	0.343732	0.7880
.2130	2.231075	0.475219	0.747178	0.271959	0.345564	0.7870
.2140	2.224317	0.476004	0.749059	0.273055	0.347399	0.7860
.2150	2.217591	0.476782	0.750932	0.274150	0.349235	0.7850
.2160	2.210897	0.477554	0.752796	0.275242	0.351074	0.7840
.2170	2.204233	0.478319	0.754652	0.276333	0.352916	0.7830
.2180	2.197600	0.479077	0.756499	0.277422	0.354759	0.7820
.2190	2.190997	0.479828	0.758337	0.278509	0.356606	0.7810
.2200	2.184425	0.480573	0.760167	0.279594	0.358454	0.7800
.2210	2.177882	0.481312	0.761989	0.280677	0.360305	0.7790
.2220	2.171368	0.482044	0.763803	0.281759	0.362158	0.7780
.2230	2.164884	0.482769	0.765608	0.282838	0.364013	0.7770
.2240	2.158429	0.483488	0.767404	0.283916	0.365871	0.7760
.2250	2.152003	0.484201	0.769193	0.284992	0.367732	0.7750
.2260	2.145605	0.484907	0.770973	0.286066	0.369595	0.7740
.2270	2.139236	0.485607	0.772745	0.287138	0.371460	0.7730
.2280	2.132894	0.486300	0.774509	0.288209	0.373327	0.7720
.2290	2.126580	0.486987	0.776264	0.289277	0.375197	0.7710
.2300	2.120294	0.487668	0.778011	0.290344	0.377070	0.7700

p	$-\log_2 p$	$-p\log_2 p$	H	$-q\log_2 q$	$-\log q$	q
.2310	2.114035	0.488342	0.779750	0.291408	0.378944	0.7690
.2320	2.107803	0.489010	0.781481	0.292471	0.380822	0.7680
.2330	2.101598	0.489672	0.783204	0.293532	0.382702	0.7670
.2340	2.095420	0.490328	0.784919	0.294591	0.384584	0.7660
.2350	2.089267	0.490978	0.786626	0.295648	0.386468	0.7650
.2360	2.083141	0.491621	0.788325	0.296704	0.388355	0.7640
.2370	2.077041	0.492259	0.790016	0.297757	0.390245	0.7630
.2380	2.070967	0.492890	0.791698	0.298808	0.392137	0.7620
.2390	2.064917	0.493515	0.793373	0.299858	0.394032	0.7610
.2400	2.058894	0.494134	0.795040	0.300906	0.395929	0.7600
.2410	2.052895	0.494748	0.796699	0.301952	0.397828	0.7590
.2420	2.046921	0.495355	0.798350	0.302996	0.399730	0.7580
.2430	2.040972	0.495956	0.799994	0.304038	0.401635	0.7570
.2440	2.035047	0.496551	0.801629	0.305078	0.403542	0.7560
.2450	2.029146	0.497141	0.803257	0.306116	0.405451	0.7550
.2460	2.023270	0.497724	0.804876	0.307152	0.407364	0.7540
.2470	2.017417	0.498302	0.806488	0.308186	0.409278	0.7530
.2480	2.011588	0.498874	0.808093	0.309219	0.411195	0.7520
.2490	2.005782	0.499440	0.809689	0.310249	0.413115	0.7510
.2500	2.000000	0.500000	0.811278	0.311278	0.415037	0.7500
.2510	1.994241	0.500554	0.812859	0.312305	0.416962	0.7490
.2520	1.988504	0.501103	0.814433	0.313330	0.418890	0.7480
.2530	1.982791	0.501646	0.815998	0.314352	0.420820	0.7470
.2540	1.977100	0.502183	0.817557	0.315373	0.422752	0.7460
.2550	1.971431	0.502715	0.819107	0.316392	0.424688	0.7450
.2560	1.965784	0.503241	0.820650	0.317409	0.426625	0.7440
.2570	1.960160	0.503761	0.822185	0.318424	0.428566	0.7430
.2580	1.954557	0.504276	0.823713	0.319438	0.430509	0.7420
.2590	1.948976	0.504785	0.825234	0.320449	0.432455	0.7410
.2600	1.943416	0.505288	0.826746	0.321458	0.434403	0.7400
.2610	1.937878	0.505786	0.828252	0.322465	0.436354	0.7390
.2620	1.932361	0.506279	0.829749	0.323471	0.438307	0.7380
.2630	1.926865	0.506766	0.831240	0.324474	0.440263	0.7370
.2640	1.921390	0.507247	0.832723	0.325476	0.442222	0.7360
.2650	1.915936	0.507723	0.834198	0.326475	0.444184	0.7350
.2660	1.910502	0.508193	0.835666	0.327473	0.446148	0.7340
.2670	1.905088	0.508659	0.837127	0.328468	0.448115	0.7330
.2680	1.899695	0.509118	0.838580	0.329462	0.450084	0.7320
.2690	1.894322	0.509573	0.840026	0.330453	0.452057	0.7310
.2700	1.888969	0.510022	0.841465	0.331443	0.454032	0.7300
.2710	1.883635	0.510465	0.842896	0.332431	0.456009	0.7290
.2720	1.878321	0.510903	0.844320	0.333416	0.457990	0.7280
.2730	1.873027	0.511336	0.845737	0.334400	0.459973	0.7270
.2740	1.867752	0.511764	0.847146	0.335382	0.461959	0.7260
.2750	1.862496	0.512187	0.848548	0.336362	0.463947	0.7250
.2760	1.857260	0.512604	0.849943	0.337339	0.465938	0.7240
.2770	1.852042	0.513016	0.851331	0.338315	0.467932	0.7230
.2780	1.846843	0.513422	0.852711	0.339289	0.469929	0.7220
.2790	1.841663	0.513824	0.854085	0.340261	0.471929	0.7210
.2800	1.836501	0.514220	0.855451	0.341230	0.473931	0.7200
.2810	1.831358	0.514612	0.856810	0.342198	0.475936	0.7190
.2820	1.826233	0.514998	0.858162	0.343164	0.477944	0.7180
.2830	1.821126	0.515379	0.859506	0.344128	0.479955	0.7170
.2840	1.816037	0.515755	0.860844	0.345089	0.481968	0.7160
.2850	1.810966	0.516125	0.862175	0.346049	0.483985	0.7150

p	$-\log_2 p$	$-p\log_2 p$	H	$-q\log_2 q$	$-\log q$	q
.2860	1.805913	0.516491	0.863498	0.347007	0.486004	0.7140
.2870	1.800877	0.516852	0.864814	0.347963	0.488026	0.7130
.2880	1.795859	0.517207	0.866124	0.348916	0.490051	0.7120
.2890	1.790859	0.517558	0.867426	0.349868	0.492079	0.7110
.2900	1.785875	0.517904	0.868721	0.350817	0.494109	0.7100
.2910	1.780909	0.518244	0.870009	0.351765	0.496142	0.7090
.2920	1.775960	0.518580	0.871291	0.352711	0.498179	0.7080
.2930	1.771027	0.518911	0.872565	0.353654	0.500218	0.7070
.2940	1.766112	0.519237	0.873832	0.354595	0.502260	0.7060
.2950	1.761213	0.519558	0.875093	0.355535	0.504305	0.7050
.2960	1.756331	0.519874	0.876346	0.356472	0.506353	0.7040
.2970	1.751465	0.520185	0.877593	0.357408	0.508403	0.7030
.2980	1.746616	0.520491	0.878832	0.358341	0.510457	0.7020
.2990	1.741783	0.520793	0.880065	0.359272	0.512514	0.7010
.3000	1.736966	0.521090	0.881291	0.360201	0.514573	0.7000
.3010	1.732165	0.521382	0.882510	0.361128	0.516636	0.6990
.3020	1.727380	0.521669	0.883722	0.362053	0.518701	0.6980
.3030	1.722610	0.521951	0.884927	0.362976	0.520769	0.6970
.3040	1.717857	0.522228	0.886126	0.363897	0.522841	0.6960
.3050	1.713119	0.522501	0.887317	0.364816	0.524915	0.6950
.3060	1.708396	0.522769	0.888502	0.365733	0.526992	0.6940
.3070	1.703689	0.523033	0.889680	0.366647	0.529073	0.6930
.3080	1.698998	0.523291	0.890851	0.367560	0.531156	0.6920
.3090	1.694321	0.523545	0.892016	0.368470	0.533242	0.6910
.3100	1.689660	0.523795	0.893173	0.369379	0.535332	0.6900
.3110	1.685014	0.524039	0.894324	0.370285	0.537424	0.6890
.3120	1.680382	0.524279	0.895469	0.371189	0.539520	0.6880
.3130	1.675765	0.524515	0.896606	0.372092	0.541618	0.6870
.3140	1.671164	0.524745	0.897737	0.372992	0.543720	0.6860
.3150	1.666576	0.524972	0.898861	0.373890	0.545824	0.6850
.3160	1.662004	0.525193	0.899978	0.374785	0.547932	0.6840
.3170	1.657445	0.525410	0.901089	0.375679	0.550043	0.6830
.3180	1.652901	0.525623	0.902193	0.376571	0.552156	0.6820
.3190	1.648372	0.525831	0.903291	0.377460	0.554273	0.6810
.3200	1.643856	0.526034	0.904381	0.378347	0.556393	0.6800
.3210	1.639355	0.526233	0.905466	0.379233	0.558517	0.6790
.3220	1.634867	0.526427	0.906543	0.380116	0.560643	0.6780
.3230	1.630394	0.526617	0.907614	0.380997	0.562772	0.6770
.3240	1.625934	0.526803	0.908678	0.381876	0.564905	0.6760
.3250	1.621488	0.526984	0.909736	0.382752	0.567041	0.6750
.3260	1.617056	0.527160	0.910787	0.383627	0.569179	0.6740
.3270	1.612637	0.527332	0.911832	0.384499	0.571322	0.6730
.3280	1.608232	0.527500	0.912870	0.385370	0.573467	0.6720
.3290	1.603841	0.527664	0.913901	0.386238	0.575615	0.6710
.3300	1.599462	0.527822	0.914926	0.387104	0.577767	0.6700
.3310	1.595097	0.527977	0.915945	0.387968	0.579922	0.6690
.3320	1.590745	0.528127	0.916957	0.388829	0.582080	0.6680
.3330	1.586406	0.528273	0.917962	0.389689	0.584241	0.6670
.3340	1.582080	0.528415	0.918961	0.390546	0.586406	0.6660
.3350	1.577767	0.528552	0.919953	0.391402	0.588574	0.6650
.3360	1.573467	0.528685	0.920939	0.392255	0.590745	0.6640
.3370	1.569180	0.528813	0.921919	0.393105	0.592919	0.6630
.3380	1.564905	0.528938	0.922892	0.393954	0.595097	0.6620
.3390	1.560643	0.529058	0.923859	0.394801	0.597278	0.6610
.3400	1.556393	0.529174	0.924819	0.395645	0.599462	0.6600

p	$-\log_2 p$	$-p\log_2 p$	H	$-q\log_2 q$	$-\log q$	q
.3410	1.552156	0.529285	0.925772	0.396487	0.601650	0.6590
.3420	1.547932	0.529393	0.926720	0.397327	0.603840	0.6580
.3430	1.543720	0.529496	0.927661	0.398165	0.606035	0.6570
.3440	1.539520	0.529595	0.928595	0.399000	0.608232	0.6560
.3450	1.535332	0.529689	0.929523	0.399834	0.610433	0.6550
.3460	1.531156	0.529780	0.930445	0.400665	0.612637	0.6540
.3470	1.526992	0.529866	0.931360	0.401494	0.614845	0.6530
.3480	1.522841	0.529949	0.932269	0.402321	0.617056	0.6520
.3490	1.518701	0.530027	0.933172	0.403145	0.619271	0.6510
.3500	1.514573	0.530101	0.934068	0.403967	0.621488	0.6500
.3510	1.510457	0.530170	0.934958	0.404788	0.623710	0.6490
.3520	1.506353	0.530236	0.935842	0.405605	0.625934	0.6480
.3530	1.502260	0.530298	0.936719	0.406421	0.628162	0.6470
.3540	1.498179	0.530355	0.937590	0.407234	0.630394	0.6460
.3550	1.494109	0.530409	0.938454	0.408046	0.632629	0.6450
.3560	1.490051	0.530458	0.939313	0.408855	0.634867	0.6440
.3570	1.486004	0.530503	0.940165	0.409661	0.637109	0.6430
.3580	1.481969	0.530545	0.941010	0.410466	0.639355	0.6420
.3590	1.477944	0.530582	0.941850	0.411268	0.641604	0.6410
.3600	1.473931	0.530615	0.942683	0.412068	0.643856	0.6400
.3610	1.469929	0.530644	0.943510	0.412866	0.646112	0.6390
.3620	1.465938	0.530670	0.944331	0.413661	0.648372	0.6380
.3630	1.461959	0.530691	0.945145	0.414454	0.650635	0.6370
.3640	1.457990	0.530708	0.945953	0.415245	0.652901	0.6360
.3650	1.454032	0.530722	0.946755	0.416034	0.655171	0.6350
.3660	1.450084	0.530731	0.947551	0.416820	0.657445	0.6340
.3670	1.446148	0.530736	0.948341	0.417604	0.659723	0.6330
.3680	1.442222	0.530738	0.949124	0.418386	0.662004	0.6320
.3690	1.438307	0.530735	0.949901	0.419166	0.664288	0.6310
.3700	1.434403	0.530729	0.950672	0.419943	0.666576	0.6300
.3710	1.430509	0.530719	0.951437	0.420718	0.668868	0.6290
.3720	1.426625	0.530705	0.952195	0.421491	0.671164	0.6280
.3730	1.422752	0.530687	0.952948	0.422261	0.673463	0.6270
.3740	1.418890	0.530665	0.953694	0.423029	0.675765	0.6260
.3750	1.415037	0.530639	0.954434	0.423795	0.678072	0.6250
.3760	1.411195	0.530609	0.955168	0.424558	0.680382	0.6240
.3770	1.407364	0.530576	0.955896	0.425320	0.682696	0.6230
.3780	1.403542	0.530539	0.956617	0.426078	0.685014	0.6220
.3790	1.399730	0.530498	0.957333	0.426835	0.687335	0.6210
.3800	1.395929	0.530453	0.958042	0.427589	0.689660	0.6200
.3810	1.392137	0.530404	0.958745	0.428341	0.691989	0.6190
.3820	1.388355	0.530352	0.959442	0.429091	0.694321	0.6180
.3830	1.384584	0.530296	0.960133	0.429838	0.696658	0.6170
.3840	1.380822	0.530236	0.960818	0.430583	0.698998	0.6160
.3850	1.377070	0.530172	0.961497	0.431325	0.701342	0.6150
.3860	1.373327	0.530104	0.962170	0.432065	0.703689	0.6140
.3870	1.369595	0.530033	0.962836	0.432803	0.706041	0.6130
.3880	1.365871	0.529958	0.963497	0.433539	0.708396	0.6120
.3890	1.362158	0.529879	0.964151	0.434272	0.710756	0.6110
.3900	1.358454	0.529797	0.964800	0.435002	0.713119	0.6100
.3910	1.354759	0.529711	0.965442	0.435731	0.715486	0.6090
.3920	1.351074	0.529621	0.966078	0.436457	0.717857	0.6080
.3930	1.347399	0.529528	0.966708	0.437181	0.720232	0.6070
.3940	1.343732	0.529431	0.967332	0.437902	0.722610	0.6060
.3950	1.340075	0.529330	0.967951	0.438621	0.724993	0.6050

p	$-\log_2 p$	$-p\log_2 p$	H	$-q\log_2 q$	$-\log q$	q
.3960	1.336428	0.529225	0.968563	0.439337	0.727380	0.6040
.3970	1.332789	0.529117	0.969169	0.440051	0.729770	0.6030
.3980	1.329160	0.529006	0.969769	0.440763	0.732165	0.6020
.3990	1.325539	0.528890	0.970363	0.441472	0.734563	0.6010
.4000	1.321928	0.528771	0.970951	0.442179	0.736966	0.6000
.4010	1.318326	0.528649	0.971533	0.442884	0.739372	0.5990
.4020	1.314733	0.528522	0.972108	0.443586	0.741783	0.5980
.4030	1.311148	0.528393	0.972678	0.444286	0.744197	0.5970
.4040	1.307573	0.528259	0.973242	0.444983	0.746616	0.5960
.4050	1.304006	0.528122	0.973800	0.445678	0.749038	0.5950
.4060	1.300448	0.527982	0.974352	0.446370	0.751465	0.5940
.4070	1.296899	0.527838	0.974898	0.447060	0.753896	0.5930
.4080	1.293359	0.527690	0.975438	0.447748	0.756331	0.5920
.4090	1.289827	0.527539	0.975972	0.448433	0.758770	0.5910
.4100	1.286304	0.527385	0.976500	0.449116	0.761213	0.5900
.4110	1.282790	0.527227	0.977023	0.449796	0.763660	0.5890
.4120	1.279284	0.527065	0.977539	0.450474	0.766112	0.5880
.4130	1.275786	0.526900	0.978049	0.451149	0.768568	0.5870
.4140	1.272297	0.526731	0.978553	0.451822	0.771027	0.5860
.4150	1.268817	0.526559	0.979051	0.452493	0.773491	0.5850
.4160	1.265345	0.526383	0.979544	0.453160	0.775960	0.5840
.4170	1.261881	0.526204	0.980030	0.453826	0.778432	0.5830
.4180	1.258425	0.526022	0.980511	0.454489	0.780909	0.5820
.4190	1.254978	0.525836	0.980985	0.455150	0.783390	0.5810
.4200	1.251539	0.525646	0.981454	0.455808	0.785875	0.5800
.4210	1.248108	0.525453	0.981917	0.456463	0.788365	0.5790
.4220	1.244685	0.525257	0.982373	0.457116	0.790859	0.5780
.4230	1.241270	0.525057	0.982824	0.457767	0.793357	0.5770
.4240	1.237864	0.524854	0.983269	0.458415	0.795859	0.5760
.4250	1.234465	0.524648	0.983708	0.459061	0.798366	0.5750
.4260	1.231075	0.524438	0.984141	0.459704	0.800877	0.5740
.4270	1.227692	0.524224	0.984569	0.460344	0.803393	0.5730
.4280	1.224317	0.524008	0.984990	0.460982	0.805913	0.5720
.4290	1.220950	0.523788	0.985405	0.461618	0.808437	0.5710
.4300	1.217591	0.523564	0.985815	0.462251	0.810966	0.5700
.4310	1.214240	0.523338	0.986219	0.462881	0.813499	0.5690
.4320	1.210897	0.523107	0.986617	0.463509	0.816037	0.5680
.4330	1.207561	0.522874	0.987008	0.464134	0.818579	0.5670
.4340	1.204233	0.522637	0.987394	0.464757	0.821126	0.5660
.4350	1.200913	0.522397	0.987775	0.465378	0.823677	0.5650
.4360	1.197600	0.522154	0.988149	0.465995	0.826233	0.5640
.4370	1.194295	0.521907	0.988517	0.466611	0.828793	0.5630
.4380	1.190997	0.521657	0.988880	0.467223	0.831358	0.5620
.4390	1.187707	0.521403	0.989237	0.467833	0.833927	0.5610
.4400	1.184425	0.521147	0.989588	0.468441	0.836501	0.5600
.4410	1.181149	0.520887	0.989933	0.469046	0.839080	0.5590
.4420	1.177882	0.520624	0.990272	0.469648	0.841663	0.5580
.4430	1.174621	0.520357	0.990605	0.470248	0.844251	0.5570
.4440	1.171368	0.520088	0.990932	0.470845	0.846843	0.5560
.4450	1.168123	0.519815	0.991254	0.471439	0.849440	0.5550
.4460	1.164884	0.519538	0.991570	0.472031	0.852042	0.5540
.4470	1.161653	0.519259	0.991880	0.472621	0.854649	0.5530
.4480	1.158429	0.518976	0.992184	0.473207	0.857260	0.5520
.4490	1.155213	0.518690	0.992482	0.473792	0.859876	0.5510
.4500	1.152003	0.518401	0.992774	0.474373	0.862496	0.5500

p	$-\log_2 p$	$-p\log_2 p$	H	$-q\log_2 q$	$-\log q$	q
.4510	1.148801	0.518109	0.993061	0.474952	0.865122	0.5490
.4520	1.145605	0.517814	0.993342	0.475528	0.867752	0.5480
.4530	1.142417	0.517515	0.993617	0.476102	0.870387	0.5470
.4540	1.139236	0.517213	0.993886	0.476673	0.873027	0.5460
.4550	1.136062	0.516908	0.994149	0.477241	0.875672	0.5450
.4560	1.132894	0.516600	0.994407	0.477807	0.878321	0.5440
.4570	1.129734	0.516288	0.994658	0.478370	0.880976	0.5430
.4580	1.126580	0.515974	0.994904	0.478930	0.883635	0.5420
.4590	1.123434	0.515656	0.995144	0.479488	0.886299	0.5410
.4600	1.120294	0.515335	0.995378	0.480043	0.888969	0.5400
.4610	1.117161	0.515011	0.995607	0.480595	0.891643	0.5390
.4620	1.114035	0.514684	0.995829	0.481145	0.894322	0.5380
.4630	1.110916	0.514354	0.996046	0.481692	0.897006	0.5370
.4640	1.107803	0.514021	0.996257	0.482237	0.899695	0.5360
.4650	1.104697	0.513684	0.996462	0.482778	0.902389	0.5350
.4660	1.101598	0.513345	0.996662	0.483317	0.905088	0.5340
.4670	1.098506	0.513002	0.996856	0.483853	0.907793	0.5330
.4680	1.095420	0.512656	0.997043	0.484387	0.910502	0.5320
.4690	1.092340	0.512308	0.997225	0.484918	0.913216	0.5310
.4700	1.089267	0.511956	0.997402	0.485446	0.915936	0.5300
.4710	1.086201	0.511601	0.997572	0.485971	0.918660	0.5290
.4720	1.083141	0.511243	0.997737	0.486494	0.921390	0.5280
.4730	1.080088	0.510882	0.997896	0.487014	0.924125	0.5270
.4740	1.077041	0.510517	0.998049	0.487531	0.926865	0.5260
.4750	1.074001	0.510150	0.998196	0.488046	0.929611	0.5250
.4760	1.070967	0.509780	0.998337	0.488557	0.932361	0.5240
.4770	1.067939	0.509407	0.998473	0.489066	0.935117	0.5230
.4780	1.064917	0.509031	0.998603	0.489572	0.937878	0.5220
.4790	1.061902	0.508651	0.998727	0.490076	0.940645	0.5210
.4800	1.058894	0.508269	0.998846	0.490577	0.943416	0.5200
.4810	1.055891	0.507884	0.998958	0.491074	0.946194	0.5190
.4820	1.052895	0.507495	0.999065	0.491570	0.948976	0.5180
.4830	1.049905	0.507104	0.999166	0.492062	0.951764	0.5170
.4840	1.046921	0.506710	0.999261	0.492551	0.954557	0.5160
.4850	1.043943	0.506313	0.999351	0.493038	0.957356	0.5150
.4860	1.040972	0.505912	0.999434	0.493522	0.960160	0.5140
.4870	1.038006	0.505509	0.999512	0.494003	0.962969	0.5130
.4880	1.035047	0.505103	0.999584	0.494482	0.965784	0.5120
.4890	1.032094	0.504694	0.999651	0.494957	0.968605	0.5110
.4900	1.029146	0.504282	0.999711	0.495430	0.971431	0.5100
.4910	1.026205	0.503867	0.999766	0.495900	0.974262	0.5090
.4920	1.023270	0.503449	0.999815	0.496367	0.977100	0.5080
.4930	1.020340	0.503028	0.999859	0.496831	0.979942	0.5070
.4940	1.017417	0.502604	0.999896	0.497292	0.982791	0.5060
.4950	1.014500	0.502177	0.999928	0.497751	0.985645	0.5050
.4960	1.011588	0.501748	0.999954	0.498206	0.988504	0.5040
.4970	1.008682	0.501315	0.999974	0.498659	0.991370	0.5030
.4980	1.005782	0.500880	0.999988	0.499109	0.994241	0.5020
.4990	1.002888	0.500441	0.999997	0.499556	0.997117	0.5010
.5000	1.000000	0.500000	1.000000	0.500000	1.000000	0.5000

Appendix C

Gaussian Distribution Function

$$\Phi(x) = \frac{1}{\sqrt{2\pi}} \int_{-\infty}^{x} e^{-\frac{1}{2}y^2}\, dy$$

x	0.00	0.01	0.02	0.03	0.04	0.05	0.06	0.07	0.08	0.09
0.0	.5000	.5040	.5080	.5120	.5160	.5199	.5239	.5279	.5319	.5359
0.1	.5398	.5438	.5478	.5517	.5557	.5596	.5636	.5675	.5714	.5753
0.2	.5793	.5832	.5871	.5910	.5948	.5987	.6026	.6064	.6103	.6141
0.3	.6179	.6217	.6255	.6293	.6331	.6368	.6406	.6443	.6480	.6517
0.4	.6554	.6591	.6628	.6664	.6700	.6736	.6772	.6808	.6844	.6879
0.5	.6915	.6950	.6985	.7019	.7054	.7088	.7123	.7157	.7190	.7224
0.6	.7257	.7291	.7324	.7357	.7389	.7422	.7454	.7486	.7517	.7549
0.7	.7580	.7611	.7642	.7673	.7704	.7734	.7764	.7794	.7823	.7852
0.8	.7881	.7910	.7939	.7967	.7995	.8023	.8051	.8078	.8106	.8133
0.9	.8159	.8186	.8212	.8238	.8264	.8289	.8315	.8340	.8365	.8389
1.0	.8413	.8438	.8461	.8485	.8508	.8531	.8554	.8577	.8599	.8621
1.1	.8643	.8665	.8686	.8708	.8729	.8749	.8770	.8790	.8810	.8830
1.2	.8849	.8869	.8888	.8907	.8925	.8944	.8962	.8980	.8997	.9015
1.3	.9032	.9049	.9066	.9082	.9099	.9115	.9131	.9147	.9162	.9177
1.4	.9192	.9207	.9222	.9236	.9251	.9265	.9279	.9292	.9306	.9319
1.5	.9332	.9345	.9357	.9370	.9382	.9394	.9406	.9418	.9429	.9441
1.6	.9452	.9463	.9474	.9484	.9495	.9505	.9515	.9525	.9535	.9545
1.7	.9554	.9564	.9573	.9582	.9591	.9599	.9608	.9616	.9625	.9633
1.8	.9641	.9649	.9656	.9664	.9671	.9678	.9686	.9693	.9699	.9706
1.9	.9713	.9719	.9726	.9732	.9738	.9744	.9750	.9756	.9761	.9767
2.0	.9772	.9778	.9783	.9788	.9793	.9798	.9803	.9808	.9812	.9817
2.1	.9821	.9826	.9830	.9834	.9838	.9842	.9846	.9850	.9854	.9857
2.2	.9861	.9864	.9868	.9871	.9875	.9878	.9881	.9884	.9887	.9890
2.3	.9893	.9896	.9898	.9901	.9904	.9906	.9909	.9911	.9913	.9916
2.4	.9918	.9920	.9922	.9925	.9927	.9929	.9931	.9932	.9934	.9936
2.5	.9938	.9940	.9941	.9943	.9945	.9946	.9948	.9949	.9951	.9952
2.6	.9953	.9955	.9956	.9957	.9959	.9960	.9961	.9962	.9963	.9964
2.7	.9965	.9966	.9967	.9968	.9969	.9970	.9971	.9972	.9973	.9974
2.8	.9974	.9975	.9976	.9977	.9977	.9978	.9979	.9979	.9980	.9981
2.9	.9981	.9982	.9982	.9983	.9984	.9984	.9985	.9985	.9986	.9986
3.0	.9987	.9987	.9987	.9988	.9988	.9989	.9989	.9989	.9990	.9990
3.1	.9990	.9991	.9991	.9991	.9992	.9992	.9992	.9992	.9993	.9993
3.2	.9993	.9993	.9994	.9994	.9994	.9994	.9994	.9995	.9995	.9995
3.3	.9995	.9995	.9995	.9996	.9996	.9996	.9996	.9996	.9996	.9997
3.4	.9997	.9997	.9997	.9997	.9997	.9997	.9997	.9997	.9997	.9998
3.6	.9998	.9998	.9999	.9999	.9999	.9999	.9999	.9999	.9999	.9999

(Reprinted by permission from Modern Probability Theory and Its Applications, by Emanuel Parzen, John Wiley & Sons, Inc., 1960)

INDEX